FROM

PEKING TO MANDALAY

FROM
PEKING TO MANDALAY

A JOURNEY FROM NORTH CHINA TO BURMA THROUGH TIBETAN SSUCH 'UAN AND YUNNAN

R. F. JOHNSTON, M. A., F. R. G. S.

WITH MAP AND ILLUSTRATIONS

GYAN

Published by

Gyan Publishing House
5, Ansari Road
Daryaganj, New Delhi-110002
Phone: 011-47034999, 9811692060
E-mail: books@gyanbooks.com

Distribution Network
gyanbooks.com
India, USA, Canada, UK, Australia, France

ISBN: 978-81-212-9276-4 (PB)
First Published, 1908

2nd Impression 2023

Printed at: Gyan Press, Delhi.

FROM PEKING TO MANDALAY

Author: R. F. JOHNSTON

FROM PEKING TO MANDALAY

CROSSING THE YALUNG RIVER. (*See p.* 191.)

[Frontispiece.

FROM

PEKING TO MANDALAY

A JOURNEY FROM NORTH CHINA TO BURMA THROUGH TIBETAN SSUCH'UAN AND YUNNAN

BY R. F. JOHNSTON, M.A., F.R.G.S.

MEMBER OF THE ROYAL ASIATIC SOCIETY
DISTRICT OFFICER AND MAGISTRATE, WEIHAIWEI

WITH MAP AND ILLUSTRATIONS

NEW YORK
E. P. DUTTON & COMPANY
1908

TO

DAVID PLAYFAIR HEATLEY

WHOSE PRESENCE IN THE EAST WOULD BRING HAPPINESS
TO EXILE, AND WHOSE ABSENCE IN THE WEST HAS
CAUSED HIS BANISHED FRIEND TO TURN
MANY TIMES WITH LONGING TO
THE SETTING SUN.

CONTENTS

LIST OF ILLUSTRATIONS

FROM PEKING TO MANDALAY

CHAPTER I

INTRODUCTION

THE journey of which an account is given in the following pages was not undertaken in the special interests of geographical or other science nor in the service of any Government. My chief object was to gratify a long-felt desire to visit those portions of the Chinese Empire which are least known to Europeans, and to acquire some knowledge of the various tribes subject to China that inhabit the wild regions of Chinese Tibet and north-western Yunnan. Though nearly every part of the Eighteen Provinces has in recent years been visited and described by European travellers, my route between Tachienlu and Li-chiang was one which—so far as I am aware—no British subject had ever traversed before me, and of which no description in book-form has hitherto appeared in any European language.

From the ethnological point of view the Chinese Far West—to which the greater part of this book is devoted—is one of the most interesting regions in the world, and presents problems the solution of which would settle many of the vexed questions relating to the origin and inter-relations of the

Asiatic peoples. As for its geographical interest, it may be sufficient to say here that the principalities of Chala and Muli contain what are probably the highest spots inhabited by man on the face of the globe, and that several of the passes crossed by my little caravan are loftier than the highest of the passes existing along the route traversed by the British expedition to Lhasa. My own contributions to geographical and ethnological lore are of the slenderest; but if I can persuade some of my readers that Tibetan Ssuch'uan and western Yunnan are worth visiting, be it only for the glory of their mountain scenery, I shall consider that my book has fulfilled the most useful purpose to which it aspires.

For those who are seized by a craving to revert for a time to something like the nomadic life of our remote forefathers, or to pass like the old Hindu ascetics into "the homeless state," there can be no country in the world more full of charm than some of the wilder and less-peopled regions of the Chinese Empire. There are enormous areas in that country covered with primeval forests in which man's foot has never trod, lofty mountains whose peaks are crowned with sparkling diadems of eternal snow, grand and savage gorges in which Nature has carved for herself in indelible letters the story of the world's youth, and gloomy chasms through which rush the mighty rivers that carry to the Indian Ocean and the Pacific snows that melted on the white roof of the world. And amid all this magnificence and desolation there are lovely valleys and stretches of garden-land that might have been chosen as the Edens of a hundred mythologies, and which in historic times have been the homes of religious recluses and poets, who, like others of their kind in Western lands, found in silence and solitude a refuge from the bitterness and pain of the world, or a hermitage in which, amid scenes of perennial beauty, they could weave their flowers of thought into immortal garlands of human words.

It is a mistake to regard the Chinese as essentially a prosaic race, caring only for material things and nothing at all for what we should call things of the spirit. If they have less power of artistic creation than the Japanese—and even that may be doubted—they are quite as sensitive as the people of any other race to the magic of beauty in either nature or art; and especially do they—like our own Ruskin—take a vivid delight in the loveliness of mountain scenery. There is a well-known story of a Chinese scholar who, like the scholars of most lands, was blest with few of this world's goods, and, unlike a great many of them, was noted for his zealous devotion to the service of his country's gods. One night he heard the voice of an invisible being that spoke to him thus: "Your piety has found favour in the sight of heaven; ask now for what you most long to possess, for I am the messenger of the gods, and they have sworn to grant your heart's desire." "I ask" said the poor scholar "for the coarsest clothes and food, just enough for my daily wants, and I beg that I may have freedom to wander at my will over mountain and fell and woodland stream, free from all worldly cares, till my life's end. That is all I ask." Hardly had he spoken when the sky seemed to be filled with the laughter of myriads of unearthly voices. "All you ask?" cried the messenger of the gods. "Know you not that what you demand is the highest happiness of the beings that dwell in heaven? Ask for wealth or rank, or what earthly happiness you will, but not for you are the holiest joys of the gods."

To those of our own day—and there are many such—whose highest ideal of happiness is that of this poor Chinese scholar, to roam at will through the beautiful places of the world, or perhaps even to dwell in some lonely hermitage far removed from

> "The weariness, the fever and the fret
> Here, where men sit and hear each other groan,"

it must be a bitter reflection that man is by his own works dooming himself to lose for evermore the privilege of freedom and the solace of isolation. When an authoritative voice informs us, in connection with wireless telegraphy, that "our ultimate ideal must be instantaneous electrical communication with every man on earth, ashore or afloat, at a cost within the reach of every one," what becomes of the unhappy man who finds one of the greatest joys of travel in the very fact of his utter loneliness, and in the knowledge that he is for the time being severed from all possibility of communication with his civilised fellow-men? The writer I have just quoted[1] assures us that owing to the recent triumphs of science "a severance of communication with any part of the earth — even the Antipodes — will henceforth be impossible. Storms that overthrow telegraph posts, and malice that cuts our cables, are impotent in the all-pervading ether. An explorer like Stanley in the tropical forest, or Geary amid ice-fields, will report daily progress in the *Times*. . . . Sir William Preece's dream of signalling to Mars may (say by utilising Niagara for the experiment) yet be realised." Thus even a flight to the virgin continents of another planet will not give the future traveller the delicious sense of freedom that comes from the knowledge of complete isolation or of entire severance from the cares of civilised life. How can we expect our mistress Nature to be gracious to us if we, with our unholy inventions, woo her so much more rudely and roughly than did her lovers of the golden time when the earth was young? For my own part I rejoice that a wireless-telegraphy apparatus has not yet become an indispensable item in every traveller's equipment, and that no law has yet been enacted penalising any individual who presumes to sever himself from communication with his fellows.

If it appears churlish and ungrateful to speak of the pleasures of separation from all those comforts and delights that Western civilisation has placed within our grasp, and without which

[1] Mr J. Henniker Heaton, M.P., in *The Nineteenth Century and After*, September 1906.

the normal European would hardly find life worth living, it is only fair to remember that no one is in a position to appreciate such comforts and delights so heartily as the man who has been temporarily deprived of them; though the depth of his appreciation will, of course, vary according to the extent of his dependence on the amenities of civilised life during his ordinary existence as a social unit.

The journey described in this book was not the first undertaken by me in the countries of the Far East. Towards the close of 1902 I travelled through the French province of Tong-king (erstwhile tributary to the Chinese Empire) and ascended the Red River to the high plateau of Yunnan. After traversing that province from east to west I reached the town of Ssumao, and thence struck southwards into the Chinese Shan States and the French Protected States of Upper Laos. A journey of many days in a dug-out canoe down one of the most beautiful rivers of that country gave me a delightful opportunity of becoming acquainted with the domestic life of the Lao-Shans—surely among the most attractive and hospitable races in the world. Leaving my canoe at the charming little Laos capital, Luang Prabang, I proceeded down the Mekong on a raft and visited the ruins of the obliterated kingdom of Vien-chan. There I left the Mekong and wandered overland through the great dry plain of eastern Siam to Korat. From Korat I was speedily conveyed by the prosaic means of a railway to the perplexing city of Bangkok, with its curious medley of East and West, old and new, its electric trams, its royal white elephants, its gilded pagodas and State umbrellas, and its forlorn collection of European legations. Except for the baggage-coolies hired at intervals along my route, I was for the greater part of this four months' journey unaccompanied by friend or servant. At one point, indeed, I was literally alone: for in the country of the Lao-Shans my four baggage-coolies, owing to some unreasonable dread of perfectly non-existent dangers, suddenly left me to my own devices, and returned to their homes, obliging me to abandon all my baggage except what I was able to carry in my own hands and pockets. It was then that my eyes were first opened to the fact that civilised man encumbers himself with a great many material possessions which he could quite well do without; for at no time did I suffer the least inconvenience from the loss of any of the articles which up to that point I had considered absolutely essential to my comfort and well-being. Servants and heavy baggage can indeed easily be dispensed with in any tropical country in which the natives are not unfriendly, and provided that the traveller is willing to subsist entirely on such food as the country affords; and it is undoubtedly the case that a traveller with few *impedimenta* can penetrate with ease into remote places that are inaccessible to one whose train includes numerous coolies and beasts of burden. One who is travelling with some definite scientific object in view must, of course, carry a suitable equipment of scientific instruments, and may require a retinue of servants and surveyors; but it is the mere wanderer—especially he who wanders in search of things strange and beautiful—not the scientific explorer, whose requirements I am here considering. It is perhaps unwise to render oneself absolutely dependent for supplies on the friendliness of natives, but in my own case it so happens that I have never met with inhospitable treatment from any of the Asiatic peoples among whom I have travelled, whether Chinese, Tongkingese, Tibetans, Shans, Siamese, or Burmese. I leave it to others who have had different experiences to tell their own tales.

At other times during my residence in China I have found opportunities to make tours, either in connection with official business or on leave of absence, in other parts of the Far East. In China I have made several excursions into the interior of the provinces of Kwangtung, Kwangsi, Kiangsi, and Shantung. In 1904 I travelled through the German colony of Kiaochou and the provincial capital, Chinan-fu, on my way to the little town of Ch'ü Fou, where I visited the tomb of Confucius and was entertained by the Duke K'ung, said to be the seventy-sixth descendant of the great sage in a direct line; and on the same occasion I ascended the famous sacred mountain of T'ai Shan, where the Emperor Shun is said to have sacrificed to heaven in the third millennium B.C. At the close of the same year, while the Russo-Japanese war was still raging, I was enabled through the kindness of a distinguished naval officer to pay an interesting visit to the capital of the distracted kingdom of Korea.

The journey described in the following pages was of a more ambitious character than those just mentioned, and occupied the greater part of a year. My intention was to ascend the Yangtse to the province of Ssuch'uan, and thence to make my way across that province to those principalities of eastern Tibet that now own allegiance to the emperor of China. I intended if possible to make my way southward through those states, and so enter the province of Yunnan; whence, as I knew from the narratives of former travellers, I should have no difficulty in making my way into Upper Burma. The details of my route I left to be determined by circumstances. Though I was occasionally subjected to minor disappointments and delays, the assistance of the various local officials and the friendly spirit shown by the people among whom I travelled enabled me to carry out my plans with success.

CHAPTER II

PEKING TO ICHANG

THE first part of my journey was accomplished with great rapidity, and my description of it will not occupy long in the telling. I had no desire to spend a longer time than was absolutely necessary in northern China, and was glad enough to avail myself of every facility for reaching Ichang—the port on the Yangtse where steam navigation ceases—as soon as possible. The recent completion of the northern section of the great trunk railway of China has rendered it possible to travel from Peking to Hankow in four days,[1] and so makes it unnecessary to undertake a long and somewhat dreary journey on horseback or in springless carts over hundreds of miles of dusty plains and impossible roads.

I left Wei-hai-wei on 6th January 1906 in the steamer *Shuntien*, and reached the ugly and depressing little port of Chin-wang-tao on the 8th. In the evening of the following day, after a night spent in Tientsin, I reached the capital, and was glad to exchange the discomfort of a monotonous

[1] Since reduced to thirty-six hours.

A FLEET OF JUNKS.

[*To face p.* 10.

railway journey for the luxury of that excellent Peking hostelry the "Hôtel des Wagons Lits." The next four days were spent in paying visits at the British Legation and elsewhere, and in fighting ineffectual battles against an unusually aggressive dust-storm. No one, except perhaps a traveller in the desert of Gobi or over the sand-dunes of Khotan, can form any conception of the penetrating power of Peking dust. Parched throats, husky voices, bloodshot eyes, are the price that must be paid for the pleasure of a walk through the streets of Peking during a dust-storm; even one's own residence is no sanctuary, for double window-sashes and padded doors are alike powerless to withstand the scourge. Most of the legations are fairly well protected by their lofty park-walls, but how to keep an ordinary Peking house or hotel free of dust is as insoluble a problem as that which baffled Alice's Walrus and Carpenter.

Peking being now one of the ordinary objectives of the modern globe-trotter, I will not encroach upon the province of the compiler of tourist guide-books by attempting a description. Even the Englishman who has never left his native soil knows something of the city that defied all the Powers of Europe seven years ago, and paid so bitterly for her defiance. There have, of course, been great changes in Peking since those dark days; but away from the railway stations and the legation quarter, with its bristling guns, its battlemented walls and its heterogeneous army of foreign guards, there is little to show that Peking was so recently in the grip of a victorious and remorseless enemy. Its streets, temples, shops and palaces are very much as they were in 1900, showing the same mixture of grandeur and sordidness, splendour and decay. As for its people, who will venture to say how much or how little they have changed? That they love the people of Europe no better than they did eight years ago may be taken for granted: I am not aware that we have done anything to win their affections. That they have learned something of the secret of European prowess, and have realised why our arms were resistless, even against their Boxer champions, is no doubt true; and if this lesson does not, for some strange reason, fill them with admiration and reverence for Europe, it is certainly teaching them where to seek a cure for the ills of their own country. Events are now making it clearer every day that a true spirit of national feeling is rising among the people, and that the best minds in China are devoting themselves to the problem of their country's salvation. Nowhere is this state of things more obvious than in Peking, but it is not only in the capital that the new spirit is working strange wonders among the Chinese people. China is, indeed, rapidly growing to be more than a mere geographical term. The racial solidarity that is the underlying cause of her wonderful power of passive resistance shows no signs of disintegration at the present time, and it will form the best possible foundation for a new national patriotism. Only ten years ago an English traveller and politician, predicting the partition of China, explained that he used the word "China" only for convenience, for "there is really no such thing as 'China' at all."[1] For such a view there was some excuse at a time when humbled China was lying wounded and helpless at the feet of victorious Japan, but few, I fancy, will be inclined to endorse it now.

The position of Peking at the present time is one of peculiar interest, for all the different forces that are now at work to make or mar China issue from, or converge towards, the capital. There, on the Dragon Throne, beside, or rather above, the powerless and unhappy emperor, the father of his people and their god, sits the astute and ever-watchful lady whose word is law to emperor, minister, and clown alike. There dwell the heads of the Government boards, the leaders of the Manchu aristocracy and the great political parties, the drafters of new constitutions and imperial decrees, and the keen-witted diplomatists who know so well how to play against European antagonists the great game of international chess. To Peking come the memorials of viceroys and provincial governors; indictments and denunciations against high officials for ultra-Conservatism or for Radicalism; bulky petitions from visionary students who have studied Western politics, and hope against hope that their proposed measures of reform may chance to come under the imperial eye. And there the great Powers of the West, reproducing in miniature the mighty armed camps of Europe, watch each other with jealous eyes from the gates of their embattled legations.

[1] *The Far East*, by Sir Henry Norman, p. 593.

The Lu-Han railway, by which I left the Capital on 18th January, brought me to Hankow on the evening of the 16th. The total distance is 1,228 kilometres, or about 759 miles. The provinces traversed by this great trunk line are Chihli, Honan, and Hupei. The line for the most part lies through a rich, flat country, studded with innumerable trees, villages, and farmsteads, but presenting no features of special interest to the ordinary traveller. The train stopped every evening, and resumed the journey early each morning, the first stage being completed at Shun-tê-fu, in Chihli. The second day we entered the province of Honan and crossed the Yellow River by the great bridge which has been the subject of so much criticism and discussion in engineering circles in the East. The construction of this bridge — a screw-pile structure almost two miles long — was by far the most serious and costly work that faced the French and Belgian engineers in the course of their labours, the chief difficulties consisting in the enormous rise and fall in the river and the shifting sands and almost fathomless mud of its bed. What must strike most travellers who are devoid of any technical knowledge of engineering are the great length of the bridge, the flimsiness of its appearance (for its massive supports are sunk far below the bed of the river), and its narrowness. Whether it is really fit to stand the strain of an abnormal summer flood, and whether its piers have been sunk sufficiently deep to ensure permanent stability, are questions which time and experience alone can solve. It had only been opened a few

SOUTH BANK OF YELLOW RIVER, WITH VIEW OF RAILWAY BRIDGE.

[To face p. 14.

weeks before I crossed it, and since then traffic has had to be suspended more than once. Only one train could pass over the bridge at a time, and each was taken across by a special light engine.

The second day's journey was completed at Chêng-chou, half an hour's journey from the south bank of the Yellow River. Here I found a quasi-European inn named the "Hotel Pericles," kept by an Italian ex-railway employee. Macaroni and chianti and the genial conversation of our host, Mr P. Mouchtouris, and two of his compatriots, afforded a cheerful interlude in a somewhat monotonous journey.

At the close of the third day we found ourselves at a place called Chu Ma-tien—a railway depôt only, not within sight of any large centre of population. On the following day we passed through the mountainous country that divides the provinces of Honan and Hupei, with scenery the most picturesque to be found anywhere between the two railway termini. Hankow itself, which was reached a few hours later, lies on the flat banks of the Yangtse, at a distance of about 600 miles from Shanghai. On the opposite bank of the great river lies the provincial capital, Wu-ch'ang, the seat of Government of the viceroy or governor-general; while on the same side of the river as Hankow, but separated from it by the Han river, lies Han-Yang. These three places together form what is practically one vast city of something like two million inhabitants: a city so favourably situated in the heart of China that it can hardly fail to become a commercial capital of pre-eminent importance. The large European trading community is fully alive to this fact, and building land is rapidly increasing in value. It is the terminus of the ocean-going vessels, and the starting-point of the smaller cargo and passenger-steamers bound for Ichang, about 390 miles further up the river. Hankow also derives great advantage from its position—denoted by its name—at the mouth of the Han, one of the Yangtse's greatest tributaries, itself navigable for native cargo boats for no less than 1,200 miles. Finally, Hankow is at present the terminus of China's only trunk railway, that by which I travelled from Peking, and it will soon be similarly connected with Canton in the south. It is perhaps no exaggeration to say that there is hardly a city in the whole world that has a greater commercial and industrial future before it than Hankow.

That the railway will pay, and pay enormously—especially when the connections with Canton and Kowloon are completed—is a matter beyond all possibility of doubt. That it will be of real benefit to the people of China is more to the point. It will undoubtedly enable the native merchants and farmers to send their goods and produce to markets which were formerly unattainable by them, and will go far towards minimising the misery caused by local famines. There is plenty of evidence that the Chinese are everywhere anxious and delighted to avail themselves of the wonderful new force that has been introduced into their country: the old days when the

Shanghai-Wusung railway had to be sold by the foreign owners to the Chinese Government, and was then deliberately wrecked and abolished to appease the prejudices of anti-foreign mobs,[1] have passed for ever away. The final proof—if one were needed—that the Chinese Government has definitely surrendered its old anti-railway policy, lies in the fact that it is itself promoting the construction of purely Chinese lines such as that from Peking to Kalgan; lines not only owned by Chinese capitalists, but actually engineered and constructed by Chinese engineers and contractors. The recent opposition of the Government to the construction of such lines as that from Kowloon to Canton, or from the Burmese frontier to T'êng-yüeh, lies simply in the rapidly-growing national hostility to the monopolisation of Chinese industrial enterprises by foreign capital, and the interference of foreign Powers—based on their subjects' pecuniary stake in the country—in the internal affairs of the empire. Therefore, though we hear a great deal just now about the difficulties placed by Chinese officialdom in the way of the employment of foreign engineers and foreign capital in railway construction and the exploitation of mines, this must not be interpreted as a reluctance on the part of China to have railways built or to have the mineral wealth of the country opened up. It is merely that the Chinese wish to build their own railways, and to work their

[1] But there is another side to this story which does not reflect much credit on the foreigners concerned. This aspect of the matter has been fully detailed by Mr Chester Holcombe, in *The Real Chinese Question*, chap. i.

own mines, in order that international disputes and political dangers may be avoided and that China may be exploited for the primary benefit of the Chinese Government and people, rather than for the benefit of foreign Governments and foreign capitalists. The European points out that the Chinese, either from want of money or from lack of technical knowledge and experience, are incapable of giving effect to these admirable ideals, however much they might wish to do so; to which the Chinese retort that rather than tolerate foreign interference, they prefer to wait until these disadvantages can be obviated, even if the country's advance in wealth and civilisation is thereby retarded. This attitude, even if economically unsound, is quite a natural one in the circumstances; but, unfortunately, there are a number of people in Europe and in the Far East who seem to regard any attempt made by China to keep or regain control of her own resources as a kind of international crime, which must, if necessary, be punished by gun-boats and bayonets. We resent the introduction of a Chinese element into British Columbia, Australia, and South Africa, but we make bitter protests against the "anti-foreign feeling in China" if the responsible statesmen of that country refuse to silence the cry of "China for the Chinese."

The Viceroy Chang Chih-tung—one of those able statesmen who prevented the spread of Boxerism in the Yangtse valley and so saved foreign commercial interests there from a serious disaster—was one of the first high officials in

China to realise the benefit that would accrue to all classes of the community from the construction of railways. "Is there any one power," he wrote, "that will open the door of learning for the scholar, the farmer, the workman, the merchant, and the soldier? To this question we reply emphatically, there is, and it is the Railway. The potentialities of the scholar lie in extensive observation; of the farmer, in finding a ready sale for farm products; of the workman, in the increase of machinery; of the merchant, in cheap and rapid transit; and of the soldier, in the quick despatch of the munitions of war. . . . The Railway is the source of the wealth and power of Western countries. . . . How can the people of our Flowery Inner Land progress, or even exist, without railways?"[1] This emphatic declaration by one of the greatest and most patriotic of Chinese officials is significant in more ways than one. China is to have railways, not merely as a means of rapid transport for merchandise and produce, but for the purpose of consolidating the military strength of the empire.

It must be a matter of serious regret to Chinese statesmen that the resources of the country—both in capital and in engineering skill—were not sufficient to enable China to undertake the whole financing and construction of the great trunk railway; and there can be little doubt that as soon as China is in a position to act upon Article V. of the Belgian Agreement, which she

[1] *China's Only Hope*, by Chang Chih-tung, translated by S. I. Woodbridge, 1901.

is entitled to do any time after 1907, she will refund all the Franco-Belgian capital advanced to her under the terms of that Agreement, and take over entire control of the whole northern section of the railway. It would probably be to the entire advantage of legitimate foreign trade and enterprise in China that she should do so, and the eventual benefit to be derived by China herself would be incalculable—provided, of course, that she honourably fulfilled her commercial treaties with the Western Powers.

On arrival at Hankow I spent two days in making such meagre preparations as I considered necessary for my long journey into the interior; for Hankow—being only four days distant by steamer from Shanghai—is the last town where it is possible to purchase European stores at a reasonable price.

Shallow-draft steamers with excellent accommodation for both Chinese and Europeans leave Hankow for Ichang two or three times a week. The traffic is divided among British, Chinese and Japanese companies. It was by a Japanese steamer that I started for the Upper Yangtse on 18th January. Our journey was not devoid of unforeseen incident. All went well until the 21st, when we ran on a shoal. All our efforts to get off proved unavailing till the 23rd, when by means of the process known to naval men, I understand as kedging, we hauled ourselves into deep water. This, however, was not effected without breaking a chain-cable and losing a valuable anchor, which sank irrecoverably in the mud. Our Japanese captain then announced that the vessel drew so much water that he could not then attempt the only available channel, and that there was no alternative but to return to Hankow and discharge some of the cargo. This caused intense dissatisfaction among the hundreds of Chinese passengers, most of whom were on their way to their homes to spend Chinese New Year's Day (which fell on 25th January) with their families. Some of the passengers, I was informed, actually threatened to use force to compel the captain to proceed, and were only pacified when they were given the option of going ashore in the ship's boats, and finding their own way to their several destinations. Twenty or thirty passengers availed themselves of this offer, and were packed into a single boat towed by the ship's steam-launch. On their way to the shore some unfortunate accident caused the boat—which was by no means over-crowded—to upset, and all the passengers were thrown into the water. I never learned the exact number of those who were drowned, for no proper tally of the passengers who had embarked appears to have been kept, but it was almost certainly not more than three. The rescued passengers were all bundled into the steam-launch, the boat (which was bottom upwards) temporarily abandoned, and the survivors brought back to the ship. The families of the poor fellows who paid so severe a penalty for their anxiety to reach their homes were doubtless waiting to welcome them with all the exuberant joy that the New Year festival brings into even the poorest Chinese household; and it was sad to reflect that in all probability no word of the tragedy would reach them until those whom they were waiting to greet were laid down at the doors of their homes in their coffins.

This sad event did not complete the chapter of our accidents. After we had anchored for the night some miles lower down the river, on our return journey to Hankow, our vessel was swung round by a back-eddy and crashed into several junks moored close to the shore. The damage, fortunately, was not very serious, and was promptly paid for by the captain of our ship. On the following day the ship's compradore came to me and asked if I could give him any medicine for a Chinese passenger who was showing signs of lunacy or delirium. As I had no remedies of the kind required, I could only recommend him to keep his patient under careful control until we reached Hankow. But about the middle of the day the poor man eluded the vigilance of those who, I presume, were looking after him, and deliberately jumped overboard. The ship was immediately stopped, a boat lowered with great promptitude, and the man rescued: he had never sunk below the surface, and it was obvious that he owed his safety entirely to his thickly-wadded winter garments, which were tied tightly at the waist and ankles and served as a temporary life-buoy. The cold waters of the wintry Yangtse had a more beneficial effect upon him than any drug, for on our arrival at Hankow he appeared to be completely restored to health. Just before we dropped anchor off the Hankow bund, one of the Chinese crew fell down the companion and damaged his ankle. Whether any further disasters occurred on board this unlucky vessel is unknown to me, as the same evening I hastily transferred my luggage, my dog and myself to the ship *T'ai Yuan*, which was due to leave for Ichang early the following morning. I was not surprised to hear that the loss to the owners owing to this unfortunate journey was estimated at not less than $10,000. Fortunately for the shareholders, the company is subsidised by the Japanese Government.

The *T'ai Yuan*, which was the property of the same company, was evidently smiled upon by a less malevolent star, for nothing except an hour's fog on the second morning interfered with our passage to Ichang. On arriving at the little treaty port of Sha-shih, on the morning of 30th January, I found from conversation with one of the Customs officials stationed there that the news of the tragedy described above had reached that port in a very distorted form. He asked me if it were true that twenty passengers had been drowned! In the evening of the same day we cast anchor at Ichang, where the number of the men reported to have lost their lives had risen to thirty.

CHAPTER III

ICHANG TO WAN-HSIEN, THROUGH THE YANGTSE GORGES

JUST before Ichang is reached, the appearance of the Yangtse valley undergoes a sudden change. The great flat plains of the Lower Yangtse are left behind, and rugged hills creep gradually up to the river's edge. Ichang owes its importance to the fact that it is situated at the eastern entrance of the great gorges of the Upper Yangtse, at the highest point of the river which is at present attainable by steamers. Its distance from the mouth of the Yangtse is almost exactly 1,000 miles. Its situation on the left bank of the river, facing a striking mountain the shape and size of which are said to be almost identical with those of the Great Pyramid of Egypt, is very picturesque. The town is not large, the population being barely 40,000, including about thirty or forty Europeans, the majority of whom are missionaries. There are also consular and customs officials, and a few merchants. The port has been opened to foreign trade for many years, but there has not as yet been any great commercial boom. It is, indeed, little but a port of trans-shipment. The main item in the out-going trade is native opium, for the poppy is grown very extensively in the valleys above Ichang. The town will therefore be considerably affected by the new anti-opium regulations.

Cargoes arriving by steamer and destined for the markets of the rich province that lies beyond the gorges are at Ichang transferred to large river junks. These junks, if they are fortunate enough to escape the manifold dangers of rocks and rapids, are hauled through the gorges by small armies of trackers, and take a month at least—sometimes far more—to cover the 400 miles between Ichang and Chung-king. With a favourable wind they can travel under their own sail in the smooth water between the rapids, but even then, owing to the strong current, the rate of progress is slow.

The right of steam navigation on the Upper Yangtse from Ichang to Chung-king and Hsü-chou-fu (Sui-fu) has existed since 1894, but the problem of the rapids is still an unsolved one, and steam-boats can only attempt the journey at a great risk. The dangerous portion is the 200 miles between Ichang and Wan-hsien. Mr Archibald Little successfully navigated his *Lee-chuen* through the gorges in 1898, but few attempts have since been made to connect Ichang and Chung-king by steam, though it is obvious that owing to the great cost and risk of the present methods of carrying on trade with the markets of Ssuch'uan, the development of a flourishing trade with that exceedingly rich and prosperous province is a matter of great difficulty. France, no doubt, hopes that by the extension of her Yunnan railway beyond Yunnan-fu the trade of Ssuch'uan will to some extent be diverted to Tongking and Haiphong, but she is, of course, fully cognisant of the fact that once the problem of the Yangtse rapids is solved by engineering skill, any such trade as she may have captured will inevitably find its way back to its natural channel. It is to be hoped, therefore, in the interests of China and Great Britain, that the problem will before long be tackled in real earnest by competent persons; it is certainly not one on which the opinion of amateurs is of any value. British river gun-boats have surmounted the obstacles on several occasions,[1] and a couple of such vessels are now kept in permanent commission in the tranquil waters between Wan-hsien and Hsü-chou-fu. In summer they also ascend the Min river (which enters the Yangtse at Hsü-chou-fu) as far as Chia-ting, a distance from Shanghai of about 1,680 miles.

Apart from the serious question of the rapids, there is no doubt that the Yangtse, with its tributaries, forms a magnificent system of navigable rivers. Not only can gun-boats ascend the Min river as far as Chia-ting, but native craft further ascend at all times of the year as far as Ch'êng-tu, the capital of Ssuch'uan, a distance of 133 miles above Chia-ting, and over 1,800 miles from Shanghai. The main stream of the river known to Europeans as the Yangtse is navigable only to P'ing-shan, 40 miles above Hsü-chou-fu, making

[1] It was accomplished very successfully by a British river gun-boat as recently as the summer of 1907.

a total distance from the Pacific Ocean of about 1,600 miles. It is on account of the shorter navigable distance of the main stream that the Chinese popularly regard the so-called Min as the true Great River. Chia-ting is within a day's journey of Mount Omei, and from the summit of Mount Omei one can see the Great Snow Mountains which form the eastern buttress of the Tibetan plateau. It is thus possible to penetrate by steam-boat or other vessel so far into the interior of China as to be within sight of her western boundary. This fact may surely be adduced in support of the contention that China possesses the finest system of navigable waterways in the world.

At Ichang, through the kind assistance of Mr H. H. Fox, British Consul at that port, and by the courtesy of the local Chinese officials, I procured a "red-boat" to convey myself and my faithful bull-terrier Jim up the rapids and through the gorges to Wan-hsien. The so-called red-boats are Chinese Government life-boats. There are several stationed in the neighbourhood of each of the most dangerous rapids, and they are manned by skilful and daring water-men. Every year a large percentage of the trading junks are wrecked in the rapids, and the annual loss of life, great as it is, would be appalling if it were not for the red-boats. This life-saving institution is maintained by Government with the assistance of voluntary contributions. A subscription towards the up-keep of the service is granted annually by the British Admiralty. There is no institution in

China which reflects more credit on the government of the country, and is more deserving of unqualified praise.

In a red-boat I was more cramped in space than I should have been in one of the large house-boats usually chartered by European travellers, but my rate of progress was much more speedy. My only shelter was a mat-awning, open at both ends, and as the thermometer rarely went above 45°, and at night often went down to 36°, I should have suffered some inconvenience from the cold had I not been able to exercise myself by scrambling along the rocks and boulders ahead of my trackers. The red-boat in which I travelled was, of course, specially detached for my use and exempted from the performance of its ordinary duties, though for part of the way it acted as escort to a naval officer who was going up the river in one of the ordinary house-boats to join his ship.

So many descriptions—good, bad, and indifferent—of the wonders of the Yangtse gorges have already been thrust into the hands of a more or less grateful public, that most of my readers may be glad to learn that I do not intend to add to the number. The travellers who in recent years have endeavoured to emulate the excellent accounts of such pioneers as Mr Archibald Little are so numerous that I would in all diffidence suggest to those who may hereafter desire to publish their "impressions" of the gorges, that it would be a graceful act on their part to pay a small fine—let it be a large one if the public receives their work with cordiality—towards the funds of the life-boat service. It would certainly be impossible to find a worthier object for their generosity. All I will venture to say myself—though I have already paid my fine—is that no description of the scenery of the gorges can do justice to the reality. For though I have beheld scenery more beautiful and quite as grand, I never saw anything in my travels that filled me with a deeper sense of awe. Perhaps one of the secrets of the fascination of the gorges is the ever-present contrast between the dumb forces of nature and evanescent humanity. For ages past human muscle has matched itself in a brave struggle with those titanic forces. The very rocks themselves, the standing symbol of changelessness, reveal something of the history of this unending strife. The smooth grooves worn deep into the jagged summits of innumerable crags have been scooped out by the ropes hauled by a hundred generations of dead trackers, and just above the water-line the deep holes in the hard lime-stone made by the poles of millions of toiling junkmen in past centuries are still used as hooks and points of leverage by their descendants of to-day. When it is remembered that more than a hundred trackers are sometimes required to haul a single junk against the current of the greater rapids, and that a junk may take half a day in covering a distance of 200 yards, some idea will be formed of the permanent difficulties that confront, and always have confronted, the indomitable Chinese navigator on these inland waters.

Much has been written by former travellers on

the subject of the terribly hard lives led by the Yangtse trackers, but I am not sure that the degradation of the tracker and the wretchedness of his life have not been greatly over-stated. Hard as the work is, the trackers' mode of life can be by no means unhealthy, and their daily food is, from the Chinese point of view, both plentiful and good. Better than all, their work is in its way interesting, and of such a nature that it can never become really monotonous. That they take a genuine satisfaction in its accomplishment, quite apart from the reward they are to receive, seemed to me, as I watched them at their labours, an obvious fact. I fancy that Ruskin would have supported the view that the tracker's lot is by no means so pitiable as that of myriads of factory hands in the hideous industrial centres of modern Europe. Personally, if I had to choose between hauling junks over rapids in the magnificent gorges of the Yangtse, and pulling cranks and levers in a dismal Lancashire factory, I should not for a moment hesitate in my choice: and I should not choose the cranks and levers.

My journey from Ichang to Wan-hsien occupied eleven days. We started on 2nd February, reached Pu-tai K'ou (the boundary between the provinces of Hupei and Ssuch'uan) on the 6th, passed through the Fêng Hsiang gorge—perhaps the grandest of all the defiles—on the 8th, and beached ourselves under the walls of the city of Wan-hsien on the morning of the 12th. Here I paid off my hardy boatmen, and prepared for my overland journey to Ch'êng-tu.

CHAPTER IV

WAN-HSIEN TO CH'ÊNG-TU

WAN-HSIEN, though one of the most beautifully situated cities on the Yangtse, is, like most Chinese towns, more pleasing at a distance than close at hand. It lies on a slope at a bend of the river 200 miles above Ichang, and 1,200 miles from the ocean. It is not yet an open port, though I was shown a spot said to have been selected by the British consular authorities as the site of the future Consulate. The only resident Europeans are a few missionaries and a postal agent. The trade of the city is brisk and developing, for the numerous roads that lead from here into the interior of the province are much used by the native merchants of Ssuch'uan for the conveyance of their goods to the river. In time to come Wan-hsien will no doubt reap a large profit from its advantageous position at the point of contact of several main arteries of traffic.

At Wan-hsien I was very hospitably entertained for a day and a night by the Rev. J. C. Platt, of the China Inland Mission, who was also most courteous in assisting me in the engagement of coolies for the next stage of my journey.

My caravan consisted of three coolies to carry my sedan chair (purchased at Wan-hsien), which

I very seldom used, three to carry my baggage, and a temporary "boy," or personal servant, who was engaged to accompany me as far as Ch'êng-tu, the capital of the province. I was also furnished by the *chih hsien*, or district magistrate, with the usual escort of two or three Chinese soldiers who, whether they are wanted or not, always accompany Europeans on overland journeys in China. From this point onwards my method was to engage temporary coolies and "boys" at various stages of my journey, discharging them as soon as I had passed out of the district in which their local knowledge rendered them specially useful. I lived entirely on native food, except on the rare occasions on which I enjoyed the hospitality of European missionaries. My knowledge of Chinese rendered me independent of interpreters or guides, though the changes of dialect were sometimes disconcerting.

The journey from Wan-hsien to Ch'êng-tu consisted of fourteen long stages, the total distance being nearly 400 miles.[1] The road lies through one of the fairest and most fertile portions of the great province of Ssuch'uan, and is one of the best I have met with in the interior of China: a circumstance which is partly due to the fact that Chinese officials generally use this road in travelling from the east of China to the provincial capital. The inns are numerous and—from the Oriental point of view—fairly comfortable. The innkeepers, so far from showing any aversion to entertaining foreigners, tout eagerly

[1] For Itinerary, see Appendix B.

A CHINESE "BRAVE."

[*To face p. 32.*

for their custom, and generally greet one with the amiable remark "*t'zŭ hou ta jên*" ("At your Excellency's service") as one enters their courtyards. The people are peaceful and industrious, and annoy foreigners only by their insatiable curiosity. Europeans have not very often travelled by this road, as they generally prefer—having a good deal of heavy baggage—to keep to the Yangtse as far as Chung-king, and thence ascend the Min river; but there are now several missionary stations between Wan-hsien and Ch'êng-tu, and the country is quite well known to foreigners. The road lies partly over undulating hills, generally cultivated almost to their summits with rice, rape, wheat, maize, and many other crops, and partly over rich and densely-populated plains. The scenery is always picturesque, and sometimes,—among the hills—exceedingly beautiful. The villages, farm-houses, and temples are generally situated amid little forests of feathery bamboo. The hill-sides are studded with charming little *châlets*, and very often the submerged rice-fields in their immediate vicinity give the appearance of artificial lakes in an English park, especially when the banks or balks are lined with graceful vegetation. My dog, I was glad to find, attracted much greater attention than I did myself: for bull-terriers are unknown in China. Delighted cries of "*K'an yang kou*" ("Look at the foreign dog!") greeted us whenever we entered a village street, and in some places delight was tempered by amazement. "Call that a dog?" I heard a village patriarch remark rebukingly. "It's a bear!"

My readers may rest assured that my four-footed travelling companion was no more like a bear than a unicorn.

Though the climate of Ssuch'uan is always comparatively mild, the mornings were generally chilly enough to make walking a pleasanter mode of progression than chair-riding. The method adopted by the peasantry to keep themselves warm struck me as distinctly novel. They carry in their hands little wicker-baskets, in which is a diminutive metal receptacle containing glowing charcoal. This is the Ssuch'uanese equivalent to a European lady's muff; but sometimes they hide it away under their clothes, in which case their appearance is apt to be rather comic.

My second night after leaving Wan-hsien was spent in the small district city of Liang-shan, where the late Mrs Bishop, as she relates in her *Yangtse Valley and Beyond*, was mobbed and assaulted. No such unpleasant experience awaited me, and I found the people orderly and good-humoured. The evening of the fourth day brought me to Ta Chu, where I found an unusually good inn. Those who have travelled much in China need not be reminded of the joy with which one finds comfortable quarters awaiting one at the end of a tiring day's journey; the experience is none too common. During the fifth day's march I passed several out-crops of coal. It seems to exist in great abundance, though mining operations do not appear to have been carried far below the surface. The coal is used in the inns of this district, and burns well.

On the sixth day we crossed the Ch'ü river in a ferry-boat. This stream, which is navigable for local craft, rises in the high range of hills in the north-east of Ssuch'uan, and for part of its course is known as the Pai Shui, or White Water. Ch'ü-hsien and Kuang-an are the only fair-sized towns on its banks, the point at which I crossed being between these two towns. The river joins the Chia-ling, with other tributaries, at Ho-chou, and so goes to swell the Yangtse at Chung-king. The water is remarkably clear. The summer rise, judging from the appearance of the banks, is probably not more than 10 feet, if so much.

On the eighth day from Wan-hsien I reached the prefectural city of Shun-ch'ing-fu,[1] once a prosperous industrial centre but now somewhat decayed. A great industry here used to be the preparation of vegetable dyes from the safflower, but the trade has been killed by the introduction of aniline dyes from Austria. Sericulture, however, is still a flourishing industry. Three or four years ago a disaster befell the city in the shape of floods, which destroyed whole streets and undermined portions of the city wall.

Soon after leaving Shun-ch'ing our road lay over an excellent four-arched bridge called the Jung An Ch'iao ("Everlasting Peace Bridge"), and we then began the ascent of a hill commonly known locally as the Hsi Shan, or West Hill. Here there are cavern-shrines, and a number of

[1] The word *fu* attached to so many Chinese place-names is usually translated "prefecture," which is an administrative division including several *hsien* or district-magistracies. *Chou* also signifies an administrative division or "department," smaller than a *fu*.

honorific portals and tablets, which indeed are exceedingly common along all the main roads of Ssuch'uan. Many of the inscriptions consist of "legends of good women," but the great majority commemorate the virtues of local officials. The carved figures on the buildings of the Hsi Shan are curious and interesting, and would probably repay study. Some distance beyond this point I observed a large flat rock close to the road, bearing the significant inscription: *Ch'i ssŭ wu kao chuang* ("Die of anger but don't go to law"). This is part of a well-known proverb which goes on to say: *O ssŭ wu tso tsei* ("Die of hunger but don't be a thief"). It would be well for the peasantry of China — who as often as not ruin themselves over their law-suits — if they would pay as much respect to the first of these injunctions as they generally do to the second.

On the 25th February my road descended from an undulating range of hills to the edge of the great plain, in the middle of which is situated the provincial capital, Ch'êng-tu; but it was not till the close of the following day, the fourteenth since leaving Wan-hsien, that we entered the city.

As in all wealthy centres, the contrast between the rich and poor in the Ch'êng-tu plain is very striking. I never met so much evidence of great wealth elsewhere in China, and certainly never encountered so many beggars. One of them, seeing that I was alone and on foot—for I had left my chair some distance behind—offered to carry me to Ch'êng-tu on his back. Another tried to impress upon me the advantages of his wheelbarrow as a mode of conveyance, though its wooden wheel was nearly broken in half. The number of bad characters in the city and neighbourhood seemed to me unusually large, and I was constantly warned against highway robbers. I hardly expected to have the good fortune to meet so picturesque a villain as a real highwayman, but such was my fate during my last day's journey before entering Ch'êng-tu. There were two of them, armed with pistols that were not only loaded, but could be discharged—a feature that is not characteristic of all Chinese fire-arms. They were lurking behind some bamboos on the side of the road, apparently waiting for an opportunity to attack and plunder any one whose docility of appearance marked him out as a suitable victim. One of them took fright at the sudden apparition of the three soldiers of my escort, who were walking in front of my chair, and bolted. He was immediately followed by his companion, and close on their heels came my scarlet-coated warriors, emboldened, no doubt, by the knowledge of the fact that they were three to two. I caused my chair to be put down in order that I might the better observe the race, and the fight which I supposed would ensue. But there was no struggle. Both the highway-men, encumbered by the weight of their unwieldy pistols and a couple of heavy knives, were speedily overtaken and captured, and, when brought back to me, threw themselves to the ground and made a piteous appeal to my generosity. They explained that they had found the knives and pistols in a field, and were trying to find the original owner in order to return them to him, and that they had no idea (until we demonstrated the fact by firing off the weapons) that the pistols were loaded. Whether they took up the same line of defence in the presence of the magistrate to whose care I consigned them, I do not know, nor have I learned their subsequent fate.

The Ch'êng-tu plain, with its marvellous system of irrigation and its three or four crops a year, is the richest and most populous district in the whole of the Chinese Empire. This extraordinarily productive plain is about 90 miles long by 70 wide, and supports a population estimated at no less than 4,000,000, of whom about 350,000 reside within the capital itself. It is studded with many prosperous towns and villages, and is cultivated to its utmost extent. Among the crops are rice, wheat, tea, tobacco, maize, the opium-poppy, which was not yet in bloom, and the yellow rape that turned hundreds of acres of land into seas of bright gold. The plain is connected by a navigable waterway (the Min) with the Yangtse, and it is in the heart of the richest province in China. The city of Ch'êng-tu has been identified with Marco Polo's Sindafu. "This city," wrote Marco in the thirteenth century, "was in former times a rich and noble one, and the kings who reigned there were very great and wealthy." Of the Min river—which had not then been subdivided to the same extent as at present into artificial channels for irrigation—he says: "The multitude of vessels that navigate this river is so vast that no one who should read or hear the tale would believe it. The quantities of merchandise also which merchants carry up and down this river are past all belief."[1]

Ch'êng-tu is a city of less importance now, but it is still one of the greatest and most prosperous in China. Its population is much smaller than that of Canton, but its general appearance is more attractive as well as far more imposing. Its streets are broad and clean, and its wall exceedingly well preserved. In mediæval times it was a frontier city of great political and strategic importance, for the Tibetan principalities extended then as far east as the lofty mountains that flank the Ch'êng-tu plain on the west. Even now large numbers of Tibetan traders are often to be seen in the streets of Ch'êng-tu, though most of their commercial transactions are carried on at the city of Kuan-hsien, about 80 miles away, a place which is also remarkable for the sluices which regulate the waters of the Min and divert them, as occasion demands, into the irrigation canals. The governor-general of Ssuch'uan, whose yamen is in Ch'êng-tu, is more like a real viceroy than any other provincial ruler in China, for he it is who, on behalf of the emperor, holds sway over, and receives the embassies of, the various Tibetan princes and tribal chiefs of the extreme west. There is at present a project to connect Ch'êng-tu by rail with a point on the Yangtse, probably in the neighbourhood of K'uei-chou-fu, a town which I passed on my way from Ichang

[1] Yule's *Marco Polo*, edited by Cordier, vol. ii. pp. 36-37.

to Wan-hsien. The provincial government—for the railway project is entirely a Chinese one—is at present actively engaged in trying to raise the funds necessary for so large an undertaking, one method being—so I was told—to compel every local official to take a definite number of shares, the number to vary according to the official's rank and reputed wealth, each shareholder being permitted to get rid of his shares in the best way possible by distributing them among the well-to-do people subject to his jurisdiction. In passing through the towns and villages of eastern Ssuch'uan, I noticed many Chinese proclamations giving the people an outline of the railway scheme, pointing out the great benefits to the trade and prosperity of the province that would result from its fulfilment, and inviting or commanding popular co-operation. It may be that this railway will offer one solution of the problem of the Yangtse rapids: in any case, the enthusiasm with which the scheme was being discussed in both official and commercial circles was another proof of the gradual breaking-down of the old Chinese prejudice against railways.

Though so remote from the sea-board, the people of Ch'êng-tu — or perhaps I should say the officials — are among the most progressive and enlightened in China. This is especially so in the matter of education. The city possesses a Provincial College, where about three hundred young men are now being educated in Western as well as in Chinese branches of learning. There is an Englishman who lectures on chemistry and physics, there are several Japanese lecturers, and a staff of Chinese teachers who have a knowledge of European languages. I have heard of an enterprising Chinese schoolmaster who once advertised that in his establishment English was taught "up to letter G." They are more ambitious than that in the college of Ch'êng-tu. Among the local industries the most important is that of silk-weaving. For this, as well as for other industrial purposes, foreign machinery and Western methods are being gradually imported and adopted.

Those who are acquainted with Baber's charming descriptions of Ssuch'uan and Yunnan[1] —descriptions which can never be superseded, though they are often neglected nowadays—will remember that he was much interested in a curious circular monolith which he discovered on the side of an artificial hill or mound in Ch'êng-tu. He was unable to get any satisfactory account of its history, though tradition said that it marked the grave of an emperor's son. It is, indeed, not improbable that the mound, which is oblong in shape, with a depression in the middle, and resembles, as Baber remarked, a half-buried dumb-bell, was raised in memory of some distinguished prince or leader of old times, perhaps when the Ch'êng-tu plain was still occupied by the so-called Man-tzŭ. I visited the spot, and found that the stone was still lying in the position in which he saw it. The portion that appears above the soil presents something of the appearance of the tilted

[1] First published in the Royal Geographical Society's *Supplementary Papers*, vol. i.

end of a huge stone barrel, badly damaged at one corner. The diameter of the circular face—of which barely half can be seen—I found to be about 17 feet. The greatest length of the visible body of the barrel is only about 2 feet 3 inches, but it is impossible to say how much of it is underground. An excavation of the mound at the spot where the stone lies might lead to some interesting results: but Baber was assured that any attempt to dig would cause the sky to darken and goblins to appear, so he left it alone, and I decided to follow his example.

Something of the grandeur of Ch'êng-tu in its most palmy days may be realised by a reference to extant Chinese books, as well as from the eulogies of Marco Polo. From the *Shu Hua Shih*[1] we learn that under the T'ang dynasty (618-905 of the Christian era) it was a great art centre, and a long list of paintings and frescoes relating to the Buddhist religion are mentioned in that work as hanging on the walls of the palaces of Ch'êng-tu. Some of the temples are worthy of a long visit, though the finest in the district is not in the city itself but in the neighbouring town of Kuan-hsien, where Li Ping and his son, the deified founders of the great irrigation system of the Ch'êng-tu plain, have had raised in their honour a temple that is said to be the most beautiful in China. But as has been well remarked of Li Ping by a recent English traveller,[2] the perennially fertile fields around Ch'êng-tu are his finest monument.

[1] 書畫史.
[2] Clive Bigham, in *A Year in China*, p. 125.

CHAPTER V

CH'ÊNG-TU TO OMEI-HSIEN

MY next objective after leaving Ch'êng-tu was the sacred summit of Mount Omei, one of the most famous of the many historic mountains of China. I left Ch'êng-tu on 1st March in a small, leaky, and most uncomfortable craft, which took me down the Min river to Chia-ting in four days, the total distance being slightly over 130 miles. The Kuan-hsien sluices having not yet been opened to give the great plain its spring flooding, there was very little water in the stream till we reached Chiang K'ou[1] on the morning of the third day, and in some places it was necessary to pull the boat over mud shoals. At Chiang K'ou the various subdivided waters (of which the branch that brought me down from the east gate of Ch'êng-tu was one) reunite and form a river which is broad and deep enough at all seasons of the year for cargo-junks of a considerable size. This is the Min river, which, as already stated, is regarded by the Chinese of central Ssuch'uan as the true Upper Yangtse. The far greater but unnavigable stream which rushes impetuously from the Tibetan mountains in the north-west and is joined by the Min at Hsü-chou-fu,[2] is known by the Chinese for a great part of its course as Chin Ho (Gold River) and as the Chin Sha

[1] 江口. [2] See Map.

Chiang[1] (the River of Golden Sand). The name Min being apparently unknown to the Chinese, Baber suggested that it had been invented by the early Jesuit geographers.[2] If so, it was no doubt derived from the range of mountains known to the Chinese as the Min Shan (岷山) in the north-west of the province, for it is there that the river rises. But all the rivers of China have a multitude of names; in fact the Chinese do not appear to be endowed with a proper sense of the continuity of rivers, and the country people who dwell on the banks of a stream from which they derive their livelihood are seldom aware of where it comes from or whither it goes. This circumstance has been a source of embarrassment to many European travellers, whose passion for geographical exactness is incomprehensible to the rustic mind in China.

The scenery of the Min is always picturesque. The river flows for the most part through richly cultivated districts, broken only here and there by low hills. Nearly opposite the town of P'êng-shan-hsien, on the third day from Ch'êng-tu I visited a fine twelve-storied pagoda (the So Chiang T'a or Lock-River Pagoda), which, unlike most buildings of the kind, is in sufficiently good repair to enable one to ascend it by a spiral staircase. The pagoda is built of hard brick and the staircase is of sandstone blocks. The scenery on the

[1] It will be observed by those acquainted with Chinese that here and elsewhere I have, for the sake of uniformity, transliterated all Chinese names according to the sounds of Pekingese, except in the case of a few stereotyped words.

[2] It is used, however, in the official Annals of the province (*Ssuch'uan T'ung Chih*).

A CHINESE WALLED CITY.

[To face p. 44.

river becomes finer as one approaches Chia-ting. Well-wooded hills come close to the water's edge, and broken cliffs covered with verdure reveal openings into fairy vistas of greenery and mysterious grottoes that would have delighted the soul of a Keats.

The town of Chia-ting, which I reached on the evening of 4th March, is beautifully situated on the right bank of the Min, just above its junction with the T'ung (more generally known as the Ta Tu) and Ya rivers. From this point onwards the three streams flow in a broad, navigable river for a distance of about 180 miles, when they join the Yangtse at Hsü-chou-fu. My river-journey, however, ended at Chia-ting.

Apart from its proximity to the sacred mountain of Omei, Chia-ting is interesting for its temples, its prehistoric cave-dwellings, its sericulture, and for the white-wax industry. High on a rocky hill on the left bank of the river is a remarkable monastery known as "The Monastery of the Voice of the Waters." It was founded in the T'ang dynasty, nearly twelve hundred years ago, and restored in 1667 by the munificence of a Provincial Judge. It bears the alternative name of "The Great Buddha Monastery," the reference being to a huge image which has been carved out of the face of a cliff that overhangs the waters of the Min. The story goes that a holy monk named Hai T'ung came to this locality in the eighth century of our era and determined to perform some act of religious devotion which would save the surrounding country from the ruin and desolation caused by the overflowing of the three neighbouring rivers. He therefore spent nineteen years in hewing out of the rock an immense image of Maitrêya Buddha. The carving, which is in bold relief, must have been a work of immense labour and considerable danger; but its artistic merits are obscured by the partial decomposition of the rock and the growth of vegetation in the fissures. Parts of the body are almost indistinguishable. The whole figure is about 386 feet high. An exceedingly steep and rather perilous scramble down a cutting in the precipice enabled me to study the great figure from various points of vantage, and also to inspect some little rock-shrines containing innumerable small Buddhas. It is doleful to reflect that in spite of Hai T'ung's piety and extraordinary industry the three rivers have not yet ceased to cause periodical floods.

Amongst other objects of great interest in the monastic grounds are some of the prehistoric cave-dwellings which were first described by Baber. One of these caves, in close proximity to the monastery, has been diverted from its original uses (whatever they may have been), and is now a Buddhist chapel, with altar, bell, and images all complete. These caves, of which there are many in the neighbourhood of Chia-ting and a great quantity in other parts of what is known as the "Red Basin" of Ssuch'uan, constitute one of the unsolved problems of Chinese archæology. I visited several of them during the two days I spent at Chia-ting, but am not in a position to add much to the information already available, or to offer any novel theory regarding their origin.

The caves are entirely artificial, and have been hewn out of the sandstone by people who were evidently skilful in the handling of their tools. There is little evidence of a strong artistic instinct, but it is curious to note that the decoration, such as it is, bears no resemblance to any Chinese work, and seems rather of Hindu type. The square or oblong doors are generally on the face of a cliff, and the majority are at the present time quite inaccessible without the use of ropes and ladders. In some cases the cliffs are honey-combed with caves, the insides of which have never been trodden by human foot for untold ages. Other caves, however, are quite easily accessible. The interiors vary in details, but in general design they are alike. The door leads into a long room, which is in most cases connected with other rooms, and there are holes and grooves in the walls which show that there must at one time have been wooden partitions. Within the rooms, which are quite lofty and broad enough for human habitation, there are cistern-like troughs, deep recesses, bench-like seats, and projections that may have been used as shelves: all of which are hewn out of the rock and remain immovable. No one can now say definitely whether the caves were used as strongholds, as tombs, as houses or as places of worship. Arguments may be adduced in support of each and all of these theories. The inaccessibility of the majority of the cave-apertures lends support to the stronghold theory. Perhaps they were reached by temporary ladders which were drawn up on the approach of an enemy. Possibly the enemies to be feared in those remote days were wild beasts as well as human beings. The narrow rooms, with their immovable stone coffers and shallow recesses, suggest mausolea; yet the existence in some cases of fire-places (without chimneys) and stone projections that were evidently intended to be sat upon are more suggestive of dwelling-places. As regards the temple theory, all that can be said is that some of the more accessible of the caves have been turned into Buddhist shrines, as in the case already mentioned; but there is no evidence whatever that they were originally intended for religious purposes. On the whole, it seems probable that the caves were actually used as the ordinary dwelling-places of a primitive people that lived chiefly by hunting and fishing, had attained a fair degree of civilisation and social organisation, and found themselves in constant danger of attack by hostile tribes, perhaps Tibetans, by whom—if not by advancing Chinese—they were eventually scattered or exterminated.

All I propose to add by way of comment is this. In the *Journal* of the Royal Asiatic Society for July 1904 and January 1906, Mr E. Crawshay-Williams described some mysterious rock-dwellings which he discovered at Raineh, in Persia. Now from his description of those caves I gather that they must be exactly similar in situation, size, and general appearance to those which we are now considering. Unfortunately, neither the Raineh caves nor those of Ssuch'uan contain inscriptions. Whether the resemblance is purely accidental or has some deeper significance is a question which I leave to archæologists. It might, if we had corroborating evidence, tend to show that regions so far apart as Persia and the Min valley of Ssuch'uan were once inhabited by allied races, perhaps of Indian origin. As we shall see later,[1] there is, indeed, some reason to believe that the Chinese cave-dwellers were connected with the Vaggians or Licchavis, a race that attained to great political strength in the extreme north-east of India, and which—according to one authority at least—is identical with the Yüeh-chi.[2] The latter, however, who after their disastrous defeats by the Hiung-nu on the confines of China in the second century B.C. migrated to western Asia, never seem to have penetrated so far west as Raineh in Persia. Their empire was founded on the ruins of the Græco-Bactrian dominion in Sogdiana and on the left bank of the Oxus, and their ambitions led them south rather than west. It may be that future explorers will discover in other regions caves of a similar pattern to those of Persia and China, and in that case it may be possible to trace the migrations of the cave-dwellers and so find a clue to their identification. The caves noticed by the abbé Huc on the fringe of the Mongolian desert, and those that exist near the Yamdok lake on the road to Lhasa[3] have not been described fully enough to justify our drawing many deductions. The rock-cut caves on the Murghab near the Afghan frontier, and those of Bamian close to the

[1] See chap. xv. p. 286 (note 1).

[2] S. Beal in the *Journal* of the Royal Asiatic Society, January 1882, p. 39. His view does not seem to have attracted much attention.

[3] See Waddell's *Lhasa and its Mysteries* (John Murray, 1905), pp. 289-290.

Indian Caucasus on the road between Kabul and Turkestan,[1] have many characteristics in common with those of Ssuch'uan, but appear to have served only religious uses. Professor Parker has discovered in the records of the T'ang dynasty (seventh to tenth century A.D.) what appear to be references to the existence of a race of cave-dwellers in Ssuch'uan as late as that time, and a further reference to cave-chiefs (one of whom was named T'ien Shih Ch'iung) in records corresponding to the year 1012 of our era.[2] But there is nothing to prove that these were the descendants of the original cave-dwelling race, and the probabilities are rather against their being so.

What the Chinese themselves say is that the caves were inhabited by the "Man-tzŭ" in prehistoric times; but Man-tzŭ is a term which has a very elastic meaning, for, as we shall see below,[3] it has been made to embrace Tibetan border tribes, Lolos and "savages" generally. It must reluctantly be admitted that until a proper archæological enquiry has been made into the subject and the more inaccessible caves have been thoroughly searched for relics, the only theory with which no fault can be found is the illuminating one propounded by Baber. "My own theory," he said, "which I offer with diffidence, is that these excavations are of unknown date, and have been undertaken, for unexplained purposes, by a people of doubtful identity."

On 6th March I set out for Omei-hsien, the

[1] See *Journal* of the Royal Asiatic Society, January and July 1886.
[2] See *China Review*, vols. xv. and xix.
[3] See chap. xv.

little city that lies at the foot of Mount Omei. The distance from Chia-ting is only about 16 miles, and was easily covered during the day. My retinue consisted of three chair-bearers, three baggage coolies and a useless "boy" whom I had picked up at Ch'êng-tu and hoped to get rid of as soon as I could find a suitable man to take his place. The road led us over the river Ya and across a great plain almost entirely occupied by myriads of the dwarf ash-trees which are used in connection with the production of the famous white wax. The wax-insects, which are brought annually in baskets from the Chien-ch'ang valley south of the Ta Tu, are placed on the branches of this tree, and in due time proceed to cover themselves and the branches with a thick coating of the wax. The branches are then cut off and the wax carefully removed. The whole process has been carefully described by Sir Alexander Hosie in several Foreign Office reports and in his *Three Years in Western China.*

The inns of Omei-hsien are unusually good, and as the pilgrim season had not yet begun I was able to select the best quarters that the city could provide. Western readers must not suppose that even the best of Chinese inns would meet with commendation in England or America. If in China I am shown into a room that has been moderately well swept, and possesses a wooden floor which does not give way, and walls without holes; that contains a steady table, an unbroken chair, a window recently papered, and that does not smell too offensively of stale opium; and if the room is not next door to the stables and opens into a yard that is reasonably clear of garbage and filth, and is not the common resort of peripatetic pigs and diseased dogs,—I then consider that good fortune has brought me to an inn that may be described as excellent. The furniture is, of course, in all cases of the simplest description, the principal guest-room generally containing only a table and a couple of chairs. The walls are either of bare stone or brick, or of mere lath and plaster. Sometimes they are adorned with a few hanging scrolls containing "antithetical couplets" or crude paintings—probably New Years' gifts to the landlord from his "foolish younger brothers." Washing-stands, dressing-tables and side-boards and similar luxuries are unknown, and the bed consists either (in north China) of a *k'ang*, which is built of bricks, or (in the warmer regions) of a couple of planks placed on trestles. For several reasons a camp-bed is to Europeans an indispensable part of even the most modest travelling equipment. If such are the good inns, what is to be said of the worst? Earthen floors saturated with damp and filth and smelling of decaying refuse; windows from which the paper (glass being, of course, unknown) has been torn away; tables which collapse under the weight of the traveller's frugal dinner unless they are propped up by his portmanteau and gun-case; roofs from which hang trailing cobwebs spun by spiders of a vanished generation; walls of mud through which the village urchins make holes by the simple pressure of their grimy fingers; wicked-looking insects of uncouth shapes that issue at night-time from a hundred gloomy lurking-places and crawl over

CHILDREN OF CHINA.

[*To face p.* 53.

the edge of one's rice-bowl; an entire lack of means of illumination except a single sputtering wick protruding from a saucer filled with rancid oil: these are but a few of the more obvious discomforts of many a Chinese hostelry. The inns of the large towns are with a few exceptions no better than those of the villages, and often much less comfortable on account of the greater amount of noise and dirt. As a rule it is preferable, if possible, to complete a day's march at a village rather than in a town; not only for the sake of quietness and peace, but also because one is less likely to be disturbed by inquisitive crowds if one ventures outside the door of the inn.

The people of Omei-hsien, however, are unusually amiable. Many of them earn their living by attending to the wants of pilgrims to the great mountain, and vie with each other in their efforts to show civility to the stranger within their gates. Not many Chinese venture to climb Mount Omei so early in the year as March, as it is still covered with snow for several thousand feet of its height; but I observed a large number of Tibetan pilgrims on their way to and from the mountain, and ascertained from them that there was no great difficulty in the ascent. On the morning of the 7th March, therefore, I left my servant (who was appalled by the mere shadow of the mountain) to look after my baggage in Omei-hsien, and started the ascent in the company of the two soldiers of my escort. The town of Omei-hsien lies at 1,500 feet above sea-level: the summit of the mountain is about 9,500 feet higher.

CHAPTER VI

MOUNT OMEI AND CHINESE BUDDHISM

THE forests and ravines of Mount Omei[1] teem with mystery and marvel, for there are legends that carry its story far back into the dim days when the threads of history meet together in the knots of myth. There is hardly a peak ungarlanded with the flowers of romance, hardly a moss-grown boulder that is not the centre of an old-world legend. The many stories of wonderful visions and wizard sounds that have come to the eyes and ears of the pilgrims to the shrines of Omei may raise a smile of amusement at human credulity, yet they are easily enough explained when we remember how strangely both sights and sounds may be affected by mountain-mists; and it is seldom that the giant bulk of Omei is bathed from peak to base in clear sunshine.

> "The swimming vapour slopes athwart the glen,
> Puts forth an arm, and creeps from pine to pine,
> And loiters, slowly drawn."

It is, indeed, true that "many-fountain'd" Omei would lose a great part of its spell if the mists were to melt away into garish daylight. No more

[1] 峨眉.

could the pilgrim pour into the ears of wondering listeners tales of how, when ascending the mountain amid gloom and silence, he had suddenly heard his own praises of the Lord Amitabha re-chanted by spirit voices; how a rift in the curtain of white cloud had suddenly disclosed landscapes of unearthly loveliness, with jewelled palaces and starry pinnacles such as were never raised by the hands of men; how he had caught glimpses of airy forms that passed him with a sigh or a whisper, but left no traces in the forest or the snow and made no sound of footfall; or how when approaching unwittingly the edge of some terrible abyss he had felt the touch of a ghostly finger that led him back to safety.

It is believed that the Lolos, who are not Buddhists, worshipped on Mount Omei a triad of deities of their own, and it is at least certain that men of that race are sometimes met on Omei's slopes. But the earliest legendary associations of the mountain are in Chinese minds naturally connected with those mythical progenitors of the Chinese people — Fu Hsi and Nü Wo. This carries us back to the twenty-ninth century B.C. Both these mysterious persons have their "caves" on Mount Omei, but they are in such inaccessible situations that no mortal eye has ever seen them. The first of the legendary hermits was a holy man named T'ien Chên Huang Jên,[1] the Heavenly Sage and Imperial Man. He lived in the age of phœnixes and unicorns; and on Mount Omei he once received a visit from Huang Ti,[2] the

[1] 天眞皇人. [2] 黃帝.

Yellow Emperor, who flourished in the twenty-sixth century B.C. Though one of the few of the world's monarchs who appear to have lived long enough to celebrate the centenary of their succession to the throne, Huang Ti wished to attain the crowning distinction of immortality. It was to acquire the elixir of life from the Heavenly Sage that Huang Ti paid him his memorable visit. A short record of the conversation between the Sage and his imperial disciple has been preserved, and we may gather from it that Huang Ti derived from the interview a good deal of sound practical advice, but the Sage seems to have skilfully evaded the main point. He kept his secret, but made such excellent personal use of it that he is supposed to have lived for at least a millennium or two, and indeed his death has not yet been recorded. In order to keep count of time he acquired the useful habit of changing his name with each successive epoch,[1] and his name in the Chou dynasty—which occupied the throne about a millennium and a half after the Yellow Emperor's time—was the singularly appropriate one of The Old Man.

Omei-shan — like other sacred mountains in China—has always been famous for the medicinal value of its roots and herbs, and the monks still derive no little benefit from their sale. Perhaps it was among these herbs that The Old Man found his elixir of life, and if so he did not remain in exclusive possession of the secret. The records

[1] 隨時易名.

of Omei are full of accounts of recluses and others whose span of life extended far beyond the normal. One of them is known to legend as Pao Chang,[1] but more popularly as Ch'ien Sui Ho Shang,[2] or "The Monk of a Thousand Years." The period of his long and useful life is given in the records. He was born in the twelfth year of Wei Lieh Wang of the Chou dynasty, and died in the eighth year of Kao Tsung of the T'ang dynasty at the ripe old age of precisely one thousand and seventy-one. He was a native of India, but came to China in the Chin dynasty (265-419 of our era) and went to worship at the shrine of P'u Hsien Bodhisattva on Mount Omei, where he spent the declining centuries of his life. According to another account his arrival at Omei was a good deal earlier than the Chin period, for his name is connected with the most famous of all the Omei stories—one which refers to the reign of Ming Ti of the Han dynasty.

This story relates to the foundation of what may be called the Buddhistic history of Omei and the beginning of its long religious association with its patron saint, P'u Hsien Bodhisattva. We are told that in the reign of Ming Ti (58-75 of the Christian era) a certain official named P'u[3] happened to be on Mount Omei looking for medicinal herbs. In a misty hollow he suddenly came upon the footprints of a deer. They were

[1] 寶掌.   [2] 千歲和尚.

[3] This name (蒲) is not to be confused with the P'u (普) of P'u Hsien. The sound is the same but the Chinese characters are different.

shaped not like the footprints of an ordinary deer but like the flower of the lotus. Amazed at the strange sight, he followed the tracks up the mountain. They led him continually upwards until at last he found himself on the summit, and there, at the edge of a terrible precipice, they disappeared. As he gazed over the brink he beheld a sight most strange and wonderful. A succession of marvellous colours, luminous and brilliant, gradually rose to the surface of the vast bank of clouds that lay stretched out below, and linked themselves together in the form of a glorious iridescent aureole. P'u, full of wonder at so extraordinary a spectacle, sought the hermitage of the famous "Monk of a Thousand Years" and told him his strange story. "You are indeed happy!" said the monk. "What you have seen is no other than a special manifestation to you of the glory of the great Bodhisattva P'u Hsien: fitting it is, therefore, that this mountain should be the centre from which his teachings may be spread abroad. The Bodhisattva has certainly favoured you above all men." The end of the whole matter was that P'u built, on the spot from which he had witnessed the sublime manifestation, the first of the Buddhist temples of Mount Omei, and dedicated it to P'u Hsien Bodhisattva; and the present monastic buildings known as the Hsien Tsu Tien and its more modern neighbour the Chin Tien occupy in the twentieth century the site chosen for the original P'u Kuang Tien, or Hall of Universal Glory,[1] in the first century.

[1] The word P'u, which means Universal, is also the first character in the name of P'u Hsien.

This story is interesting as carrying back the Buddhistic traditions of Omei to the very earliest days of Buddhism in China. My readers will probably remember that it was in the same epoch —the reign of Ming Ti—that the emperor had his famous vision of the Golden Man, which is supposed to have led to the introduction of Buddhism into China under direct imperial patronage. The story is also of interest as embodying the first record of the remarkable phenomenon known as the Glory of Buddha, which has always been one of the principal attractions of the mountain and may well have been the real cause —as the story itself indicates — of its special sanctity.

The other curiosities of Omei are so numerous that most of them cannot even be referred to. Near the foot of the mountain is a scooped-out rock which is said to have once formed a bath in which pilgrims were required to go through a course of purification before ascending the mountain. This, if true, is curious and suggestive. There is a spot shown where a miraculous lotus-plant—the lotus is sacred to the Buddha—used to blossom in every season of the year. There is a flying bell, the tolling of which has been heard in many different parts of the mountain, though it is never moved by human hands. There are rock-inscriptions written by emperors and empresses and by the great Sung dynasty poet, Su Tung-p'o. Not far from the Wan-nien monastery — perhaps the second oldest on the mountain—is a stream called the Black Water.

In the T'ang dynasty a wandering monk, looking for a home, came to this stream and wished to cross it, for he espied on the further bank a spot which he thought would make an excellent site for a hermitage. But the stream was turbulent and violent and he could not cross. Suddenly out of the midst of the torrent came a huge tiger. The tiger looked at the monk, and the monk, unabashed, looked at the tiger. The wild beast recognised a teacher of the Good Law, and lay down at his feet, tamed and obedient. The monk mounted on his back and was carried safely across the water. The tiger has gone and the monk has gone, but the story must be true, for a bridge was built to span the Black Water at the spot where the miracle occurred, and it is known as the Tiger Bridge to this day. In another place there is a great split rock inside which a mighty dragon slumbered for untold ages. One night in a terrible thunderstorm the rock was cleft asunder by lightning. The dragon flew away and was never seen again, but the story is true, because the sundered rock is still there and can be touched.

The numerous caves on the mountain have endless stories connected with them. One is supposed to be the haunt of nine great demons. Once upon a time some audacious monks determined that they would probe its mysteries. They advanced some distance into the interior without accident, when suddenly they were met by a prodigious bat that breathed fire. The monks turned round and walked away, wiser and sadder.

Another cave—the Thunder Cavern—is the haunt of a ghostly dragon, who lurks in the depths of a gloomy tarn. This cave, with its lake, has probably a very ancient history, for it seems to be associated in some way with animistic worship, of which there are many traces on Omei.[1] In seasons of drought it is or was formerly the custom to go to the cave with offerings of rich silks. If rain did not speedily fall as a result of the offerings, the correct procedure was to insult the dragon by throwing into his cave a dead pig and some articles of a still more disagreeable nature. This infallibly raised the wrath of the dragon, who immediately issued forth from his damp and gloomy home and roared. This meant thunder, and then the rain fell and all was well.

Mount Omei has several famous trees. Of one of them this story is told. In the Hui Tsung period (1101-25) of the Sung dynasty there was a very old tree, which about the year 1112 was torn open by a violent storm. Inside it was found a Buddhist monk, alive, in a state of ecstatic trance. The whole of his body was covered with his long hair and whiskers, and his nails were so long that they encircled his body. The emperor having heard of this living relic of the past, directed that he was to be carefully conveyed to the capital. Having with difficulty induced him to emerge from his tree, the messenger asked him his name. "I am the disciple," he replied, "of Yüan Fa-shih of Tung Lin. My name is Hui Ch'ih. I came to Omei on pilgrimage and entered

[1] See Note 1 (p. 411).

into meditation in this tree. How is my master Yüan? Is he well?" "Your master Yüan," said the imperial emissary, "lived in the time of the Chin dynasty, and died seven hundred years ago." Hui Ch'ih answered not a word, but turned his back and resumed meditation in his tree. A somewhat similar story is as follows. In the fourteenth century of our era there was a monk who had chosen for the scene of his meditations the hollow interior of an ancient decayed tree. There he sat cross-legged in silent contemplation until he was about eighty years of age. His piety apparently communicated some mysterious vitality to the tree, for suddenly it underwent an extraordinary change: the withered branches put forth fresh shoots, green foliage reappeared, and the gaping fissure in the trunk closed up, leaving the contemplative monk inside. The chronicler goes on to remark with ill-timed levity that the monk had begun by taking possession of the tree, but the tree had ended by taking possession of the monk. It is understood, however, that the accident by no means interrupted his meditations, and that he is still sitting cross-legged in the darkened interior of his sylvan retreat, wrapped in profound reverie.

There is a legend that the Buddha himself visited Mount Omei, and his footprint in a rock is still shown near the summit, though in this age of little faith its outline is scarcely recognisable. As one of the monasteries also possesses an alleged Buddha's tooth it is clear that the fame of Omei ought to be as far-reaching as that of Adam's Peak and Kandy combined; but Ceylon and

China are not the only countries that rejoice in the possession of footprints and teeth of the Buddha.

The local myths that have gathered round the name of the patron saint of Omei, P'u Hsien[1] Bodhisattva, who is said to have brought the sacred books of Buddhism from India to China on the back of an elephant, and deposited them on the mountain, are quite devoid of historical foundation, for P'u Hsien was merely one of the numerous figures invented by the Mahayana Buddhists to fill up the broad canvas of their vast symbolical system.[2] He represents, or rather is, the Samanta Bhadra of Indian Buddhism, and figures as such in that great Chinese Buddhist work, the *Hua Yen Ching*,[3] one of the voluminous productions of Nāgārjuna.[4] The monks of Omei have invented the famous elephant-ride simply because Samanta Bhadra is always associated with an elephant in such authoritative Mahayana works as the Saddharma-Pundarîka. The third last chapter of that work (in Kumarajiva's translation) deals with P'u Hsien, who is represented as declaring to the Buddha that he will "mount a white elephant with six tusks" and take good monks under his special protection, shielding them from gods, goblins and Mara the Evil One. The monks of Omei say that having come to the mountain on his elephant he established himself

[1] 普賢.

[2] He must not be confused with the Adi-Buddha or primordial deity of Red Lamaism, though the name is the same.

[3] 華嚴經. See especially *chüan*, 7-10.

[4] 龍樹 (*Lung Shu*) in Chinese.

there as a teacher of the Law of Buddha, and attracted three thousand pupils or disciples. It is quite possible that one of the original Buddhist hermits or monks of Omei acquired so great a celebrity that he became identified in the popular imagination with P'u Hsien. Something of the kind certainly happened in the case of other Bodhisattvas — Manjusri and Avalokiteçvara, for instance. But all trace of historic truth soon vanished in myth. In a Buddhistic work that relates to Omei, P'u Hsien is described as the eldest son of the Buddha himself. "The Tathâgata (Buddha) sits on a great lotus consisting of 1000 leaves. Each leaf has 3000 Universes. Each Universe has a Buddha to expound the Law, and each Buddha has a P'u Hsien as eldest son (*changtzŭ*)." This is not an attempt to identify P'u Hsien with Rahula, the son of the historical Buddha; it refers to the Mahayana doctrine that Samanta Bhadra or P'u Hsien is the spiritual son or reflex of the celestial Vairocana, one of the five mythical Buddhas, just as Gautama Sakyamuni (the historical Buddha) was supposed to be the earthly embodiment of the celestial Bodhisattva Avalokiteçvara, the spiritual son or reflex of the celestial Buddha Amitabha. As regards the significance of the elephant, it need only be mentioned here that in Indian Buddhistic mythology this animal (apart from its sacred association with the well-known dream of the Buddha's mother) is symbolical of self-control.[1]

The earliest religious buildings on Mount Omei

[1] See *Dhammapada*, chap. xxiii. *S.B.E.* vol. x. p. 78.

CHINESE BUDDHIST MONKS IN "UNDRESS."

[*To face p.* 65.

were no doubt solitary hermitages, erected by recluses whose religious enthusiasm impelled them to find in the deep recesses of its forests and gorges a welcome retreat from the noise and vanity of a world that they despised. As time went on, richly-endowed monasteries—nobler and more splendid than any now existing—rose in its silent ravines and by the side of its sparkling water-courses, and opened their doors to welcome those whom spiritual ecstasy or longing for a life of philosophic contemplation, or perhaps the anguish of defeated ambition, drove from the haunts of men. But gradually as religious fervour died away, the mountain recluses and solitary students of early days were succeeded by smaller men, distinguished neither for piety nor for scholarship. It must, indeed, be confessed that no tradition of sound learning has been kept up in the Buddhist Church in China. To some extent the lack of scholarship among Chinese Buddhists may perhaps be traced not too fancifully to the practice and teaching of Bodhidarma,[1] the so-called twenty-eighth patriarch of the Indian Buddhists, and the first of the patriarchs of China. He it was who, having landed in China early in the sixth century of our era, at once made it his business to discourage book-learning in the monasteries and to inculcate the doctrine that supreme enlightenment or mystical union with the Buddha can only be achieved by disregarding all exoteric teaching and by passive contemplation. By the recognition of all phenomena, including one's own personality, as illusory, the mind was to

[1] See Note 2 (p. 412).

be maintained in a condition of intellectual quiescence and receptivity, whereby it would be in a fit state to enter into communion with the Absolute. Of Bodhidarma the story is told that he sat for nine years in one position looking at a wall, which is a crude way of explaining that he was a contemplative mystic. In China his teachings have undoubtedly had a sterilising influence on thought, somewhat similar—though for different reasons—to the baneful influence exercised in Europe by the too-exclusive devotion of the mediæval schoolmen to Aristotle and Thomas Aquinas.

It may seem a far-fetched hypothesis to attribute part of the present degeneracy of the Buddhist monkhood in China to the teachings of a wall-gazing recluse who died nearly fourteen centuries ago. It might be urged that in searching for the cause of the present state of decay one need only point to the low orders of society from which the monks are recruited, the disfavour with which Buddhism is and always has been regarded by the orthodox Confucian, and the contempt which the thoroughly practical and worldly-minded Chinese layman almost invariably feels and expresses for the monastic profession. That these causes have powerfully assisted in accelerating the corruption that we witness to-day is unquestionably true; but there is a good deal of historical justification for the view that they are results rather than causes of Buddhist decay, and that the first and third would never have come into existence if Buddhism in China had not sunk into a state of intellectual torpor. If it had retained sufficient vigour and independence to reject all esoteric teachings and alien dogmas, even the great controversies with Confucianism would probably never have assumed the bitterness they did. Unfortunately, the extravagances of the later Mahayana doctrines and the foolish eclecticism which led the Buddhist Church to admit into its own system the crudities and banalities of corrupt Taoism, rendered the Buddhist position liable to attack at indefensible points, and compel us to admit that the controversial victories gained by Confucianism over its rival were the victories of light over darkness. It is strange that the repeated defeats and persecutions of Buddhism in China have not had the effect of bringing about either extinction or reform.

Chinese Buddhism is *sui generis*, and without a qualifying adjective it can scarcely be said to be Buddhism at all. This is no place to attempt a sketch of the history of that great religion in either its orthodox or its heretical aspects, but a few words may be necessary to enable the general reader to judge for himself whether Buddhism in China — quite apart from its present stagnant condition or the corruption of the monkhood—is entitled to the name it bears.

If there is one tenet of real Buddhism—by which I mean the doctrines on religious, philosophical and ethical subjects taught or sanctioned by the historical Buddha—which is more characteristic of that system than any other, it is the doctrine of the non-existence of the *attā* (*âtman*) or "soul." It was this doctrine, among others, which made Buddhism a Brahmanical heresy, for it involved the rejection of the Vedas as the final and supreme authority on matters of religion. The crude impression of some people that Buddhism teaches the "transmigration of souls" is absurd, for the simple reason that in the Buddhist system "souls" in the Western sense do not exist. What survives the death of the individual and transfers itself to another living being is not his soul but the cleaving to existence, a *tanha* or thirst for life, an unconscious—or semi-conscious—"will to live"; and with this *tanha* is inevitably associated *karma*, the integrated results of action or character. Buddhism regards the cleaving to existence as the outcome of the worst kind of ignorance or delusion —the mistaking of the phenomenal for the real, the false for the true; and until this delusion has been completely removed and the character purified from all lusts and all evil tendencies, the reintegration of karma in a world of pain, sorrow, sickness and death cannot by any possibility be avoided. Karma,[1] apart from its technical connotation, signifies "action" or "deeds." In the Buddhist sense it represents the accumulated results of the past actions and thoughts which every individual has inherited from countless multitudes of dead men, and which he will hand on, modified by the newly-generated karma of his own life-span, to countless

[1] The Pali word is *Kamma*, which, like the Sanskrit, simply means "doing; action; work; labour; business." See Childers' Pali Dictionary, *s.v.* *Kammam*. Mr A. E. Taylor, in his admirable work *The Elements of Metaphysics*, describes the Buddhist karma as "the system of purposes and interests" to which a man's "natural deeds give expression."

generations yet unborn. It is karma which forms the character of each individual, and determines the condition of life in which he finds himself placed. The man dies, and his conscious individuality ceases to be; but his karma continues, and determines the character and condition of life of another individual. Each individual may make or mar the karma that he has inherited: if he spoils it he may literally sink lower than the beasts; if he improves it he may literally rise higher than the gods. But to the Buddhist the final goal to be aimed at was not a continued personal existence, either in this world or elsewhere: it was the total extinction of reproductive karma by the attainment of Arahatship or Nirvana, and final release from the ever-circling wheel of existence, with its endless rotation of birth, disease, sorrow and death.[1]

On the question of a *primum mobile* — the force which produced the conditions under which arose the will-to-live with its illusions, and which brought into being the first appearance of karma

[1] Cf. Virgil, *Æneid*, vi. 719-721:

"O pater, anne aliquas ad caelum hinc ire putandumst
Sublimes animas iterumque ad tarda reverti
Corpora? Quae lucis miseris tam dira cupido?"

The whole passage from 703 to 751 is of great interest to those who like to trace Buddhistic thought in non-Buddhistic literature. Lines 66-68 of the Third Georgic are equally striking in this respect:

"Optima quaeque dies miseris mortalibus aevi
Prima fugit, subeunt morbi tristisque senectus
Et labor et durae rapit inclementia mortis."

It was just such reflections as this that filled the heart of the Sakya prince with pity and love for mankind. *Sunt lacrimae rerum et mentem mortalium tangunt*, the beautiful utterance of "the chastest and royalest" of poets, expresses the feeling that prompted the Great Renunciation and gave to the world a Buddha.

—Buddhism is agnostic or silent,[1] just as it is on the question of the existence of a supreme God. What Buddhism emphatically teaches is that karma once produced, continues ceaselessly to reproduce itself, carrying with it the modifications impressed upon it by the successive individuals through whom it has "transmigrated"; that the only way to release karma from the wheel of phenomenal existence is to eradicate the desire for a continuance or renewal of conscious personality; and that this end can only be attained by following the Noble Eightfold Path,[2] leading to Nirvana, which was pointed out by the Buddha. Mystical and fanciful interpretations of the meaning of Nirvana were forthcoming at an early date, but the canonical scriptures know nothing of such interpretations. It is quite clear that Nirvana was not the infinite prolongation of individual existence in a state of spiritual beatitude nor an absorption into a pantheistic Absolute; nor was the word intended to be a euphemism for death. It was simply a release from the thraldom of sense and passion; a "blowing-out" of personality and selfishness, of ignorance and delusion; an enfranchisement which in this present life would confer the boon of "the peace which passeth all understanding," and after this life would prevent rebirth, or rather reintegration of karma, in a world of pain and sorrow. To the Buddhist the whole world of sense, in which while subject to karma we live and move and have our being, is an illusion and unreal,—far more so than to the Platonist, to whom the phenomenal

[1] See Note 3 (p. 412). [2] The Chinese 八聖道分.

world is the reflexion, though an imperfect one, of an ideal archetype; and as the early Buddhist believed that the idea of self or personality was closely interwoven with the net of illusion, he was quite consistent when he held that the destruction of the one must involve the destruction of the other, and that release from the net is a desirable consummation. Nirvana may thus be described as full enlightenment as to the unreality and impermanence of phenomena, the removal of delusions about the self, and the eradication of the cleaving to life. Those who attained this enlightenment were the saints or "arahats" of primitive Buddhism.[1] The Buddha himself, it must be remembered, never laid any claim to godhead or even to personal immortality. His disciples reverenced him as the Fully Enlightened Sage, the Blessed One, the Teacher of gods and men, and he was the expounder of truths by the grasp of which men would be enabled to realise the condition of arahatship; but in the last resort it was to themselves and not to Buddha that men must look for salvation. "Therefore, O Ananda," said the Buddha in one of his last discourses, "be ye lamps unto yourselves. Be ye a refuge to yourselves. Betake yourselves to no external refuge. Hold fast to the truth as a lamp. Hold fast as a refuge to the truth. Look not for refuge to any one besides yourselves."[2]

How vastly different are the teachings of

[1] See Note 4 (p. 413).

[2] The Mahâ-Parinibbâna Suttanta, translated by Rhys Davids (*Sacred Books of the East*, vol. xi. p. 38).

Chinese Buddhists from those of the simple creed promulgated by the Buddha is obvious to all who have visited a Chinese monastery, or glanced at the wearisome sutras, in which the unorthodox dogmas are so elaborately set forth. The Brahmanical belief in the *âtman* or "soul" is practically reintroduced; arahatship is no longer the ideal to be aimed at by the virtuous man; Nirvana ceases to have any intelligible meaning; faith takes the place of works as a means to salvation. Celestial (Dhyâni) Buddhas are invented as heavenly reflexes of the various human Buddhas that are supposed to have lived on earth, and some of them receive worship as immortal gods; arahats are regarded as inferior to a class of mythical Bodhisattvas, who purposely refrain from entering into the state of Buddhahood in order that they may continue to exercise a beneficent influence among the beings who are still bound to the wheel of existence; the most glorious lot attainable by the ordinary man is held to be not a release from delusion and the pains of birth, sickness, and death, but a final rebirth in the glittering Paradise of the West. In this Paradise reigns the Lord of Eternal Life and Boundless Light, the great Dhyâni Buddha Amitabha; on his right and left are enthroned the Bodhisattvas Mahâsthâma and Avalokiteçvara,[1] the lords of infinite strength

[1] Avalokiteçvara is the Chinese Kuan Yin, generally represented in China (where temples to this divinity are exceedingly numerous) as a female, and known to Europeans as the "Goddess of Mercy." The change of sex is due to an identification of this Bodhisattva with a legendary Chinese princess, who devoted herself to saving human lives, especially from the dangers of the sea. She has thus become in a

and pity, the saviours of mankind. To win utter happiness in Sukhâvatî, the Western Paradise, is the object of the longings and prayers of the devout Chinese Buddhist. The name of Sakyamuni Buddha means little to him, and he may even be ignorant of who the Buddha was, and where he lived; but the names of "O-mi-to-fo" (Amitabha Buddha)[1] and of Kuan Yin P'u Sa (the Bodhisattva Avalokiteçvara) stand to him for everything that is holiest and most blissful. To such an extent have Amitabha and his attendant Bodhisattvas taken the place of the "Three Refuges"[2] of orthodox Buddhism that one almost feels justified in suggesting that the prevailing (though not the only) form of Buddhism in China should once and for all be differentiated from that of Burma and Ceylon, by the adoption of the name of Amitabhism, just as the corrupt religion of Tibet has rightly been given the special name of Lamaism.

If the Mahayana teachers in China had been satisfied with substituting the doctrine of a more or less sensual heaven for that of the orthodox arahatship or Nirvana on the ground that it was more suited to the comprehension of the ordinary

special sense the guardian deity of sailors; but she is also worshipped by women as the goddess who grants male offspring. Mahâsthâma is the Chinese Ta Shih Chih, the Bodhisattva of Great Strength. Eitel, in his *Handbook of Chinese Buddhism*, says that this Bodhisattva is perhaps the same as Maudgalyâyana; but this is a mistake, as is quite clear from the fact that, in certain sutras, such as the Amitâyur-Dhyāna Sutra, they figure as separate personalities.

[1] The Japanese Amida.

[2] "The Buddha, the Dharma, and the Samgha": *i.e.* the Buddha, the law and doctrine of the Buddha, and the Church or Community of Brethren established by the Buddha.

layman, and would be more effective in teaching the people to lead virtuous lives, their distortion of the early teachings might, perhaps, to some extent be justified; but unfortunately the form which the new doctrine took at a very early stage shows that no such theory was in their minds. Instead of exhorting to strenuous lives of virtue and good works, they went out of their way to teach that nothing was really necessary to salvation but loud and frequent appeals to the name of Amitabha Buddha and zealous repetitions of the appropriate sutras. One of the principal sutras of this class contains the following emphatic statement:—"Beings are not born in that Buddha country of the Tathâgata Amitâyus as a reward and result of good works performed in this present life. No, whatever son or daughter of a family shall hear the name of the blessed Amitâyus, the Tathâgata, and having heard it, shall keep it in mind, and with thoughts undisturbed shall keep it in mind for one, two, three, four, five, six or seven nights,—when that son or daughter of a family comes to die, then that Amitâyus, the Tathâgata, surrounded by an assembly of disciples and followed by a host of Bodhisattvas, will stand before them at their hour of death, and they will depart this life with tranquil minds. After their death they will be born in the world Sukhâvatî, in the Buddha country of the same Amitâyus, the Tathâgata. Therefore, then, O Sâriputra, having perceived this cause and effect, I with reverence say thus, Every son and every daughter of a family ought with their whole mind to make

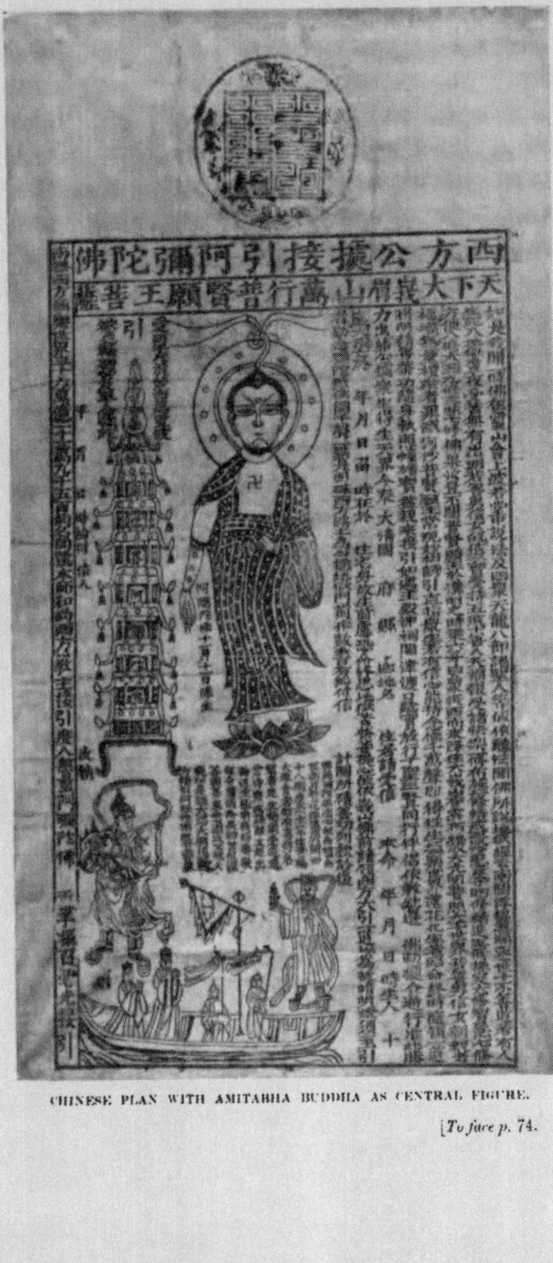

CHINESE PLAN WITH AMITABHA BUDDHA AS CENTRAL FIGURE.

[*To face p. 74.*

fervent prayer for that Buddha country."[1] Numerous Buddhist tracts are in existence and widely circulated among the people, in which it is explicitly stated that if a man calls sufficiently often on the name of Kuan Yin, he will be delivered from any danger or difficulty in which he may be placed, quite regardless of his deserts. There are popular stories in which it is told that even if a man be guilty of grave crimes for which he has been imprisoned and condemned to death, the knife of the executioner will break in pieces and do him no hurt provided only he has, with a believing heart, summoned to his aid the "Goddess of Mercy." Stories of this kind, even if educated men do not believe in them, can hardly have a beneficent effect upon morality, and hardly redound to the credit of the monks who invented them.

To blame the Chinese Buddhists, however, for failing to preserve their religion from corrupt influences is hardly fair: for it must be admitted that the stream of Buddhist literature and tradition that flowed for centuries into China from Northern India and Nepal issued from a source that was already tainted. Sakyamuni Buddha probably died in the fifth century B.C. Buddhism did not obtain a foothold in China till five or six centuries later, and it was not till the fourth century of our era that native Chinese began in large numbers to take the vows as Buddhist monks. By this time primitive Buddhism had already been cruelly distorted.

[1] The Smaller Sukhâvatî Vyûha, translated by Max Müller (*Sacred Books of the East*, vol. xlix.).

Where it was at all possible, the Mahayana dogmas were read into the simple scriptures that formed the Asokan canon; where the utmost ingenuity failed to find the germs of these dogmas in the canon, the doctors of the Mahayana school deliberately set themselves to compile a series of colossal forgeries by putting forth new sutras, purporting to have been uttered by the Buddha himself, but containing an entirely new book of doctrine.[1] Part of it was probably brought from Persia and Arabia, and nearly all was totally inconsistent with the primitive doctrine of the Buddha. Like the founder of the Mormons in after-ages, the pious forgers — let us hope they were unconscious of their guilt—pretended to be merely the "finders" of the new sutras. Sometimes they were said to have been discovered in caves guarded by demons. Nāgārjuna, for instance, who was one of the worst offenders, is supposed to have found in "the palace of the Dragon" the great Hua Yen sutra, already referred to, a work which justifies us in regarding Nāgārjuna as one of the principal inventors or adapters of the Mahayana doctrines, or at least as one of those who grafted them on the original Buddhistic stock. The Chinese admire him so much that they have elevated him into the position of a Bodhisattva, and celebrate his birthday on the 25th day of the seventh moon. Among the principal speakers in the Hua Yen sutra are the Buddha himself and the mythical Bodhisattvas P'u Hsien and Manjusri. The Mahayana doctrine concerning this order

[1] See Note 5 (p. 414).

of being is, as I have said, totally unknown to early Buddhism; and out of or beside this central doctrine of the Mahayana system grew up a cluster of dogmas which, like some parasitic weed, could only have the effect of choking and killing the original plant of which the Buddha himself had sown the seed. The Chinese "fathers" were not primarily responsible for all this. The vast mythology that culminates in the doctrine of Amitabha's heaven was accepted in China only too readily, but it was not a Chinese invention. If the history of these fanciful dogmas can be more readily traced in China and Tibet than elsewhere, it is only because Buddhism practically ceased to exist in the country of its origin. What Chinese Buddhism might have been if it had sought to establish itself upon the Asokan canon instead of upon a bundle of crude myths and grotesque allegories may be realised easily enough by comparing it with the Buddhism of Burma and Siam, which—in spite of their tolerance of a system of animistic worship alien to Buddhism—have preserved almost intact the body of doctrine that they inherited through Ceylon from the orthodox Church. What with the growth of the mystic schools derived from Bodhidarma, the Tantra schools with their magic spells and incantations, the Lin Tzŭ school that teaches religion in the form of enigmas, the Wu Wei school with its doctrine of a Golden Mother, the hideous demonology introduced into Buddhism by a debased wonder-working Taoism, and the innumerable schools that unite in their praises of the bejewelled Western Heaven which can be attained merely by repeating the name of Amitabha Buddha or Kuan Yin P'u Sa, it is no wonder that Buddhism in China has fallen a victim to the fangs of its own grotesque offspring.

In the following chapter some further remarks on Mount Omei will, I trust, serve to emphasise the observations already made, and will perhaps help the European reader who has not visited China to form some conception of the theory and practice of Chinese Buddhism at the present day. I hope I may be excused if I depart so far from the usual practice of travellers in China as to refrain from entering into a discussion of the general question of religion, especially in connection with Christian propaganda. For my own part, I may perhaps venture to express the hope and belief that the missionary question is one which time will solve at no very distant date. As soon as a reformed China has earned for herself—by the reform of her legal codes and judicial procedure—the right to demand the total abolition of foreign consular jurisdiction within Chinese territory, missionaries will cease to be a thorn in the flesh of Chinese officialdom. They may obtain fewer converts, but they will at least have the satisfaction of knowing that such converts as they may then gain will not be actuated by the desire to secure foreign protection against the laws of their own country; whereas the official classes will no longer have cause to regard missionaries as a political danger. There is no doubt that many of the outbreaks of fanatical hatred against foreigners are directly or indirectly traceable to the missionary question.[1] In spite of this fact it will be generally conceded that, like most Orientals, the Chinese are, in purely religious matters, inclined to be extremely tolerant: far more so, needless to say, than Western peoples usually are. History proves that the Chinese people are not hostile to foreign religious doctrines as such, but only when foreign religions tend to introduce disintegrating forces into the social fabric. Similarly the official classes are not inimical to foreign religions as such, but only when foreign religions threaten the stability of the political fabric and the independence of the State. These dangers will no longer operate when foreign missionary enterprise absolutely ceases to have even the semblance

[1] Any one who is not hopelessly narrow-minded can thoroughly sympathise with the missionary position. The missionaries as a body are men of religious enthusiasm. They believe they have been summoned by their Master to preach to non-Christians a faith which they believe to be the only true faith; and some of them believe that an acceptance of this faith is "necessary to salvation." From their point of view, all missionary work is entirely justified; and from any point of view the work the Christian missions have done in alleviating sickness and pain in China is wholly admirable. As regards the purely religious aspect of the question, I am glad to refrain from expressing a personal opinion. It is a subject which requires to be handled with extraordinary delicacy, for many people are unable to discuss it dispassionately, and it gives rise to endless arguments which from the nature of the case are and must be utterly devoid of persuasive power. Now that Religion, as distinct from any systematised Creed, has taken its place among the recognised subjects of philosophical investigation (and psychological also, as in Professor James's brilliant book, *The Varieties of Religious Experience*), we may expect to hear missionary work discussed (at least by educated persons) with less bitterness and strong language than has sometimes disgraced the controversialists on both sides. A short and incomplete but very interesting discussion of the missionary question from an obviously impartial point of view may be found in Professor Knight's *Varia*, pp. 31-35. (John Murray: 1901.)

of a connection with international politics, and foreign missionaries become in all respects amenable to the courts of the country in which they live and work. Whether the change will tend to spread the doctrines of Christianity in China with greater rapidity, or will, on the other hand, bring about its ultimate extinction, is a question regarding which it would be rash to prophesy. Given fair field and no favour it might well seem that the disorganised forces of a corrupt Buddhism would be ill fitted to cope with such strenuous and well-equipped adversaries as the Churches of Christendom: yet perhaps it is more likely that the ultimate victory will rest with neither. The clashing of forces that must assuredly result from the weakening of the hold of Confucianism on the educated classes and the introduction of new political and social ideals may lead to an intellectual upheaval tending to the destruction of all religion. Even to-day, the only vigorous element in the heterogeneous religious systems of China consists in that expansion of the ideal of filial piety which takes the form of the cult of ancestors: a cult which has done so much in the past to preserve, consolidate and multiply the Chinese people and make them peaceful, law-abiding and home-loving, and which has nevertheless been condemned as idolatrous by the two great branches of the Christian faith. It was this rock of Chinese orthodoxy that shattered the power of the Church of Rome in China, and that rock is still a danger and an obstruction in the troubled waters through which glide the frail barks of the Christian missions. On the whole, it seems improbable that the dogmas, at least, of any of the Christian Churches will ever find general acceptance on Chinese soil. The moral and spiritual regeneration of China is more likely to be brought about by the growth of a neo-Confucianism frankly accepting such adaptations as the social and political conditions of modern times may render necessary; and if this is insufficient to satisfy the spiritual aspirations of the people, there may arise a reformed Buddhism drawing its inspiration either from the simple faith of Burma, Siam, and Ceylon, or—far more probably—from one of the complex systems (near in kinship to those of China but with a vitality of their own) that have evolved themselves upon the soil of Japan.

CHAPTER VII

MOUNT OMEI

VERY few of the buildings now existing on Mount Omei can boast of antiquity, for a damp climate and the ravages of fire have in the past made short work of their fragile timbers. The monasteries are humble structures, being simply one-storied bungalows of wood. Compared with the richly-carved teakwood *wats* of Siam and *kyaungs* of Burma, they are unpretentious buildings with little decoration, and what there is possesses small artistic merit. Over the doorways and under the eaves hang sundry massive wooden boards, resplendent with richly-gilded characters, giving the name of the monastery and brief quotations from the Buddhist scriptures. Most of the tablets containing inscriptions or quotations have been presented by devout pilgrims, but the periodical regilding of the characters is paid for out of the corporate funds. The interiors are generally more imposing; for every monastery on Mount Omei is also a temple, and the decoration of the halls containing the images of the Buddha and his saints is generally on a fairly lavish scale. The larger temples have a series of such halls one behind the other, with courts or quadrangles intervening, the sides of each quadrangle being occupied by the monks' living quarters. There are also spacious quarters for visitors. The office in which the financial and other secular affairs of the monastery are administered is generally a small room on the left side of the first hall of images, corresponding to a room on the other side which is used as a kind of porter's lodge. In the latter room the monks spend a great deal of their time in the cold weather, and sit huddled round a charcoal brazier. From the middle of the room they can see, through the open door, every one who enters and leaves the temple by the main entrance; and one of them is generally deputed to attend on every group of visitors or pilgrims. All pilgrims bring their own food with them — the Chinese their rice, and the Tibetans their *tsamba*; but those whose appearance entitles them to respect, or who have given a substantial donation to the funds of the establishment, are invited to drink tea and eat sweetmeats, and warm themselves by the charcoal fire. The Buddhistic injunction to avoid taking life is rigorously obeyed on Mount Omei by visitors as well as residents, all of whom conform to a strictly vegetarian diet. The only persons who ever disregard this rule are some inconsiderate Europeans. Small subscriptions—generally in the form of copper "cash" — are placed on an offertory plate, or on the altar table in front of one of the principal images, and are deposited there by the pilgrims after they have finished their devotions. Those who wish to leave a permanent record of their visit, or whose donation exceeds a *tael* (say three shillings), inscribe their names or paste their cards in the subscription book, with a statement of the amount of their donations. An ingenious plan has been devised to relieve pilgrims of the necessity of carrying large quantities of coin up the mountain, and at the same time to invalidate excuses of want of money. In the town of Omei-hsien, where every pilgrim spends the night before beginning the ascent, he is visited by a banker or broker, who offers him little paper notes or chits called *fei tzŭ*, bearing various face-values from ten taels down to one hundred cash (about twopence). They are printed from wooden blocks, and in many cases the amount of money represented is inserted in writing. The pilgrim selects as many *fei tzŭ* as he thinks he may require or can afford, and pays over their face-value to the banker. The notes are handed as occasion requires, or benevolence prompts, to the temple treasurers, or are deposited on the altars, and are received in the temples as readily as coin. When a considerable collection of them has been made in any monastery they are sent down to the banker, who deducts his very small commission and settles the account either by sending silver in return, or by crediting the monastery with the amount in his books.

The monasteries naturally vary in size. Some of them are the homes of a score or more of monks and acolytes, while the smaller ones shelter but three or four. When a monastery is destroyed by fire or other cause, its elderly or infirm inmates lodge themselves temporarily in one of the neighbouring religious houses, while the more energetic go forth on a pilgrimage—sometimes as far as the Eastern sea-board—carrying with them a donation book for the purpose of collecting funds for rebuilding. When the monastery arises again from its ashes it is practically a new foundation with new endowments, even its name being sometimes altered. In spite of the apathy concerning religious matters that strikes every European observer as characteristic of China to-day, it is a significant fact that large subscriptions for religious purposes can always be obtained from the Chinese layman notwithstanding his protestations of contempt for the monastic ideal and for the idle and useless lives led by the vast majority of Chinese Buddhist monks.

Passing by the Pao-ning monastery, which is situated on the plain between the city and the mountain-base, I visited the monasteries of the White Dragon (Pai Lung Ssŭ), and the Golden Dragon (Chin Lung Ssŭ), and stopped for the night at the Wan-nien Ssŭ, formerly the White Water Monastery of P'u Hsien. This is one of the largest establishments on the mountain, and its written history goes back to the third century, if not further. It contains many objects of interest, the chief of which is the life-size bronze elephant discovered, or rather first described, by Baber. The very curious spiral-roofed brick building in which it stands—believed by Baber to have been erected by Hindu Buddhists not later than the sixth century of the Christian era—is unfortunately so small and shut in that it is impossible either to photograph the elephant or to view it from a proper standpoint. Baber believed that this edifice was, next to the Great Wall, the oldest building in China of fairly authentic antiquity, and he considered that the elephant was the most ancient bronze casting of any great size in existence,—perhaps fifteen centuries old. I have some reason, however, to doubt the alleged antiquity of both building and elephant.[1] Upon the animal's back is a bronze statue of P'u Hsien P'u Sa (Samanta Bhadra Bodhisattva), who, as I have said, is supposed to have come from India to Mount Omei on an elephant. Among modern curiosities at the Wan-nien Ssŭ is a small alabaster image of Gautama Buddha, which was recently brought from Burma by a Chinese Buddhist monk who had been on pilgrimage to the shrines of Mandalay and Rangoon. The same pilgrim presented a coloured print of the great Shwe Dagon pagoda at Rangoon, which is regarded by the monks of Wan-nien as a precious work of art, though its intrinsic value is, of course, trifling. There is also, in a separate building called the Hai Hui T'ang,[2] a supposed tooth-relic of Buddha, which is treated with strange lack of reverence.[3] But it is only an elephant's molar, and the monks know it.

[1] See Note 6 (p. 414). [2] 海會堂

[3] See Note 7 (p. 417).

Wan-nien Ssŭ is situated at a height of about 3,500 feet above the sea-level. The summit of the mountain (11,000 feet[1]) is therefore still a long way off; but as I succeeded in reaching it on the evening of the day on which I left Wan-nien Ssŭ, in spite of the fact that the path was often obliterated by snow and ice, I satisfied myself that the difficulty of the climb has often been much exaggerated. In dry weather, indeed, there is no reason why a healthy man of average physical vigour should not accomplish in one day the whole climb from base to summit: though such a feat of endurance would prevent him from paying much attention to the objects of interest on the way. The mountain sides are luxuriantly wooded, and it is only when the path approaches the edge of a precipice or a steep slope that any extensive view can be obtained during the greater part of the ascent. The silver fir, evergreen-oak, pine, cypress, laurel, birch, chestnut, spruce, *nan-mu*, maple (several species) and *camptotheca acuminata* are all to be met with, and there are innumerable flowering plants and ferns; but the character of the flora naturally varies a great deal at the different altitudes. On the exposed parts of the summit there is little but dwarf bamboos, junipers and rhododendrons, though in sheltered places I noticed the silver fir, liquidambar, yew, willow, pirus, and several kinds of shrubs. Other trees, like the alder, Chinese ash, and banyan, are confined to the plain

[1] This is the usually accepted estimate; but Sir A. Hosie has recently stated it to be only 10,158 feet.

or to the lower slopes. The banyans[1] of the Omei plain are magnificent trees, some of them of enormous girth.

Below Wan-nien Ssŭ I left behind me spring warmth and sprouting vegetation. By the time I had reached a height of 4,000 feet there were patches of snow on the roadside; 2,000 feet higher all visible trace of the path was gone, icicles hung from the leafless trees, while small acolytes from the monasteries, clad in their wadded winter garments, were busily sweeping away the snow in front of the gateways. When I left Omei-hsien my thermometer registered 64° Fahr. At Wan-nien Ssŭ the temperature had sunk to 49°; on the summit of the mountain there were 18 degrees of frost after sunset.

The next temple to Wan-nien Ssŭ is the Kuan Hsin Ting,[2] a poor building which was apparently in sole charge of a child of nine. The next is the Hsi Hsin So.[3] These words may be interpreted as "The Haven of the Tranquil Heart," but they also mean "The Pilgrim's Rest," for *hsi hsin* are the words used to translate or explain the Sanskrit term *sramana*,[4] an ascetic or monk. The records of the mountain explain the name by saying that when the pilgrim reaches this place, he can no longer hear the growlings and mutterings of the "dusty world": his heart therefore becomes as peaceful as his surroundings. In the building is a large image of Maitrêya, the "Buddha of the Future," who

[1] *Ficus infectoria.* [2] 觀心頂. [3] 息心所.
[4] Literally, "the quelling of the passions."

is supposed to be in the Tushita heaven, awaiting incarnation.

Passing by the Ch'ang Lao P'ing[1] temple, the next is the Ch'u Tien,[2] otherwise known as the Tsu Tien. *Tsu* is a kind of red-eyed duck, and the allusion is to the duck-like shape of a neighbouring rock. The temple contains rather life-like images of the eighteen *lo-han*.[3] These Chinese words represent the Sanskrit *arhat* or *arahat*, "venerable" or "worthy." We meet with arhats in the oldest Buddhist scriptures. They were the worthiest and most enlightened of Buddha's disciples; men who fully understood the doctrine as it was delivered to them by their master, and accepted it as a final statement of truth. Arahatship, as we have seen in the last chapter, is the goal aimed at by all true Buddhists, and implies a release from all delusion, ignorance and sorrow. In technical language the arahat is the man who has acquired the "four distinctive qualifications" (*patisambhidâ*) and has attained the state of "final sanctification." In the hands of the Mahayanists the arahats come to be persons possessing magical powers,[4] such as that of moving without support through space, in which respect they are the nearest approach to the mysterious Tibetan beings invented by the self-styled "theosophists": but

[1] 長老坪.

[2] 開山初殿. See Note 8 (p. 418).

[3] 阿羅漢.

[4] In the early Buddhist scriptures we learn that super-normal powers were even then supposed to be characteristic of the arhats, but it was generally considered undesirable to put such powers to the test.

arahatship as an ideal becomes altogether subordinate to that of Bodhisattship, the state of the holy man who, having arrived at the stage next preceding that of Buddhahood, voluntarily refrains from taking the final step, in order that he may remain as a teacher and saviour among men. In the Chinese Buddhistic system there are several classifications of the arahats or *lo-han*: we find them in groups of twelve hundred, five hundred, eighteen and sixteen. The twelve hundred are only met with, so far as I am aware, in books; but many large temples in China contain images of the five hundred. In Canton, for example, there is what Europeans have rather foolishly named the Hall of the Five Hundred Genii. Some wag once fancied he saw a resemblance in one of the figures there to Marco Polo, and for some reason or other the idea struck the professional Canton guides as such a happy one that for many years past they have been in the habit of deluding thousands of European and American travellers with the belief that Messer Marco has been turned into a Chinese "god." The mistake assumes a somewhat grotesque character when we remember that, according to the Chinese belief, each of the five hundred lo-han is destined at some remote period to become a Buddha.[1] In the majority of Chinese temples—as in those of Mount Omei—the number of lo-han represented by images is only eighteen; but there is a difference of opinion among the

[1] See the Saddharma-Pundarīka, translated by Kern in the *Sacred Books of the East*, vol. xxi. The Chinese version is known as the Miao Fa Lien Hua Ching (妙法蓮華經).

followers of different schools as to the identity of two of these. In Korea and Japan the temples generally contain sixteen lo-han, while Tibetan Lamaism sometimes recognises sixteen and sometimes eighteen.[1] The two extra ones seem to have been added as an after-thought by Chinese Buddhists in comparatively modern times.

Above the Temple of the Red-eyed Duck comes the Hua Yen Ting.[2] As already mentioned, the name *Hua Yen* is that of a famous sutra "discovered" by Nāgārjuna. The temple contains the eighteen lo-han and figures of Sakyamuni Buddha and the two Bodhisattvas P'u Hsien and Manjusri.[3] Behind these three central figures is a small Kuan Yin (Avalokiteçvara). On leaving this temple the road strikes downwards for a short distance, and, soon after recommencing the ascent, we arrive next at the monastery known as the Lien Hua Shih[4] ("Lotus Flower Stone"), where there is a holy relic consisting of the curiously-

[1] See an article on this subject by T. Watters, in the *Journal of the Royal Asiatic Society*, April 1899. See also Edkins, *Chinese Buddhism*, pp. 249 and 394-395.

[2] 華嚴頂.

[3] Manjusri (文殊師利) is a Bodhisattva who in China is practically worshipped as the God of Wisdom. Like Ti Tsang, Kuan Yin and others, he is supposed to have had a human prototype, or rather to have been incarnated in the body of a historical personage. But the truth probably is that any person of superlative wisdom was liable to be identified by his admirers with Manjusri. There is an interesting reference to him in I-Tsing's *Records of the Buddhist Religion*, translated by J. Takakusu (Oxford: Clarendon Press, 1896), p. 169. The translator comments on the fact that Manjusri was even by the people of India supposed, at one time, to be somehow connected with China, and the actual place of his residence was identified as Ping Chou in Chih-li.

[4] 蓮花石.

shaped stone from which the place derives its name. I found a number of Tibetan pilgrims rubbing coins on it; the coins to be afterwards carefully preserved as charms. The stone is said by the monks (on no authority that I can discover) to have been brought up from deep waters by miraculous agency, and to have floated on the surface like the flower of the lotus. The lotus myth in Buddhist cosmology is based on a very picturesque allegory, with which most of my readers are probably acquainted. Its meaning has been accurately described in the following words by E. J. Eitel, who, though he possesses the usual bias against "heathendom," is a fairly sympathetic writer on Buddhist subjects. "The idea conveyed in this flowery language of Buddhism is of highly poetic and truly speculative import, amounting to this: that as a lotus flower, growing out of a hidden germ beneath the water, rises up slowly, mysteriously, until it suddenly appears above the surface and unfolds its buds, leaves, and pistils, in marvellous richness of colour and chastest beauty of form; thus also, in the system of worlds, each single universe rises into being, evolved out of a primitive germ, the first origin of which is veiled in mystery, and finally emerges out of the chaos, gradually unfolding itself, one kingdom of nature succeeding the other, all forming one compact whole, pervaded by one breath, but varied in beauty and form. Truly an idea, so far removed from nonsense, that it might be taken for an utterance of Darwin himself."[1]

[1] *Three Lectures on Buddhism*, pp. 60-61.

Visitors to Buddhist temples cannot fail to observe how frequently the lotus allegory has been made to subserve religious and artistic purposes, and we have seen in the last chapter how it has been associated with the story of the beginning of P'u Hsien's worship on Mount Omei. The images of the Buddhas and Bodhisattvas are nearly always represented as sitting or standing in the centre of a huge open lotus, and even P'u Hsien's elephant stands on the same sacred plant.

As regards the stone in the Lien Hua monastery, I may add that it does not bear the smallest resemblance to a lotus or any other plant, and apparently it is not supposed to do so. Its original crude shape has evidently never been tampered with, though its surface has been worn smooth by constant rubbing.

Into the same temple another stone—not a sacred one—has found its way. It is a huge boulder, many tons in weight, that was brought down the mountain side some years ago by an avalanche, and crashed into the back of the main hall, where, for superstitious reasons—and perhaps because its removal would be a matter of immense difficulty—it has been allowed to remain. On a hanging scroll above the central images I noticed a Chinese transliteration[1] of the well-known Tibetan formula, "*Om Mane Padme Hom* (or *Hung*),"[2] generally translated—but this is a controversial matter—"Hail! The Jewel in the Lotus." The

[1] 唵 嘛 呢 叭 𡁠 吽.

[2] ཨོཾ་མ་ཎི་པད་མེ་ཧཱུྃ་

first word *Om* or *Aum* is the well-known sacred syllable of Brahmanism; practically it is simply a *syllaba invocationis.* The Jewel may mean the Buddha, or his Law (Dharma), or the Buddhist Church (Sangha), or all three combined, or more probably signifies Avalokiteçvara (the Chinese Kuan Yin and Japanese Kwannon), who in Lamaism is supposed to be incarnated in every successive Grand Lama. But, as a matter of fact, very few of the Tibetans who mutter the sentence as they walk or turn it in their prayer-wheels, or carve it on stones and rocks by the wayside, can give any clear idea of what they mean by it. Like the Chinese *Nam-Mo* (or *Nan-Wu*) *O-mi-to-Fo*[1] ("Praise be to Amitabha Buddha"), it is regarded as a kind of *dhâranî* or mystic spell, the constant repetition of which will lead the believer to a life of bliss in Sukhâvatî, the Western Paradise. The only Chinese whom I met on the mountain besides the residents were Buddhist monks on pilgrimage, and the invocation to Amitabha was constantly on their lips; the other was repeated with equal persistence by the Tibetan pilgrims. During part of my climb the mountain was enveloped in a thick mist, which muffled the sound of footsteps; but there was seldom a moment that I did not hear one or other of these mystic sentences floating weirdly in the air above me or below.

A steep climb soon brought me to the Hsi Hsiang Ch'ih[2] ("The Elephant's Bath"), where a

[1] 南無阿彌陀佛.
[2] 洗象池.

temple has been built close to a pool of water where P'u Hsien's famous elephant is said to have bathed after his long journey. The temple contains images of Sakyamuni Buddha, P'u Hsien and Manjusri. Behind them, in the same hall, are three beautifully gilded figures, larger than life-size, representing Amitabha Buddha attended by Kuan Yin and Ta Shih Chih[1] Bodhisattvas. These are the three beings who are supposed to preside over the Western Paradise; their images are therefore frequently found together, Amitabha always in the centre. In another hall is an image of Kuan Yin unattended.

The next temple is known as the Great Vehicle[2] or Mahayana monastery. Here are images of Sakyamuni, Manjusri and P'u Hsien, who are also constantly associated in this manner; and behind them, facing in the opposite direction, is a large Maitrêya, the Coming Buddha. After a fairly steep ascent thence and a short descent the path rises to the Pai Yün Ku Ch'a[3] ("The Old Monastery of the White Clouds")—which at the time of my visit I found to be a most appropriate name. Here there is a colossal sedent image of Chang Liang,[4] a warlike hero who died in the second century of our era, after he had made an ineffectual attempt to achieve immortality by starving himself. He was subsequently canonised by the name of Wên Ch'êng.[5] In another hall are Sakyamuni Buddha, Manjusri and P'u Hsien, supported by the eighteen lo-han.

[1] 大勢至. [2] 大乘寺. See Note 9 (p. 418).
[3] 白雲古剎. [4] 張良. [5] 文成.

In ascending to the next temple, the Lei Tung P'ing,[1] all pilgrims are expected to preserve absolute silence. The Lei Tung or Thunder Cavern is that which shelters the irascible Dragon of rain and thunder, to whom I referred in the last chapter. An inscription that hangs in the temple apparently refers to his controlling powers over lightning and rain-clouds.[2] The slightest sound of the human voice, either in laughter or in speech, is liable to produce a terrific whirlwind and thunderstorm.

Next above this perilous locality comes the Chieh Yin Tien[3] — the Temple of Amitabha. The words *chieh yin* mean "to receive and lead," and are applied to Amitabha because he it is who is supposed to assist the faithful to reach the Western Heaven in which he reigns. The first hall contains a richly-gilded colossal statue of this Buddha, standing upright. Behind him is a figure of Wei To[4] (*Vêda*), a Bodhisattva who is regarded as a *vihârapâla*, or tutelary deity of the Buddhist monkhood. He is responsible for seeing that the recluses do not suffer through lack of nourishment, and that the monastery is properly supplied with necessaries. The second hall contains the eighteen lo-han in bronze. There are also the usual images of Sakyamuni and his attendant Bodhisattvas, and a colossal gilded P'u Hsien sitting on a lotus on the back of a white elephant.

[1] 雷洞坪. [2] 掣電飛雲. [3] 接引殿.

[4] 韋陀 or 護法韋陀: *Veda Fidei Defensor*—a Hindu deity who was regarded as one of the protectors of the four "Continents" of the world or Universe.

In the right-hand corner of this well-populated hall is another triad of divinities: Yo Shih Fo,[1] a mythical Buddha who dwells in an eastern world, with Ti Tsang and Kuan Yin Bodhisattvas on his left and right. This is a favourite Buddha in China, and is supposed to hold in the East a position somewhat analogous to that of Amitabha in the West. In the popular imagination he has replaced the Motionless (*wu tung*) Buddha Akchôbhya (A-ch'u-p'o) and is worshipped as the healer of sickness. Ti Tsang[2] is one of the great Bodhisattvas, like P'u Hsien, Ta Shih Chih and Manjusri. The principal seat of his worship in China is in the province of Anhui. He is the benevolent being who seeks to save human beings from the punishments of hell. His prototype is said to have been a Siamese prince.

A steep ascent from this interesting monastery leads to the Ku T'ai Tzŭ P'ing,[3] the "Ancient Temple of the Prince Royal." It is said that this building is named after a prince of the Ming dynasty, but the monks of to-day prefer to regard the T'ai Tzŭ as Sakyamuni Buddha himself, in the character of Prince Siddharta, son of the king of Kapilavastu. The figure representing him is attired in real robes, richly embroidered. On his right is P'u Hsien, seated on a white tuskless elephant. As already mentioned, P'u Hsien's elephants are generally characterised by their six

[1] 藥師佛, whose common title *Lui Li Fo* (琉璃佛) translates the Sanskrit *Vaidūrya*, *lapis lazuli*. This precious stone seems also to have been associated with a favourite Assyrian deity, Ênu-rêstū.

[2] 地藏. [3] 古太子坪.

tusks. On the prince's left is Kuan Yin; and behind these three central figures are images of Ti Tsang, Ta Shih Chih, Wên Ch'êng (Chang Liang) and Manjusri, all of whom have been described.

The next is the Yung-ch'ing Ssŭ[1] or Eternal Happiness monastery. Here a many-armed Kuan Yin faces the entrance, and behind him (or her) is an Amitabha. The only new figure among the rest is that of Bodhidarma or Ta-mo, the St Thomas of the Catholic missionaries.[2] He sits cross-legged with the first finger of the right hand raised. A small P'u Hsien is seated on an elephant with four tusks, the other two being lost. In this hall I observed some heaps of broken statues in bronze and iron, the remains of a ruined temple. From here a level path leads to the K'ai Shan Jou Shên Tsu Shih Tien,[3] which, as the name partly indicates, contains a gruesome relic in the shape of the mummified body of a former abbot, attired in the robes he wore in life. The dried shrunken face has been lacquered with great care, and no one would guess that the figure was not made of clay or bronze. It is not the only mummy on the mountain. From here a short steep path leads to the Eagle-wood Pagoda,[4] a monastery named after a miniature nine-storied bronze pagoda, the gift of a Ming empress. The next temple bears the imposing inscription of "The

[1] 永慶寺.

[2] See above, p. 66.

[3] 開山肉身祖師殿.

[4] 沉香塔. The aloes or eagle-wood is so-called because it sinks (*ch'ên*) in water. It is supposed to be the aloes-wood mentioned in the Bible.

August Guard of the Gate of Heaven,"[1] where there is a large Sakyamuni with the usual attendant Bodhisattvas. Next comes the Ch'i T'ien Ch'iao[2]—The Bridge of the Seventh Heaven—where there is a small temple in which the three Bodhisattvas — P'u Hsien (in the middle) and Manjusri and Kuan Yin (on the right and left)—sit in a row in front of a solitary image of Sakyamuni. The next temple is the P'u Hsien Pagoda,[3] where the patron saint of Mount Omei, as is natural, occupies the place of honour in the middle of the hall facing the entrance. Behind him is Amitabha, and at the back of the hall, right and left, are Sakyamuni and Kuan Yin. On the left side of the hall is an image of one of the favourite personages in the Chinese theogony—Ts'ai Shên, the "God of Wealth."[4] This god is so popular in China that Buddhism could not afford to neglect him, but as he is really a Taoist divinity he is only allowed to appear in a Buddhist temple as an act of grace. The same may be said of Kuan Ti,[5] the God of War, Lung Wang[6] the Dragon Raja or Naga-king, and the San Kuan.[7]

From this temple a short walk over a wooden-paved path, kept clear of snow by sedulous sweeping, leads to the Hsi Wa Tien[8] — the Pewter-Roofed Hall. At one time there were three "halls," with roofs of pewter, bronze and iron respectively.

[1] 威鎮天門 [2] 七天橋
[3] 普賢塔. [4] 財神 or 財帛星神.
[5] 關帝. [6] 龍王.
[7] 三官. [8] 錫瓦殿.

The metal roofs have vanished, though the names remain. "Pewter - roof" is specially appropriate to a Buddhist monastery, for pewter is the only metal that Buddhist monks may — in theory — possess. Each monk is supposed to carry a pewter-headed staff when he goes on pilgrimage or on his begging-rounds; and when he lodges at a monastery he is said to *kua hsi*, which literally means "to hang up the pewter." In south China there is a spring called the Pewter Spring, because it bubbled up at the bidding of a thirsty monk who struck the ground with his staff.

Another short climb brought me at last to the summit of Mount Omei, where, at a height of about 11,000 feet, I found welcome and rest in the spacious monastery that proudly describes itself as "The Golden Hall of the True Summit."[1]

Though I was not expected by the monks—for my two soldiers had failed to keep up with me in spite of my efforts to send them on as my ambassadors — I was at once made comfortable in a large, clean apartment on the first floor; and when my hosts heard that I was a humble student of their religion they soon provided me with as ample a vegetarian banquet as I could have desired, and treated me with great kindness.

An hour after my arrival I stood outside the temple gateway watching the sun set below

[1] Chêng Ting Chin Tien (正頂金殿). There is another Chin Tien or Golden Temple on the summit of a range of mountains north-east of Tali-fu in Yunnan (the Chi Shan) which is also a noted centre for Buddhist pilgrimages. A short account of the temples of this mountain is given in a Foreign Office Report by the late Mr Litton. (China, No. 3: 1903, pp. 4-6.)

a wild white ocean of clouds that laved the mountain side about 2,000 feet below me and turned the summit of Mount Omei into a snow-draped island. The air rapidly grew bitterly cold, and I was glad to seek warmth indoors by the side of my charcoal fire. My dilatory escort, carrying my modest baggage, came wearily in just as it began to grow dark.

The next morning held in store a wonderful surprise. The vast ocean of white clouds had entirely disappeared, and the wide country that lay far below me was bathed in the glory of brilliant sunlight. The sun rarely reveals himself in his full splendour in Ssuch'uan—so rarely that when he does so the dogs are said to bark at him [1]—and on Omei's summit sunshine is rare even for Ssuch'uan; but by good fortune it was on one of those exceptional occasions that I spent there the whole of one memorable day.

There are several monasteries on or near the summit. The one in which I lodged for two nights is crowned with a gilded ball that scintillates on its roof. Just behind the various buildings of this monastery is the tremendous precipice from the edge of which fortunate pilgrims witness the phenomenon known as the "Glory of Buddha." [2] As mentioned in the last chapter, this is the appearance of a gleaming aureole floating horizontally on the mist a few thousand feet below the summit. This beautiful phenomenon, to which is probably due the special sanctity of Mount Omei, has not yet been quite satisfactorily explained. It

[1] 日出則犬吠. [2] 佛光.

has been likened to the famous Brocken Spectre, and to the Shadow of the Peak in Ceylon, but the brilliant and varied colours of "Buddha's Glory"—five colours, say the Chinese—give it a rainbow-like beauty which those appearances do not possess.[1] The pious Buddhist pilgrim firmly believes that it is a miraculous manifestation of the power and glory of the Buddha—or of his spiritual Son P'u Hsien—and is always much disappointed if he has to leave the mountain without catching a glimpse of it.[2] The necessary conditions of its appearance are said to be a clear sky above and a bank of clouds below, and as those conditions were not fulfilled for me I must sorrowfully confess that I cannot describe the spectacle from personal experience. But the circumstance that deprived me of that privilege enabled me to have a superb view of the surrounding country. Nearly 10,000 feet below me to the north and east lay the rich rolling plains of central Ssuch'uan; to the south the silver streak of the Ta Tu river and the wild mountains that enable the mysterious Lolo races to maintain their solitary independence; slightly to the south-west appeared the huge mass of the

[1] A somewhat similar phenomenon, described as an "anthelia," may be witnessed in Ceylon. Sir James Emerson Tennent, in his *Ceylon* [Longmans: 1859, 2nd edition], states that phenomena of this kind may have "suggested to the early painters the idea of the glory surrounding the heads of beatified saints." He adds this description: "To the spectator his own figure, but more particularly the head, appears surrounded by a halo as vivid as if radiated from diamonds. The Buddhists may possibly have taken from this beautiful object their idea of the *agni* or emblem of the sun, with which the head of Buddha is surmounted. But, unable to express a *halo* in sculpture, they concentrated it into a *flame*."—Vol. i. 72 *seq.*

[2] See Note 10 (p. 419).

"JIM" ON THE SUMMIT OF MOUNT OMEI.

[*To face p.* 102.

Wa mountain, with its extraordinary flat summit and its precipitous flanks; and, grandest sight of all, clear and brilliant on the western horizon stood out the mighty barrier of towering peaks appropriately known by the Chinese as the Ta Hsüeh Shan — Great Snow Mountains. Those are the peaks—some of them 20,000 feet high, and more—that keep watch and ward over the lofty Tibetan plateau on the one side and the rolling plains of China on the other: the eastern ramparts of the vast Himālayan range, whose icy fingers seem ever to grope outward into the silent abyss of space as if seeking to grasp the fringe of a mightier world than ours. Even at a distance of nearly 100 miles as the crow flies the pinnacles seemed too lofty to be real; but it was pleasant to know that a few weeks hence I should be in the midst of the great mountains, perhaps learning something of their hidden mysteries.

The narrow gallery behind the monastery from which one watches for a manifestation of Buddha's Glory is carefully railed, for a fall from this spot would mean a sheer drop of more than a mile down the face of a precipice which, as Baber has remarked, is perhaps the highest in the world. Many are the stories told by the monks of men and women who in moments of wild religious exaltation have hurled themselves down to win death and paradise in one glorious instant by throwing themselves into the bosom of their Lord Buddha: true stories, which have well earned for this terrible precipice the name of

"The Rejection of the Body."[1] Less sinister names which have been given it are the Diamond Terrace and the Silvery Boundary,—the latter[2] perhaps because Mount Omei is regarded as the eastern buttress of the Great Snow Mountains; or perhaps the words refer to the view of those mountains on the western horizon. Near the edge of the cliff are the remains of a once famous bronze temple, which was several times struck by lightning and has never been restored since the date of the last catastrophe. Some of the castings are exceedingly fine and well worthy of preservation. A Chinese proverb says that Heaven grants compensation for what the lightning has destroyed,[3] but in this instance it seems to have failed of fulfilment.

The temple at which I stayed harbours about twenty monks and acolytes, and visitors both lay and monastic are constantly coming and going. I observed there the performance of an interesting custom, whereby the monks who come on pilgrimage from distant monasteries produce papers of identification and have them stamped with the seal of each of the monasteries they visit. As their journeys are made that they may "gain merit," not only for themselves but also for the religious communities which they represent, it is important that on their return they should be able to produce duly authenticated certificates that they have actually attained the objects of

[1] 捨身崖. There is a similar Suicide's Cliff near the summit of T'ai Shan. *Shê shên*, it may be remarked, has a double meaning.

[2] 銀色界.

[3] 雷打天補.

CHINESE PLAN OF MOUNT OMEI, SURMOUNTED BY THE SEAL OF THE MONASTERY OF THE GOLDEN SUMMIT.

[*To face p.* 105.

their pilgrimage. In many cases the establishment visited also grants Buddhist tracts or plans of its own buildings. One such crude plan—representing the mountain of Omei with its principal religious houses—is reproduced here on a reduced scale. The monastic seal (in red in the original) appears at the top. Some yellow-robed monks from a large monastery near Pao-ning-fu in north-eastern Ssuch'uan, and a small group of lamas from Litang, on the Tibetan border, were having their papers sealed at the time of my arrival at the Golden Summit.

During my day's rest I attended two religious services, besides a "choir-practice" of young boys who had not yet become fully-fledged monks. The services were well intoned, and, considering one's strange surroundings, had a singular impressiveness. The ordinary daily prayers are very simple, consisting in little more than repeated invocations of Buddhas and Bodhisattvas: they are "praises" rather than prayers. The ordinary Morning Service or Matins (Tsao K'o)[1] begins with a procession of monks into the principal hall or chapel—*Ta hsiung pao tien*,[2] "The Precious Hall of the Great Lord (or Hero")—where, after circling round the central figure of Sakyamuni, keeping one bared shoulder towards the image, they take their seats on low benches on left and right. In front of Sakyamuni are lighted candles

[1] 早課.

[2] 大雄寶殿. The first two characters, rendered Great Lord or Hero, represent the Sanskrit Vīra, used as the epithet of a Buddhist saint.

and burning sticks of incense. The service then begins by the general invocation, *Nam Mo Pên Shih Shih Chia Mou-ni-Fo:*[1] "Praise to our Lord Sakyamuni Buddha." This is followed by *Nam Mo Tan Lai Mi Lei Tsun Fo:*[2] "Praise to the Honoured One Maitrêya, the Buddha that is to be." The Buddhas of the past and future having thus been honoured, a bell is sounded to announce a change in the manner of address, when somewhat similar phrases of adoration, interspersed with short hymns of praise, are sung in honour of some of the great Bodhisattvas, those selected at the service attended by me being the following, in the order named: *Wên Shu Shih Li*[3] (Manjusri, the Lord of *Ta chih,*[4] Great Wisdom); *P'u Hsien*[5] (Samanta Bhadra, the patron saint of Mount Omei); *Hu Fa Chu T'ien P'u Sa*[6] (all the Bodhisattvas, Defenders of the Faith); *San Chou Kan Ying Hu Fa Wei To Tsun T'ien P'u Sa*[7] (the Honoured Bodhisattva Wei-To,[8] the Distributer of Rewards and Punishments throughout the three Continents, Defender of the Faith); *Jih Kwang Pien Chao* and *Yüeh Kuang Pien Chao*[9] (the Bodhisattvas of the Far-Shining Light of the Sun and of the Moon—who are regarded as attendant on Yo-Shih Fo, the Healing Buddha of the East); *Tsêng Fu Ts'ai Shên*[10] (the Bodhis-

1 南無本師釋迦牟尼佛.
2 南無當來彌勒尊佛. 3 文殊師利.
4 大智. 5 普賢. 6 護法諸天菩薩.
7 三洲感應護法韋陀尊天菩薩.
8 韋陀. 9 日光 and 月光遍照菩薩.
10 增福財神.

attva who increases happiness and wealth — the Chinese "God of Wealth"[1]); and finally *Shih Fang P'u Sa*[2] (the Bodhisattvas of the Ten Quarters of the Universe).

The most interesting part of the service consists in the short "lections" of extracts from the scriptures, which take the place of the lessons and sermons of Christian churches. The lections are followed by short hymns, some of which have been specially composed for liturgical purposes and are not to be found in the sacred books. Several processions and prostrations take place during the service. The intoning when heard from some distance is often not unlike a Gregorian chant, but the words are uttered rather too quickly, especially in the constantly-repeated invocations.

The Evening Service or Vespers (Wan K'o[3]) begins with a solemn invocation to the mythical Buddha of the Western Paradise, the sublime Amitabha.[4] Then follow the praises of Yo Shih Fo, the Healing Buddha, who "averts calamity and lengthens human life."[5] Two Buddhas, as in the Morning Service, having thus been invoked, the next to be lauded are a new selection of the great Bodhisattvas, in the following order: *Kuan Yin* or *Kuan Shih Yin*, the "Goddess of Mercy," and *Ta Shih Chih*, the Bodhisattva of Great Strength,[6] the two who under Buddha Amitabha

[1] See above, p. 99. [2] 什方菩薩. [3] 晚課.

[4] 極樂世界阿彌陀佛.

[5] 消災延壽藥師佛.

[6] 大慈觀世音 and 大勢至 (Avalokiteçvara and Mahâsthâma: see footnote, p. 72).

preside over the Western Paradise; *Ti Tsang Wang*,[1] who saves men from the terrors of hell; *Wei To*, Defender of the Faith—the only divinity whose name is included in both Morning and Evening Services; *Chia Lan Shêng Chung P'u Sa*[2] ("the holy Bodhisattvas, Protectors of the Monasteries," of whom Kuan-Ti, the Taoist "God of War," is one); *Li Tai Tsu Shih P'u Sa*[3] (the Patriarchs, the Bodhisattvas of Successive Ages); *Ch'ing Ching Ta Hai Chu P'u Sa*[4] (all the Pure Bodhisattvas of the Great Ocean: *i.e.* of life and death or continual metempsychosis).

"Buddha's Glory" is not the only marvel that the fortunate pilgrim may hope to behold when he reaches the Golden Summit. Night, on Mount Omei, has its treasures hardly less glorious than those of day. These take the form of myriads of little lights, moving and glimmering like winged stars in the midst of an inverted firmament. They are known as the Shêng Têng (Holy Lamps),[5] and have been described to me—for alas! I saw them not—as brilliant specks of light darting hither and thither on the surface of the ocean of mist on which in daytime floats the coloured aureole. A fanciful monk suggested to me that they are the scintillating fragments of the "Glory of Buddha," which is shattered at the approach of night and

[1] 地藏王.

[2] 伽藍聖衆菩薩. The two first characters represent the Sanskrit Sanghârâma, the park or dwelling-place of monks, equivalent to a *vihara* or monastery.

[3] 歷代祖師菩薩.

[4] 清淨大海諸菩薩.

[5] See Note 11 (p. 419).

reformed at the rising of the sun. Foreigners have supposed that they are caused by some electrical disturbance; but the monk's explanation, if the less scientific of the two, is certainly the more picturesque.

The monastery in which I was entertained is probably the largest on the summit, but by far the most famous is its neighbour, the Hsien Tsu Tien,[1] which is believed to occupy the site of the original temple to P'u Hsien that according to the legend was built by P'u Kung in the Han dynasty after he had tracked the lily-footed deer to the edge of the great precipice and had beheld the wonderful sight thenceforth known as the "Glory of Buddha." The temple contains a large sedent image of the patron saint, and behind it is a terrace from which may be seen the manifold wonders of the abyss. Not far from this building is the Monastery of the Sleeping Clouds,[2] and further off are the temples of the Thousand Buddhas (Ch'ien Fo) and the White Dragon.[3]

I regretfully left the summit of Mount Omei on my downward journey early on the morning of 10th March, and, after many a slip and sprawl on the snow, reached the Wan-nien monastery in the afternoon. Here I spent a night for the second time, and continued the descent on the following morning. Just below the temple of the Pai Lung (White Dragon) which I had already visited, the road bifurcates; and as both branches lead eventually to Omei-hsien, I naturally chose

[1] 先祖殿. See Note 12 (p. 420).

[2] 峰頂卧雲庵.

[3] 白龍池.

the one that was new to me. By this time I had left far behind me the snow and icicles of the higher levels, and had entered a region of warm air and bright green vegetation. The change was startling, as though by some magic power the seasons had been interchanged.

> "I dreamed that as I wandered by the way
> Bare winter suddenly was changed to spring,
> And gentle odours led my steps astray,
> Mixed with a sound of waters murmuring."

Shelley's dream would have been realised on the slopes of Mount Omei.

Between the bifurcation of the roads and the foot of the mountain there are a number of monasteries, few of which possess any feature calling for special remark, except the romantic beauty of their situations. The most conspicuous are the Kuang Fu Ssŭ,[1] or "Monastery of Abounding Happiness"; the Lung Shêng Kang,[2] or "Mountain Ascending Dragon," from which there is a splendid view of the Golden Summit; the Kuan Yin Ssŭ,[3] or "Monastery of Avalokiteçvara"; the Chung Fêng Ssŭ,[4] "Half-Way Monastery"; and the Ta O Ssu,[5] the "Monastery of Great O" (*i.e.* Omei Shan, Mount Omei), which is a spacious building, often visited by holiday-making Protestant missionaries from Chia-ting. After passing this building the downward path leads across a small bridge, called the "Bridge of the Upright Heart" (Chêng Hsin

[1] 廣福寺. [2] 龍昇岡. [3] 觀音寺.
[4] 中峰寺. See Note 12 (p. 420).
[5] 大峨寺. See Note 12 (p. 420).

Ch'iao[1]), to the monastery named Hui Têng Ssŭ[2] ("The Spiritual Lamp"), from the neighbourhood of which the view of the mountain summit is of exceptional beauty. A charming road leads thence past several other monasteries, down to the level plain, whence the walk to Omei-hsien is easy. Before I reached the city the great mountain had vanished from my sight and I never saw it again: from peak to base it had disappeared into impenetrable mist. There was only the soft sound of a distant monastery bell to assure me that somewhere in the clouds the sacred mountain might still be looked for not in vain.

I have dwelt long upon the Buddhistic associations of Omei; and perhaps the reader is wearied by an account of temples and of forms of belief that he considers grotesque and uncouth. I should be sorry if I were to leave him with the impression that Omei possesses no interest beyond the glimmer that is shed upon it by the Light of Asia. If every monastery were to crumble into dust, if the very memory of Buddhism were to be swept utterly away from the minds of men, Omei would still remain what it was before the first Buddhist recluse had built there his lonely hermitage—it would still be a home of portent and mystery, the abode of nameless spirits of mountain and flood, the source of inspiration to poet and artist, the resort of pilgrims from many lands, each of whom—whatever his faith—would find, as he gazed from the edge of the Golden Summit into the white abyss below, a manifestation of the Glory of his own God.

[1] 正心橋. [2] 慧燈寺.

CHAPTER VIII

OMEI-HSIEN TO TACHIENLU

An easy journey of four days from Omei-hsien brought me to the prefectural city of Ya-chou-fu. During the first day the road lay through the northern portion of the same well-cultivated plain that stretches to the south-east as far as Chia-ting. Large areas were devoted to the cultivation of the small ash-tree which is used to assist in the production of the insect-wax. The yellow blossom of the rape was everywhere in bloom, and pervaded the air with the most delicate of perfumes; while the wheat-fields were just beginning to wear their spring raiment of bright green. Towards evening my road lay across the river Ya to the small magisterial town of Chia-chiang, where I spent the night. Next day, soon after starting, we again crossed the Ya in a ferry-boat and thence proceeded for a few miles along the right bank. Near the ferry-crossing I noticed on the left bank numerous shrines and small caves hollowed by nature and by art out of the face of a cliff. Sticks of incense were burning in front of several of the miniature images contained in them. From this point onward the road lay through a very picturesque district studded with groves of fine trees and two or three good pagodas, and beautified by the fresh blossom of peach and cherry and by wild primroses that seemed to grow out of the solid rock. In the afternoon we again crossed to the left bank of the river in order to reach the magisterial town of Hung Ya, the main street of which we passed through. Another six miles brought us to the poor village of Chih-kuo-chên. The accommodation was very bad, as I had passed beyond the ordinary stage. The whole river-valley from Chia-chiang upwards is the resort of great numbers of wild-duck, a few of which fell to my gun, though the season was late, and they were not at that time plentiful. A curious feature of the shallower waterways of this district is the basket-bridge. Large wicker baskets are filled with loose stones and deposited in the bed of the river at even distances of about 10 feet. Planks of that length are placed on the top of them and constitute the bridge. This device has the merit of cheapness, but as soon as the basket is rotted by the action of the water, the stones gradually subside, and the planks are submerged. The Ya river, here as elsewhere, is too full of rocks and rapids for navigation. Long timber rafts, however, make the journey from Ya-chou to Chia-ting at all seasons of the year, except in the height of the rainy season, and serious accidents are rare.

Next day the road led tortuously through the river-valley and crossed the stream several times. After one ferry-crossing I was faced by a stiff climb of about 800 or 1,000 feet leading to a pass where there is a primitive tea-house. A corresponding descent on the other side soon led us back to the river's edge, at a point where the stream is very turbulent. We crossed by a bridge called the "Bridge of the Goddess of Mercy" (Kuan Yin Ch'iao), formed of long slabs of stone, and immediately afterwards passed through the village of the same name. Another 4 or 5 miles brought me to the small town of Ts'ao Pa, where I spent the night. This town lies in a plain surrounded by hills in every direction except the east and north-east. It lies on the left bank of the river at a point where the current is gentle and the bed very broad and shallow.[1]

On the morning of the following day, 14th March, I reached Ya-chou-fu, the seat of government of a taotai, whose jurisdiction extends to the Tibetan border. The town is important as being on the "mandarin" road from Peking to Lhasa, and also as being the centre of a great tea district.[2] It is in the plains surrounding Ya-chou that the inferior tea which is considered good enough for the Tibetan market is grown, and from here it is carried in long, narrow bundles on the backs of coolies to Tachienlu. There it is cut into cakes or bricks, packed in yak-hides, and carried by Tibetans all the way to Lhasa, and even to the borders of India.

At Ya-chou I was most hospitably entertained by the members of the American Baptist Mission, who, judging from the friendliness with which they

[1] From here a road leads direct to the capital, Ch'eng-tu, which can be reached in three stages.

[2] See Note 13 (p. 421).

were greeted in the streets, were evidently on excellent terms with the people. The Mission has established a dispensary and a school, and at the time of my visit was engaged in the construction of a large hospital. To make invidious comparisons between different missionary bodies in China is unbecoming for a traveller who has been treated by all with every possible courtesy; but if I venture to refer to the American Baptist Mission with special praise, it is only because the members of that Mission whom I have had the good fortune to meet happen to have been persons of broad sympathies and more than ordinary culture and refinement.

The hospitalities of Ya-chou induced me to break my journey here for one day, which I spent in exploring the town and neighbourhood. It is situated in a rather confined plateau nearly surrounded by hills, including one mountain, the Chou Kung Shan, which, as a place of pilgrimage, is a humble rival of Omei.[1] At Ya-chou I paid off the somewhat uncouth "boy" whom I had engaged at Ch'êng-tu, and found a successor to accompany me to Tachienlu. I also engaged a new set of coolies. A sedan-chair which I had bought on leaving the Yangtse at Wan-hsien had been with me the whole way, but I very seldom used it, except when entering and leaving large towns. At Ya-chou I might as well have left it behind, and so reduced the number of my coolies by half; for I did not enter it after the day I left that city. I abandoned it finally at Tachienlu.

[1] See Note 1 (p. 411).

Almost immediately on leaving Ya-chou on the next portion of my journey I entered into the mountainous region that fringes the Tibetan plateau. Marco Polo evidently passed through the Ya-chou plain on his journey from Ch'êng-tu to Yunnan-fu *viâ* the Chien-ch'ang valley. In his day Ya-chou must have been a frontier town on the extreme west of Cathay, for all the mountainous region beyond belonged to Tibet. Like most border regions this district was the scene of constant warfare, and Messer Marco draws a pitiful picture of its utter desolation. It was infested, apparently, by wild beasts, as well as by wild men. But since his day the political boundary of China has been moved steadily westwards, and the province of Ssuch'uan now nominally includes a vast tract of country that was once, and still to a great extent is, inhabited by Tibetans or allied tribes.

On 16th March, a few miles' walk from Ya-chou brought me to the Flying Dragon Pass (Fei Lung Ling), about 3,600 feet high. Hosie, describing this road, says that "a long pull over a frightful road brought us to the summit";[1] but the weather must have been against him, for I experienced no difficulty, and found the road no worse than roads in China usually are. About 65 *li* (barely 20 miles) from Ya-chou brought me to the village of Shih-chia Ch'iao, where I spent the night in a rather good inn. Next day I went up the right bank of a stream that flows north-east to meet the Ya, and after

[1] *Three Years in Western China*, p. 95.

twice crossing it reached the small district town of Jung-Ching, in the streets of which I smashed a carved Buddha-headed mountain-pole that I had bought on Mount Omei, in my efforts to beat off a dog that presented every appearance of insanity. Late in the afternoon I reached the end of the stage at Huang-ni-p'u, a small straggling village on the slopes of the mountain range that was to be crossed on the following day. The pass, which is known as the Great Elephant (Ta Hsiang Ling) is 9,200 feet high — less than 2,000 feet lower than the summit of Mount Omei. Huang-ni-p'u lies at a height of about 3,870 feet; so the actual climb that faced us on the 18th March was about 5,330 feet. The pass, according to one interpretation, derives its name from the elephant on which P'u Hsien rode from India to Mount Omei; but that legend, as we have seen, has no basis in fact.[1] I started the ascent early in the morning, amid the glorious weather that had smiled upon me ever since I entered Ssuch'uan; and my dog Jim and I climbed the pass amid slush and snow with a rapidity which entirely baffled the efforts of the two soldiers who formed my escort to keep up with us. I reached the summit about midday, and rested in one of the numerous refreshment shanties that cater for the tea-coolies, of whom I passed many hundreds during the journey from Ya-chou to Tachienlu. The weights that these men carry on their backs are enormous. A single man carries as much as 300 and sometimes 400 pounds

[1] See Note 14 (p. 421).

weight.[1] They receive twenty or thirty cents a day each, according to the weight carried, and spend about three weeks on the journey. An unburdened traveller traverses the same distance in eight days. The coolies walk very slowly, as a slip might have dangerous consequences. My own greatest difficulty in making the ascent of the Ta Hsiang Ling was to pass these people on the narrow path, especially when a string of them stood sideways to rest their burdens on their wooden props: for they never unload themselves on the road, owing to the great difficulty of getting the burden on to their backs again. I saw only one man meet with an accident. He was passing under an overhanging ledge of rock, and tried to dodge a long ice stalactite. This unbalanced him, and he fell on the path with his huge load uppermost. Till we had extricated him I saw nothing but his legs; but he rose up smiling, and some friendly hands assisted him in replacing his burden.

The temperature at the summit was not lower than 43° in the shade, according to my thermometer, but that was at midday. The snow was melting fast under a hot sun. The view from the ridge was on both sides magnificent. There was no mist, and the bright sunshine made the distant peaks with their white caps stand out with marvellous vividness against the deep-blue sky.

Having descended from the snowy heights of the Great Elephant Pass, and so having left the

[1] Baber mentions an instance of a coolie who "must have had, at the lowest computation, more than 400 English pounds on his back."

TEA-CARRIERS ON THE ROAD TO TACHIENLU.

APPROACH TO TACHIENLU.

[To face p. 118.

plains of China out of sight for many weeks to come, I found myself in the little city of Ch'ing-ch'i-hsien, which in spite of its diminutive size and remoteness from Western influences is so far advanced in civilisation as to possess a girls' school. There is also a temple dedicated to Kuan-Ti (the so-called "God of War"), which was an appropriate circumstance, as soldiers and military supplies were being duly hastened through the town in connection with the border warfare that was being carried on between the Chinese and Tibetans south of Batang. I noticed a versified proclamation in the streets warning the people not to be alarmed at the sight of the soldiers, and promising that all supplies required for their use would be paid for at current market rates. I passed several small bodies of troops between Ya-chou and Tachienlu, and as far as I could observe they were very well-behaved. There were no foreign-drilled troops among them, and they carried the old-fashioned firearms that China is now rapidly learning to discard. What was perhaps a more noteworthy circumstance was the fact that the troops were being regularly paid, and that the commissariat arrangements worked without a hitch. I heard few details of what was actually taking place at the front until I reached Tachienlu, but it was evident that the provincial authorities were dealing with the trouble in a thoroughly energetic manner. The difficulties of sending military supplies and munitions of war from Ch'êng-tu to the borders of Tibet must have been enormous. Ta Hsiang Ling was only one of a number of great passes that had to be crossed before the scene of warfare could be reached. The dragging of field artillery over a succession of wild mountains where the highest of the passes rises to more than 15,000 feet, is a feat which can perhaps be best appreciated by those who helped to perform a similar one during the British march to Lhasa.

Ch'ing-ch'i-hsien was at one time a city of great strategic importance, and was the scene of many a fierce struggle between the Chinese and the Lolos—who have now retired many miles to the south. At other times, too, the Chinese have been hard put to it to defend themselves against the quasi-Tibetan tribes and Mantzŭ who still inhabit the mountains to the west. Its natural position, at the edge of a ravine or natural moat, is a very strong one, and a besieging force armed with primitive weapons would have very little chance of taking it by storm unless they first secured the Great Elephant Pass: for on that side only the city has no natural protection except the mountain range itself.[1]

Immediately on leaving Ch'ing-ch'i by the west gate we descended into the ravine which protects it on the west and south, and crossed the sparkling mountain stream from which the city derives its name. The road then gradually ascends along the flank of some bare hills, picturesque but with little cultivation. It then descends and passes between high hills, issuing thence into a broad valley in which flows the stream Liu Sha ("Shifting Sands"). On its left bank is the village of Fu Chuang.[2] A little

[1] See Note 15 (p. 422). [2] Also known as Man Chuang (蠻庄).

further on the valley gradually contracts, leaving only an insignificant area for cultivation. What there is of it is said to be very rich, chiefly owing to the periodical inundations, which render it suitable for rice. The hills are mostly bare, and trees are few except in the neighbourhood of houses. The next place of any importance is known as Ni (or I) T'ou Courier Stage, which is a large village of comparative importance, and contains excellent inns. Here we spent the night to recuperate our energies in anticipation of the pass that lies just beyond.

Ni T'ou lies about 4,900 feet above the sea-level, and the summit of the Fei Yüeh Ling is 9,000 feet high, only slightly less than the Great Elephant. For a considerable part of the way the path led up the valley of the Liu Sha, which rises in the mountains on the east side of the pass. Above Ni T'ou it is simply a turbulent mountain stream rushing downwards through a picturesque gorge.[1] The final climb of 1,500 feet is very steep, but the dangers and difficulties of the pass have been much exaggerated not only by the Chinese chroniclers—who, like all the *literati* of their country, are sure to have been bad pedestrians —but also by at least one European. The *Hsi Tsang T'u K'ao* quite unnecessarily describes it as "the most dangerous place in China."[2] The view from the top—which is a narrow ridge—is less grand than that from the Ta Hsiang Ling, owing to the proximity of other lofty ranges.

[1] See Note 16 (p. 422).

[2] 內地第一險阻也.

One of the poets of the present dynasty (Hsü Chang) has declared in a pleasant poem that the ascent of this mountain is like the soaring of a swan, the descent like the swooping of a hawk. This is a picturesque description, but it could hardly be applied with appositeness to a certain Buddhist monk who was met on the pass some years ago by a Western traveller.[1] The monk was doing a pilgrimage from P'u T'o (Chusan) to Lhasa, and had already been seven years on the road. His somewhat slow progress was accounted for by the fact that at every two steps of his journey he prostrated himself at full length on the ground. He was quite cheerful, and anticipated that in two or three years more he would reach Lhasa. Without assuming that there was anything either swanlike or hawklike in my movements I may claim to have crossed the Fei Yüeh Ling rather more rapidly than the monk, and I reached the end of the day's stage—the village of Hua-lin-p'ing—early in the afternoon.[2] Shortly before arriving there I turned off the road to visit a picturesque temple which I espied embowered in a grove of trees on the right bank of a mountain torrent. It is dedicated to Kuan Yin, but the Guardian Deity of the Kao Shan ("Lofty Mountain") also has a shrine in the temple grounds. Behind the main hall, which contains the eighteen lo-han in miniature, and a cast-iron bell dated the second year of Tao Kuang (1822), there is a timber-built monastery in which a few

[1] Rockhill, *The Land of the Lamas*, p. 305.
[2] See Note 17 (p. 422).

monks reside. Higher up is a pavilion which contains among other things a black wooden tablet recording the names of those who had subscribed towards the restoration of the building after its destruction by wind and rain. The grounds of the temple are well laid out, and there is a fine view.

Hua-lin-p'ing is a village of two streets, one of them broader and cleaner than is usual in Chinese villages. Most of the inhabitants, however, are not pure Chinese. A proclamation on the walls stated that a large number of coolies were being employed by Government on transport service, in connection with the border war, and that if any such coolie used any military supplies for his own purposes or sold them to civilians he would be punished with relentless severity; and that a like fate would befall any civilian who bought such goods from him.

There is great abundance of coal in the hills about Hua-lin-p'ing, and it is freely used by the poorest peasants for heating and cooking purposes. Judging from the coal which was brought to me in a brazier it appeared to be of excellent quality, for it burned well, and gave out considerable heat with hardly any smoke. The temperature in these mountain villages was generally low enough to make artificial warmth very desirable; but the fumes of charcoal are not conducive to cheerfulness or to health, and coal was a welcome surprise.

For the remaining three days of my journey to Tachienlu the scenery was of great beauty and grandeur. I have seldom seen anything more magnificent than the view of mighty mountains that greeted me as I left Hua-lin-p'ing, and continued to face me nearly all the rest of the way. The lustre of the snow, the rich azure of the sky and the sombre shadows of the gorges and ravines combined to make a series of pictures which no words can describe, and which time can never efface from the memory. There are scenes which an artist could never be weary of painting, a poet never weary of describing: yet both would assuredly fail to communicate the secret of their loveliness to those who had never seen. There are times, of course, when the glories of the scenery are hidden by clouds or dimmed by rain and mist, and many a traveller must have gone through this country with very little idea of the wonderful sights that were hidden from him; but the good fortune that accompanied me to the summit of Mount Omei did not forsake me for even half a day during my long walk to Tachienlu, for the sun was never eclipsed by a cloud, and the lustrous peaks that towered skyward never once robed themselves in fog.

From Hua-lin-p'ing the road descends steeply till it reaches the beautiful valley of the Ta Tu. This great river I had not seen since I left Chia-ting, where it joins the Min. Like the Ya river, its current is too swift and the rapids are too dangerous to admit of navigation. Between Lu Ting Ch'iao (which I reached the same day) and the junction with the Min the fall of the river is no less than 3,750 feet.[1]

[1] See Note 18 (p. 423).

The road to Lu Ting keeps to the left bank of the river, sometimes at a height above it of several hundred feet, and sometimes (as at the village of Lêng Chi) close to the river bank. Lu Ting, which gives its name to an important suspension bridge, is about 20 miles from Hua-lin-p'ing. Shortly before reaching it I passed safely over a somewhat dangerous section of the road, where from a steep bank rocks and stones frequently crash down over the path and into the river, with disastrous results to unwary passengers. Hosie describes how a large stone the size of his head narrowly missed striking him, and how he saw the body of a man who had been struck dead, his weeping wife and friends trying to remove the corpse without endangering their own lives. The vicinity of Lu Ting must be beautiful at all seasons, but it was particularly so at the time of my arrival there, on account of the wonderful display of myriads of fruit-tree blossoms. Had I come at a later season I should no doubt have been able to endorse Rockhill's verdict as to the excellence of the peaches.[1] The town itself is small and dirty, but its position renders it of some commercial importance, for through it all the trade that follows this main route between China and Tibet must pass. The iron suspension bridge towards which all the streets of the town converge affords the only means of crossing the Ta Tu. This fine bridge, which has been several times repaired since its construction more than two hundred years ago, is about 120 yards long.

[1] *Land of the Lamas*, p. 304.

It may now be regarded as the iron chain that connects China and Chinese Tibet.[1] Geographically and ethnologically the Ta Tu river is the eastern boundary of Tibet, for, though the steady advance of Chinese influence has caused the political boundary to be moved further and further west, the races that inhabit the western side of the Ta Tu are still predominantly Tibetan, Mantzŭ, or Hsi Fan,[2] and the tribal chiefs are still left in complete control of their mountainous territories. The Chinese have indeed driven a wedge into this region as far as Tachienlu in order to maintain control over the high-road to Lhasa; but they interfere very little with the government of the country. Beyond the Ta Tu the country is not divided into magisterial districts, and the jurisdiction of the Ch'ing-ch'i magistrate extends only as far as Lu Ting. Recent maps of China make the province of Ssuch'uan extend further west even than Batang, but the whole of the region I have referred to should properly be marked on the maps as Chinese Tibet,[3] or as Tibetan Ssuch'uan. There is, of course, an extraordinary mixture of races and languages in this wild border region, but the prevailing type is anything but Chinese; and in religion, history and social customs the people who inhabit this territory obviously belong to one of the numerous allied races of which Tibet is composed to-day.[4]

After crossing the bridge the road leads along

[1] See Note 19 (p. 423). [2] See chap. xv.

[3] I observe that it is so marked in Waddell's map attached to his recent book on the British expedition to Lhasa.

[4] For a brief discussion of the ethnology of this country, see chap. xv.

the right bank of the Ta Tu for a distance of nearly 20 miles. Villages are few and the population is scanty. In the hamlet of Ta P'êng Pa I rested in an eating-house kept by a Chinese, who, to my surprise, greeted me in Pekingese. As I sipped my tea he cheerfully informed me that he had been a Boxer, and had left Peking immediately after the allies had entered it. I fancy he must have done so under a cloud; but I did not press the subject, and amiably accepted his assurance that, in spite of troublesome political estrangements, he was sentimentally attached to all foreigners. After Ta P'eng Pa there is a long upward climb, followed by a short and sudden descent to a wooden bridge crossing a mountain stream. From here there is a magnificent view of the snowy mountains in the south-west.

As this road is frequently tramped by Tibetan pilgrims on their way to Mount Omei, I was not surprised to find a number of wayside shrines. If the name of Thomas Atkins is—I hope it is not—scribbled over the walls of the Lhasa cathedral, it is satisfactory to know that Tibetan feelings cannot have been outraged thereby; for no more inveterate wall-scribbler exists than your Tibetan pilgrim. I found abundant evidence of this in the shrines just referred to, as well as in the temples of Chia-ting and Mount Omei.

Twenty-five *li* beyond Ta-P'êng Pa the road suddenly branches off to the left, leaving the valley of the Ta Tu, and entering that of its tributary the Lu, or, as the Tibetans call it, the Do river. A steep descent soon led us to our resting-place, the village of Wa Ssŭ Kou ("The Ravine of the Tile-roofed Monastery"). It consists of one street, behind which are a few small maize-fields, orchards and walnut trees in the level ground between the village and the water's edge. A small temple, presumably that from which the village is named, overlooks a rather cranky iron suspension bridge. This bridge crosses the Lu to a steep path which climbs along the opposite mountain side in the direction of the valley of the Ta Tu, or Chin Ch'uan ("Gold Stream")[1] —as the Ta Tu is called above the junction with the Lu. The path leads into the territory of a tribal chief, subordinate to the Tibetan prince who rules at Tachienlu. Hosie states that respectable Chinese settling there are allowed to take unto themselves temporary native wives, on payment to the chief of three taels (less than half a sovereign) per wife. "They are free," he adds, "to leave the country when they choose, but the wives and children must remain."[2] I spent an afternoon exploring the fringe of this region, the northern part of which was in the eighteenth century the scene of a long and terrible struggle between the imperial troops and the Chin Ch'uan chiefs. Near the summit of the steep path that creeps along the precipitous face of the cliff opposite Wa Ssu Kou, there is a small shrine dedicated to Kuan Yin, who is here regarded as the protectress of a road which, without her protection, might subside into the turbulent river hundreds of feet below.

The next day I walked the remaining distance

[1] Gold-washing is carried on here to a considerable extent, as in nearly all the rivers of western Ssuch'uan.

[2] *Journey to the Eastern Frontier of Tibet*, pp. 24-25.

—about 15 miles—to Tachienlu.[1] The road keeps to the right bank of the river the whole way, and gradually ascends from 5,300 feet at Wa Ssŭ Kou to 8,400 feet at Tachienlu. This is sufficient to indicate that the Lu river is a wild torrent with many waterfalls. In summer, after the melting of the snows, it must present the appearance of a continuous white cascade; even in spring its waters are turbulent enough. I reached Tachienlu early in the afternoon about five hours in advance of my sluggish followers, and found a warm welcome in the hospitable house of Mr and Mrs Moyes, well known by name to those who have studied the interesting history of missionary enterprise among the Tibetans.[2]

Tachienlu is a long, narrow little city which has had to adapt its shape to that of the mountains by which it is hemmed in. The summits of these mountains are covered with snow all the year round, and some are very lofty. According to Bretschneider's map, one of them is estimated at 25,592 feet, and another at 24,900 feet. Outside the walls of the city there is hardly a foot of level ground, except along the banks of the river, which, on entering the city, cuts it into two parts. It is the great emporium of trade between China and Tibet, being the point at which Tibetans and Chinese come from west and east, respectively, to exchange the produce of the two countries.[3]

[1] See Note 20 (p. 424).

[2] Mrs Moyes (then Mrs Rijnhart) is the well-known author of the book, *With the Tibetans in Tent and Temple*, in which she ably describes the life of adventure and hardship which she led in the far interior of Tibet, where she lost both husband and child.

[3] See Note 21 (p. 425).

The contribution of China to this trade is chiefly tea, with limited quantities of tobacco and cotton; that of Tibet mainly consists of musk, gold-dust, skins and various mysterious concoctions used for medicines. The population of the town is predominantly Tibetan, there being about seven hundred Tibetan families to about four hundred Chinese.[1] In addition to the Tibetan families, however, must be reckoned a great number of lamas, most of whom live in large lamaseries outside the city walls. Many of the houses—especially the large inns—are of the well-known two-storied Tibetan type, and on their flat roofs flutter innumerable prayer-flags giving to the winds the universal Tibetan hymn of praise, *Om mane padme hom.* The streets are generally noisy with the sounds that always accompany buying and selling in Eastern countries; but rarely so noisy as to stifle the pious murmurings of red-frocked lamas. For Tachienlu, like all Tibet, is priest-ridden. Even the Chinese seem to succumb, after a few years of residence there, to the wiles of priest-craft, and constantly seek the assistance of lamas in exorcising demons and invoking the protection of the saints of lamaism. Many of the lamas make a good deal of money by securing temporary engagements as domestic chaplains; and the deep, sonorous voices (assiduously cultivated from youth upwards) in which they intone their dirge-like spells and unintelligible prayers, penetrate far beyond the walls of their improvised chapels.

[1] Hosie, *Journey to the Eastern Frontier of Tibet.*

CHAPTER IX

TACHIENLU

I REMAINED in Tachienlu, where I found excellent quarters in a Tibetan inn, from 23rd March to 15th April. During this period of more than three weeks I exchanged visits with the Chinese prefect and the Tibetan chief or "king" of Chala, and made excursions to various places of interest in the vicinity. My main object in staying so long in one place was that I might devote some attention to the Tibetan language, of which I had previously acquired a very rudimentary knowledge. With this end in view I engaged a native teacher, a pleasant and mild-mannered old gentleman, who, in the approved Tibetan fashion, put out his tongue at me most respectfully whenever I chanced to pronounce or spell a word correctly. He officiated at the king's court as a kind of soothsayer. I hoped that my acquaintance with him might lead me to endorse the opinion of Marco Polo, that among the Tibetans are to be found "the best enchanters and astrologers that exist in all that quarter of the world." They, he goes on to remark, "perform such extraordinary marvels and sorceries by diabolic art that it astounds one to see or even hear of them."[1] Ser Marco was more fortunate than I was, for no blandishments on my part could wring any necromantic secrets from my soothsayer. But perhaps he had none to impart.

The climate of Tachienlu, as might be expected at an altitude of over 8,000 feet, is very bracing. The temperature sometimes sank to the freezing point, and snow often fell during the night, but the days were almost uniformly bright and sunny. There was a slight shock of earthquake on 30th March, and I was told that the occurrence was a common one; certainly it caused no consternation. The people of Tachienlu are generally healthy and vigorous, but the annual recurrence of typhus fever is a great scourge. The poorer class of Tibetan house is exceedingly dirty, and it can only be the fine climate that prevents Tachienlu from being frequently devastated by terrible epidemics.

I have already observed that west of the river Ta Tu the country is ruled by tribal chiefs, and is not under the direct rule of China. The chiefs are never interfered with so long as they abstain from political intrigues, and are punctual in the payment of their small tribute to the Chinese Government. The Chinese, however, fully recognise the importance of controlling the main road into Tibet proper; they have, therefore, stationed an officer of prefectural rank (*chün liang fu*) at Tachienlu, and his duty it is to protect Chinese interests, and keep a watch over

[1] Yule, *Marco Polo* (Cordier's edition), vol. ii. p. 49.

the movements of the Tibetan chiefs and kings. He exercises jurisdiction over the Chinese of the district — there are very few outside the town itself — but has no judicial or administrative control over the rest of the population. His official duties are chiefly connected with transport and commissariat arrangements, and in keeping up regular communications between the governor-general in Ch'êng-tu and the amban[1] or *ch'in ch'ai* at Lhasa. At the time of my visit his hands were full owing to the frontier war, and he was also burdened with the responsibility of looking after the new amban, who arrived in Tachienlu shortly before me on his way to Lhasa, and was still there when I left three weeks later. His predecessor, it may be remembered, was brutally murdered at the instigation of the lamas on the Tibetan frontier; and it was freely admitted by the new amban's numerous retinue that his courage, which had steadily diminished as he proceeded westwards, had vanished altogether when he reached Tachienlu. When it appeared that the frontier war showed no signs of coming to an end he applied, I understand, for leave to proceed to Lhasa by way of India; but this request was promptly refused by his superiors at Peking. Some yak-loads of his baggage started for the west shortly before I left the city, and I presume he had made up his mind to make a start soon afterwards. The turbulent

[1] The word *Amban*, now so well known to Europeans, is Manchu, and is applied to many high Chinese officials serving in the Mongolian and Tibetan dependencies of China, besides the Resident at Lhasa.

condition of the tributary states which had culminated in the murder of some French missionaries and the assassination of the amban seems to have forced the Chinese Government to give its serious attention to the problems of the frontier. As usually happens in China, the policy determined on was one of ruthless severity. Two large lamaseries were destroyed by the Chinese troops, several of the leading lamas were put to death, and the rest driven westward at the point of the sword. Two tributary Tibetan chiefs, of rank nearly equal to that of the king of Tachienlu, were found guilty of treasonable intrigues, and promptly executed. All these persons, if the stories told of them were true, seem to have deserved their fate. The events had occurred some time before my arrival in Tachienlu, but as the war was still in progress, and the lamas of the extreme west were known to be the implacable enemies of China, future possibilities still agitated the minds of Chinese and Tibetans alike. The loyalty of the chief or king of Chala was probably above question, and he was quite powerful enough to control any restlessness that might show itself among the lamas of his own principality; but there was some reason to believe that pressure was being brought to bear on the Chinese Government from an unknown source to induce it to abolish all the territorial chieftainships, and parcel out the whole country into regular magistracies under Chinese officials right up to the nominal frontier of Tibet proper. It was rumoured that Tibet itself was to be turned into a Chinese province, and furnished with the usual hierarchy of Chinese officials — the main object probably being to frustrate the supposed designs of England on that country—and that Ssuch'uan was to be divided into two separate provinces. In view of all these possibilities, it is clear that the position of the tributary princes of Ssuch'uan was, and probably still is, a somewhat precarious one; and that the king of Chala, who could at any moment be placed under lock and key by the prefect at Tachienlu, would probably be the first to suffer from the change of policy. It would not be difficult for an unscrupulous Chinese official to trump up vague charges of treason which might quickly lead to the king's overthrow. Among other rumours I heard that the Ya-chou taotai was expected to move his headquarters temporarily or permanently to Tachienlu, and that the king's palace had already been selected as a suitable residence for him. The king had not apparently been consulted in this little matter. How the local politics of Chala have developed since I left that distracted kingdom I have had no opportunity of learning; but if in another five years the king is still swaying the fortunes of his little monarchy he will deserve a good deal of credit for his skilful manipulation of affairs during a very trying period.

The territory of this potentate, including that of the small chiefs subordinate to him, extends from the Ta Tu river on the east to the Yalung on the west, and for about seventeen days' journey from north to south. The name of his principality is spelt in Tibetan *Lchagg-la*, but, as usual in Tibetan words, it is not pronounced as it is written. Lchlags (pronounced *cha*) is the Tibetan for "iron," and *la* means a mountain-pass. The Chinese transliteration[1] of the word would in the Pekingese dialect read Chia-na: but in western Mandarin the *i* is elided, and the *n* is sounded like an *l*. The king's own name in Chinese is Chia I Chai.[2] His Tibetan title, *gyal-po*, which means "king" or "ruling prince," sufficiently well expresses the nature of the authority which he exercises.[3] Rockhill describes him as "one of the most powerful chiefs of eastern Tibet, for among them he alone demands and obtains obedience from the lamas dwelling in his principality."[4] He rules by hereditary right, and has absolute power over the lives and fortunes of his subjects. The Chinese in his territory are exempt from his jurisdiction, but they are so few in number, except in the city itself, that the exemption counts for little. Beyond the periodical payment of a small tribute, the only concession which he is obliged to make to the suzerain power is the privilege of *ula*. This word is neither Chinese nor Tibetan, but is in universal use in Mongolia and Tibetan countries.[5] *Ula* is a system whereby all Tibetans living in the neighbourhood or within a certain distance of a caravan route are com-

[1] 甲那. [2] 甲宜齋.

[3] See Note 22 (p. 425).

[4] *Land 'of the Lamas*, p. 276.

[5] The Chinese is 烏拉, which is merely phonetic. The word *ula* is Mongolian. Rockhill observes that *ula* (*oulák*) was known in India in mediaeval times.—(*Land of the Lamas*, p. 52.)

pelled to furnish Government officials (Chinese and Tibetan) with men, baggage-animals, and food, either free of all cost or for a very small fixed sum. The system has given rise to great abuses, and has in some places caused so much distress among the people that whole villages have been abandoned and rich valleys left uncultivated. The subjects of the king of Chala were groaning under the weight of the *ula* system at the time of my visit, and I heard the king himself lamenting the sufferings which—owing to the greed and harshness of Chinese military officials—it caused his people. The burden at that time was more than usually heavy, for the Chinese Government insisted on exacting its full rights of *ula* in connection with the carriage of military supplies to the scene of warfare.

The only three official buildings of any importance in Tachienlu are the residences or yamêns of the king, the prefect or *chün liang fu* and a Chinese colonel (*hsieh-t'ai*). Of these by far the largest is the king's. I visited him a day or two after my arrival, and was received very cordially. He is a man of about forty years of age, of rather delicate appearance, but active and vivacious. He speaks Chinese (with a strong Ssuch'uan accent) in addition to his own language, and has adopted Chinese dress. His position in Tachienlu cannot be a very pleasant one, owing to the peculiar nature of his relations with the Chinese Government. The prefect appears to regard him as a kind of enlightened savage, and apparently considers that the most effective method of demonstrating the superiority of the suzerain power is to treat the vassal with the least respect possible. The Chinese regard all Tibetans much as they used to regard Europeans—as barbarians outside the pale of true civilisation. I heard it stated that if a Chinese in Tachienlu kills a Tibetan he is merely mulcted in two packets of tea, but that if a Tibetan kills a Chinese the lives of three Tibetans must pay the forfeit; I cannot, however, vouch for the truth of this. The king would be glad to remove the centre of his government to another part of his territories and leave Tachienlu to the absolute control of China; but this he is not allowed to do. A few years ago a lama versed in magic spells prophesied to the king that if he spent any one of the next three consecutive New Year seasons in Tachienlu great misfortunes would fall upon him, but that if he spent them elsewhere all would be well. The king, who like all Tibetans is prone to superstition, lent a willing ear to the wisdom of the lama, and spent the last and first months of the next two years in one of his mountain retreats. When the third New Year season came round the frontier war had commenced, and the king's presence was urgently necessary in Tachienlu in connection with the transport arrangements; but his superstitious dread of unknown calamities again decided him to retire to the mountains. He came back in due course to find that he was in trouble. The *ula* arrangements had suffered by his absence, and the Chinese officials held him to blame. Since then he has been zealously endeavouring to regain the confidence of his Chinese masters, with only partial success. His friendly intercourse with the few Europeans he has met is regarded somewhat suspiciously by the Chinese as well as by the lamas; and it is possible that when the days of trial and tribulation come to him he will look—I fear he will look in vain—to his European friends for protection and support. With two or three of his Protestant missionary friends he has actually entered into "sworn brotherhood,"[1] an old Chinese custom whereby close friends enter into a mutual compact which creates between them a kind of fictitious relationship. This may explain a not quite accurate passage which occurs in Waddell's recent book, *Lhasa and its Mysteries*.[2] He says that "the Tibetan chief of Dartsendo (Tachienlu), the king of 'Chala,' is especially well-disposed towards foreigners; and when the Dalai Lama threatened to punish him on this account, he is reported to have become 'sworn brothers' with the Protestant Christian *Tibetans*." Colonel Waddell adds that the king of Chala was said to be building forts in his country, and could put ten thousand fighting men in the field; but I know no reason for supposing that the king's intentions are other than entirely pacific.

A few weeks' residence in Tachienlu served to open my eyes to the fact that scandal and gossip are not confined to Western societies. Even the

[1] *Huan-t'ieh* (換帖), literally "the exchange of cards."

[2] See p. 358 of that work.

Tibetan is sufficiently civilised to take an intelligent interest in his neighbour's sins. One story which caused much hilarity among the Smart Set of Tachienlu concerned the wife of a certain court official. A distinguished person of royal lineage (not the king) is a man who is known to be of an amorous disposition, and has been the hero of several pathetic romances. He gazed upon the court official's lady and saw that she was fair. Steps were immediately taken to send the husband on a mission to a far country, he having been assured that his domestic interests would be carefully protected in his absence. The lady, reluctantly or otherwise, speedily bestowed her caresses on her exalted lover. For some time all went well; but, unlike the less fortunate Uriah in the Biblical story, the official returned to his family in safety, discovered the intrigue, and promptly repudiated his lady. The tragedy of the situation consists in the fact that she was also repudiated by her "royal" lover, his fickle affections having meanwhile found another object. The lady subsequently consoled herself by marrying a Chinese merchant, and is said to be still carrying on a monotonous existence within the curtained recesses of that gentleman's private house. The episode is one which might perhaps be commended to Mr Stephen Phillips for dramatic treatment.

Court intrigues have given rise to incidents more sombre than this. The last king, elder brother of the present one, is said to have had the date of his death foretold to him by a certain lama. When the date was close at hand, the king took ill and died, after two days' illness, exactly on the date prophesied. For some dark reason the lama—who should probably have been tried for murder—succeeded in acquiring such potent influence over the dead man's successor, the present king, that he persuaded his Majesty to adopt his daughter. Quite apart from the fact that lamas have no right to possess daughters at all, it does not seem to be quite clear what the lama stood to gain by this proceeding. The king was at that time childless, but he has since acquired a daughter of his own. I saw both the lama's child and the king's during a visit to the Summer Palace in the mountains, and was astonished to find that the lama's daughter—a little girl of eight—was being brought up as a boy, and was attired in boy's clothes. There was some mystery connected with the whole affair which I failed to fathom. As may be gathered from stories of this kind, the lamas do not enjoy a good reputation. Their private morals are not above reproach, and they are too fond of meddling in mundane affairs; but they do not wield the great political power of which in other Tibetan states the lamas have gradually possessed themselves.

The heir to the "kingdom" is the king's younger brother, a very amiable man whose love of outdoor sports would endear him to the heart of many an Englishman. He does not meddle with questions of *la haute politique*, and loves to spend his time in the delightful mountain residence to which I have just referred as the Summer

Palace, a place known in Chinese as the Yü Lin Kung. I was invited to spend a few days there as the king's guest, and was received and most hospitably entertained by his brother. It is a large, rambling building, beautifully situated in a lonely spot among the mountains about 8 miles from Tachienlu. One of the greatest attractions of this place is a hot sulphur spring, the water from which is made to flow into a capacious tiled bath. The Tibetans are said to be an unclean race—and I will not gainsay it—but they delight in hot water when they can get it. The neighbouring forests are strictly preserved for sporting purposes, and afford splendid cover for pheasants and other game. Our "bag" was an insignificant one; but I was filled with admiration for the zeal of the king's brother, who was armed only with an old-fashioned muzzle-loading weapon of venerable appearance and doubtful efficiency. He deserved success, if he failed to command it. Behind the palace are some of the tombs of the royal family. They are surrounded by clusters of prayer-flags—strips of white cloth tied to the top of sticks or slender poles and bearing the usual prayer formulas. Close by is a rivulet in which there is a large prayer-wheel: a large wooden cylinder, appropriately inscribed, placed perpendicularly in a strong framework of timber. Through the cylinder runs a fixed wooden pin, and the whole structure is so arranged that the lower end of the cylinder is always in the water. The flow of the stream causes it to revolve unceasingly, and each revolution is supposed to be equivalent to

VIEW FROM THE "SUMMER PALACE" NEAR TACHIENLU.

[*To face p.* 142.

a single utterance of the words, *om mane padme hom*. The prayer-flags and prayer-wheels may thus be regarded as continually engaged in saying masses for the souls of the dead princes. In my subsequent travels through the Tibetan states I found wheels and flags of the same kind in great abundance; and they are, of course, well known to all who have travelled anywhere in Tibet. As a rule, a cluster of flags is all that marks a Tibetan graveyard, especially in places where cremation is the general method of disposing of the dead. Prayer-wheels may be found wherever there is flowing water; and I observed that the Tibetans—who have not as much objection as the Chinese to imbibing cold water—would often stop to drink just below a prayer-wheel, as if under the impression that the water, which had performed the pious act of turning the wheel, had acquired thereby some mysterious sanctity. In connection with this I may mention that holy water is not a monopoly of Roman Catholic countries, for it is quite commonly used for ritualistic purposes in lama temples. As every reader knows, this is not the only respect in which there are resemblances or coincidences—sometimes startling enough—between the ceremonial usages of lamaism and Catholicism.

Prayer-wheels[1] may be turned either by water or by hand. The ordinary small hand-wheel is constantly seen in the hands of both lamas and laymen. Old men, especially, who are anxious to

[1] For the origin of the Prayer (or perhaps rather *Praising*) Wheel, see Rhys Davids' *Hibbert Lectures* (1881), p. 138 (4th ed.). See also Tylor's *Primitive Culture*, ii. 372-373 (4th ed.)

devote their slender remnant of life in acquiring new merit or destroying bad karma, hardly ever go out of doors without their wheels. They twirl them with their fingers as they walk, and years of practice enable them to do it without any conscious effort: indeed, I fancy that many old men would twirl an imaginary wheel if the reality were taken from them. It is curious to note that the older a wheel is—that is, the more it has been twirled—the more valuable it becomes; for few Tibetans will exchange an old wheel for a new one, and only the direst poverty will induce them to sell this most precious of all their possessions to a curio-hunter. Another form of hand-wheel is similar in size and appearance to a water-wheel. It is inserted perpendicularly in specially-constructed recesses, and may be twirled round its pin by any devout passer-by. Sometimes it is found in the wall of a temple, and not infrequently in a private house. In the latter case it is generally found inside the house on the right-hand side of the main doorway as one enters. Every one who goes in or out gives it a revolution or two. The stranger on entering thus confers a kind of benediction on his host, and at the same time accumulates a little merit for himself. The custom is an amiable one, and certainly does no one any harm. Not content with flags and prayer-wheels, the Tibetans are also very fond of erecting piles of stones on which are loosely-placed innumerable flat slabs, of varying shapes and sizes, each bearing the *om mane* formula in large, carved letters. These are variously termed *obo*,[1] *mani-drombo* and *mani-dong*. They were specially numerous in the country through which I passed after leaving Tachienlu, but there are many of them also in the immediate neighbourhood of that town. Lamaism shares with other forms of Buddhism the rule that sacred objects should, as far as possible, be kept on the right-hand side. Where an obo or mani-drombo occurs, therefore, the road always bifurcates so as to enable the devout traveller to keep it on his right whichever way he is going. The inscribed slabs are the pious gifts of pilgrims, or of any person who wishes to conciliate or show his respect to the unseen powers. Every lamasery has among its inmates one or two masons who are employed by such persons in carving the inscriptions.

Before reaching Tachienlu I had purposely left undecided the route to be followed thereafter, as I was only too well aware of the obstructions which the authorities would be certain to put in my way when I attempted to leave the main routes. I had a vague idea of making an effort to cross the frontier into Tibet proper, and so proceeding to Lhasa by the route which no European has traversed since the days of the abbé Huc; but it soon became obvious that this would be impossible—at least so long as a state of war existed on the border. The Chinese prefect had no doubt acquainted himself with the fact that I was engaged in the study of Tibetan, and when I called upon him he showed

[1] A Mongolian word which the Chinese have naturalised as *o-pu* (阿卜).

considerable anxiety and curiosity as to my intentions. The new amban showing no eagerness to avail himself of a unique opportunity to add a British adviser to his staff, and the undertaking being otherwise impossible in the face of Chinese and Tibetan opposition, I was obliged to give up the idea of a ride to Lhasa, and had to fall back on my original intention of travelling through the Sino-Tibetan states of the Yalung valley to the north-west of Yunnan. If I were prevented by official opposition from following this route as well, I decided to return to the Ta Tu river, and find my way down the Chien-ch'ang valley to Yüeh-hsi and Ning-yüan-fu, the route which has been made famous by the journey of Marco Polo, and has been in recent years traversed by E. C. Baber and Sir A. Hosie. With regard to this route I was told that the road was much infested by robbers—Lolos and others—and that many of the inn-keepers had entered into a league with them to drug and rob, and, if necessary, murder their visitors. There was only one way to avoid molestation, and that was by the discovery and use of the robbers' password. The utterance of this word on appropriate occasions would not only ensure safety, but would remove all difficulties about transport and supplies. The person (a Chinese in Government employment) who gave me this information, and who may, for all I know, have had personal dealings with the gang, was so obliging as to give me the password itself, which consisted, he said, of the single word *Ku* ("old"). As I did not, after all, follow this interesting route, and therefore had no opportunity of testing the efficacy of the word, I can only express the hope that the timely information now given will be of service to future travellers.

The Yalung valley is one of the least-known portions of the Chinese empire. In 1895-96 M. Bonin, a French Colonial official, travelled from Tali-fu to Tachienlu by a route which to a certain extent coincided with that taken by myself, and three years later a Swedish missionary, Mr E. Amundsen, travelled in the reverse direction by a road which was evidently almost the same as my own. But no Englishman [1] had traversed the same route before me, and as I had no opportunity of reading the narratives published by either M. Bonin or Mr Amundsen until my return to civilisation, I unfortunately derived no benefit from their previous experience: but their accounts, though interesting, are very meagre in detail and of tantalising brevity.[2] A glance at the map will show that my route lay across the mountains to the south-west of Tachienlu. On crossing the Yalung it enters the Muli or Huang Lama, and thence it crosses the Yunnan frontier a few miles north of Yung-ning-fu. Short as the total distance appears on the map, the series of great mountain ranges over which the road passes makes the journey a long one and arduous. A

[1] Major H. R. Davies, whose admirable survey and exploration work are well known, visited the Muli lamasery before me, but our routes only touched at that point. He has unfortunately published no account of his journey from Mien-ning-hsien to Chung-tien.

[2] For M. Bonin's see the *Bulletin de la Société de Géographie*, 1898, pp. 389 *seq.* For Mr Amundsen's, see the *Geographical Journal* for June and November 1900.

few Yunnanese merchants[1] choose this route to Ssuch'uan in order to avoid the likin-stations in the Chien-ch'ang valley; but the great difficulties of arranging for the safe transport of merchandise over snowy passes and unbridged rivers have given it a bad reputation.

Even at Tachienlu I was unable to gather much information about the country. The king himself appeared to have a very scanty knowledge of the southern part of his own territory. As soon as he and the Chinese prefect heard of my intention—and it was impossible to conceal it from them—the strongest objections were immediately raised. The road was impassable, the mountains were covered with snow that never melted, the lamas were hostile, the whole country was infested with robbers and wild beasts, and I should find neither food nor means of transport. I had already satisfied myself by private enquiry among the Tibetans and some Yunnanese merchants that the route was feasible, and that nothing was to be feared beyond the ordinary difficulties and hardships of travelling in a very wild region sparsely populated. I felt that if the road were safe and easy enough for an occasional trading caravan, it should also be safe and easy enough for an Englishman burdened with little beyond clothes and gun. I therefore declined to put faith in the exaggerated descriptions with which the officials endeavoured to frighten me, and insisted upon the right conferred upon me by my passport to travel where I chose. We exchanged several messages

[1] How few, may be judged from the fact that I met only one caravan in the course of a month's journey.

on the subject, and in personal interviews I made it as clear as possible that none of the difficulties which they had mentioned seemed to me sufficiently imposing to justify me in altering the route on which I had determined. The prefect, however, was particularly strenuous in his efforts to dissuade me from my purpose, and pointed out that he would be powerless to grant me any protection during the journey, and that the risks and dangers would be considerable. I need hardly say that his concern was not for me personally, but was due to his fears of what might happen to himself in the event of my coming to grief. From this point of view his attitude was reasonable enough. The upshot of a long discussion was that the king of Chala and the prefect allowed me to set out on my consenting to sign declarations in English and Chinese to the effect that all responsibility for my safety was to rest with myself. The first of these declarations ran as follows:

> "This is to certify that I have been fully informed by the Ming Chêng Ssŭ (king of Chala) that the road by which I intend to travel from Tachienlu to the borders of Yunnan, *viâ* the southern portions of his territory and the country known as Huang Lama, is beset with great difficulties, and that my journey will be very arduous and possibly dangerous. Having been fully assured of these circumstances, and having nevertheless decided to traverse the country in question, I wish it to be understood that I undertake the journey at my own risk and on my own responsibility, and that the king of Chala

is not to be held responsible for any delay or accident that may occur in the course of such journey so far as it lies within his territory."

This document was handed to Mr Moyes, to be used by him to save the king from blame in the event of an accident. A similar declaration, containing the name of the Chinese prefect instead of that of the king, was handed directly to that official before my departure. I perhaps created an unwise precedent; but as the prefect seemed determined to prevent my departure unless I relieved him of all responsibility, I was left with no option. The British Consular authorities, I knew, would do nothing: they had already declined to countenance my travelling by this route.

The fears of the officials with regard to possible dangers were in some respects justifiable. A great part of the country between the Yalung and the borders of Tibet proper was and is under the direct or indirect control of lamas, who show very little respect for Chinese suzerainty. It was only recently that two French missionaries were cruelly butchered by the lamas somewhere near the Tali-Batang trade route; and a young Scotsman named Forrest, who had been collecting botanical specimens in the same locality, only escaped with his life after being hunted by the lamas with dogs, and suffering extraordinary privations. The country into which my road should lead me after crossing the Yalung was also directly ruled by lamas; and while I was in Tachienlu there were rumours to the effect that the lama-prince of that region, though far from the scene of actual fighting, was not only secretly supporting the rebels, but had caused the roads in his territory to be torn up and blocked in order to prevent the advance of Chinese reinforcements from Yunnan. The war, indeed, was not progressing altogether favourably for the Chinese. It was whispered that on one occasion a whole regiment had been cut to pieces during a night attack. The Tibetans had eluded the sentries, who were probably asleep, rushed the camp, put out the fires, slaughtered many defenceless soldiers, and then quietly vanished, leaving the Chinese to shoot and stab each other in the extremity of their panic. Other rumours stated that five hundred Chinese troops had joined the Tibetans, and were receiving from them twelve *tiao* (about thirty shillings) a month each—much larger pay than they drew from China; and that the tributary prince of Litang — the state that adjoins Chala on the west—was only waiting to hear of another serious reverse to the Chinese troops before throwing in his lot with the rebels. Probably these rumours were much exaggerated, but they caused much uneasiness to the Chinese of Tachienlu, who for a long time past had been living in constant dread of a massacre. I heard that some time before my arrival the Tibetans were expected to attempt a great *coup* by making a sudden descent on Tachienlu itself, and any Tibetan in the city who was suspected of treasonable dealings with the rebels was imprisoned or closely watched. The principal Chinese merchants sent the bulk of their goods to Wa Ssŭ Kou or Lu Ting Ch'iao, and were ready to start for the east themselves at the first signs of serious trouble. The worst of the panic had passed away before my arrival, chiefly owing to the vigour and severity with which the Government was dealing with the insurrection and the large numbers of Chinese soldiers that almost daily passed through Tachienlu on their way to the front.

Whether the prefect was sincere in his apprehensions regarding my safety if I insisted on crossing the wilder parts of the eastern Tibetan states I have no means of knowing; at any rate, he appeared to regard the written declaration already quoted as sufficient to relieve him of all responsibility in the matter; and as soon as that question was settled, both he and the king showed themselves ready to give me every reasonable assistance, and placed no further obstacles in my way. The king deputed a man of his own—a Tibetan who spoke a little Chinese—to act as my guide to the boundary of his territory on the Yalung river, and the prefect and colonel ordered three soldiers to escort me as far as the town of Yung-ning, just within the Yunnan frontier. I had also previously engaged a young man, whose father was a Chinese and his mother a Tibetan from Lhasa, to act as my personal servant, and this youth accompanied me almost as far as the frontier of Upper Burma. As a speaker of both Tibetan and Chinese, he proved a useful member of my party. The king was also obliging enough to accord to me the valuable privilege of *ula*, which would (within his territory) obviate all difficulties about transport. The *ula* was in this instance no hardship for the people, as I undertook to pay more than double the ordinary rates for all animals required for my use.

1.

2.

4.

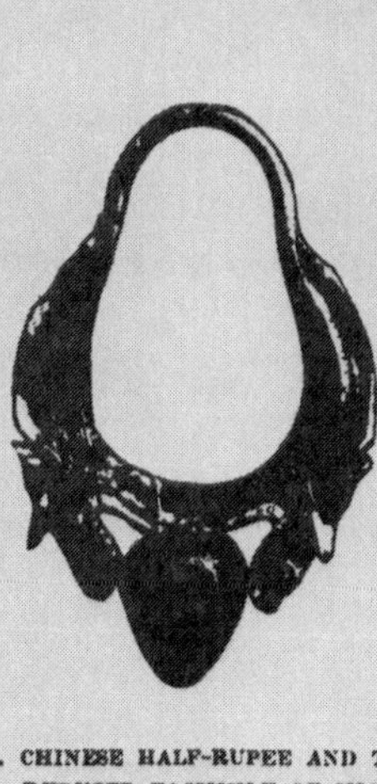

3.

1. CHINESE HALF-RUPEE AND TIBETAN COINS.
2. REDUCED FACSIMILE OF SILVER PLAQUE WORN BY WOMEN IN THE YALUNG VALLEY.
3. CLAY VOTIVE TABLETS FROM MULI, WITH MINIATURE BUDDHAS.
4. EAR-RING WORN BY MO-SO WOMEN OF YUNG-NING.

[To face p. 152.

CHAPTER X

TACHIENLU TO PA-U-RONG, YALUNG RIVER

I SET out from Tachienlu on 15th April. My caravan consisted of three mules to carry my baggage and silver[1] (very light loads which in level country might have been carried by a single mule), two riding mules for myself and my servant, and four for my escort. Half a mile

[1] The complications and variations in currency and money values constitute one of the greatest vexations to a European traveller in China. As is well known, the ordinary medium of exchange in China for small purchases is the "cash" (*t'ung ch'ien*) of which about 1,000 (sometimes more and sometimes less) are equivalent to a dollar (Mex). In larger transactions silver sycee or "broken" silver is used, in which case payments are made by weight and according to the "touch" or fineness of the silver. The ingots are cut up by the use of sycee-shears into small or large portions as required. The larger ingots—which in Ssuch'uan are generally of the approximate value of ten taels each (equivalent to nearly two pounds)—usually bear the guarantee "chops" of bankers and large merchants. In the west of Ssuch'uan the Indian rupee became many years ago a well-known and much appreciated coin, and very largely took the place of broken silver. Its convenient size and shape specially commended it to the Chinese and Tibetan merchants who had trade relations with Burma, Tibet and India: and as its exchange-value in and about Tachienlu was in excess of its face-value many Yunnanese merchants used to bring mule-loads of rupees to that city from Tali-fu, thereby making a very considerable profit. The coin was generally known as the *lama-t'ou* or Lama's Head—Queen Victoria's head being supposed to be that of a lama—and also as *yang ch'ien* or "foreign money," the same term that is often applied in other parts of China to the Mexican and British dollars. Recently the provincial Government prohibited the circulation of Indian rupees in Ssuch'uan, and began to issue a

beyond the city I crossed the stone bridge known locally as the Gate of Tibet, close under the walls of a gloomy lamasery, and entered the long defile that leads into the heart of the great mountains. The road gradually rose to a height of about 2,250 feet above Tachienlu, and at the hamlet of Chê-to—about 10,650 feet above sea-level, and about 40 *li* from Tachienlu—I found a haven for the night in a ruinous hut.

As far as Chê-to my route followed the Litang-Batang road that leads into Tibet proper, and I met several yak caravans bringing goods to Tachienlu. Outside my quarters at Chê-to hung a proclamation in Chinese and Tibetan informing the people that the insurrection of the I-jên (barbarians) gave all good men a favourable opportunity for proving their loyalty to Govern-

similar coin of its own at the Mint in Ch'êng-tu. The new coin is almost exactly equivalent in value to the Indian rupee, and resembles it in size and appearance: but it bears the head of the emperor of China instead of that of the emperor of India. It is interesting as being the first Chinese coin, so far as I am aware, to bear the sovereign's head. Probably had it borne no head at all it would have been regarded with suspicion and dislike by those who had for years been accustomed to the Indian rupee. One of the Ssuch'uanese coins (a half-rupee) is illustrated in the text, along with the obverse and reverse of a Tibetan coin also in common use about Tachienlu and western Ssuch'uan. I found the new Ssuch'uan rupee was accepted fairly willingly by the people between Tachienlu and Pa-U-Rong, less willingly by those of the Muli country. South of Yung-ning I again had recourse to broken silver; but west of Tali-fu the Indian rupee is generally accepted, and at the town of Hsia Kuan, near Tali-fu, Indian rupees can be bought in any quantity by travellers and merchants bound for Burma. The Indian rupee is now a rare coin in Ssuch'uan, but sometimes it is treated like broken silver, being cut into pieces and sold by weight. I have in my possession several mutilated rupees which were weighed out to me as small change. The late queen-empress's head has been treated with small respect by the silver-merchants.

"THE GATE OF TIBET."

[To face p. 154.

ment by ready compliance with the regulations about *ula*; but the dead bodies of no less than four yaks lying by the road-side between Tachienlu and Chê-to offered a grim comment on the results of those regulations.

At Chê-to my road left the caravan-route and led into a wild region where during a day's march I passed only one lonely house, near which we encountered the only representative of the local population—a sad-faced old woman sitting astride a mottled yak. The day's journey (the second stage from Tachienlu) was long and arduous. The road from Chê-to rose steadily, but not steeply, through a confined valley, following the left bank of a stream. About midday we were picking our way laboriously through deep snow, and early in the afternoon we reached the summit of the pass of Chê Ri La, 17,400 feet above the sea-level.[1] The pass is a double one, the two summits being divided by a long valley which appears to have been at one time the bed of a glacier.[2] High as we were, there were peaks in the north-east that still towered several thousand feet above us, and to the south and south-west we saw nothing but a vast ocean of billowy mountains with innumerable trough-like valleys. The descent was a difficult one on account of the snow, which was almost too deep for our

[1] See Note 23 (p. 428).

[2] It has been pointed out by Griesbach that the central Himālayan glaciers are receding, and once extended much lower than at present. Apparently the same is the case in the "Himālayas" of Tibetan Ssuch'uan. I saw few living glaciers; but in many ravines there were evident traces of lateral and terminal moraines.

mules, one of which fell never to rise again. A fertile valley opened before us as we descended, and we soon struck the right bank of a stream flowing down from the snows of the range we had just crossed. A beautiful forest of firs covered the slopes on the eastern side. About 3,000 feet below the summit we came upon the first signs of human habitation—a herd of yak. Five *li* further we came to a few cultivated fields and a large two-storied house, which proved to be the beginning of the straggling hamlet of A Te, where we spent the night. In this valley the high peaks are all hidden, and though its elevation is about 13,000 feet the gently-sloping hills are well forested. Here for the first time I caught sight of the great white pheasant known as the machi.[1]

This day's march was a fair sample of our daily toil for the next few weeks. It was a continuous march up and down the snowy or forest-clad slopes of the loftiest mountains in China; and no doubt the journey would have been monotonous and arduous enough had it not been for the magnificence of the ever-changing scenery. The food which I shared with my followers was of the roughest and plainest. We lived almost entirely on *tsamba*—parched barley-meal, mixed with yak butter and the peculiar concoction which the Tibetans believe to be tea, and kneaded by one's own fingers into a thick paste. Occasionally—for I had to be very sparing

[1] This I take to be the *crossoptilon Tibetanum*. It is quite unknown in China proper.

of my cartridges—I contributed a pheasant to the table, and in two or three places we were able to buy goats. The goats trotted along with our caravan until we were hard up for food, and then they trotted no longer. White pigeons were numerous in the deeper valleys. Villages were very few—we seldom passed more than two in a day, and sometimes none at all, and as a rule they were nothing but the sorriest hamlets. We were generally able, however, to arrange our stages in such a way that we could spend the night under cover. We had no tent, and the nights were always too bitterly cold for sleeping out of doors. I was clothed in thick Peking furs, and wore boots lined with sheep-skin. During the day I wore smoked glasses to protect my eyes from snow-blindness. A couple of extra pairs I lent to two of my escort, and the rest wore the yak-hair eye-shade which the Tibetans call *mig-ra*. We found the villagers friendly and hospitable, and we never had any difficulty in getting accommodation when we came to a hamlet; and as we paid well for all supplies — a matter which sometimes caused evident surprise — we were always given the best that the village could produce or could spare. I did not meet a single Chinese between Chê-to and Li-chiang in Yunnan[1]—a journey that occupied about a month—and the Chinese language was entirely unknown.

Tibetan houses are gloomy stone buildings with small windows, and the rooms are both dark and

[1] See Note 24 (p. 428).

dirty. I was sometimes grateful to the darkness for concealing some of the dirt, but my sense of smell unfortunately remained painfully acute. The windows are necessarily small, as paper is too scarce to be used as a protection against the wind, and glass is of course unknown. The apparent size of the houses is deceptive. A building that presents the outward appearance of a substantial two- or three-storied dwelling-house with many rooms, shrinks into a dismal and draughty collection of stables, courtyards, and dungeon-like living-rooms, when one gets inside. As often as not, the greater part of the ground-floor is used as a cattle-shed, and off this a short passage leads into the family common-room. The upstairs rooms—reached by clambering up a block of wood, with carved notches to serve as steps—are generally only granaries and barns, full of beasts that crawl and bite. In some cases I was provided with the luxury of a room to myself; but more often I had to share the living-room with men, women, children, and disagreeable animals that love the night. My slumbers would certainly have been unpleasantly disturbed if I had been less worn out at the end of each day's journey. There are no fire-places or chimneys. The fire is kindled in the middle of the room, and the smoke escapes by the door and windows or through holes in the wall, but much of it does not escape at all, and the effect is trying to the eyes; while the black streaky soot, that clings to the walls and hangs on spiders' webs dangling from the roof, adds to the general effect of gloom and discomfort.

On arriving at our destination each night, we all crowded round the fire and consumed our *tsamba*, while our hostess exercised a pair of muscular arms in vigorously stirring up our tea and butter in a big wooden churn,[1] whence she ladled it out into a big pot, from which each of us poured what he wanted into his own bowl. Tibetan tea —made of the twigs of the tea-plant, and its coarsest leaves — has been much maligned: I always found it drinkable if one added plenty of butter and forgot it was meant to be tea. If as tea it is horrible, as a soup it is almost agreeable. The yak-butter, taken by itself, is insipid and unpleasant; but the Tibetans can make a kind of cream-cheese out of it, and I found this fairly good when I could get nothing better. Conversation with my kind hosts was apt to be stilted, even with the assistance of my semi-Tibetan boy. Fortunately my bull-terrier formed a topic of never-failing interest. His three simple tricks had delighted the genial monks of Mount Omei and the village children of central Ssuch'uan, and indeed his mere appearance—so different from that of Chinese dogs—had filled them with wonder; but when the simple herdsmen of the Yalung valley saw the strange foreign beast lying down at the word of command, or sitting on his hind legs and balancing a lump of *tsamba* on the end of his nose, the prevailing feeling seemed to be something not very far removed from religious awe.

Every valley seemed to have a dialect of its

[1] The Tibetan *ja-ndong*.

own, and occasionally my servant found it hard to make himself understood. As none of my hosts appeared to have heard of England, it was difficult to satisfy their curiosity about myself, and I fear they often failed to understand what I meant by saying that my country was outside the Chinese empire, and that it had an emperor all to itself. On the whole, I was far less troubled by the inquisitiveness and curiosity of the people than in China proper: and, indeed, I was glad to find that the three soldiers who formed my Chinese escort were often regarded with greater curiosity than I was myself. The children appeared to look upon us as a new kind of wild beast, and I fear we often unwittingly brought tears to their eyes. Our mules were changed, under the rules of the *ula* system, at nearly every village. A riding-mule was generally procurable for myself, though as a rule I performed at least half the day's journey on foot. When mules were unobtainable we employed yaks, and if yaks were not to be had my baggage was carried by Tibetan men, and still more frequently by women. This last circumstance was a source of great gratification to my three soldiers, who hardly knew more Tibetan than I did myself, but were never at a loss in exchanging lively banter with the damsels who accompanied us. Once or twice I was seized with the unworthy suspicion that the village patriarchs were careful to entrust us with only the least attractive of their women-folk: otherwise, I was at a loss to account for the circumstance that whereas every Tibetan village possessed several good-looking girls, the women who carried our baggage were almost invariably plain.

The people of eastern Tibet are totally unlike the Chinese in appearance, though the extraordinary mixture of races produces a large variety of types. As a rule, the men are tall, very well made, with well-marked features, noses of European shape, and eyelids that are often quite free from the peculiarity which produces in many Eastern races the well-known appearance of an obliquity of the eyes. As specimens of vigorous, stalwart manhood they are much more noteworthy than the people of Lhasa and Central Tibet. They are born mountaineers and have healthy, well-bronzed faces. Sometimes, indeed, they are as dark in complexion as the Burmese.[1] They wear goat-skin or yak-skin clothes, and well-lined leather boots, reaching nearly to their knees, that protect their feet from snow and frost-bite. Most of them are attired in a garment that might be regarded as the prototype of the Scots kilt. The women wear skirts, and, as their feet are of course unbound, they do not walk with the mincing gait of the lily-footed lady of China. I have been told by persons who take an interest in the human form that the average woman of Chinese Tibet is decidedly handsome. It is unfortunate that she does not often wash her face. She is certainly more genial and vivacious than the quiet and timid Chinese woman. She climbs mountains as nimbly as her husband, and the loads she carries are just as heavy; nor does she hesitate to join

[1] See Note 25 (p. 428).

in amiable conversation with her husband's male friends when she meets them on the road.

Marco Polo, who only touched the fringe of the Tibetan countries, describes in his naïve way some of the peculiar social customs of the people of those lands "as a good story to tell, and to show what a fine country that is for young fellows to go to";[1] and a much later traveller — Cooper — amusingly describes how he unexpectedly found that he had gone through a ceremony of marriage with a Tibetan damsel when he innocently thought that he was merely having a picnic under a grove of walnut trees.[2] No such hymeneal experience fell to my lot, though walnut trees were common enough in the deep valleys. Nor am I able to endorse Marco Polo's somewhat hasty criticism that the Tibetans are "an evil generation, holding it no sin to rob and maltreat: in fact they are the greatest brigands on earth." I took no special care of my money and baggage, yet I never met a robber, and never—so far as I am aware—lost even a handful of *tsamba*. "These people of Tibet are an ill-conditioned race. They have mastiff dogs as big as donkeys." This further remark of Messer Marco's is nearer the truth if we take "ill-conditioned" to mean "unclean," and allow for a considerable exaggeration about the size of the dogs. No Tibetan household is complete without one or two of those uncouth animals. The breed has changed since Marco's day, for the

[1] Yule's *Marco Polo* (Cordier's edition), vol. ii. p. 45.
[2] *Travels of a Pioneer of Commerce.*

dogs are not mastiffs (though these are still well known throughout Tibet proper), but a large long-haired dog that somewhat resembles a collie. They are exceedingly savage towards strangers and of great value as watch-dogs. Their physical strength is enormous. The usual custom is to allow them to go loose at night and to chain them up in the yard or in front of the house during the day, the theory apparently being that any one who wanders out of doors after nightfall must be a knave, and deserves any ill-fate that may befall him. Their bark is most peculiar: not sharp and crisp like that of most European dogs, but with a sepulchral and "far-away" sound as if each dog kept his own ghost in his stomach and it was only the ghost that barked.

The villages are surrounded by fields which—considering the great elevation of even the deepest valleys—are wonderfully productive. In many cases, where the valleys are very narrow, the cultivated land has all been reclaimed from virgin forest. Up to 10,000 feet, and in some places at greater elevations, there is a good deal of wheat and maize; in sheltered valleys, buckwheat, oats, beans, peas and barley are cultivated with considerable success up to over 13,000 feet. The mountain flora surprised me immensely by its richness and variety. Wild-flowers — many of them quite unknown to England and perhaps to Europe—grew luxuriantly in the deep ravines into which we dipped between the parallel ranges, and the mountain slopes up to 14,000 feet at least were generally covered with immense primeval forests of pine and fir. In the great forests the pine was the first to die out on the higher levels; the fir asserted itself to 2,000 or 3,000 feet higher, and the hardiest of all was the tree-rhododendron, which I have seen growing at a greater height than 16,000 feet. There is some variation in the line of perpetual snow on the different ranges and even on the two sides of the same range; on an average it was not below 16,500 feet, though there were several passes at a lower elevation on which I was told the snow only disappeared for two or three months in the summer.[1] Next to the pines and firs the commonest trees are other coniferæ such as the spruce and juniper, and evergreens such as the yew and cypress. Among deciduous trees the poplar,[2] horse-chestnut and wild cherry are common at heights varying from 8,000 to 12,000 feet. The Chinese oak (*quercus sinensis*), which has evergreen leaves, is also to be met with very frequently. Besides the rhododendron there are many hardy shrubs to be found at elevations almost as great, such as brambles, *aucuba*, the viburnum, artemisia, a kind of hydrangea, the clematis, and wild-gooseberry. The wild-flowers are naturally not numerous on the summits of the lofty ranges, but in the neighbourhood of the banks of the Yalung and other rivers and in the warmer valleys I found innumerable flowering plants to which, had I been

[1] It is now well known that in parts of the Himālayas which form the watershed of the great Indian rivers the line of perpetual snow is as high as 18,000 or even 20,000 feet.

[2] There is a fine poplar grove close to Tachienlu, fringing the "royal" parade-ground. Sarat Chandra Das (*Journey to Lhasa and Central Tibet*) mentions a poplar at Lhasa which is supposed by the Tibetans to have sprung from the hair of the Buddha.

a botanical expert, I should have been glad to put names, but which were, after all, quite as beautiful nameless. The familiar plants included wild roses, edelweiss, gentian, spiræa, and several varieties —some almost certainly unknown to botanists—of the primula.

Had my principal object in visiting these remote mountains been to study their fauna or to shoot big game, I should no doubt have been amply rewarded for my toil; but, as it was, I cannot say much of the country from a sportsman's point of view, for I carried no rifle, and shot only to supply the needs of my frugal table. Most of the wild animals kept well out of my way, and I did not go in search of them. The musk-deer and horned stags are common denizens of the mountains, and there are also the wolf, fox, antelope, bear, panther,[1] wild ass, wild goat and wild sheep. Sometimes, when camping in the forest —which we had to do several times after crossing the Yalung—my followers insisted upon keeping up a big fire all night, and begged me to discharge my gun once at least to frighten away the beasts of prey. This precaution was judged necessary on account of the mules, which on such occasions were turned loose to find their own fodder. Instinct apparently prevented them from wandering far from the camp, for we never had the least difficulty about catching them in the morning.

The heights of the passes which we crossed varied between 12,000 and 17,500 feet, and some of them were above the line of perpetual snow.

[1] The *felis fontanieri*, besides other members of the Cat tribe.

The climbing was sometimes very steep work, but it never became really difficult except on the few occasions when we experienced high winds and snow-storms. The cold was then so intense that the thickest furs did not afford adequate protection. The rarefied air made rapid motion impossible, and prevented one from getting warm through exercise. The mules stopped to recover breath at intervals of a hundred yards, and though I never suffered from the least trace of mountain-sickness I often found walking strangely laborious. We made slow progress, of course, sometimes not more than 10 or 12 miles in a day, but nearly every stage took us from dawn to sunset to accomplish. The tops of the passes were generally sharp ridges, in some cases culminating in a sheer wall of frozen snow and ice through which my men had to dig out a path for the mules and for ourselves. Stone cairns (*lab ch'a*) surmounted by sticks and rags crown the summit of every pass; they were always greeted by my men with shouts of joy, and sometimes they added a stone to the cairn or tied an extra bit of rag to one of the protruding sticks.[1] But

[1] Customs of this kind seem to exist or to have existed all over the world. For Tibet, see Sarat Chandra Das's *Journey to Lhasa and Central Tibet*, and several recent works. Frazer, in the *Golden Bough* (2nd edn. vol. iii. pp. 4-6), has an interesting note in which he mentions the same or similar customs in the Solomon and Banks Islands, Nicaragua, Guatemala, Central and South Africa, Bolivia, Burma and Korea. He says: "The act is not a religious rite, for the thing thrown on the heap is not an offering to spiritual powers, and the words which accompany the act are not a prayer. It is nothing but a magical ceremony for getting rid of fatigue, which the simple savage fancies he can embody in a stick, leaf, or stone, and so cast it from him." Gipsies have a custom of leaving heaps of stones and

the steep descents were sometimes quite as arduous and dangerous as the upward climbs, especially when it was necessary—owing to the excessive steepness—to descend in zig-zags, or when a miniature avalanche tore down in our direction bringing stones and boulders in its frozen clutches.

But, on the whole, I found the difficulties of this almost unknown route by no means so serious as I had been led to expect. I never for a moment regretted that I had so obstinately declined to be guided by the timid officials at Tachienlu, and never found myself without a good reserve of strength and energy at the end of every day's march. I should be indeed sorry if my description of the route should deter others from undertaking the same journey. Granted health, strength, a first-rate digestion, and an average fund of cheerfulness, there is no reason whatever why any of my readers who longs to behold Nature in her supreme glory should not forthwith pack up his hand-bag—he should take little else—and follow in my steps with a light heart. Would that I could bear him company: for the spirits of the mountain and the forest never cease, in hours of solitude, to haunt the mind of him who has known them once and learned something of their spell.

bits of stick at cross-roads, to guide members of their band who have fallen behind. I do not propose to argue from this fact that the gipsy race was originally a Tibetan tribe, in spite of the facts that both gipsies and Tibetans love a wandering life, and that the gipsies of Persia and the Tibetans use almost the same word for "tent," which is *guri* in Persia and *gur* (གུར་) in Tibet.

The reader who does not propose to undertake any such expedition may be recommended to glance but lightly at many of the pages that follow. The details of my daily march through the mountains of Chinese Tibet to the borders of Yunnan will hardly be of interest to any but those who are themselves travellers or are contemplating a journey of a similar kind.

My route from Tachienlu to the frontier of Yunnan may be divided for descriptive purposes into three sections: the first, from Tachienlu to the village of Pa-U-Rong, on the banks of the Yalung or Nya Ch'u, occupying eleven days; the second, from the west bank of the Yalung to the lamasery of Muli, seven days; and the third, from Muli to Yung-ning in north-western Yunnan, three days.

Of the first section, the two first stages from Tachienlu have already been described. On the third day from Tachienlu (17th April), my road led in a most tortuous manner through three long valleys, fairly well populated and sprinkled with villages. The first village, about 8 miles from A Te, is Du Sz Drung, situated at the point where the road emerges from the first and turns into the second valley—the direction as far as Du Sz Drung being south-west, and thereafter almost due west. Opposite the next village of Dza Ri K'u is a conspicuous conical hill; a little further on the valley (lying N.N.E. and W.S.W.) becomes very much broader, and is dotted with several isolated houses and a village named Ring I Drung. Here we changed *ula*. Immediately afterwards, we struck off to the south into the third valley, keeping to the left bank of a stream named the Dja Ki Ch'u. In the villages of these valleys I observed several cases of goitre, a complaint which is common in the highlands of Ssuch'uan and the lofty tableland of Yunnan. Curious octagonal stone towers, now seen for the first time, are a conspicuous feature in the landscape of both these valleys. The towers which are described by Gill[1] as existing further north in the country explored by him are evidently of the same pattern. Baber, who knew of them only from Gill's account, has made the following observations on the subject. "What the use of these buildings may have been is unknown, but the presumption is that they were watch-towers; for the present purpose it is enough to know that they are universally said to have been erected by the Menia, and that there is nothing resembling them west of the Yalung on the main road."[2] My own observation corroborates the information given to Baber. I passed a large number of the towers, but none further west than Ri Wa, which was still five days' journey from the Yalung by my route. All were built on the same plan, and have eight corners, as shown in the ground plan on the following page. That they were used as watch-towers and beacon-stations is highly probable, for they are generally placed in positions from which the watchers would have an uninterrupted view up and down the valleys; but as I observed

[1] *River of Golden Sand*, vol. ii. p. 136.
[2] Royal Geographical Society's *Supplementary Papers*, vol. i. p. 96.

several of them close together, when one would have been sufficient according to the watch-tower theory, it is probable that they must have been used also as fortresses. At the advance of an enemy the tribesmen very likely drove their cattle and other animals into the large room on the ground floor,[1] and used the upper stories for their own protection. Missiles could be discharged from the roof and from the narrow holes that served also as windows: just as was the case with the old peel-towers of the Scottish border. I explored several of the towers, but found no inscriptions. They are nearly all in a dilapidated condition, but some have been kept in good preservation and are used as granaries and store-houses. In one case at least the tower has been made to serve as the wing of a modern house of the ordinary Tibetan type, and the interior has been partially reconstructed.

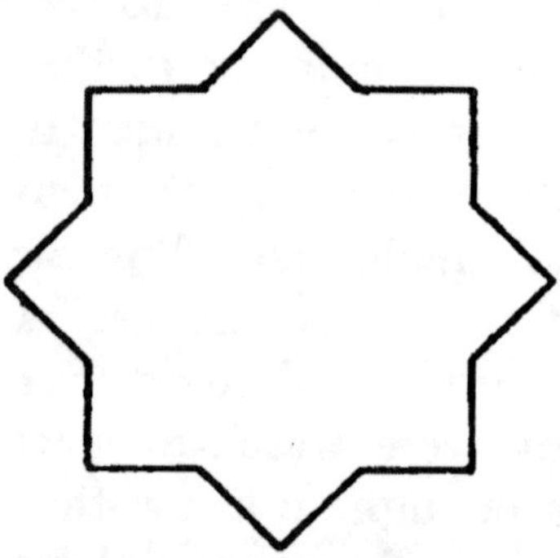

Two or three miles of easy riding through the third valley brought us to a curious wooden bridge by which we crossed the Dja Ki Ch'u, which, having been joined by several tributaries at the intersection of the valleys, was now a fairly large river. It joins the Yalung, but its

[1] Sometimes, however, the door is several feet above the level of the ground, so that ladders of some kind must have been used for entrance and exit.

OCTAGONAL TOWER AT RI WA.

[*To face p.* 170.

valley is apparently impracticable for travellers, for our road soon left its banks. We had changed *ula* for the second time at Ring I Drung,[1] and we did so again at a place called Ba Lu, where there is a single hut. At last, after a march of about 16 miles for the day, we put up at a solitary house named P'un Bu Shi. The valley here lies N.N.E. and S.S.W. Just beyond our quarters, on the left bank of the river, a small tributary descended from a valley, containing some houses, in the south-east. Leaving this valley on our left we continued the next day to keep to the valley of the Dja Ki Ch'u, which, however, twice changes its name during the day's march. We soon passed a conspicuous ruined tower a couple of hundred feet above the road on our (the right) bank of the river. The lofty mountains were all invisible, and the hills that bounded our valley were smooth and low, with plenty of pasturage and a fair amount of forestation. In one small area I noticed sheep, goats, yak, ponies and pigs all pasturing together, and all apparently on the most amiable terms with one another.

A second tower, higher up than the first, stands about 2 *li* beyond the latter. About a mile beyond this the valley narrows to a gorge, where cultivation ceases. The name of the river at this point was given to me as A-mi-chi-ts'a, which is also apparently a name of the people who inhabit the westerly end of the valley. In

[1] The word *Drung* or Dr'ong (གྲོང་) is the Tibetan word for Village.

the gorge the lower slopes were well wooded, but a good deal of tree-felling was going on. The abundance of timber makes the people wasteful, for they selected their trees with an obvious disregard of their age or condition. For about 20 *li* we went through the forest by a winding path and then crossed the river by a well-made wooden bridge of the same peculiar construction as that crossed on the previous day. This brought us to the left bank of the river, which in this locality is known as the Li Ch'u. Very soon afterwards, emerging from the gorge, we came to a solitary house at the entrance to a valley which lies approximately south-east and north-west. We took our frugal midday meal of *tsamba* in the cottage, then, leaving the Li Ch'u, which we never saw again, we proceeded in a south-easterly direction up the new valley, down which flows a rather large stream, the Tsa Ch'u. A rough road wound in and out amid well-wooded and picturesque scenery for a distance of about 5 miles, till we found ourselves opposite a large house on an eminence overlooking our valley, and at the entrance to another valley lying in a south-westerly direction. The house we found to be the residence of a *t'u pai hu*, or sub-chief, who received us very cheerfully and provided us with comfortable quarters for the night.

For two days our route had been an easy one, lying as it did through a series of river-valleys. The next day our toils began again. We left the hospitable headman's house on a brilliantly

HOUSE OF *T'U PAI HU.*

THE AUTHOR'S CARAVAN.

[*To face p.* 172.

fine but cold morning. There had been hard frost during the night, and the still waters were coated with ice when we started. Proceeding up the new valley towards the south, we gradually ascended for a few miles till we reached a beautiful level glade from which we had a fine view of dense pine forests that covered the hills on both sides almost to their summits. Another short climb brought us to a point from which we began the ascent of the pass of Tan Ga La.[1] We changed *ula* at the hamlet of Sho Ti Ba Dze at its foot. After another 3 miles or so the hills began to close us in on every side and the ascent began to be steep. The mountain is wooded up to the summit of the pass (15,000 feet), which we reached about mid-day. The descent began at once and abruptly, and was at first very steep. We descended about 3,000 feet into a wooded gorge where machi and other game-fowl abound. We then entered a valley of which the direction (E.N.E. and W.S.W.) was at right angles to that through which we had descended. A large brook flowed through it in a westerly direction, and, rather to my surprise, our road led us along its right bank towards the east. A walk of half a mile brought us to the hamlet of Tu or Lu Li, where we spent the night. I found lodging in a barn. The people seemed more afraid of us than was usually the case, and did not greet us with open arms; but they made up for their cold reception

[1] *La* is the Tibetan word for a Mountain Pass. *Ri*, which often occurs in the names of villages and passes, means Mountain, and *Rong* Valley.

of us by increased friendliness later on. The valley is broad and fertile enough for cultivation. As usual, the principal grain is the Tibetan barley (Chinese *ch'ing k'o*), from which *tsamba* is made. The dialect spoken differed considerably from that we had heard spoken in the morning only a few miles away. The valleys in this wild region are so sharply separated one from another that their inhabitants must always have formed more or less isolated communities; thus the rapid changes of dialect are not surprising.

Starting at daylight next morning a few hundred yards' walk brought us to the end of the cultivated part of the valley. We followed the right bank of a stream, the road gradually turning S.S.E. We then crossed to the left bank by a wooden bridge. After proceeding for 8 miles through a gorge we entered a plain several miles broad, and the road turned due south. Half a mile's further walk brought us through the hamlet of Dro Dze Drung (or San Chia-tzŭ) to that of Na K'i (or Hsia Ch'êng-tzŭ), where we changed *ula*. On the hillside on the right of the road I noticed some small caves. They are artificial, but bear no resemblance to those of the Min river, and are said to be used as herdsmen's shelters. Near these two villages are clusters of prayer-flags marking the site of a graveyard. The people of this region frequently—as already mentioned[1]—dispose of their dead by cremation. The scenery now becomes much wilder and the forest almost

[1] See above, p. 143.

A RUSTIC BRIDGE.

[To face p. 174.

ceases, giving place to rugged rock. After going S.S.W. for 2 miles, we reached the village of Dra Shê, where we again changed *ula.* This village is very poor and semi-ruinous. The longest obo or *mani-dong*[1] I had yet seen lay between the villages of Na K'i and Dra Shê. Another mile or so brought us to the dilapidated hamlet of Ri Wa (Chinese Wu Chia-tzŭ[2]), where I saw the last of the octagonal towers.[3] Soon afterwards we reached the end of our stage at a hamlet of three houses named Ko Ri Drung (Chinese Chung Ku). The stage was a short one, but I learned that no shelter was to be obtained further on. This I ascertained to be the case next morning, when we commenced the ascent of the great pass of Dji Dju La. Our path, lying S.S.W., climbed the right bank of a stream by the side of a gaunt and jagged range of precipitous mountains. The only vegetation consisted of a few stunted trees near our path, and not a shrub was visible on the black flanks and snow-crowned summits of the hills. But as we ascended the lower slopes of the pass, the path wound into one ravine after another, and in their sheltered depths I noticed large numbers of coniferous trees and rhododendrons. The

[1] See above, p. 145.

[2] Many of the villages between Tachienlu and Yung-ning have been given Chinese names by the Yunnanese, who occasionally send merchandise by this route. The Chinese name, as a rule, has no connection with the Tibetan or Man-tzŭ name. *Wu Chia-tzŭ,* for instance, means a "Village of Five Families"; *San Chia-tzŭ* a "Village of Three Families."

[3] See illustration of this tower, which is a fair sample of the rest, *to face p.* 171.

last few hundred feet of the pass were deep in snow, and along the ridge of the summit (at a height of about 17,500 feet) we were faced by a pointed wall of ice. From Ko Ri Drung to the summit—a climb that kept us busily occupied for the greater part of the day—there is no house and no cultivation. From the pass there was a grand view of snowy summits on both sides, and I was told by our yak-drivers that the pass itself is never free from snow. An icy west wind met us as we reached the top: so cold that it seemed as though it must have swept over all the frozen mountain-tops of eastern Tibet. The first part of the descent is steep. Lower down it becomes easier, and for about 10 miles we went south and south-west through a forest of firs. The weather changed for the worse as we descended, and for four hours we had to grope our way through a blinding snow-storm. After a very arduous day's march of over twelve hours' duration we were glad to find a resting-place at last in the comparatively large village of Dur (Chinese Hei Lao), where I found roomy but draughty quarters in the house of a sub-chief or *t'u pai hu*, who had gone to Tachienlu. I was told by his wife, who entertained us, that he had gone to prosecute a lawsuit which had already been dragging on for two generations.

The upland valley in which this village lies is known as Dji Dju Rong. Part of it, if I mistake not, is the bed of an extinct glacier. It was still snowing when we set out next morning. For about 8 miles we retraced our steps of the

TIBETANS OF WESTERN SSUCH'UAN.

MOUNTAIN SCENERY NEAR SIN GO LA.

[To face p. 177.

previous day, then crossed and left the stream that comes down from the Dji Dju La range and found ourselves in a beautiful open glade. It is a small flat plain, affording good pasture-land for a herd of yaks, and surrounded on all sides by forests and enormous mountains. It contains three log-cabins. From here our road lay W.S.W., and we struck up into the mountains again to the pass known as Wu Shu (or Shih) La. The forest accompanied us nearly all the way to the summit, the height of which is about 15,500 feet. The ascent is steep at first, then very gradual, and finally steep again near the top. The forest met us again on the other side, and through it we descended to the village of Wu Shu. The stage was a short one, probably not more than 11 miles. The scenery about Wu Shu is extremely beautiful. Close by the village are the remains of a ruin on a mound. It may have been an octagonal tower but it was impossible to identify it as such.

The ground was covered with snow and it was still snowing heavily when we started next day (23rd April) on what proved to be on the whole the severest day's march which I experienced throughout the whole of my long journey. We began a stiff climb almost immediately, and going south and south-west reached the summit of the first pass (Sin Go La), after a straight pull of about 5 miles. The elevation was about 15,000 feet. Before we reached the top the snow ceased to fall, and the weather for the rest of the day was brilliantly fine. From the summit we had a glorious view of lofty peaks towering far above the highest limit of the thick forests. We descended about 2,000 feet into a shallow ravine, from the further side of which we mounted about 3,000 feet to the second pass, Nai Yu La, about 16,000 feet. On the further side of this pass we descended very gradually to a confined valley, where we crossed a frozen brook and started to climb a third pass, Hlan Go La, the height of which is about 17,200 feet. This was the longest and most arduous climb of all.

I observed that on the sloping sides of the ravines dividing these three ranges hundreds of acres of forest-land had been cruelly devastated by fire. During my journey from Tachienlu to Yunnan nothing puzzled me more than the extraordinary frequency of the forest fires, which must have destroyed many thousands of acres of magnificent timber. The natives say they are caused by careless travellers, who leave the glowing embers of their camp fires to be scattered by the wind; but, as many of the fires commence and burn themselves out in pathless regions where neither natives nor travellers ever set foot, the explanation was obviously unsatisfactory. Serious as the fires are, the forests have to contend with an enemy even more dangerous. No traveller in this region can fail to notice the pale green moss that swathes itself round the trunks and branches of firs and pines, and hangs in graceful festoons from tree to tree. This is the parasitic lichen known to botanists as *usnea barbata*, and popularly as the "fairies' scarf," which dooms any tree once caught in its pendulous net to gradual decay and ignominious death. In many places I saw hundreds of fine trees — the parasite attacks young trees as well as old — stark and dead, stripped of their bark, as if they had been struck by lightning, but still draped with the vampire-like lichen that had sucked them dry. It seems to spread rapidly from one tree to another; its streamers are sometimes several yards long, and in a dense forest it only requires a moderate breeze to blow the loose end of a streamer from a tree that is already dying to its still vigorous neighbour; and so the disease spreads. Apparently the only way to protect the forests would be to cut a "fire-belt" round every group of trees that had been attacked, and so isolate it from the rest. But forestry is an unknown science in the Chinese empire, and the Government does not seem to realise the value of its neglected forests. For want of a better explanation of the forest fires I hazard the suggestion that they may be caused spontaneously by friction between the dry branches of adjoining trees that have been killed by the "fairies' scarf."

The descent from the pass of Hlan Go La into the ravine below was steep and long. A large level plain occurs during the descent, and it is after traversing it that the descent becomes steepest. We found shelter for the night, after a very arduous march, in Gur Dja (Chinese Yin Cho), a hamlet of log-huts. Clearances have been made in the valley just below (for the hamlet is perched on the side of a ravine), and there are a few fields of barley and buckwheat.

Next day we again retraced our steps to a distance of 2 or 3 miles. Then we crossed the ravine and commenced a climb on the opposite side. As usual our climb lay at first through forest, then we plunged into the snow, and found it deeper and more troublesome than on any of the other passes. At about 16,500 feet we reached the summit of the pass known as Ri Go La. The descent was sudden and steep, not without its exciting moments, and we lost a mule. We proceeded downwards in a southerly and south-westerly direction and re-entered the forest. Thence we descended several thousand feet into a deep ravine. By the afternoon we had left the snows behind us and entered into a region characterised by a luxuriance of vegetation that was almost tropical. Among other plants and grasses there were great clusters of bamboo—fragile and feathery, and so thin that it could be bent between two fingers. It was also pleasant to come upon beautiful beds of primroses and flowering shrubs. As we neared the end of the stage we met with a light shower of rain—a sure sign that we were at a comparatively low elevation and drawing near the valley of the Yalung. The village of Pei T'ai, where we spent the night, lay at an elevation of about 10,000 feet. Just before reaching it we had a short climb of 800 or 1,000 feet over the small pass of Pu Ti La, which gave us no trouble. The village of Pei T'ai is the proud possessor of three gilded pinnacles which adorn the roof of a miniature lamasery. The headman's house, in which I was entertained, almost adjoins it.

The next day's march was the last stage to the Yalung. We began by descending a rough path from the eminence which is crowned by the village. Our road then led up and down the south side of a deep ravine, with many tortuous windings. The path—such as it was—had in some places been torn away by recent landslips. Wild-flowers and wild fruit-trees were in blossom, and the young vegetation was delightfully fresh and green. Squirrels were common, and we caught sight of some beautiful long-tailed green parrots. A steep path led us down to a confined valley named Lan Yi Pa, and outside its solitary hut we stopped for our midday meal. The woman of the house, with a nose quick to scent the proximity of untold wealth, hastened to offer me, on bended knee, a present of three eggs. From here the road led steeply to the crest of a hill, and after turning several corners we found ourselves in full view of the noble waters of the Yalung.

When we reached a projecting corner of the road at a spot called Hsin Yi La, I was requested by the *ula* people to fire a shot from my gun in the direction of the village of Pa-U-Rong, which now lay at our feet and was in full view. This I did, on learning that it was a custom with which all travellers approaching Pa-U-Rong were expected to comply. The village, with its comparatively rich fields, has often been the prey of mountain robbers, and any travellers who approach without giving a warning signal are presumed to be coming with no good intent, and may find all the inhabitants of the valley fully clad in the panoply of war, ready to give them a hostile reception. From the spot where I fired the warning gun the road again descended steeply, but after crossing a deep gully we found ourselves in the large village of Pa-U-Rong, and were received by the people with friendly faces.

The valley slopes gradually towards the river, and, though it is of small area, it is thoroughly well cultivated with wheat, barley and other grain, and several kinds of vegetables. The actual banks of the river are very steep, and on them there is no cultivation. The level of Pa-U-Rong is about 7,700 feet, and the river, which has a considerable rise and fall, is on an average about 200 feet lower. The village—with two or three scattered suburbs in other parts of the valley—contains a population of perhaps two thousand, and was the largest and most prosperous centre of population we had come across since leaving Tachienlu.

We had now descended, for the time being, from the icy heights of the Chinese Alps, and were in a region of green vegetation and tranquil beauty. But the snowy peaks and passes were still in full view, and amid the rich scenery that now surrounded me it was the wild splendour of the mountains, and the snow, and the dark primeval forests that haunted me still. The scenery through which I had passed was not of the kind that could be looked at, admired and then forgotten. The purple crags and jewelled peaks rising in sombre majesty from the white slopes of the sun-lit snow-fields were sights upon which one might gaze from dawn till dark and ever find new treasures of beauty, and which, when the eye had once seen, the mind could never forget. Surely our great prose-poet—never more full of enthusiasm and spiritual insight than when describing the glories of his beloved Alps—spoke with truth when he told us that in the whole range of inorganic nature there could perhaps be found no object "more perfectly beautiful than a fresh, deep snow-drift, seen under warm light."[1] But, as Ruskin well knew, it is the dark setting of rock and crag that lends so rare a beauty to wide stretches of untrodden snow. The wild and desolate aspects of nature have indeed a charm that is different in kind from that which belongs to sylvan or merely "pretty" scenery, for they touch profounder depths in our nature than can be reached by the faery beauty of dale and wood and running water. The feelings they excite can only be compared to the deepest religious emotions of which our nature is capable. "Surely, if beauty be an object of worship," said Tyndall, "those glorious mountains, with rounded shoulders of the purest white—snow-crested and star-gemmed—were well calculated to excite sentiments of adoration."[2] Thus it is that in the

[1] *Modern Painters*, I. II. chap. iv. p. 2.

[2] See John Tyndall's description of his ascent of the Finsteraarhorn (*Glaciers of the Alps*).

presence of Nature's holiest shrines it is generally best to be alone. If we have companions, all we ask of them at such times is that they should be silent. The wonders of mountain and snow, ocean and sky, need not the explanatory or descriptive notes of any commentator when we have the reality before our own eyes. The man to whose deeper nature they do not at once appeal will not learn their secrets any the better for listening to the ecstatic ejaculations of the noisy friend who is for ever at his elbow telling him how lovely are those purple mountains, or how rich the colours of that splendid sunset. It is better to acquire the reputation of being insensible to all beauty than to force oneself to listen patiently and respond cheerfully to such well-meant chatter. The feelings that such aspects of Nature produce within us are not feelings that any man has ever yet learned to put into words. Speech, after all, can only interpret the thoughts that lie on the surface of our natures; the deeper thoughts and the nobler emotions elude the grasp of mere human language. The mystic well knows, and the poet well knows, that their sublimest visions cannot be adequately rendered, even by the use of the most splendid imagery and allegory, in the terms of written or spoken language. And similarly it is known to every lover of Nature, though he be no poet, that the deepest mysteries of Nature's loveliness are only revealed to him who possesses, in the unsounded depths of his own soul, the key that can unlock them. And what he has learned he can no more communicate to others than a Saint Teresa or a Saint Ignatius can describe in fitting words the visions that were shown to them in their mystic trances. Each of us, after all, must act as the pilot of his own soul in its solitary voyage through the unknown. The loneliness of the individual human soul is one of the saddest facts of human experience, but there are divine moments in the lives at least of some of us when by the contemplation of the supremely beautiful in Nature or in Art, or by the stirring of some profound emotion, we feel that our loneliness is a mere appearance that will pass away: moments in which we feel that we are in communion and fellowship with the perfect beauty and white truth that lie beyond the fleeting shadowland in which we daily move. And though our splendid visions may not be always present to fill us with rapture, we feel that the spiritual wisdom they have given us can at all times be drawn upon to help and guide us through the darker hours of our lonely daily life.

CHAPTER XI

PA-U-RONG TO MULI

THE Yalung river forms the western frontier of the dominions of the king of Chala. Across the river lies the country generally known as Huang Lama, which is governed by its own lama-prince. The guide whom the king had deputed to accompany me thus far, and who had proved himself a sturdy, honest fellow, had now to return to Tachienlu, leaving me to the care of the three Chinese soldiers who had been instructed to follow me all the way to the borders of the province of Yunnan. Before leaving me, the king's man was obliging enough to cross the river in order to explain to the people of the other side that I was a harmless traveller and deserving of their assistance. This was a necessary precaution, for the *ula* privilege had been extended to me only as far as the king of Chala's frontier.[1]

The king's brother had told me in Tachienlu that on the banks of the Yalung I should find a colony of "White-bone" Lolos. The Lolos—to whom I have already referred—were once a powerful non-Chinese race inhabiting a great part

[1] See Note 26 (p. 429).

of southern Ssuch'uan and the greater part of Yunnan. A large remnant of them still maintains its independence in the mountainous country between the Chien-ch'ang valley and the Upper Yangtse. The so-called *Hei-Ku-t'ou* or "Black-bones," are the aristocrats of the race, the *Pai-Ku-t'ou* or "White-bones" the "tame" ones, who do what they are told by any one who has authority over them, whether of their own race or not. The Lolos are an interesting people from the European point of view on account of their obstinate self-reliance, their dislike for the Chinese, and their mysterious history. The 12,000 square miles or so of mountain-land which still belong to them comprise one of the least-known corners of the Chinese empire;[1] but this is only owing to the jealousy of the Chinese, who object to Europeans going where they cannot and dare not go themselves. A well-conducted European able to satisfy his hosts that he had no hostile intentions would probably be well received in Lolo-land, for the people seem to be as hospitable as those of Laos and the Shan States, with whom, indeed, it is just possible that they are ethnologically connected. The European students of their language could be numbered on the fingers of one hand, and no one has yet given a comprehensive account of it. It is evident from Paul Vial's little hand-book[2]—which deals with some of the Lolo tribes of Yunnan—that there are several dialects, which probably represent several

[1] See Note 27 (p. 429).

[2] *Les Lolos*, by M. Paul Vial, Catholic missionary (Shanghai, 1898).

broad tribal cleavages. It is doubtful, indeed, whether many of the Yunnan Lolos would be able to carry on an intelligent conversation with the independent Lolos of the Ta Liang Shan.[1] During the day's holiday which I gave my men at Pa-U-Rong—for I remained there two nights — I made enquiries about the isolated Lolo colonists of whom I had heard, and discovered that the information given me was accurate. I had great difficulty in persuading one of them to come to me and tell me something of their history; and the one who finally accepted the bribe which I held out was not a brilliant specimen of the attractive race to which he belonged. He was afflicted with deafness, stupidity and extreme nervousness, had no knowledge of Chinese, and was only partially acquainted with the local dialect of Tibetan. I managed, however, to take down a small vocabulary from him[2] and extracted hesitating answers to a few of my questions. In Pa-U-Rong and its suburb villages there are some twenty-three families of Lolos. They came from the independent Lolo country, east of Yüeh-hsi, about the year 1850, the migration being due to a tribal feud. They were well received by the local *t'u pai hu*, and lands were allotted to them for which they pay an annual rent. In or about the year 1864 they addressed a petition to the king of Chala in which they begged to be enrolled among his subjects. The answer to this petition

[1] See chap. xv. below, on the ethnology of the Lolos and other border tribes.

[2] See Appendix A.

A HALT ON THE ROAD TO MULI.

[*To face p.* 188.

was favourable, and they have since been treated with every kindness, for which they are grateful. They use the Tibetan alphabet in transcribing their language,[1] but only a few of them can read and write. They call themselves *Drü*, which has the meaning of "comrades." They worship a deity called Ba Le Nim Bu and another called San To. The latter is supposed to reside on the top of one of the high mountains overlooking Pa-U-Rong on the north-east. They neither bury nor burn their dead: they tie a white veil over the dead man's face, swathe him in a shroud, and throw him into the Yalung. The poorest among them go barefooted and scarify the soles of their feet with a hot iron in order to make them hard. When the head of a family dies his property goes to his eldest son; if there is no son the widow adopts a boy, who then takes the family surname and succeeds to the property—much as is done in China. If there is no heir, the property goes to the lamas, in accordance with Tibetan custom.

The statement regarding the deity on the mountain-top is interesting as showing that when the Lolos migrate they take their gods with them and give them a new residence in a locality convenient for acts of worship. It seems to be an established fact that the Lolos have never been converted to Buddhism. Mount Omei is to them a sacred mountain, but it is to worship gods of their own and not Buddhas or Bodhisattvas that they go thither on pilgrim-

[1] There is, however, a system of written characters peculiar to the Lolos. It appears to be unknown among these colonists.

age.[1] Considering their fondness for mountains as religious centres, it does not seem rash to hazard the prophecy that when their country has been explored the highest point of the Ta Liang Shan will be found to be the Olympus of their gods. The little colony of emigrants has no doubt been obliged to conform to most of the social customs of those among whom they live, and this is sufficient to explain why among them the lamas are regarded as *ultimus haeres* of their property. As time goes on it is probable that their descendants will gradually forget their own language and the history of their race.

An old man — not a Lolo—who said his name was Shou Ji Tseri, paid me a visit in order to tell me that he was a Roman Catholic. He had been converted by a French missionary in Tachienlu over twenty years before, and though he had long since migrated to Pa-U-Rong, he and his family had remained steadfast in the faith. He assured me that he was not persecuted, and suffered no social disabilities through being a Christian.

The landlord of my house was the *t'u pai hu*,[2] and he was evidently a devout Buddhist, or rather lamaist. The room in which I was quartered was a kind of private chapel, containing a small library of Tibetan books grimy with age. More numerous than the books were bundles of charms supposed to ward off disease and ill-fortune. They consisted of small stiff cards, not unlike playing-cards in size

[1] See above, p. 55.
[2] See Note 28 (p. 429).

and appearance, covered with writing on one side, and crudely-painted pictures of horses and other animals on the other.

On the eve of my departure from Pa-U-Rong I gave my returning guide a letter in which I informed the king of my safe arrival at the limits of his territory. The lack of startling adventures was perhaps a little disconcerting after all that I had been told of the perils of the way, but I was glad to know that I had not contributed to the collapse of that amiable monarch's already rather insecure throne.

I made my exit from the kingdom of Chala by the undignified expedient of sliding down a rope. The Yalung[1] is one of the greatest tributaries of the Yangtse, but it is full of rapids and cascades, and is unnavigable. At Pa-U-Rong it is about 70 or 80 yards broad, and the current is very swift and strong. I heard that till recently it could at the season of slack water be crossed by a raft;[2] but at the time of my visit there was no raft or boat of any kind on the river (the last one had been wrecked and lost), and a single stout cable of twisted bamboo, stretched from bank to bank, afforded the only means of crossing. The frontispiece to this book, which reproduces a photograph taken by myself, shows one of my followers in the act of making the passage. Bridges of this kind are common in Tibet, and in the Himālayan gorges, but it is not often that the stream to be crossed

[1] See Note 29 (p. 430).

[2] Mr Amundsen states that he crossed by a raft made of two pieces of timber, with a plank in the middle to stand on.—(*Geographical Journal*, vol. xv. p. 621).

is so wide as the Yalung. The main roads—such as the highroad from Tachienlu to Lhasa—are generally provided with good bridges or ferries; and, as a rule, it is only when travelling by the "small roads" and by-ways of Tibet that one is compelled to cross rivers and gorges by single ropes. The abbé Huc admits that in the course of his long journey to Lhasa and back he never ventured on bridges of this kind, though he frequently saw them. Captain Gill[1] remarks that "this is a method of crossing a river that must require a considerable amount of nerve"; but he too, apparently, evaded the necessity of putting the matter to personal test. In my case there was no possibility of evasion.

The first view of this primitive substitute for a bridge certainly does not inspire one with confidence. There is one rope for crossing from the left to the right bank, and another—some 80 yards off—for the reverse proceeding. The banks on either side are high and steep, and each rope-end is firmly bound round an immovable rock or boulder. The arrangement is shown in the accompanying diagram.

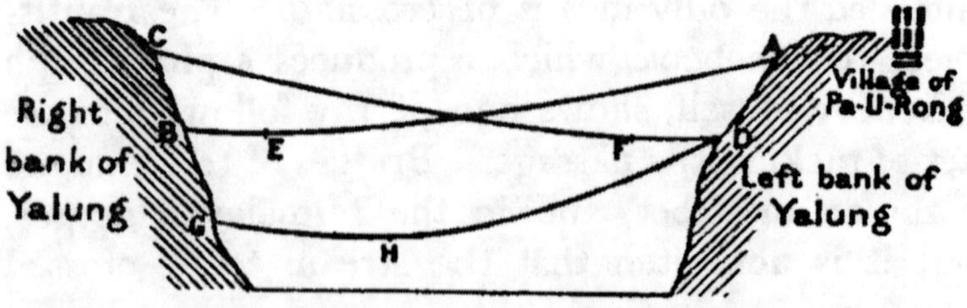

[1] In Captain Gill's *The River of Golden Sand* (John Murray), p. 121, where there is a good illustration of the single-rope bridges.

On crossing from the left bank (Pa-U-Rong side) one starts at the point A, reaching the right bank at the point B. Crossing in the opposite direction one starts at C, reaching the left bank at D. The points A and C are about 120 feet above the level of the water. B and D are about 40 feet lower. The native of the district, when about to cross the river, places a semicircular piece of tough wood, with two grooves for the fingers, on the bamboo rope, clutches it with both hands and lets himself go. He is not tied to the movable cylinder or to the rope, and he has nothing to sit on. He simply holds on with his hands, his legs hanging in the air. He descends with terrific speed to the point where the rope sags or hangs lowest (the points E and F); and having safely arrived there, he is only a few yards from the further bank, and quickly hauls himself along the remaining distance. In this manner the crossing is only a matter of a few exhilarating seconds. With us, however, the operation was a longer one. Unfortunately, the proper rope for leaving the left bank was old, and had been condemned as unsafe; all my party, therefore, were obliged to use the rope that was only intended for crossing in the opposite direction. The rope-end at the point C, however, had been temporarily brought down to the point G, as it would otherwise have been necessary for us to haul ourselves along nearly the whole length of the rope in an ascending direction, which would have been a task requiring great strength and endurance. Even as it was, instead of a rapid rush through the air across almost the whole width of the river, the weight of our bodies only took us about two-thirds of the total distance, and from that point we had to proceed by throwing our legs over the rope and pulling ourselves upwards inch by inch, hand over hand. The work was exceedingly laborious. All my party went across in this manner one by one, starting at D and arriving at G. The point H represents the place at which we had to commence hauling. In view of the fact that we were all novices at rope-climbing, each of us submitted, before starting, to having a leather thong tied under the arms, and made fast to the sliding cylinder, so that if loss of nerve or other cause had made us let go we should not have fallen into the river, but hung limply on the rope until rescued. There was, therefore, no actual danger provided that nothing gave way. In some places where these primitive bridges are in use, passengers are provided with a swinging rope - seat which hangs from the cylinder. This, of course, must relieve the strain on hands and arms very considerably. But we were furnished with no such luxury. My dog Jim was sent across by himself, his body being firmly tied up with strips of cloth suspended from the cylinder, from which the unhappy beast hung like a squirming fish at the end of a line. When he reached the point at which upward hauling became necessary, one of the natives—who seemed to delight in performing acrobatic feats above the swirling waters of the Yalung—clambered along from the right bank with an extra rope and tied it round him. He did this while he was hanging upside down with his legs round the rope-bridge. The loose end of the spare rope he took back with him to the right bank, and the dog was safely pulled by several willing hands along the remaining distance. My baggage was sent across in the same manner. I found the experience interesting and somewhat exciting. The whole village turned out to watch us cross the river, and I must confess that when I was being trussed up with the leather thong my feelings were perhaps only comparable to those of a condemned criminal who is being pinioned before execution. A fall into the river would mean almost certain death. The water seethes and bubbles in innumerable whirlpools, and is nearly as cold as ice, for it largely consists of frozen snow.

I never heard the Yalung given that name by the natives. The word is a Chinese approximation to the Tibetan Nya Rong ("Valley of the Nya"). The Tibetans all know the river as the Nya Ch'u or Nya river; but the Chinese, so far as my experience goes, never give it any other name than *Kin* [*Chin*] *Ho*, which means "Gold River,"—so that "Yalung" is really only a book-word. The number of rivers in western China, of which the word "Gold" forms part of the Chinese name, might almost fill a page. The Ta Tu river above Wa Ssu Kou[1] is the Chin Ch'uan ("Gold Stream"), the Yangtse for hundreds of miles of its course is the Chin Sha Chiang [Kin Sha Kiang], or "River of Golden Sand," and many streams of less importance bear similar names. The reason

[1] See above, p. 128.

of the popularity of the name is not far to seek, for gold in larger or smaller quantities is well known to exist in nearly all the rivers that take their rise in eastern and northern Tibet, and the Tibetans—especially the lamas—derive therefrom a very considerable profit.

Baber pointed out that the upper Yangtse, from its junction with the Yalung to about P'ing-shan (above the mouth of the Min), is "never called locally by any other name than *Kin-* [*Chin-*] *Ho*, or 'Gold River.'" M. Cordier, in quoting this passage in his sumptuous edition of Marco Polo's travels,[1] says that he imagines Baber to have made a slight mistake in saying that this part of the great river is named a *ho*, and that the word actually used is probably *kiang*. As both words mean "river" the point is of small importance, but as a matter of fact Baber is perfectly right. Not only is the Yangtse from the mouth of the Min to the mouth of the Yalung called the Kin [Chin] Ho, as Baber said, but it seems obvious that the natives regard the Yalung as the main upper stream of the same river, just as they regard the Min as the main upper stream of the Yangtse hundreds of miles lower down.[2] Baber was no doubt unaware that the Yalung was known as the Kin Ho, or he would have seen why it is that its junction with what we know as the Yangtse effects a change in the name of the latter.

In official publications, however, the local names are disregarded. In such works the

[1] Yule's *Marco Polo*, edited by Cordier. [London: John Murray.] See vol. ii. p. 67.

[2] See above, pp. 43-44.

Yangtse is given one name from its entrance into Ssuch'uan down to Hsü-chou-fu, where it comes to an untimely end by entering the Min:[1] and that one name is the Chin Sha Chiang.[2] As regards its Tibetan course, the Chinese geographical authorities attempt after their usual cumbrous fashion to give the sounds of the various Tibetan names — they write of the *Mu-lu-ssŭ-wu-su* for instance—but they recognise it as the same river. In explanation of the local idea that the Yalung is the principal stream it may be mentioned that at the point of junction the Yalung has the appearance of being larger than the Yangtse.[3]

We did not proceed far on our journey during the day on which we accomplished the feat of crossing the Yalung. We clambered up the steep slope to a height of about 1,500 feet and remained for the night in the poor hamlet of Dju Mu. We were still well within sight of Pa-U-Rong, having travelled only about 12 *li*. A change of language or dialect perplexed my servant as soon as we had crossed the river, and though it is rash to generalise from the appearance of the inhabitants of a few isolated villages, there seemed to be racial changes as well. The Tibetan-Man-tzŭ population of the kingdom of Chala seems to give place to a race-group which might be described as Tibetan-Mo-so. The men are shorter than those of the eastern watershed of the Yalung, the women

[1] 流入岷江. Similarly we read of the Han River (which flows into the Yangtse at Hankow) *joining the Min* (合岷江).

[2] See Note 30 (p. 430).

[3] This is on Mr Amundsen's authority. See *Geographical Journal*, Nov. 1900, p. 534.

plainer and stouter and of heavier build. There is no great change in the dress of the men, but the women — perhaps recognising their deficiency of personal attractiveness—show an exaggerated fondness for jewellery and trinkets, which make a ceaseless jingle as they walk. Many of the people —men as well as women — wear large earrings consisting of plain circles of silver, from which, in the case of girls, are suspended long strings of coloured beads. On both sides of the Yalung —but not far from its banks on either side—the women also wear curious silver plates or plaques which are fastened to their hair. Unmarried girls wear one and married women two of these ornaments. Some of the plaques — which vary in size from about 5 inches to more than a foot in diameter—are adorned with dainty filigree work, which would do credit to the silversmiths of any country, but the majority are simple and of rude workmanship, such as the specimen which with difficulty I succeeded in purchasing.[1] In the middle of each plaque is a silver tube containing some red substance that from a distance looks like dark coral. These little plates are regarded as ornaments, but they are also charms to ward off a certain dread disease. From a description of the ailment it would appear to be something like bubonic plague. I saw no cases of it, but I was told that it devastates the valley of the Yalung every autumn, and kills every one who does not wear a charm. It is curious to note that nearly

[1] See illustration, p. 152 (No. 2). The plaques may also be seen on the women's heads, p. 188.

all the great trough-like river-valleys of south-western China have acquired a similar reputation of extreme unhealthiness. The Red River of Tongking and Yunnan is so much dreaded by the Chinese on account of its deadly fevers that nothing will induce them to spend a night on its banks.[1] The Salwen, the valley of which forms a yawning chasm from north to south of the Yunnan plateau, has an even worse reputation, as is well known to all who have travelled from Tali-fu to Bhamo.[2] Charms against disease are worn by the men of the Yalung valley as well as by the women, but they do not take the same form. The men and boys carry a small charm-box (*ga-u*[3]) hung round their necks like a locket by a string or chain, and in the box they place little amulets[4] which they have received from the lamas. The efficacy of the charms is supposed to be impaired if they are removed from the person or put into the hands of a stranger, so it is not often that one has an opportunity of close examination.

[1] I travelled up the valley of this river in 1902, and heard much of its deadliness. Rocher, in his excellent history of Yunnan, remarks that the only people who could live on the banks of the Red River with comparative immunity were some indigenous non-Chinese tribes and Cantonese merchants. As regards the Cantonese, the jealous Yunnanese supposed that their immunity was derived from the fact that they possessed a sovereign remedy for the disease, but kept the secret of it to themselves so that they alone should obtain the benefit. Some of the Yunnanese told Rocher that they would go into battle rather than brave a visit to the banks of the Red River.—(*La Province Chinoise du Yunnan*, vol. i. pp. 229, 230, and 286.)

[2] See below, pp. 305 *seq.*

[3] གའུ་

[4] Tibetan brTen (བརྟེན་) pronounced *ten*, or Srung-ba (སྲུང་བ་) pronounced *sung-wa*, the original meaning of which is simply "protection."

The next day (28th April) we travelled a very short distance—about 6 miles. The path wound round the edge of a defile and up the mountain side west and south-west through a pine forest. We halted at a place called Tê Ben, a single house belonging to a headman, situated near the edge of a bluff that commanded a fine view of the Yalung valley, now far below us. Difficulties about transport prevented our making a longer stage. Next day, these difficulties having been overcome, our path led us over innumerable undulations, in the course of which we gradually ascended another 2,000 feet. At the hamlet of Pa Sung, which we reached during the morning, there were no animals to be hired, and our baggage was carried for the rest of the day's march by three women and a yak. One of my Chinese escort —not in love with his mountaineering experiences—was much perturbed at the discovery that he was expected to walk, and made himself so disagreeable to the villagers that they had to bribe him to calmness by making him a present of a live fowl. He accepted the fowl, and made one of the village damsels carry it for him. This incident was not discovered by me until our arrival at our destination that night, when I punished my soldier for the impropriety of his conduct by paying for the fowl and eating it myself. The yak caused us some trouble by losing itself in the forest while we were having our midday *tsamba*. It was finally discovered by its driver —a very little boy — and brought back by him triumphantly at the end of a rope. The incident pleasantly recalled to my memory the only poem in the English language, so far as I am aware, which sings the exclusive praises of the yak, an animal which, however useful to man, is indeed hardly of the kind that would naturally inspire a poet to a lyrical outburst.[1] Tibetan and Man-tzŭ children seem to be able to manage the clumsy beast with the same ease and dexterity as are shown by Chinese children in controlling the cumbrous movements of the water-buffalo; and the European who may prod a yak without the least effect in accelerating its motion, and whose mere proximity often rouses the water-buffalo to dangerous fury, can have nothing but jealous admiration for the Oriental child whose lightest touch reduces one or the other to complete docility.

From the hamlet of Pa Sung we dropped down to a deep ravine at the bottom of which is a sparkling mountain stream spanned by a rustic bridge. The ravine was full of wild-flowers—pink, red, purple and white in a setting of rich green. I noticed also that ivy—not so common a sight in the Far East as in England—clambered in great profusion round the trunks of trees and over a small obo; and some exquisite ferns, including maiden-hair, covered the steep banks of the stream and fringed our path. After climbing up the further side of the ravine our path again wound up and along the mountain-side, and brought us finally to the hamlet of Ten Ba K'a, where we

[1] The reader will not, I hope, require to be reminded of "The Bad Child's Book of Beasts," in which the poem to which I refer finds an honourable place.

lodged in the local chief's house. Our host was a fine-looking man, whose long black hair hanging down on each side of his face gave him an appearance of ferocity that was belied by the gentleness of his manners. I was accommodated in the family chapel—a large room on the first floor. Close by was a small lamasery. The village is situated at the head of a small valley which runs north-east and south-west, and from it we had a magnificent view of the snowy mountains we had left behind us on the other side of the Yalung. The valley itself—when one looks down upon it from above—is of very peculiar formation, being split up by a series of clearly-defined ridges. I could see nothing to indicate that they were glacier moraines. Next morning we climbed one of the ridges that lies immediately behind the village, and from its summit we descended into a thickly-wooded ravine, bounded on the left by lofty and picturesque cliffs. After descending a thousand feet or more we emerged from the ravine into a small partially-cultivated valley containing a village. After leaving this village, where we took our midday rest, we began a long and rather wearisome up-hill climb past a plantation of birches and through a thin forest. From the top of the pass we made a gradual descent through similar country, and struck into the valley of a large stream—the Dja Ch'u—issuing, apparently, from some high snowy peaks visible in the distance.[1] This river accompanied us from

[1] It would appear from the recent Indian Survey map prepared by Major H. R. Davies, that this must be the Litang River, and therefore starts its course much further north.

MOUNTAIN AND VALLEY ON THE ROAD TO MULI.

[*To face p.* 202.

this point practically all the way to Muli. Our path led us hundreds of feet above the river's left bank, and brought us to our night's lodging in a solitary house. Other scattered houses were visible some distance off, and I was told that they all bear the collective name of Hu Dra. Our hostess brought me as a present the best Tibetan cheese I had tasted.

The next day, 1st May, we left our quarters at Hu Dra just as the sun rose, on a beautiful fresh morning that reminded one almost too vividly of early summer in England. Even the cuckoo was not wanting. The road led us at first in a south-easterly direction high above the left bank of the Dja Ch'u for about 3 miles, then turned with that river into a valley running south-west. A mile or so beyond the bend I observed a village on the right bank, but we kept to the left, still high above the river. Nearly opposite that village we came to a couple of tumbledown huts. While we were resting here, two of my soldiers took the opportunity to disgrace May Day by indulging in a violent quarrel. For the sake of cacophony I had previously given one of these men the unmelodious name of Bloggins, owing to the singular irregularity of his features. Certainly no one could have mistaken him for a reincarnation of Plato's Charmides. To the other, for a different reason, I had given the surname of Hoggins. Before I could learn the cause of the dispute and settle it by friendly arbitration, Hoggins drew his sword and began laying it about him in a manner suggestive of slaughter and blood. The effects were not serious, as the blade of the sword, not being intended for actual warfare, broke off at the hilt. Bloggins took shelter behind a mule. The quarrel arose and subsided like a thunderstorm, for in half an hour the combatants were again on the most amiable terms with each other and drowning the memory of their disagreement in a bowl of tea.

From the scene of this bloodless combat the road continued to lead us high above the left bank of the river-valley, giving us occasional glimpses of the many windings of the stream. One has to ride with caution, as the path frequently lies along the edge of a precipice. The surface is sometimes very rough and rocky, and the road undulates a great deal as it has to cross a number of deep ravines. After riding about 65 *li* from our starting-place we reached the neighbourhood of an important lamasery, named Wa-chin Gompa,[1] well hidden in a wooded dell. The lamas objected to receiving us here, so we went on to a scattered hamlet called Ta K'oa. The Dja Ch'u here changes its name to the Ya-Rong Ch'u.

A great authority has told us that among the losses brought upon us by the fury and vulgarity of modern life, one of the saddest is the loss of a wish to gather a flower in travelling.[2] Perhaps it was because I was so far from the beaten tracks of civilisation that on that beautiful May morning the wish to gather flowers still asserted in me its vigorous vitality. The wild-flowers during that day's journey were indeed so

[1] See p. 216.

[2] Ruskin, *Proserpina*, II. IV.

numerous and beautiful that all the members of my party yielded to the temptation of decking themselves out in blossoms pink and white and blue. The dainty freshness of our summer garlands only served, I fear, to throw into stronger relief the dirt and dust of our travel-stained garments. Though there were three flower-bedecked women among my party, I was moved by no impulse to crown any one of the three as our Queen of May. It would be ungallant to give the reasons. But if none of them was conspicuous for beauty of figure or feature, I think it only fair to call to grateful remembrance the fact that one was the possessor of an alluring smile and a not unattractive dimple.

On 2nd May a pretty road lined with "English" hedgerows bursting into bloom, led us after a ride of 4 miles to a point from which we obtained a fine view of the river—a long stretch of smooth water shining in the sun, a rather violent rapid, and a series of graceful curves. From the village of Dje Ru we descended for the first time to the river-bank and crossed the stream—now called the Tong Yi—by a substantial wooden bridge about 50 yards long. I have already referred to the variety of names possessed by the rivers of this region. The stream which we knew first on 30th April as the Dja Ch'u had changed its name at least seven times before we finally left its banks three days later; but as in the case of many other Tibetan rivers, the different names often represent merely the tribal names of the various village communities that dwell on its banks, or even the names of the valleys through which it flows. In the interests of geography it would no doubt be more satisfactory if every river were given one name only, by which it could be universally known throughout the whole length of its course; but the convenience of so doing would hardly appeal to people who never saw a map, and never travel, and know nothing of their rivers except the short stretches that flow by their doors. I did not meet a single inhabitant of the Yalung watershed who was able to tell me whence any of their rivers came, or whither it went. Such questions seemed to them merely frivolous, the answers being regarded as beyond the range of possible human knowledge.

About a mile beyond the wooden bridge the river becomes the Wo Pu Tsong, and later on the Mi Ch'u. Not far beyond, a fairly large tributary—the Ba Tsam Ch'u—enters by a valley in the east, and joins the main stream at a point where, after flowing for some miles due south, it turns sharply to the south-west. Our path, following the right bank of the river, now turned into a narrow valley through which we travelled for the rest of the stage, and from which we did not emerge till the middle of the following day. This valley possesses, perhaps, the most beautiful riverine scenery met with anywhere throughout my journey, though it is not on the same grand scale as the scenery of the Yangtse gorges or the valley of the Ta Tu. After travelling along an undulating road for about 5 miles, we came to a place which possesses the abrupt name of

Wu, where—on the flat roof of one of the two huts forming the hamlet — we had our midday meal. Just before reaching this spot we passed a place where two landslips, one on each side of the river, had very recently taken place. Part of the subsiding banks having fallen into the water, a violent rapid had been formed across the river.

In this extremely beautiful valley the river is known as the Li Ch'u. It is an unnavigable stream

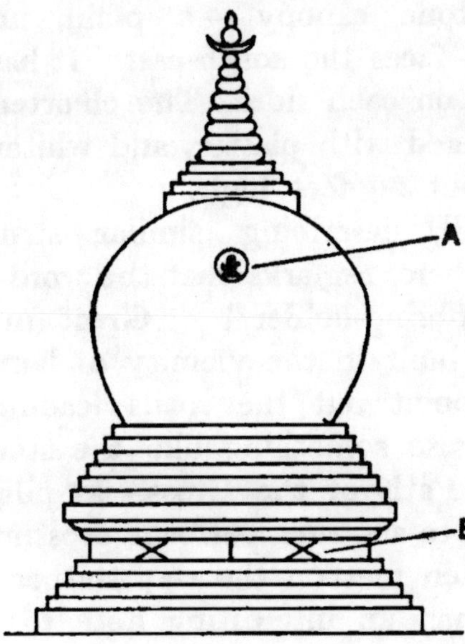

A—Recess with miniature Buddha, on the S.E. side.
B—Conventional lions in relief, two on each of the four sides.

containing a considerable body of water sometimes nearly 100 yards broad, but occasionally narrowed to 80. An easy walk through the most charming sylvan scenery brought us, a few miles beyond Wu, to a wooded glade, where—as the moon had already risen and there was no sign of a village—I decided to camp out. There is here an obo covered with the usual inscribed slates; and close by stands a square stone building with a wooden roof. This building serves as a kind of canopy for a *ch'o-ten*[1] (ch'orten), or small lamaist pyramid, which occupies the whole space inside. My sketch of this ch'orten, which is of a type very common in Tibetan lands, will convey an idea of its appearance.

The stone canopy — a plain, unpretentious building[2]—faces the south-east. It has four doorways, one on each side. The ch'orten itself is of stone, covered with plaster, and whitewashed, and stands about 20 feet high.

Rockhill, describing similar structures met with elsewhere, remarks that the word "ch'orten" means "offering-holder." "Great numbers" he says "are built in the vicinity of lamaseries, and serve to point out the roads leading to them. They are also something like the stations in the Catholic 'Path of the Cross,' as pilgrims, when journeying to a shrine, perform prostrations before each ch'orten met on the way thither."[3] Colonel Waddell has an interesting note to explain the symbolical character of this type of building. He says that ch'ortens are "symbolic of the five elements into which a body is resolved upon death: thus . . . the lowest section, a solid rect-

[1] Spelt in Tibetan mCh'od-rTen.

[2] See illustration, p. 207.

[3] *Land of the Lamas*, p. 63.

THE AUTHOR'S CAMP, 2ND MAY.

[*To face p.* 208.

angular block, typifies the solidity of the *earth*; above it *water* is represented by a globe; *fire* by a triangular tongue; *air* by a crescent—the inverted vault of the sky; and *ether* by an acuminated circle, the tapering into space."[1] The Tibetan ch'ortens may thus be regarded either as the tombstones of dead lamas or as chambers for preserving the relics of Buddhist saints. In the latter case they are analogous to the far more imposing pagodas of China or the dagobas of Burma and of Anuradhapura in Ceylon.

Outside the stone building containing the ch'orten I spent the night of 2nd May. We were now in a sheltered ravine and in a fairly warm latitude. We were therefore independent of walled shelter, and, as we carried with us our own *tsamba*, we were in no want of food. The spot we had chosen was indeed an ideal resting-place. The utter peacefulness of our beautiful valley, the murmur of the stream only a few yards away, the soft shimmer of moonlight interwoven with the network of fresh foliage that curtained mysterious fairylands beyond, combined to create an earthly paradise that might almost make one cease to long for a heavenly one. If Shakespeare had visited the Far East, he would surely have chosen just such a spot as this for the scene of a new Midsummer Night's Dream. It was sad to reflect that until æroplanes come into general use it could never be made accessible to lovers of nature except those who were willing to cross

[1] *Lamaism in Tibet*, pp. 262-264.

the vast ranges of snowy mountains that hem it in; but I could not restrain a feeling of exultation at the thought that never—I hope this is no rash prophecy—would the shriek of a steam-engine disturb here

> "The silence that is in the starry sky,
> The sleep that is among the lonely hills,"—

and that our boisterous civilisation would be content to leave this one nook of beauty for ever undefiled. If any of my readers is yearning to seek in some quiet hermitage rest and release from the pains and feverish joys of modern life, some home of ancient peace amid lovely scenery, let him turn his pilgrim steps towards the far lands of the Tibetan border, for his ideal would be surely realised in some such valley as this.

It was with regret, not shared, I fear, by my unemotional companions, that I left my camping-ground on the morning of the next day. For half the day, however, our path still lay through the southern portion of the same beautiful valley, and amid scenery no less charming than that of the day before. A short distance beyond our camp a turn in the path brought us opposite to a ravine opening towards the east, on the river's left bank. The sun rose behind it as I passed, and shed a rich glow on rocks and caseades and masses of pure green foliage. A walk of 5 or 6 miles brought us to a crazy wooden bridge[1] over which we crossed with some trepidation to the left bank, and about 8 miles further

[1] See accompanying illustration.

RUSTIC BRIDGE CROSSING LITANG RIVER ON THE ROAD TO MULI.

[To face p. 210.

on we again crossed to the right. Beyond this the scenery becomes wilder, and the river-valley gradually opens out into a region where rocks and hills lie about in fantastic confusion. Passing oboes, prayer-flags and prayer-wheels in great numbers, we climbed up a steep and winding path that gradually led us far away from the Li Ch'u and brought us to a scattered mountain village named Ku-Dze, where we rested. One of my men had gone in advance of us in order to arrange for new means of transport; and when I arrived at the village I found that the hospitable headman had converted four tumbledown, roofless walls into a delightful arbour with a thick, soft carpet of green leaves and walls of pine-branches, and a doorway festooned with feathery bamboo. In this Arcadian retreat I was provided with an appropriate repast of milk and eggs.

From this village to the lamasery of Muli—the capital, if it may be called so, of the Huang Lama territory—is a distance of about 14 miles through pleasant undulating country and over an easy road. At one point, however, we found the main path blocked by a huge landslip, and for a distance of several miles we were obliged to take a rough and rocky path that gave us a good deal of trouble. We did not arrive at Muli till after sunset. There is nothing to show that one is anywhere near a human habitation until suddenly, after turning a corner, one comes in full view of a mass of white walls only a few hundred yards away. This is the lamasery of Muli. To all appearance it is a compact, unwalled town composed entirely of white-plastered houses. In reality it is a large monastery and nothing else, for all the buildings that look like ordinary houses are only the separate cells or dwelling-places of the lamas. Two or three of them, in their dark-red gowns, were waiting to receive me. These were the people who, I had been led to understand, were fanatically anti-foreign, and whose hostility rendered it a dangerous experiment to travel through their country. If their feelings were of a hostile nature, they certainly evinced a wonderful power of self-control, for their reception of me was altogether courteous and friendly. They lodged me in a comfortable two-floored building only a few yards from the lamasery, and sent me presents of fuel and food.

CHAPTER XII

MULI TO YUNG-NING

THE territory ruled over by the lama-prince of Muli[1] is to Europeans, as it is to the Chinese themselves, almost an unknown corner of the Chinese empire. One may search in vain through books of history or travel for any description of it. Even the *Ssuch'uan T'ung Chih*—a work that describes the province in nearly two hundred volumes—devotes to it only a single page. Baber does little more than refer to it by name. He describes it as "a country of which almost nothing is known, lying south of Litang and west of the Yalung. I can only learn," he adds, "that the language of its inhabitants is unintelligible to Tibetans. The Chinese call it the 'land of the Yellow Lamas.' The Mili of D'Anville's map is probably its chief monastery."[2] Hosie, in his recent report of a journey through Litang and Batang to the border of Tibet proper, refers to it as "the State of Mili, or Muli—better known as Huang Lama ('Yellow Lama')." As regards this name "Huang Lama," there appears to be some

[1] See Note 31 (p. 431).

[2] Royal Geographical Society's *Supplementary Papers*, vol. i. p. 96. The conjecture about the monastery was correct.

confusion of ideas, either on the part of the natives of the state or on the part of the Chinese. *Huang* means "yellow," but another word of identical sound though differently written means "imperial,"[1] and I was assured by the lamas themselves—who may have been deliberately misleading me—that the *huang* which is applied to their territory or its rulers is the second of these. According to this theory, the state of Muli is the land of the Imperial Lamas (or Lama), not the land of the "Yellow Lamas." The Muli lamas do, however, belong to one of the Gélupa or reformed sects, and therefore wear the "yellow hat" in religious ceremonials.

Unfortunately, the lama-prince was not at Muli at the time of my arrival there, and three or four subordinate lamas, who called upon me and with whom I conversed in Tibetan with the assistance of my servant, were either disinclined or unable to impart much information. But as far as I could gather, it appears that "a long time ago"[2] the principal lama of this country rendered valuable services to the Chinese Emperor, and received as a reward the title of "Huang Lama," and was confirmed in the spiritual and temporal sovereignty of the whole principality of Muli. It is evident, however, that Muli has for centuries past been regarded as a debatable land: sometimes the kings or Grand Lamas of Tibet and sometimes the emperors of China have been regarded

[1] 黃 (Yellow) and 皇 (Imperial).

[2] Judging from the dates in the *T'ung Chih*, it cannot have been earlier than 1729.

as suzerains. According to one story which was told me by a lama, Muli-land was at one time an integral part of the "monarchy" of Tachienlu, and was ceded to a certain lama by one of the kings of Chala as a reward for having cured the king of a painful disease. However this may be, the dignity of prince-lama is now, and long has been, the exclusive monopoly of one family. The system of succession is therefore totally different from that generally in vogue in Tibet proper, where the prior of a lamasery is either selected by the Dalai Lama or by the whole body of lamas, or—in the case of the greater establishments—is chosen as an infant to fill that high office because he is believed to be the reincarnation of the prior or abbot last deceased.[1] The ecclesiastical title of the lama-prince of Muli is *k'an-po*,[2] a word which may be translated lord-abbot or bishop—and it is by that title that he is familiarly known in his own territory; but in virtue of his civil powers he is also a *gyal-po* or "king," and is just as powerful within his own limits as the king of Chala. The Muli *gyal-po* being a lama cannot marry, but when he dies his successor is chosen from among his brothers or nephews. If an otherwise eligible heir is under the age of eighteen or thereabouts, he is passed over in favour of any suitable elder relative who

[1] "Nearly every great monastery," says Waddell, "has its own reincarnate Lama as its chief."—(*Lamaism in Tibet*, p. 230. For the numbers of these reincarnated saints, see *ibid.*, p. 243.) These are the personages generally known by Europeans as Living Buddhas. One of them presides over the great lamasery in Peking.

[2] Spelt mk'an-po (མཁན་པོ་)

may be a lama. Notification of the death of the *k'an-po* or *gyal-po* must be sent to the emperor at Peking, and at the same time the name of a suitable heir, selected from the eligible members of the "royal" family, is submitted for the imperial consideration. His succession is as a matter of form ratified by the emperor, and he forthwith enters upon his duties and honours. News of the *k'an-po's* death and the accession of his heir is also sent to Lhasa, but the approval of the Dalai Lama is not now essential to legalise the succession. Subject to the suzerainty of China the *k'an-po* is invested with full ecclesiastical and civil powers in virtue of his double position, but in practice he generally confines himself to civil and judicial administration, and leaves the management of ecclesiastical affairs to lamas of lower rank. He has three centres of government, all of which are also lamaseries: their names are Muli, Lha-k'ang[1] and Khon.[2] Muli, the chief lamasery and headquarters of the government, contains about four hundred and fifty lamas; Lha-k'ang and Khon between one and two hundred each. At these centres the *k'an-po* resides alternately, generally remaining a year at each. I was told that this custom was originated in order that the *k'an-po* might acquire a thorough knowledge of the different parts of his territory, and that his ear should always be open to receive his people's

[1] This word literally means the "house of a god, or shrine" (ལྷ་ཁང་) It is the same lamasery as that otherwise known as Wa-chin, referred to on p. 204.

[2] See Note 32 (p. 431).

complaints. Important lawsuits are decided by the *k'an-po* himself, but smaller suits and petty criminal cases are dealt with by officials of lower rank. The government is emphatically a hierarchy, for every official — executive and judicial — is a lama. The only apparent exceptions to this rule are the *Bei-ze*, village headmen, who, however, hold no official rank, and are merely the patriarchs or most substantial landholders of the different villages. The *bei-ze* is empowered to settle simple local disputes, but he has no prestige outside his own village. His rank is inferior to that of any one who has donned the robe of a lama or novitiate (*tra-pa*). The highest officials after the *k'an-po* are the *ch'an-dzö*,[1] a kind of lord high treasurer, the *ku-ts'ab*[2] or "commissioner," and finally the *nyer-ba*, whose chief duties appear to be connected with the food-supply. All these dignitaries are appointed by the *k'an-po*, and hold office during his good pleasure.[3]

In matters affecting Chinese interests the *k'an-po* is expected to communicate with the district magistrate of Yen-yüan, the prefect of Ning-yüan, or the taotai of Ya-chou. If one of the parties to a lawsuit is an independent Chinese, the case is sent to the Yen-yüan magistrate, who deals with it according to ordinary Chinese procedure, or passes it to his superiors. But such cases hardly ever arise in practice, as the only

[1] ཕྱག་མཛོད་ (ch'ag-mDzod), literally the "treasury-hand."

[2] སྐུ་ཚབ་ (sku-ts'ab), literally "vice-gerent" or "lieutenant."

[3] See Note 33 (p. 431).

people in Muli-land who call themselves Chinese are a few half-castes who as dependents of one of the Huang Lama lamaseries are subject to the *k'an-po's* jurisdiction. The *k'an-po* himself is expected to proceed at least once in twelve years to Wu T'ai Shan,[1] the sacred mountain of Shansi, whence, after the performance of certain religious duties, he is supposed to go to Peking to do homage to the emperor. His presents to the Court on such occasions take the form of gold and skins. Within his territory he has complete control of finances, but he pays a small annual tribute to China. All local revenue is said to be paid in kind, and, as in China, mainly consists in a land-tax assessed according to the productive capacity of the land. In addition to ordinary taxation the people whose holdings adjoin the main roads are subject to the same system of *ula* that presses so hardly on many of the subjects of the king of Chala. The *k'an-po* also derives considerable revenue from the gold-workings in his territory. Gold-washing and mining rights are vested in the lamas, who exercise a jealous control over the output of the metal and exact large royalties. The gold is generally disposed of in the markets of Litang and Tachienlu. The only remaining tax of importance is levied on tea, which in the Muli territory is very expensive and beyond the means of many of the inhabitants.

The present *k'an-po* (whom, owing to his

[1] Known by the Tibetans as Re-wo-tse-nga. The monastery there is said to be the oldest in China, and is visited annually by thousands of pilgrims, Tibetan, Mongolian, and Chinese.

absence at Khon, I did not meet) was in May 1906 a man of about thirty-seven years of age, and had presided over his little state for about seventeen years. He succeeded his elder brother. His full designation as given to me was Ha-ba-de-li-gyal-po.[1] The permanent rank of the *k'an-po* in his capacity of Barbarian Chieftain is that of an *An Fu Ssŭ.*[2] His territory is said to be larger than that of the king of Chala, but it is poorer and has a smaller population.[3]

Within the Muli lamasery the rules of the reformed sects of Lamaism are observed with fair strictness, and no woman is allowed under any pretence to enter its coenobitical precincts. This is very different from the lax state of affairs that prevails in the large lamaseries at Tachienlu and further west. The houses or cells are for the most part buildings of two stories. In spite of their clean whitewashed exteriors they have a somewhat forbidding aspect, as, like all Tibetan buildings, the windows are small and have neither glass nor paper. Boarded windows are apt to give an impression of desolation to which it takes a long time to become accustomed. The lamasery is built on the slope of a mountain on which the various buildings rise above one another tier upon tier. The first view of it is very striking, for the configuration of the hill conceals it from sight until one is within a very short distance of its walls, and

[1] Spelt Ha-dBar-bDe-Ligs (ཧ་དབར་བདེ་ལེགས་རྒྱ་ལ་པོ་).

[2] See Note 34 (p. 432).

[3] For further information regarding the position of the ruler of Muli and the history of his state, see Note 34 (p. 432).

then almost every separate building becomes simultaneously visible.[1] To a traveller approaching from the south-west the view is even more remarkable; for the whole mass of buildings is entirely hidden from sight until he is within a stone's throw of its nearest walls, and then it appears suddenly to rise out of the ground before him in a blaze of whiteness. Nearly all the buildings face east and north-east, with their backs to the mountain. In front of the lamasery there is a gentle slope down to a valley running north-east and south-west, through which flows a small stream, the Rong Ch'u or "Valley Water." This stream flows to swell the waters of the Li Ch'u, which is visible from Muli at a distance of about 8 miles, and which flows in a south-easterly direction to join the Yalung. On the slope in front of the lamasery are terraced fields of wheat, barley and buckwheat, and pasture-lands for goats and yak. Behind and above the lamasery is a forest, consisting mostly of oak-trees and coniferæ. It is full of pheasants, but, as shooting is prohibited in the vicinity of the lamasery, they are of no use to a hungry sportsman. Above the forest is a precipitous range of crags. On the south side of the valley are sparsely-wooded hills. Two buildings in the lamasery stand out conspicuously, one above and the other below the lamas' dwellings. The lower one, with not very conspicuous gilded pinnacles, may be regarded as the cathedral, for it is there that the ordinary services taken from the Kah-gyur and Tang-gyur—the

[1] Travellers to Mecca have recorded the same fact with regard to that city.

LAMASERY OF MULI.

[*To face p.* 220.

scriptures of Lamaism — are daily celebrated. I attended one of the services in the company of two of my lama hosts, but was requested not to go beyond the threshold of the open door. A large choir of lamas and acolytes were on their knees, intoning the usual chants in a manner that would not discredit the choirs of some English churches. The singers had evidently been well and skilfully trained, and though the music had none of the magnificent harmonies of European music, it was by no means unpleasant to the ear, and once or twice I was vaguely reminded of Palestrina. As the interior of the building was shrouded in deep gloom, I asked if I might enter and look round when the service was over, but was told that it would continue without intermission for eleven days and nights, during which time different choirs of lamas would successively relieve each other. This surprising assertion was probably merely designed to prevent my unsanctified feet from desecrating the sacred floor; or perhaps my hosts, who may have been told that Europeans were noted for their predatory instincts, feared that I might take advantage of the darkness to purloin some of the sacred utensils. The other conspicuous building to which I have referred stands on an elevation overlooking the rest of the lamasery, and was closed up when I arrived at Muli. It is the residence of the *k'an-po*, and in it special services are held during one month in each year, from the middle of the fourth to the middle of the fifth Chinese "moon," roughly corresponding to July. During that month no animal may be slaughtered, and the lamas are restricted to a purely vegetable diet. This is the only time that the Buddhist injunction to destroy no living animal is observed at Muli. Smoking, however, which is nowhere referred to, so far as I remember, in the Buddhist scriptures, is at all times strictly prohibited.

Muli is much smaller than some of the huge lamaist establishments in other Tibetan states, where there are sometimes as many lamas collected in one lamasery as there are undergraduates at Oxford. Muli has only four hundred and fifty, and this number includes the *tra-pa* [1] or novices, who are not, strictly speaking, entitled to be called lamas Most of the lamas have been to Lhasa, and all must go there on pilgrimage before they can be allowed to hold high office. One of my hosts informed me that the journey to Lhasa occupied three months, but that the difficulties of the road were less serious than those which I had myself met with during my journey from Tachienlu.

Tibetan is the official language of the state, and most of the lamas can speak it; but they have also a language of their own, of which I attempted to compile a small vocabulary.[2] It certainly appears to be allied to Tibetan, but would be unintelligible to any one acquainted with that language only. It seems to show a considerable admixture of Mo-so, and perhaps of other less-known tribal dialects. The Tibetan alphabet is used for the transcription of sounds. When I asked what different races inhabited Muli-land I was only given a little vague informa-

[1] གྲྭ་པ་

[2] See Note 26 (p. 433).

tion which may be far from accurate. Unfortunately the dialect of Tibetan spoken by the lamas who visited me was not always intelligible to my servant, far less to myself, and I am by no means satisfied that my questions were always clearly understood, or that the replies given me were properly interpreted. The Njong, I was told, are the predominant race, and it is of their language that I have given a few words in the Appendix. I have suggested in another place[1] that they may be more or less closely connected with the Mo-so of to-day. Less numerous are the Man-tzŭ (always a vague term), Lolos, Pa-No, Po-Nyi and Pa-Chi. The Pa-No and Po-Nyi, whoever they may be, appear to have languages of their own. The Pa-Chi are said to be of mixed Chinese and Man-tzŭ descent, and speak a dialect which my servant could make nothing of. Finally there are a number of Miao-tzŭ, an aboriginal race of which we still find vestiges in Kwang-si, Yunnan, Kuei-chou and other parts of China. It was curious to find representatives of that race or tribe so far west as the borders of Tibet,[2] and it would be interesting to ascertain if they have preserved any traditions of their origin. Unfortunately, it does not seem likely that there are any educated men among them. Even in Muli-land they are a despised race, and are the only people who are debarred from becoming lamas. The names of

[1] See pp. 280-281.

[2] Major H. R. Davies informs me that he found some Miao-tzŭ between Mien-ning-hsien and the Yalung on the way to Muli, but that is much further east.

other race-types of Muli given in the *T'ung Chih*[1] are somewhat puzzling, and I can make little of them.

The lamas themselves are by no means well educated, and apart from the lamas no one can read or write. As in all countries where lamaism has established itself, laymen are allowed and indeed expected to remain in complete ignorance of letters. In Burma and Siam, where a far purer form of the Buddhist religion is observed, the monks are the schoolmasters of the people, and the monasteries are the village schools; but no such scholastic work is undertaken by the lamas of Tibetan countries, who believe that nothing is worth studying except what is in their sacred books, and that only lamas are worthy to study them. It is no wonder that the people of Tibet are the most ignorant and superstitious of any semi-civilised race in Asia.

In manners and customs there does not seem to be any particular in which Muli-land stands alone. The dead bodies of both lamas and laymen are disposed of by cremation. In the case of lamas the ashes are carefully collected from the funeral pyre, ground into fine powder and preserved in urns. The cremated bodies of laymen are treated with less respect, for the ashes are merely thrown over precipices or into mountain caverns.[2] In some parts of the eastern Tibetan states—including those which like Chala and Muli

[1] See Note 34 (p. 432).

[2] Cf. Marco Polo's description of the burial customs of certain Yunnan tribes, vol. ii. pp. 122-123. (Cordier's edition, 1903.)

have been annexed to the Chinese empire — the bodies of the dead are left exposed on the mountain sides until every particle of flesh has been torn off the bones by vultures and beasts of prey;[1] and elsewhere—especially in the case of the very poor, who cannot afford the expense of cremation—the corpses are simply thrown into the nearest river, without any ceremony.

I rested at Muli from the 3rd of May—the day of my arrival—till the morning of the 6th, when I resumed my march towards Yunnan. From Muli to Yung-ning, which is situated a few miles beyond the border, is a journey of three stages, and up to that point — or rather to the frontier of Yunnan — my path continued to lie through the territory of Muli. The lamas did everything possible to render this part of my journey pleasant. They granted me the privilege of *ula* (for which I paid the same rates as in the territory of Chala), sent an *avant-courier* to warn the villagers to give me proper treatment, and deputed one of their probationers or *tra-pa* to escort me to Yung-ning. Our first stage was a short one. We began by going up the valley of the Rong Ch'u towards the S.S.W. About 4 miles from Muli we descended to the bed

[1] See Rockhill, *Land of the Lamas*, pp. 286-287. See also p. 81, where he states that "the remains of the dead are exposed on the hillsides in spots selected by lamas; if the body is rapidly devoured by wild beasts and birds of prey, the righteousness of the deceased is held to be evident, but if it remains a long time undevoured, his wickedness is proved." See also the *Zend-Avesta*, *Sacred Books of the East*, vol. iv. pp. 74-75 and 97-98. It is interesting to note that Friar Odoric's account of "Tebek" is almost literally true, if we except the remark about the tusked ladies.

of the river, and crossed to the right bank. A winding path led us up the steep slope of the south side of the valley, and while we were still not more than 7 miles from Muli we halted. The prospect of a steep climb over a pass on the following day seemed to break the spirit of my followers, as they declared it was impossible to proceed further that day. The pass is apparently a notorious haunt of robbers. There was a solitary farmhouse at the place where we halted; but as it was rather more squalid and filthy than usual, I decided to camp out of doors. Towards evening a thunderstorm drove me into the house, but I was speedily expelled again by the smoke and charcoal fumes, and established myself under an improvised awning on the roof.

On the following day we had a long and somewhat arduous march over the pass of Shi Li La, the height of which is about 15,500 feet.[1] The path bears at first towards the east and south-east, and gradually ascends to a ridge, which is separated from the true summit by a narrow valley running north-east and south-west. From this point to the summit the climb would be easy in dry weather, but the thawing snows made the path slippery and disagreeable. From the summit we found the descent at first steep and rocky, but, as soon as we had left the snow behind us, we found ourselves descending an easy road through a forest containing many magnificent firs. Some of them measured 15 feet in circumference, 5 feet above

[1] See Note 36 (p. 434).

THE AUTHOR'S MULETEERS, NEAR YUNG-NING.

[*To face p.* 226.

the ground. Between 3,000 and 4,000 feet below the summit of the pass, we crossed a stream, and went uphill for a few hundred feet, thereafter descending into a broken and very picturesque valley, in the middle of which we found the first inhabited spot we had seen in the course of a 30-mile ride. This was the hamlet of Li She Tzŭ, the inhabitants of which are Mo-so, a race of which I shall have more to say below.[1] From this point to Yung-ning, and some distance beyond it, we found every village inhabited almost exclusively by people of this race.

Leaving Li She Tzŭ at dawn on 8th May, we rode over an undulating road, generally wooded, and at about 5 miles changed mules at the village of Li Rang Tzŭ. This proved to be the last village of Muli-land, and of the province of Ssuch'uan, for a march of barely 4 miles beyond it led us across the boundary of the province at the top of a low range of wooded hills. We were then in Yunnan. The descent into the next plain was steep, and the road execrable. There we entered the first of the Yunnanese villages—Djo-Dji—where I was received by the local headman. Though a Mo-so, he was acquainted with Chinese, as well as his own language, and was attired in a Chinese long coat with bright brass buttons that had once adorned the uniform of a British soldier. From a metal case which he held in his hand he drew one of his cards. As he presented it to me, he told me that he was well acquainted with Western foreigners, for he had

[1] See below, chap. xv.

seen two besides myself. They, he added, were two Frenchmen, who had passed through the village quite recently, and who—judging from his description—must have been engaged in surveying.[1] He spoke of them with great warmth of feeling, for it appeared that they had presented him with a valuable memento in the shape of an empty sardine-tin. This was the metal box which he had converted into a card-case, and of which he was evidently very proud. The district in which this village is situated is fairly rich and well populated. A series of cultivated plains, divided from each other by rounded hills, extends the whole way from the frontier of the province to the town of Yung-ning, which we reached after passing through a number of prosperous villages, inhabited by Mo-so, of which the largest were Wo La, Yi Ma Wa, A-ko Am-ni Wa, and A-gu Wa. In these villages the houses were nearly all mere cabins, built of pine-logs, the roofs being thin wooden boards weighted with heavy stones to keep them from blowing away; but the dress of the women is in striking contrast with the poverty of their dwellings. Their hair, which is roped round the head, is lavishly adorned with strings of beads and silver ornaments, and their skirts are brilliantly coloured.[2] But while wife and daughter are allowed to array themselves in all the finery that the family possesses, the husband is content to wear the meanest sack-

[1] From information obtained later I gather that these travellers were the Count de Marsay and the Count L. de Las Cases.

[2] One of their earrings is illustrated at p. 152.

YUNG-NING.

[*To face p.* 229.

cloth, and carries no ornaments. Some of the men, in imitation of the Chinese, shave the front of their heads and wear queues.

Yung-ning, in spite of the prominence given to it on the maps, is a large straggling village rather than a town. It has no walls, its houses are humble structures mostly built of wood, and its only conspicuous building is an imposing lamasery. Its population is purely agricultural. The people are of mixed Mo-so and Tibetan race, and the prevailing religion is Lamaism. The town—if it must be so called—is the capital of a district bounded on the north and east by the provincial frontier, on the south by the Yangtse or River of Golden Sand, and the Chinese sub-prefecture of Yung Pei, and on the west by the tribal district of Chung-tien. The district of Yung-ning is ruled by a hereditary native chief, a personage of less importance than the "kings" of Chala and Muli, but still of considerable rank and influence. Like many other tribal chiefs who, during the last few centuries have been brought by cajolery or force of arms under the dominion of China, the Yung-ning chief holds the hereditary rank of a Chinese official. In China proper, as I need hardly say, official rank is not hereditary; but in subduing the wild "barbarian" districts of Ssuch'uan and Yunnan the Chinese Government found their task facilitated by making an ingenious compromise with the chiefs. Each chieftain who placed himself and his territory under the suzerainty of China, and undertook to be guided in all matters of political importance by Chinese advice, was not only confirmed in his position as tribal ruler, but received the title and rank of a Chinese official to be borne by his heirs and successors in perpetuity. The ruler of Yung-ning thus bears the hereditary rank and title of prefect, and it is for this reason that in the maps his capital is marked as a *fu* or prefecture. In all matters affecting Chinese interests he is practically the subordinate of the sub-prefect of Yung Pei, a Chinese official whose rank is nominally inferior to his own. Yung Pei is a small city lying about six days' journey south of Yung-ning, forming the centre of a Chinese administrative subdivision.

The day after my arrival at Yung-ning I received a call from the chief. As he knew no Chinese we had to converse through the medium of his Chinese secretary. The chief was a young man of about twenty-eight, amiable enough, but intensely shy and ill at ease in the presence of a foreigner. He wore the uniform of his Chinese rank, and showed himself well acquainted with the Chinese rules of ceremony and etiquette.

The plain of Yung-ning is situated about 9,500 feet above sea-level, in a warm latitude, and produces a great variety of crops. Part of it is given up to the cultivation of rice, for it is well watered by a considerable stream, which bisects the town and flows through the middle of the plain. I saw here, for the first time since I had left central Ssuch'uan, that patient and indispensable partner of the Chinese ploughman in the rice-field, the water-buffalo. The stream is named the K'ai Chi[1]

[1] 開基.

and is spanned by a handsome stone bridge which, according to the inscription on a tablet close by, was rebuilt as recently as the thirtieth year of the present reign (1905). The stream produces excellent fish.

The town contains, besides quasi-Tibetans and Mo-so, a considerable number of Li-so (Leesaw), who speak a language of their own. During the day and a half I spent in Yung-ning I took the opportunity to note down a list of Li-so words, in order that I might compare them with the Mo-so words I had picked up during the three days' march from Muli. The vocabularies will be found in Appendix A.

In many respects the social customs of the Mo-so are identical with those of eastern Tibet. Polyandry, for example, prevails among them to a great extent. It is quite common for a woman to have three or four husbands, or even more. With regard to the prevalence of this practice in Tibetan countries, Baber[1] has observed the curious fact that polygamy is the rule in the valleys while polyandry prevails in the uplands, the reason apparently being that women are numerous in the valleys, where the work is light and suitable to their capabilities, but form only a small minority of the population of the mountains, where the climate is severe and the work of the herdsmen not suited to females. "The subject," he says, "raises many curious and by no means frivolous questions, but I cannot help thinking it singular that the conduct of courtship and

[1] See Royal Geographical Society's *Supplementary Papers*, vol. i. p. 97.

matrimony should be regulated by the barometrical pressure." In the Mo-so country, however, the practice of polyandry seems to be almost, if not quite, as prevalent among the people of the plains as among those of the mountains; it exists, for instance, in the villages situated on the banks of the upper Yangtse, less than two days' journey south of Yung-ning. The children of a woman who has several husbands are apparently regarded as the legitimate offspring of all of them: an arrangement facilitated by the fact that the husbands are generally closely related to each other,[1] and that the Mo-so, like the Tibetans, have no regular surnames. In one of the Sino-Tibetan states north-west of Tachienlu the sovereign power is said to be always in the hands of a woman. This is the principality of Sa-mong (so spelled in Tibetan) in the north-east of Derge. If this "regiment of women" is not connected with an ancient matriarchal custom it may be the result of ages of polyandry, though I am not aware

[1] "In Ceylon the joint husbands are always brothers, and this is also the case among the tribes residing at the foot of the Himalaya mountains." (Lord Avebury's *Origin of Civilisation*, 6th ed. p. 153.) A fuller account of polyandry in Ceylon may be found in Tennent's *Ceylon* (Longmans, 1859, 2nd ed. vol. ii. pp. 428 *seq.*). Tennent points out that polyandry can be traced back to very ancient times. It "receives a partial sanction in the Institutes of Manu," and is referred to without reproach in the Mahabharata. Herbert Spencer (*Principles of Ethics*, pt. ii. ch. 13) says that in Tibet, "polyandry appears more conducive to social welfare than any other relation of the sexes. It receives approval from travellers, and even a Moravian missionary defends it: the missionary holding that superabundant population, in an unfertile country, must be a great calamity and produce 'eternal welfare or eternal want.'" See also *Principles of Sociology*. Polyandry is forbidden in the Shan States, though polygamy is sanctioned. (See *Gazetteer of Upper Burma*, pt. i. vol. i. p. 325.)

that the queen of Sa-mong takes to herself more than one prince-consort.[1]

The funeral ceremonies of the Mo-so are much the same as those of the Tibetans and the people of Muli. The dead are generally cremated or left to the vultures and beasts of prey. In case of cremation, the ashes are scattered or thrown into a ravine or river. Such rough-and-ready methods of disposing of the dead seem to point back to a time when the people that practise these customs were nomads, having no fixed habitation and unable to raise permanent memorials to their dead. The Mo-so, who have settled close to the banks of the Yangtse, hold the richest lands, and are perhaps the most civilised members of their race. They, perhaps influenced by the example of the Chinese, seem to be gradually modifying the national customs with regard to the disposal of the dead. After cremation they carefully wash the ashes in the waters of the Yangtse, and then deposit them in artificial caves roughly hewn by themselves out of the loose crumbling soil of the river's right bank. But the ashes are not inurned, and no record of the deceased is preserved on tablets or monuments.

[1] See Note 37 (p. 434).

CHAPTER XIII

YUNG-NING TO LI-CHIANG

At Yung-ning I parted with some regret from my three Chinese soldiers—including Hoggins and Bloggins—who had acted as my escort all the way from Tachienlu. They had carried out their orders to the letter in seeing me safely into Yunnan, and in many ways had rendered me faithful and valuable service. Attended by such men a traveller in the wilds of Chinese Tibet has indeed but little to complain of. They were always cheerful, obedient and respectful, never once grumbled at the hardships of the road or the difficulties that we sometimes had about obtaining food, and at the end of a day's journey were always busy about my personal requirements before they looked after themselves. I rewarded them with treble the pay I had promised them at Tachienlu, and still felt that I was in their debt. They started off on the return journey in the company of the lama who had acted as my guide from Muli, and I was glad to learn some months afterwards that they had arrived safely at Tachienlu. The lama, of course, left them at Muli. The Tibetan servant whom I had engaged at Tachienlu remained in my service for some weeks longer, until I had arrived at T'êng-yüeh near the frontier of Burma.

I started from Yung-ning on 10th May, with an unusually large retinue. The mountain pass that separates the Yung-ning plain from the Yangtse was said to be one of the most dangerous roads in western China, owing to the presence of large bands of Lolo robbers. The Yung-ning chief was therefore kind enough to send no less than twelve armed men to escort me to the banks of the river. Two of the twelve were soldiers in uniform; the rest were honest rustics who were probably less afraid of the Lolos than of their borrowed firearms, which on their own admission they had never been taught to use. Our general direction during the morning was W.S.W., over an undulating road that at first led us through cultivated fields and afterwards gradually ascended the side of a wooded mountain. Early in the afternoon we reached, after a long climb, the summit of the Ge Wa pass or Ge Wa Ya K'ou, the height of which is about 13,000 feet. From the summit there was no view towards the south as it was hidden by forests, but a backward glance afforded a beautiful view of the Yung-ning plain, the afternoon shining brightly on its many shades of green. We descended the west side of the pass by a bad road, and all distant views were concealed until we had gone down about 3,000 feet. Then a panorama of very lofty mountains, crowned with snow, opened out before us in the south-west. After passing one or two log cabins and a few fields of scanty vegetation we reached our night's quarters in a sorry hut. The whole of the next morning was occupied in continuing the long descent to the Yangtse valley. The road is not very steep, but the surface is crumbling and rocky. We first caught sight of the great river when we were between 2,000 and 3,000 feet above it. The glimpse revealed to us a tortuous channel of which the general direction was from north-west to south-east. The mountains slope almost to the water's edge on both sides, but there are several small villages perched above the banks, and there is a considerable amount of cultivation. Yet it is curious to observe that the Chinese, as distinct from the natives, are convinced that this broad valley—like all other river-valleys in the west—is dangerous to the health of "civilised" beings. We had our midday meal outside a solitary house called Lan Ga Lo, not far from which is a village. Thence we descended, always in full view of the river, to the village of La Ka Shi, which lies close to a small stream called the Si Dji or Si river. From there we proceeded along the left bank of the Yangtse, two or three hundred feet above it, for a distance of half a mile, then descended to the water's edge by a very steep zig-zagged path.

The crossing of the river was effected by means of a ferry-boat; but, as there was only one boat and we had mules to take across, it was not till two hours afterwards that we were all safely deposited with our baggage on the right bank. It was difficult work to get the animals into the boat. The second boat-load (consisting of two of them)

THE YANGTSE RIVER, NEAR YUNG-NING, ABOVE THE FERRY.

[*To face p.* 236.

nearly found a watery grave, for a mule became panic-stricken when the boat was only a third of the way across, and stamped about so much that the rather crazy craft sprang a leak and had to be hurried back. The current was much less swift than that of the Yalung, and we were not carried down stream more than about 30 yards during the passage; but we were told by the ferryman that the water had only recently begun to rise above the usual winter level. The melting snows in summer naturally make a great difference in the speed of the current and the level of the water. Where we crossed, the river was more than 100 yards broad, but just above that point it forces its way through a narrow channel formed by some jutting rocks.[1] The rapids render the river quite unnavigable. The height of the Yangtse above sea-level at this point is about 5,200 feet. A local Chinese name for this portion of the river is Pai Shui Ho ("White Water River"), but, like all rivers fed by melting snows and glaciers, it was very brown and muddy when we crossed it. The Mo-so name is Gi Dji, which simply means "The River."

It is only within the last ten years that geographers have known anything about the great bend in the Yangtse that brings it to within a day's journey of Yung-ning. The bend is, of course, caused by the vast mountain range that extends to the north of Li-chiang—a range that proved impenetrable even to the turbulent waters of the greatest river in China, and forced

[1] See illustration *to face page* 236.

it to take a northerly course that added scores of miles to its total length.[1] M. Bonin was, I believe, the first traveller to make this discovery, and his observations were subsequently confirmed by Major Davies and Major Ryder.

On reaching the right (south) bank of the Yangtse, we at once commenced a stiff uphill climb. Close to the river's edge I noticed some of the small artificial caves or recesses mentioned above,[2] in connection with the burial customs of the Mo-so. Not far from these, but not quite so close to the river's edge, were a number of holes, large enough to admit a man, and partly covered by loose planks. These, I was told, were the shafts of gold-mines, but I could get no information as to the output, and no doubt the methods of working are exceedingly primitive. When I asked my guides whether the gold of this district had not attracted Chinese miners, they told me a naïve story of how some years ago some Chinese "from the east" came and set up a mining establishment there, ruthlessly driving the natives to the neighbouring mountains. Soon afterwards the Chinese miners found themselves harassed day and night by continuous showers of stones and rocks, which killed not a few of their number and wrecked their huts. After patiently enduring these calamities for a

[1] A similar great bend, only recently discovered, occurs in the course of the Yalung. In travelling between Mien-ning-hsien, north of Ning-yuan-fu, and Muli, the Yalung must, on account of this bend, be crossed no less than three times. The bend was discovered by Major H. R. Davies.

[2] See page 233.

THE YANGTSE RIVER AT THE FERRY.

[To face p. 238.

few days, without hope of being able to retaliate, they picked up their belongings and quietly fled away, doubtless regretting their foolhardiness in tampering with the prescriptive rights of the quarrelsome barbarians.[1]

Several hundred feet above the gold-mines I passed some old graves—not unlike a type of grave often seen in China proper. One of my mule-drivers, a Mo-so, could only tell me that they were the tombs of *pên-ti-jên*, which means nothing but "the natives," and is therefore not a very enlightening expression to use in a country inhabited by three or four different races, none of which has any exact knowledge of how it came there. The predominant races between the Yunnan frontier, north of Yung-ning, and the town of Li-chiang are undoubtedly Mo-so and Li-so, but that there are tribal differences among them seems to be evident from the fact that the Mo-so north of the Yangtse are under the rule of the chief whom I met at Yung-ning, while south of that river they are subject to another chief who resides at Li-chiang. At one time, indeed, it is well known that all the Mo-so were governed by a king whose capital was at Li-chiang, but the present Li-chiang chief—whose influence is gradually waning owing to Chinese encroachments—is not the representative of the ancient Mo-so king.

After climbing about 2,000 feet above the river, we halted for the night in the flourishing

[1] A similar story, apparently, was told to Mr Amundsen with reference to a locality in the Muli territory.

village of Fêng K'o, where I found excellent quarters in the upper story of an empty house. Next day we crossed the little upland valley in which Fêng K'o is situated, and gradually ascended along the mountain-side in a south-westerly direction, following to some extent the course of the river now far below us. About 8 miles from Fêng K'o we turned west into a defile, having in front of us, to the south and south-west, a range of rocky mountains with snowy peaks probably over 18,000 feet high. Another 2 or 8 miles brought us to a brisk, clear stream, which we followed up to a little temple or shrine close by which the water bubbles out of a fountain in a rock. The water is excellent, and there is good camping-ground for a small party. I strongly recommend travellers who may traverse this route hereafter to make this a stage if possible. Lightly-equipped travellers might make it the second stage from Yung-ning, and heavily-laden caravans might make it the third. From this attractive spot we marched steadily uphill for a few miles and rested outside a couple of cottages. Thence, after a luncheon of eggs, we resumed our upward journey for several hours, finally following an undulating track along one of the mountain ridges. It began to cloud over about this time. The tops of the neighbouring mountains were hidden in mist, and towards evening rain fell heavily. This part of the country is a dreary waste of wild mountains without a trace of human habitation. We went on till nightfall, then camped in the forest. As we had no tent, and were sheltered only by the gaunt arms of fir-trees, the prospects of a comfortable night were somewhat dismal; but fortunately the rain ceased to fall before midnight and we were troubled only by the dripping branches. In one respect the rain was useful, as it afforded us all the water we required for drinking and cooking purposes. We had found no spring-water in this part of the forest.

The rain began to fall again next day while we were at breakfast, and continued off and on all the morning. In the afternoon it cleared up, and for the rest of the way to Li-chiang the weather was perfect. Our road gradually led us uphill, and took us over the pass known by the Mo-so as Go Ka A, the height of which is about 15,000 feet. The descent is steep and rocky. Both sides of the pass are well wooded. All the afternoon we continued to descend, and towards evening reached a cultivated valley surrounded by an amphitheatre of hills. Here there was a scattered hamlet named T'o Ko Sho—the first village we had seen since we left Fêng K'o. While we were resting outside one of the cottages I saw a man going out to shoot pheasants with a bow and arrows.[1] As we did not await his return I am unable to give any opinion as to his skill. A few miles beyond T'o Ko Sho we camped in the forest at the end of a marshy meadow, which gave pasture to our beasts and supplied (from a brook) good water for ourselves. The forest is said to be infested with panthers; but they gave us no

[1] This is, I have been told, a common practice among the people of the Upper Mekong valley, especially about Atuntzŭ.

trouble. I was somewhat disturbed, however, by a very large and obstinate species of mosquito. Next day the road undulated in a southerly direction through the forest. We soon caught sight of some lofty and magnificent snowy peaks to the south-west—the mountains that tower some 10,000 feet above the Li-chiang plain which itself lies at an elevation of over 8,000 feet. A few more miles brought us to the village of Ming Yin Chi,[1] which with its almost-Chinese architecture, its likin-station and familiar official notices (the first seen since the first day's journey from Tachienlu), reminded us that we were entering a country where the direct influence of China succeeded in making itself felt.

The houses of Ming Yin Chi are mostly built of wood, but there are a few tiled roofs. The dress of the people is hardly distinguishable from that of the Chinese, except in the massive ear-rings and other ornaments worn by the women. Their feet, of course, are unbound. Outside the village likin-station I saw a versified proclamation in Chinese, referring to the dangerous state of the roads of the neighbourhood owing to the prevalence of brigandage, and offering rewards for the capture of the robbers. Leaving this village behind us we soon passed again into the forest, the road lying through a fairly level park-like country studded with noble pines. We continued our journey till sunset and again camped in the forest. So still and peaceful was the night that my candle burned with as steady a flame as

[1] 鳴音溪.

if it were inside a lantern. Next morning we began by climbing uphill out of the hollow in which we had camped to a *col* rather over 10,000 feet in elevation. The road then led rapidly downhill for about 3 miles and brought us to a narrow valley through which flows a stream called the Hei Shui ("Black Water"). Here I observed a sight which unfortunately is only too rare in China—the building of a new bridge. It was in fact one of three new bridges crossed during this day's journey. A party of workmen was busily engaged in top-dressing the surface of the bridge, which was almost finished, and as it is considered unlucky in China to use a new bridge before it is opened to traffic, I crossed by a temporary wooden structure a few yards lower down. The inevitable tablet commemorating the erection of the bridge and the names of the givers—for it had nothing to do with Government—was already in position on the right bank of the river. Beside this tablet is a smaller one dedicated to the Spirit of the Road. Soon after crossing the Black Water the road turns to the right, southwards.

Another road, which looks like a continuation of the old one, descends through the valley of the stream, and as I was then on foot and far ahead of my caravan I followed this road for some *li* without guessing it was the wrong one. So I had to retrace my steps, to find that the road to Li-chiang climbs over three successive small passes, divided from each other by a series of ravines. I expected when I reached each summit—the highest being about 11,000 feet in elevation—to find the city of Li-chiang lying at my feet, but I beheld only forests and the great snowy peaks. The descent from the third pass led into a barren stony valley which was once, in all probability, the bed of a glacier. If appearances are not very deceptive the shrunken glacier can still be seen high up on the mountains, some distance below the snow-line. The stony valley is the northern section of the Li-chiang plain, but though we had no more climbing we had a long and rather wearisome march of between 10 and 20 miles before we reached the city. The first section of the valley—absolutely bare and uninhabited—is approximately rather less than 2 miles broad, and on each side are scantily-wooded hills. The snowy summits towered above us on our right. The valley seems almost level, and one can gaze over its whole extent from almost any point, but it has a gentle slope towards the south. After traversing a belt of shrubby wilderness the desert gradually transformed itself into a delightful garden. The principal crop in the cultivated part of the Li-chiang plain is opium, and the pure white flower of the poppy-plant was in full bloom. Among the most attractive features of the plain are its hedges and wild-flowers—especially its luxuriant white wild-roses, the most beautiful I have ever seen. The air was deliciously fresh and warm and laden with the scent of flowers, and it was only when we caught sight of the huge wintry mountains gazing icily down upon us from the sky that we were forced to remember that "it is not always May."

An excellent broad road—one of the very best I have seen in China—traverses the greater part of the cultivated portion of the valley. A dog-cart might be driven over it with perfect safety, and in many places it is broader than a good English country road. It is lined on both sides with luxuriant untrimmed hedges, beyond which lie beautiful Gardens of Sleep—acres of white poppy. Villages are numerous in the plain, but our road did not take us through many of them. One—the village of Pei Sha—through which we rode just as the sun was setting, was very picturesque with its wild-flowers and palm-trees. The road degenerated as we approached the city. It had once been paved and was no doubt an excellent causeway in time past; but as usual in China the paving-stones had sunk crookedly and had not been repaired. It was dark before we arrived at the end of our unusually long day's journey, and in the hedges of the suburbs glimmering glow-worms took the place of the wild-roses that night had rendered invisible.

Li-chiang is a small unwalled town, only dignified by the name of a city because it is the administrative centre of a prefecture and a district magistracy. As the capital of the old Mo-so kingdom its situation was well chosen, for in the days of border warfare the strategic importance of its position must have been considerable. It stands on a small hill commanding the greater part of the plain, and is within comparatively easy reach of the Yangtse ferries, both on the east and on the west. No doubt the

Mo-so, in the days of their strength, made a point of holding the crossings at both places. Li-chiang is still the residence of a Mo-so or Nashi (Lashi) chief, but his influence is steadily waning. The great majority of the inhabitants are of mixed race, the predominating types being Mo-so, Li-so, Lolo and Min-chia.[1] There is also a pure Chinese element, which is gradually tending to increase. Li-chiang is a considerable centre of trade, and is visited by large numbers of Tibetans and "Ku-tsung" from Atuntzŭ and the valley of the Mekong, and also by traders from Tali-fu, Yunnan-fu, Yung Pei and the Chien-ch'ang valley. There is a broad market-place in the middle of the town, almost constantly occupied by loquacious crowds of buyers and sellers of many races. There is a good deal of green foliage in the outskirts, and much deflected water which flows through some of the streets like little canals. To a casual observer the streets are not very unlike those of an ordinary town in China: the shops have much the same outward appearance, and the same charactered sign-boards hang above their doors.

The morning after my arrival at Li-chiang, where I found accommodation in a very bad inn, I heard the surprising and welcome news that there were two Englishmen staying in the town, one of them being a consular official and the other a railway surveyor. As I had no idea that the British Government of Burma had any present intention of extending their railway

[1] See Note 38 (p. 435).

system to northern Yunnan I decided to call upon my compatriots and ascertain if such were the case. In the course of my enquiries into their place of residence I discovered that one of the Englishmen had left the town some days before, and that the other was a Frenchman! It finally turned out that the former was a Mr Forrest, the adventurous botanist to whose narrow escape from torture and death at the hands of the lamas I have already referred.[1] He had been making a short stay in Li-chiang, and had just left on a botanical expedition to the neighbouring hills. The Frenchman was M. Gaston Perronne, a merchant, who was engaged in the purchase of musk. He had taken a Chinese house in Li-chiang for the period of his residence there, and when I called upon him he most kindly insisted upon my staying with him until I left Li-chiang. Instead of leaving on the following day, therefore, as I had intended, I remained in Li-chiang from the evening of the 15th May to the morning of the 18th.

[1] See above, p. 150.

CHAPTER XIV

LI-CHIANG TO TALI-FU

I WAS now bound for Tali-fu, having bargained with a new set of muleteers to take me there in five days. I was anxious to press on as rapidly as possible, not only because I was now on ground that had several times been traversed and described by other Europeans, but also because the rainy season was just beginning, and might seriously hamper my movements in crossing the mountains and rivers beyond Tali-fu. I had not yet decided whether to proceed to Burma by the T'êng-yüeh-Bhamo route or to attempt to reach Lashio (the terminus of the British Shan States railway system) by Yün-chou and the Kunlon Ferry. My host, M. Perronne, was a thorough believer in the deadly unhealthiness of the Salwen valley in the rainy season, and assured me that it would be madness to attempt to cross it till the autumn. I decided, however, to wait till I reached Tali-fu before coming to a decision.

From Li-chiang my road lay in a westerly direction over a portion of the plain that I had not yet traversed. Roses, meadow-sweet, primroses and other wild-flowers made the hedges smell of England. We left the plain behind us by crossing a low range of hills from which we descended into another plain called the Lashi-Pa, in which there is a small lake. Here I was shown a path that leads west towards the Ashi Ferry on the Yangtse, only a few miles distant, and so leads to Chung-tien and Atuntzŭ.[1] The last-named place, I may mention incidentally, is said to exist no longer, part of it having been destroyed by a gigantic landslip, and the rest having been demolished in the recent war between the Chinese and the lamas. The landslip appears to have been an extraordinary occurrence, and was perhaps caused by an earthquake. Torrents of mud and stones tore like an avalanche down the side of the mountain at the base of which Atuntzŭ was situated, demolishing houses, destroying all growing crops, and burying alive whole families. The local officials dealt with the catastrophe in an interesting and characteristic manner. Possessed, apparently, by the idea that the moving masses of mud were directed and controlled by a malevolent devil, they armed themselves with muzzle-loading guns and bows and arrows, and went out and shot the mud. In due time the torrent ceased to flow, and no doubt it was universally believed that the devil had been slain by arrows and bullets. The harm already done, unfortunately, was irreparable, and what remained of the town has since, as I have said, fallen a prey to warfare.

My road instead of going west to the Yangtse

[1] Known to the Tibetans as A-jol (འཇོལ་)

bore away southwards to the left of the lake, and brought us about midday to the village of Shang La Shih or Upper Lashi, where I lunched. The plain contains several other villages, but its soil seems hardly so rich as that of the plain of Li-chiang. In the afternoon, after crossing a pass of no great elevation, we dropped down to a third valley and stopped for the night at the hamlet of Kuan Hsia, also called P'o Chiao.[1] About here I observed a good deal of ruddy soil, which reminds one of the red sand-stone basin of Ssuch'uan. There is also a small lake or tarn. During the whole of the next day we traversed the same valley, passing through many prosperous and populous villages. The valley is indeed only a narrow strip of fertile land between more or less barren ranges of hill, but what there is would be amply sufficient to support a very large population. The road is very fair, and at one time was probably an excellent highway. There are the remains of drinking-fountains along the road, and many of the bridges are still admirable and substantial pieces of work. It would I think be a mistake to say that all the decay is traceable to the ravages of the Mohammedan rebellion of the seventies. The decay had probably set in—here as elsewhere in China — long before that lurid episode had drenched the province of Yunnan in seas of blood.

On leaving the Li-chiang plain we had left behind us the country of the Mo-so or Lashi,

[1] Both names are Chinese. The first means "Below the Pass," the second "The Foot of the Hill."

and had entered a district that is perhaps chiefly inhabited by a race known to the Chinese as *Min-chia*,[1] which simply means "the people" or "the families of people." The mystery that surrounds the origin of all the tribes I have mentioned clings no less obstinately to the Min-chia. They are a very interesting and amiable people, fair in face, and with clear bold eyes that do not shun to meet the gaze of a stranger. The women, if less handsome and imposing than the tall women of eastern Tibet, have a grace and prettiness of their own, that would, I feel sure, be found exceedingly attractive by impressionable Europeans. Two days north of Tali-fu I saw a Min-chia child who would be considered beautiful in any western country. She was standing alone in a poppy-field, singing a song in a language that was certainly very different from Chinese.

> "Will no one tell me what she sings?
> Perhaps the plaintive numbers flow
> For old, unhappy, far-off things
> And battles long ago."

But the subject of the song mattered little. The child made as pretty a picture as I had ever seen in China.

My second day's journey from Li-chiang took me through a large number of villages, of which the names of the most important will be found in the itinerary. At midday we reached the departmental city of Chien-ch'uan-chou, a small town which sits among a crowd of small centres of

[1] See below, pp. 289 *seq.*

population, like a hen among her chickens. It is surrounded by a battlemented wall of the usual type, which gives it an appearance of compactness, but in origin it was probably merely an agglomeration of villages. Its population is mainly employed in tilling the surrounding fields. A few miles further we passed near the shores of a small shallow lake, from which flows a small river called the Hai Wei.[1] Just beyond the village of Han Têng, where a market was being held, we crossed the river by a handsome bridge, and almost immediately afterwards arrived at the last village of the long valley through which we had been riding all day. This was the village of Tien Wei, where we spent the night. Good quarters were provided for us in a hostelry which was quite new and therefore comparatively clean.

Since leaving the high mountains north of Li-chiang we seemed to have entered a new climate. Riding and walking during the day under a blazing sun, and with a shade temperature of 80° F., proved to be much more exhausting than climbing snowy mountains. We were now on the high Yunnan plateau, at an average elevation of about 7,000 feet; but we were gradually approaching a tropical latitude, and the season—just before the breaking of the rains—was the hottest of the year. I had long since discarded the thick garments which in the mountains near the Yalung had seemed none too warm. The nights and early mornings, however, were always deliciously cool, and I was well aware that in the

[1] Literally "Tail of the Lake."

steaming plains of Burma I should long for the comparative coolness of the Yunnan plateau. At Tien Wei the temperature an hour before our early start sank as low as 54°, and we made haste to get well on the road before the sun rose high in the heavens. Out of the valley our road lay over a picturesque range of low hills over-grown chiefly with dwarf pines. On leaving these behind we found ourselves in a small valley studded with a few villages, from which we ascended another and a higher range. From its northern slopes I had a last view of Li-chiang's snow-clad peaks, and half a mile further on we came within sight of another range of snow-crowned hills to the south. This was the lofty range—never perhaps absolutely free from snow in spite of its latitude[1]—which forms the magnificent background to the city of Tali-fu, now little more than two days distant. At the foot of the hills from which we had this view we came to a small temple and an eating-house, close to a stream crossed by a bridge called Hao Shou. The first word is the Chinese for a crane, a bird which is emblematic of longevity, and *shou* is the ordinary word for "long life"; so it is evidently intended that this bridge should last for ever. Here we halted for lunch, I secluding myself from public observation within the little temple.

About 8 miles further on we passed through the village of Niu Kai,[2] which means Ox Village,

[1] Snow is said to exist in patches on the summit of the Tali mountains all the year round; and is hawked in the streets of Hsia Kuan, near Tali-fu, in the summer months.

[2] In Yunnan the word *chieh* (which means either "street" or "village") is always pronounced *Kai*, as in the Cantonese dialect.

just beyond which we passed close to a curious hill which has the appearance of a truncated cone. It is flattened at the top, and there is a small pagoda. Hot springs issue from the base of this hill, which bears the name of Huo Yen Shan ("Fiery Flame Hill"). Perhaps it was once a miniature volcano. I may mention, by the way, that the valley through which we travelled the previous day has within the last fifteen years suffered from a disastrous earthquake, which is said to have destroyed many villages and dozens of lives.[1] A short distance beyond the hot-spring hill we halted at a good inn in the small market town of San Ying, the name of which (meaning Three Camps) seems to indicate that it was once a military centre, perhaps in the days of the Mongol invasions. In this town I bought myself an umbrella for the sum of 600 cash—about one shilling. It professed to be of English make, and to have come from Rangoon in Burma; but the mis-spelling of the name of a well-known Anglo-Indian firm, and the obvious inferiority of the manufacture, showed that it was only a crude imitation. If this is the kind of article that passes current for English goods in the west of China it is little wonder that the trade between Burma and Yunnan is not showing the elasticity which is desirable from the point of view of the material interests of both China and Great Britain.

Next day we continued our march through the valley in which San Ying is situated, passing

[1] The official *Annals* of Yunnan contain records of very many disastrous earthquakes in this province.

numerous farm-houses and small villages surrounded with rice and poppy-fields. The rose-bushes which had so frequently lined our path since we entered the Li-chiang plain had by this time shed all their blossoms. The poppy-flowers, too, were rapidly vanishing. Under the brilliant sunshine the country still looked very charming; the landscapes being very often of the kind that would have delighted the heart of a Corot. After passing through the village of Ch'ang Ying (Long Camp) a few miles' ride brought us to the southern termination of the valley, and thence the road wound gradually up the slope of low hills, mostly consisting of barren moorland. We passed a small lake or tarn, and after this the road turned south-west and brought us to the large village of Ying-shan-p'u, situated in a confined valley lying between two ranges of hills. We skirted the left side of this village close under a temple and small pagoda. We then went southwards into a ravine, near the entrance of which is a fine single-arch bridge spanning a large stream called the Pai Sha or White Sand. Our road did not lie across the bridge, but continued to lead us along the stream's left bank. The scenery in the gorge is picturesque, but the hills on both sides are barren. Little besides the prickly pear seems to thrive on them. About 8 miles beyond the bridge we emerged from the ravine into a plain. Here the Pai Sha flows with a much slower current, and in size attains the dignity of a small river. Its waters have been brought under complete control by the formation of well-constructed embankments. For a distance of several miles, indeed, the river becomes a canal, suitable for barge-traffic. Our road led us along the embankment, and for a distance of over a mile—all the way to the village of Chung So—the road is not unlike the Magdalen Walks at Oxford. The foliage is thicker and the vegetation more luxuriant and diversified than at Magdalen, but the road bears a general resemblance to Addison's Walk, and the river is very similar to the Cherwell in its width, in the laziness of its current, and—be it confessed—in its colour.[1] At a poor inn in the village of Chung So we made our midday halt. A plague of flies drove me away from it sooner than was pleasing to my muleteers; but not before I had been cajoled into entering my name in a subscription book as a contributor towards the cost of rebuilding the Tê Yüan Bridge which spans the Pai Sha close by.

After crossing this river and passing through or within sight of several other villages we arrived at the small departmental city of Têng-ch'uan-chou. Our road took us in at one gate and out at another. It seemed to be a sleepy town and somewhat decadent. It lies not far from the northern extremity of the famous Tali lake, the Erh Hai, a great part of which came into view as soon as we had ascended some rising ground, mostly consisting of red clay, a short distance beyond Têng-ch'uan. The lake is said to be

1 The Pai Sha (White Sand) river is no whit more entitled to that appellation than the Cher would be.

annually decreasing in volume, and to judge from the appearance of the land beyond its northern extremity this seems very likely to be true. Near Têng-ch'uan there are a number of little isolated ponds which evidently once formed part of the great lake, and there is a great deal of marshy land not yet fit for cultivation.

We spent the night of 21st May in a good inn near the lake side in the village of Sha P'ing. Next day we passed through Shang Kuan, the fortified village, now partly in ruins, which once formed one of the main bulwarks of the city of Tali-fu. Between the base of the high mountains on the west and the waters of the lake on the east lies a strip of land between 20 and 30 miles long, and about 3 miles broad. At each extremity of this plain is — or rather was — a fortress. The northern extremity is protected by Shang Kuan, the southern by Hsia Kuan—the two words meaning the Upper and Lower Passes or Gates. Tali-fu itself lies at the foot of the mountains about 18 miles from the former and 7 miles from the latter, and used to be absolutely safe from attack so long as those two fortified points remained intact. The plain, which was once in all probability under water, is very rich and grows every kind of grain that a beleaguered garrison could require. It was always safe against starvation, therefore, in the event of a long siege. It was only when artillery cast by Frenchmen in Yunnan-fu was brought to bear upon the walls of the two "Kuans" that the Mohammedan rebels were forced at last to yield the city.

The plain was not, when I rode through it on my last stage to Tali-fu, devoted exclusively to cereals. Hundreds of acres were given up to the opium-poppy, and thousands of men and women were at that time employed in harvesting the drug. Much of the work was carried on by Min-chia girls, who turn their healthy bronzed faces, shaded by great straw sun-bonnets, to peer curiously at the novel sight of a Western stranger. Some of the women in this district wear turbans of dark blue cloth, the front band studded with silver knobs, which from a distance make it appear as if their foreheads were crowned with some kind of tiara. Beyond Shang Kuan the road lies at a distance of about 3 miles from the lake all the way to Tali-fu. Between the road and the lake lies an endless series of cultivated fields, which even in this dry season were plentifully irrigated by streams from the mountain. The plain is dotted with villages which generally lie half buried in foliage. On the right of the road[1] the cultivation is much more scanty. There is a good deal of barren moorland, and much ground is occupied by graves. Just before reaching Tali-fu we passed some lofty thirteen-story pagodas. I entered the city by the north gate and found good quarters on the upper floor of a quiet and commodious inn.

The city itself is neither more nor less attractive than dozens of other Chinese cities. Its numerous

[1] There are two roads from Shang Kuan to Tali-fu: one lying near the lake, the other near the mountain. My road was the latter.

ruined houses, however, have a pathetic interest of their own, for they are just in the same condition as they were immediately after the great siege. Even after thirty-five years of peace Tali-fu has not recovered from the disasters of those terrible days. I spent two days and three nights in Tali-fu, during which time I explored the city, and wandered for miles beyond its walls.[1] Late one afternoon I found myself by the lake side. The view of those tranquil waters, overshadowed as they were by the great mountain-barrier on the west, was very beautiful. The blue surface of the lake was dotted with crowds of white sails rose-tinted with the light of the setting sun. Nearer at hand crowds of wild-duck floated in the midst of rippling circles, showing but little fear of the noisy little boys who swam and dived as skilfully as themselves, and whose splashing and glad laughter were almost the only sounds that broke the utter peacefulness of a perfect summer evening. Very different was that terrible scene which only a generation ago was enacted by the shores of the Tali-fu lake, when its blue waters were incarnadined with blood and its now peaceful shores rang with the despairing cries of thousands of homeless women and children. For it was Tali-fu and the borders of its lake that in 1873 witnessed the last and most tragic events of the great Mohammedan rebellion.[2] Tu

[1] Marco Polo's description of Tali-fu and the district of which it was capital (Carajan) is well worth reading. The terrifying serpents which he mentions as having "eyes bigger than a great loaf of bread," are said to have been crocodiles. (See Cordier's edition of Yule's *Marco Polo*, vol. ii. pp. 76-84.)

[2] See Note 39 (p. 435).

Wên-hsiu, the so-called "Sultan," who had so long and successfully defied all the military power of China, had fixed his court at Tali and had converted it into what he believed to be an impregnable stronghold. The closing scene of the great conflict which devastated the whole province of Yunnan, and converted many of its most flourishing towns into blackened ruins, has been several times described, but nowhere so graphically as in the account by M. Emile Rocher,[1] the brilliant and sympathetic Frenchman who was an eye-witness of much that took place during the course of that terrible civil war. The following is a crude translation of his account of the events that occurred when all hope of holding Tali-fu against the imperial troops had been abandoned.

"Tu Wên-hsiu . . . awaited with resignation the hour that would deliver him from his last agonies. His wives and several of his children, being unwilling to survive him, poisoned themselves in his presence, and the day before he left the palace he caused all articles of value that he possessed to be destroyed, or, if they could not be broken, to be thrown into the lake. On the 15th January 1873, Tu Wên-hsiu arrayed himself in his handsomest robes of ceremony, and playing the part of a sovereign to the very end of his career, ordered the preparation of his yellow palanquin—yellow being a colour that none but the emperor of China had the right to use. Before leaving his palace, he bade a last farewell to the

[1] In his valuable work *La Province Chinoise du Yunnan* (Paris, 1880).

TALIFU.

(Photograph by Dr Clark, Missionary, Talifu).

[*To face p.* 260.

city in which the best years of his life had been passed, and gazed for the last time on the chain of mountains, the 'Azure Hills'[1] on which he had loved to ramble. Before leaving his apartments he swallowed a ball of opium. . . . The road which his retinue had to follow in order to reach the south gate was crowded with people who came to prostrate themselves before their Sultan for the last time. It was a solemn procession, and many people who had not always had reason to praise the administration of the fallen Sultan could not hide their emotion. Tu Wên-hsiu, whose senses the poison had begun to paralyse, seemed to be little affected by what went on around him. Arriving at the gate of the city he made a great effort to get out of the palanquin in order to thank the people and the leaders who had accompanied him, and his children were commended by him to the care of Yang Wei.[2] An escort of soldiers, sent by Yang Yü-k'o,[3] conducted him to the village occupied by that general. The latter treated the vanquished chief with respect, and asked him several questions, to which, however, Tu Wên-hsiu had difficulty in responding. Seeing that he could only extract confused words out of the Sultan, whose moments were numbered, the general sent him on to Hsiao Kuan-i, where the Governor of Yunnan was residing, in order that the latter might at least

[1] The Chinese name for the lofty mountains behind Tali-fu is Ts'ang Shan (蒼山), "Azure Hills."

[2] Two young children survived the catastrophe. Yang Wei was the Sultan's son-in-law and principal general of his army.

[3] 楊玉科, an imperialist general.

see him alive. He was already too late . . . the Sultan breathed his last shortly after his arrival, towards seven in the evening. . . . The next day the Governor caused his head to be cut off, and a courier specially charged with the burden was sent post haste to the capital of the province, where the head was placed in honey for preservation before being sent on to Peking."

Baber, who visited Tali-fu a few years after these events, adds a graphic and pathetic touch, the truth of which was amply vouched for. He says that when Tu Wên-hsiu was brought into the presence of the imperialist general he begged with his last breath that the conquerors would be merciful. "I have nothing to ask but this—spare the people." This request—which Baber describes as perhaps the most impressive and pathetic ever uttered by a dying patriot — was treated with disregard. The real tragedy came later, and is described by M. Rocher in a passage which I translate as follows: "The Governor, under pretext of celebrating the surrender of the city, invited all the Mohammedan leaders to a great banquet. . . . He received them very well, loaded them with praises, and, just as they were going into the banquet hall, the soldiers who had been placed in readiness for the event seized upon the doomed guests. Seventeen heads simultaneously rolled on the ground. The Governor then gave the order for six guns to be fired, the signal already agreed upon for the commencement of the massacre in the city. It was the eleventh day of the occupation. What followed is indescribable. . . . After three days of this human butchery, Tali and its environs presented a pitiable spectacle. Out of a population of fifty thousand men, thirty thousand had perished during those fatal days, and the rest were all dispersed."

There is some reason to believe that the number of those said to have been slain was largely exaggerated. Curiously enough the leaders of the imperial armies who, according to our Western notions, should have been zealous to hush up the whole grim episode, were the first to spread abroad the news of the massacre and to magnify the numbers of the slaughtered; not because they took any delight in the butchery for its own sake, but because they wished to strike such terror into the scattered bands of rebels who were still at large that they would no longer have the heart to strive against the great emperor whose armies they had defied for seventeen years. That the wholesale slaughter cannot by any possibility be excused, goes without saying. But it is only fair to remember that the great object which the imperial leaders had before them was to inflict so terrible a chastisement on the rebels that they would never again be able to threaten the stability of the empire. That object was attained. Had any considerable body of men been spared it is highly probable that they would merely have carried on the warfare from another centre, and protracted, for another decade, the strife and bloodshed which had already devastated the province of Yunnan for nearly twenty years, and reduced the population—so it is estimated—from eight millions to one.

Two years before the end, Tu Wên-hsiu made a great effort to prop up his falling cause by securing the help of Great Britain. With this view he despatched his son to England in 1871, and as a token of his desire to become the vassal of the British Crown he sent Queen Victoria four pieces of rock hewn out of the four corners of the great Tali mountain. "Our unsentimental Foreign Office," as Baber says, "blind to romantic symbolism, would not suffer them to be extricated from the bonded warehouse of the Customs;" at any rate the Sultan and his unfortunate followers were left to their doom, and the Dragon flag flew once more over the walls of Tali. The mountain, if it could think and feel, might perhaps console itself for the contempt shown to its corner-stones with the reflection that since its history began nations have grown up and passed away like the wild-flowers that live and die on its green slopes, and that the great thrones and dynasties of to-day will have become empty names, signifying nothing, long before its jewelled fingers cease to traffic with the eternal stars, or to duplicate themselves in the still waters of the Tali lake.

CHAPTER XV

ETHNOLOGY OF THE CHINESE FAR WEST

In the foregoing chapters I have attempted to give some account of a portion of that wild border country which constitutes the Far West of China, and most readers will perhaps agree that of all its striking features it possesses no peculiarity so remarkable and so puzzling as the number and diversity of the races by which it is peopled. At a meeting of the Royal Geographical Society in 1904 a well-known Oriental scholar, Sir George Scott, K.C.I.E., made the remark that "the country north of Tali-fu is the place where we shall find, if we ever do find, the solution of a great many of the puzzling questions of the different races who inhabit the frontier hills." Those secluded ravines and icy mountains have served as both the cradle and the death-bed of nations. From that region have issued vigorous and ambitious tribes, bent on a career of glory and conquest; and back to it the shattered remnants of decaying races have crept home to die.

The preceding chapters may have revealed something of the nature of the country from the geographical point of view. Fathomless chasms, towering cliffs and gloomy river-gorges are to be found throughout its length and breadth; and we need hardly be surprised to find that the strange variations which characterise its climate, scenery, fauna and flora, are faithfully reproduced in the vivid contrasts that exist among its many-tongued peoples.

The comparatively short journey from Tachienlu to Tali-fu has introduced us to some of these peoples, but these do not by any means exhaust the tribal varieties of this remote part of the Chinese empire. North of Tachienlu, up to the borders of Chinese Turkestan and Mongolia, there are semi-independent races, some of which are perhaps only remotely connected with any of those mentioned in this book; while the wilder parts of the extreme north and east of Upper Burma and the Shan States contain further ethnological problems of their own, which scholars have so far indicated rather than solved.

Most of these tribes disclaim any connection with each other, but it is impossible to believe that they are all of independent origin. Probably the scattered threads of their history will never be gathered up until scholars have found time and opportunity to study their social, physical and linguistic peculiarities by prolonged residence among them. Libraries cannot assist us much when historical records are entirely wanting or are obviously unreliable, and travellers who move rapidly from place to place can do little more.

Professor E. H. Parker sums up his remarks on the subject by expressing the opinion that most of the far western tribes of China "will be found to range themselves either under the Shan or the Tibetan head."[1] This is probably true enough if we give a very wide interpretation to the word "Tibetan," and also to the word "Shan." Our knowledge of Tibet has till recently been of a very fragmentary nature, and the veil of mystery that hung over that secluded land until it was partially torn away by Lord Curzon's Lhasa expedition, and by such enterprising travellers as Sven Hedin, has prevented us from realising how far the Tibetans are from being a homogeneous race. No one who has come across the people of eastern Tibet and has also read the descriptions of western and central Tibet given us by recent writers and travellers, can fail to see that in spite of all that they possess in common the inhabitants of Tibet are a mixed people. "Long-heads" and "broad-heads," swarthy faces, white faces and yellow faces, long noses and flattened noses, oblique eyes and straight eyes, coal-black hair and brown hair, and many other physical peculiarities differentiate the people of one Tibetan district from those of another, just in the same way as they differentiate the various races of India and Indo-China. Nearly all the people of eastern Tibet have adopted the peculiar form of Buddhism which as Lamaism we have learned to associate with that country, and their languages and customs are saturated with Tibetan influences. In spite of many dialectical peculiarities I found that the people of the Yalung watershed were nearly always able to speak and

[1] *China: Her History, Diplomacy and Commerce*, p. 9.

understand Tibetan. Yet many of them are bi-lingual, and their own languages—as may be seen from the vocabularies in the Appendix—appear to be nearly as distinct from Tibetan as they are from Chinese.

Who are entitled to be called pure Tibetans—if such people exist—and who should be regarded as of hybrid or alien race, are therefore questions not very easily determined. All the country west of the Ta Tu river and the Chien-ch'ang valley may rightly enough be designated Tibetan Ssuch'uan or Chinese Tibet, if the name does not mislead us into supposing that the natives of the king of Chala's state, for instance, are of the same type as the inhabitants of Lhasa. But as these tribes are certainly not Chinese, what are we to call them if Tibetan is, strictly speaking, a misnomer?

By the Chinese many of the western tribes are more or less indiscriminately known as Man-tzŭ, Man-chia, Hsi Fan and T'u Fan. Now the words Hsi Fan and T'u Fan [1] appear at first sight to mean simply western Barbarians and aboriginal (or perhaps agricultural as distinct from pastoral or nomadic) Barbarians; but, as is now well known,[2] the old pronunciation of the second Chinese character in T'u Fan was not *fan*, but something like *po* or *p'o*, which is simply the Tibetan word Bod,[3] pronounced Bö or Beu, the

[1] 西番 and 土番.

[2] See Rockhill's *Life of the Buddha*, pp. 215-216, and T. W. Kingsmill's article in the *Journal* of the Royal Asiatic Society (China Branch), vol. xxxvii. pp. 26-27.

[3] བོད. The last letter of the Tibetan word is not pronounced, but it modifies the phonetic value of the vowel sound. As regards

name by which the Tibetans describe their own country and people, and from which we derive the second syllable of our word Tibet. The character *t'u* was similarly a Chinese approximation to the Tibetan word *teu*, meaning *upper* or *superior*.[1] T'u Fan is then simply the Chinese equivalent of our own word Tibetan, and means the Bö(d) of the Uplands; and I assume that the name *Turfan* (the oasis on the borders of Turkestan and Sungaria, where some remarkable discoveries have recently been made by exploring expeditions) has the same origin, though Turfan itself happens to lie in a very deep depression. The combination Hsi Fan, as Mr T. W. Kingsmill gives good reason for supposing, is in like manner derived from the sound Shar-bar, the name of a tribe of eastern Tibet still found near the town of Sung-p'an in north-western Ssuch'uan.

The word Man-tzŭ (蠻子)[2] is of very wide application, and at the present time conveys the meaning of "Savage Fellows" or "Sons of Savages," though it is not impossible that here too we have a rough attempt at imitating the sound of a non-Chinese word. When the Chinese had spread themselves over all northern China they used this term to describe all the uncivilised tribes whose habitations lay to the south; just as they described

the Chinese character 番, of which the phonetic value in modern Chinese is generally *fan*, we find several cases in which the sound is still *bo* or *po*. Mr Kingsmill mentions 鄱 *p'o* (as in the characters used for the P'o Yang Lake). The characters 皤, 磻 and 播 are similar instances.

[1] སྟོད་ as opposed to སྨད་ (*smad*, pron. *ma*), meaning *lower*, *inferior*.

[2] Often transliterated *Mantse*, and spelt by Marco Polo *Manji*.

the "barbarians" beyond their western frontier as Jung (戎), those beyond their northern frontier as Ti (狄), and those of the east as I (夷). These terms all appear again and again in the ancient Chinese classics, such as the *Shu Ching* and *Shih Ching*, and the references show that at the time to which they refer, that is to say as far back as the third millennium B.C., the Chinese were constantly at war with their less civilised neighbours, and by no means met with uniform success in contending with them. In the *Shu Ching*, for example, we read that "the invading barbarous tribes of the west (Jung) have greatly injured our empire."[1] The *Man* tribes are in several places described as eight in number,[2] and we learn that in the reign of the more or less mythical king Yü (2204-2197 B.C.) their country was known as the Wild Domain,[3] and that Chinese criminals were transported thither when sentenced to exile,[4] much as the Russians send their convicts at the present day to Siberia. Sometimes in the Chinese classics the name *Man* is combined with *I* or *Jung* as a definition of barbarians in general,[5] and sometimes the word *Nan* (South) is prefixed to make the definition more specific. In Mencius we hear of "this shrike-tongued barbarian of the south (*Nan Man*), whose doctrines are not those of the ancient kings."[6] Naturally enough they are often spoken of contemptuously. "I have heard of men," says

[1] Vol. ii. p. 617 (Legge's ed.).
[2] As in *Shu Ching*, vol. ii. p. 345.
[3] 荒服.
[4] *Shu Ching*, vol. i. p. 147.
[5] *Ibid.* vol. i. pp. 42, 44.
[6] Mencius, p. 255 (Legge, 2nd. ed.).

Mencius, "using the doctrine of our great land to change barbarians, but I have never yet heard of any being changed by barbarians."[1] Yet it is interesting to notice that Confucius was liberal-minded enough to admit that even a "barbarian" might—if he were truthful and honourable—be regarded as a gentleman.[2]

The name Man-tzŭ clung to the inhabitants of what is now southern China long after the Chinese had themselves begun to spread over that country, and no doubt many of the early Chinese immigrants and their descendants writhed under the derogatory epithet. About Marco Polo's time (in the second half of the thirteenth century) the southern portion of the empire—in fact, the greater part of China south of the Yellow River—was ruled by the emperors of the expiring Sung dynasty, who, owing to the successful invasions of the Chin Tartars, had been expelled from north China and had created a new capital for themselves at Hangchow (Marco's Kinsay) in the maritime province of Chekiang. The whole of their empire was known to the Venetian traveller as the land of the *Manzi* or Man-tzŭ, as distinct from the northern (Chin-Tartar and afterwards Mongol) empire which he calls Cathay. He has handed down a circumstantial account of the splendour and wealth of the so-called Manzi capital, and he was an eye-witness of many of the stirring episodes in that long series of campaigns which overwhelmed the Sung imperial house and the

[1] Mencius, pp. 253-254 (Legge).
[2] *Lun Yü*, pp. 295-296 (Legge, 2nd ed.).

Shan and Lolo princes of Tien, and established the descendants of Genghis Khan on the throne of a united China as emperors of the Yüan or Mongol dynasty.

In the Yunnanese Shan and so-called Lolo states, which were reduced to obedience by the Mongol prince Kúbláі (afterwards emperor of China, and known to history as Kúblái Khan), the native tribes were too powerful and numerous to be exterminated. Great numbers, disdaining the Chinese yoke, migrated southward to Siam; some of those who remained behind were allowed to retain their tribal organisations under Chinese suzerainty, and to a limited extent they have retained it ever since. But in other parts of southern China the "barbarians" were much more harshly dealt with, for they were gradually broken up into small bands and forced to find for themselves a scanty subsistence in the rugged and mountainous regions of Kuang-si, Kuei-chou and Ssuch'uan, and multitudes seem to have fallen back on Annam. The term Man-tzŭ, as applied to all inhabitants of south China irrespective of race or descent, was then gradually dropped, but a curious instance of its survival in quite recent times is mentioned by Professor Parker,[1] who found, in an official proclamation, the word used to describe the Chinese of the Canton province.

Various notices of the Man-tzŭ and other hill-tribes are to be found in the monumental work of the historian Ssŭ-ma Ch'ien (about B.C. 100), and in the later dynastic and provincial records;

[1] *China: Her History, Diplomacy and Commerce*, p. 310.

but in none of them do we find anything like a clear statement of the history and origin of these tribes. The fact that they were all barbarians was sufficient, in the Chinese mind, to justify their being left severely alone or lumped together under some meaningless designation made applicable to them all.[1] At Tachienlu we come in contact with representatives of all the various tribes of western China and eastern Tibet, but they are nearly all labelled either Man-chia or Man-tzŭ. The former term means "barbarian families," and in practice is applied to the people whom the Chinese choose to regard as true Tibetans as distinct from the wilder denizens of the hills and forests. The Tibetan language is *Man-hua* ("the language of the barbarians"), and the Chinese language is *Han-hua* ("the language of the men of Han"). The term Man-tzŭ may now for practical purposes be restricted to certain of the western hill-tribes to whom both Tibetan and Chinese are foreign languages, and who preserve distinct customs of their own in the matters of dress, religion and social intercourse. A considerable proportion of the people who inhabit the scattered villages of the kingdom of Chala, through which lay my route to the Yalung, are Man-tzŭ, not Man-chia. M. Bonin, who has travelled widely in western Ssuch'uan, identifies the Man-tzŭ (using the term in the narrower sense) with the Lolos. In common with many other Europeans he has observed that the word Lolo, whatever it may mean, is an opprobrious

[1] See Note 40 (p. 437).

epithet, which is not used by the Lolos themselves and should never be used in their presence. He considers that the word Lolo should be dropped altogether, and that we should substitute Man-tzŭ as the designation of both peoples. This word, he says, has the advantage of comprehending Mo-so, Hsi Fan, Ku-tsung, Menia and Li-so, who are, he considers, all of the same origin.[1] I venture to express a doubt whether we should gain much by classing under one such designation a number of peoples who, whatever their origin, have been so long separated from one another that they refuse to acknowledge any mutual connection, and to some extent have different customs and speak different languages.[2] As regards the identification of the Lolos with the Man-tzŭ, however, there is good ground for believing that it is justified. Probably no one has a better acquaintance with the Lolos than the Catholic missionary,

[1] *Comptes Rendus*, Société de Géographie, 1898. No. 8, p. 349. But see M. Paul Vial (*Les Lolos*: Shanghai, 1898). If M. Vial's theory of the origin of the word Lolo is correct, it was originally by no means a disrespectful term. He considers that it is a Chinese reduplication of a form of the word *No* or *Na*, which was the special name of one of the patrician tribes of the Lolos. He admits, however, that the term is now regarded as impolite. He says that the Lolos have now no common name for the whole race, but simply employ the various tribal names as occasion requires. The Chinese characters for Lolo (generally 玀玀) are merely phonetic. The constant use of the "dog" radical in the Chinese characters employed to represent the names of barbarous tribes is an instructive indication of the contemptuous Chinese attitude towards such people. In the word *Man* the radical is an insect or reptile.

[2] M. Bonin regards them all as of Tibetan origin; but as they separated from the main branch, he says, before the adoption of Buddhism they have preserved on Chinese soil their primitive fetish-worship. "I consider them in consequence," he concludes, "as the *avant-garde* of the Tibetans."

M. Paul Vial. He has lived for many years among the Nyi (or Ngi) Lolos of Yunnan, and has come to the conclusion that "Man-tzŭ et Lolos ne sont qu'une seule et même race."[1] His historical sketch is unfortunately too brief to be of much value. It would appear that in his opinion the great ruling power in Yunnan up to the thirteenth century was not Shan but Lolo. Indeed, his little book almost ignores the Shans altogether, though he states that, judging from linguistic evidence (which should always be accepted with very great caution) the Lolos are "brothers of the Burmese and cousins of the T'ai"—who, of course, include the Shans. Here, however, he seems to have gone a little astray, as his remarks would imply a closer relationship between Burmese and Shans than can be proved to exist; and when he says that the Lolo language has no relationship with the Chinese—which seems to be true—he overlooks the fact that the language of the Shans, whom he claims as cousins of the Lolos, is generally recognised as being related to Chinese.[2] He concludes that the Lolos, Shans and Burmese all belong to the same stock and came originally from the unexplored regions between the upper Mekong and

[1] *Les Lolos*, p. 4. See also the *Gazetteer of Upper Burma*, pt. i. vol. i. p. 615, where it is stated that the Man-tzŭ "have undoubtedly been distinct from the Lolo for centuries, but the balance of opinion seems to connect them with that tribe."

[2] See the *Gazetteer of Upper Burma*, pt. i. vol. i. pp. 272 *seq.* "The relationship of the T'ai to the Chinese races seems unmistakable. . . . The research, which has not been long begun, points distinctly to the fact that the Chinese and the T'ai belong to a family of which the Chinese are the most prominent representatives."

the Brahmaputra; but he does not account for the subsequent divergence of languages, customs and traditions.

M. Vial has also some interesting notes on a Kuei-chou tribe called the Chung-chia-tzŭ.[1] Their own tradition, he says, declares that they came from the province of Kiangsi more than eight hundred years ago, and conquered the Ke-lao. These latter are, perhaps, Marco Polo's Koloman or Toloman, who Yule thought might have been a tribe of Lolos.[2] The Chung-chia-tzŭ are different from any of the hill-tribes round them, and are apparently related neither to Lolos nor to Miao-tzŭ. According to Terrien de Lacouperie, they speak a dialect "much resembling the Siamese, of whom they are undoubtedly the elder brothers."[3] If that is so, the Chung-chia-tzŭ must be related to the Shans, for both Shans and Siamese belong to the widely-spread T'ai family. Mr Warry, it should be noticed, identifies the Chung-chia-tzŭ with the Miao-tzŭ,[4] yet from M. Vial we learn that they differ in manners, customs and language.[5]

Mr F. S. A. Bourne, a first-rate authority, classes the Miao-tzŭ by themselves, for he believes that exclusive of the Tibetans (embracing Hsi Fan, Ku-tsung and others) there are three great non-Chinese races in south China: Lolo, Shan

[1] 重家子, or 重甲子.

[2] Yule's *Marco Polo* (Cordier's edition), vol. ii. pp. 122-123. Cordier has, however, another explanation.

[3] Introduction to Colquhoun's *Amongst the Shans*, liv.

[4] See *Gazetteer of Upper Burma*, pt. i. vol. i. p. 597.

[5] *Op. cit.* p. 35.

and Miao-tzŭ. Whatever their origin may be, the Miao-tzŭ have succeeded in planting representatives of their race in various widely-separated localities. We have seen traces of them in Muliland, west of the Yalung,[1] and they are also to be found as far south as the Lao states and as far east as Kuang-tung. They call themselves Mung, Hmung or Hmêng, and it has been suggested that they are an Indo-Chinese race connected with the Môns, Peguans or Talaings.[2] M. Vial says that the Miao-tzŭ of Kuei-chou believe that they came "from the East," which is vague. In all probability no surviving race has been settled in southern China for a longer period than the Miao-tzŭ, and no attempt to connect them with the surrounding races has yet been successful.

As regards the Mo-so and Li-so, the people of those tribes whom I met between Yung-ning and Li-chiang denied there was any connection between them, and both were strenuously opposed to the idea that they were in any way related to the Lolos. Such denials, however, do not go for much, especially in the case of people who are totally lacking in any historical sense. The Mo-so of Yung-ning told me that they were an immigrant race and originally came from Mongolia, but this may be the result of confused reminiscences of their relations with the Mongol armies between

[1] See p. 223.

[2] See *Gazetteer of Upper Burma*, pt. i. vol. i. pp. 597-601. There are numerous settlements of the Miao-tzŭ in the British Shan States, and the *Gazetteer* says: "It may be hoped that more will come, for they are a most attractive race."

six and seven hundred years ago. It is a well-ascertained fact that the Mo-so once occupied a large portion of south-western Tibet, and indeed there is a kind of national epic celebrating their wars with the Tibetans. At Li-chiang, as stated above,[1] they founded a capital which was the centre of a powerful principality, and they still have a prince near the Mekong river, south of Tse-ku. At times under weak rulers they were subject to the suzerainty of the great Shan kingdom of Nan Chao, the capital of which was generally at Tali-fu or not far from it; but at other times they were practically independent of any external control. It was not till Kûblái brought his Mongol troops to Yunnan in order to break up the Nan Chao kingdom as a preliminary to the overthrow of the Sung dynasty in south China that the political power of the Mo-so was laid low. Kúblái, in order to avert the possibility of being taken in the rear by hostile tribes, turned aside from his direct march to Tali-fu in order to reduce the Mo-so. He captured Li-chiang and broke up the Mo-so power about the year 1253. He subsequently besieged and took Tali-fu. The pacification of the newly-conquered province was entrusted by Kúblái to his great Mongol general Uriangkadai, and was successfully accomplished. The Mo-so, Lolos and Shans were never again able, with any hope of success, to defy the power of the emperor of China.

[1] See pp. 239 and 245-246.

The origin of the word Mo-so is unknown.[1] They call themselves Lashi or Nashi (the *l* and *n* being interchangeable), and the Tibetans call them Djiung.[2] Perhaps they are the descendants of the Jung tribes which, as stated above,[3] are mentioned in the Chinese classics as having frequently menaced the western frontier of China; though it seems more probable that the Jung were the ancestors of the Hiung-nu. In a recent geographical work on China[4] the Mo-so are not referred to with much appreciation. They are described as deceitful and shifty, and a proverbial saying is quoted to the effect that three Chinese are necessary to deceive one Tibetan, and three Tibetans to deceive one Mo-so. Most of the eastern Mo-so speak Chinese as well as their own language, which bears various resemblances to Lolo. When I pointed out to some Yung-ning Mo-so that many common words in their language were identical with Lolo words conveying the same meaning, they admitted the fact but vehemently denied that it betokened any racial affinity. This attitude may be due to the fact that the Mo-so, once a warlike race, have settled down quietly under Chinese rule as

[1] The Chinese characters are 麽些. It is tempting, but rash, to connect the word with *Mu-hsö*, which means "a hunter" in the Shan, Wa, Palaung, Rumai and Riang languages.

[2] The Tibetans also call them Jang or Aj'angs (འཇངས་). Surely there is some justification for tracing a connection between this word, as spelt in Tibetan, with the name of the tribe *A-ch'angs* mentioned in the *Gazetteer of Upper Burma*, pt. i. vol. i. pp. 618-619. But see Sir George Scott's *Burma*, pp. 94-95.

[3] See p. 270.

[4] *Géographie de l'empire de Chine*, by Richards (Shanghai: 1905).

peaceful tillers of the ground, while the Lolos have earned the reputation of being lawless free-booters. The Mo-so resents being taken for a Lolo, just as a sturdy Dumfriesshire farmer—whose ancestor may have been an expert cattle-lifter—would resent being described as the scion of a race of highway robbers.

The Yung-ning district, as we have seen, still enjoys a measure of independence under a native prince on whom the Chinese long ago conferred the hereditary rank of prefect.[1] The Li-chiang district is now more directly under Chinese rule, but even there a Mo-so official or noble acts as a kind of assessor to the local Chinese mandarins, who are still regarded as the representatives of a foreign power. The Tibetan name for Li-chiang is Sa-T'am,[2] by which it is also known to the Mo-so.

The Mo-so under their different appellations (including Lashi or Nashi[3] and Djiung) are still

[1] See above, pp. 228-229.

[2] In Tibetan *Sa* is "earth" or "land," and *t'am* is "seal" (*sigillum*) or "offering." Possibly the Tibetan is in this case the transliteration of a Mo-so word.

[3] We have seen on pages 249-250 that the plain west of that of Li-chiang is called Lashi-Pa, or Plain of the Mo-so, and that a village therein bears the same name. M. Paul Vial mentions what he calls a *Lolo* tribe named Ashi, apparently dwelling in the south-east of Yunnan (*Les Lolos*, p. 25). Now only a few miles west of Lashi-Pa, on the road from Li-chiang to Chung-tien, there is a village called Ashi, which gives its name to a ferry on the Yangtse river. It is possible that the sound in both cases was once either Lashi or Nashi, for, when we find from experience that the *L* and *N* are interchangeable, it may well be that in some districts inhabited by Mo-so the initial has been dropped altogether. I do not know the derivation of the word Lashio, the British settlement near the Salwen valley, in the North Shan States. There is also a district called Lashi, in British territory, north-east of Myitkyina, the people of which appear to be a connecting link between the Kachins and the Burmese. (See Sir George Scott's *Burma*, p. 70.)

a very numerous though not a homogeneous race, and perhaps deserve a more careful study than they have hitherto received. I am strongly inclined to think that it is this race which constitutes the predominant element in the population of Muli-land or Huang Lama. We have seen above[1] that the people of that region call themselves Njong, and I conjecture that this is simply a thinly-disguised form of Djiung. The nasal prefix is a quite frequent linguistic peculiarity in Chinese Tibet, and occurs in many Tibetan words. The ordinary word *dro*, "to walk," for instance, is almost invariably pronounced *ndro*.[2] It may be allowed, however, that the people of Muli have identified themselves more closely than their brethren of Yunnan with the predominant Tibetan race, and have come more directly under Tibetan influences in respect of language and religion. For the people of Muli-land are, as we have seen, Buddhists of the Tibetan type, whereas with the Mo-so of Yunnan Lamaism is only a veneer that covers an even more uncouth system of witchcraft and sorcery, founded on the pre-Buddhistic Bon-pa.[3]

The Li-so,[4] judging from their language only, would appear to be rather closer to the Burmese than to the Mo-so. In the Yung-ning district, however, Li-so and Mo-so live together on amicable

[1] See above, p. 222.

[2] As in the common expression, *ka-li ka-li ndro a*, "walk slowly" or "there's no hurry."

[3] For some account of the Bon religion see Rockhill's *Life of the Buddha*, pp. 205 *seq.*, and Sarat Chandra Das's *Journey to Lhasa*.

[4] 力梁.

terms, and both express contempt or hatred for the Lolos. The Li-so are quite as widely scattered as the Mo-so, and may be found, apparently, in the Shan States and the Kachin highlands as well as in Yunnan and Ssuch'uan. They appear to be very closely related to the La'hu of the British Shan States, and they evidently regard themselves as racially distinct from the Shans, for they refuse to ally themselves in marriage with that people.[1] The Li-so language was examined by Prince Henry of Orleans, who found it like that of the La'hu or Muh-sö and that of the Lolos. He records a tradition among the Li-so that they came originally from Nanking, on the lower Yangtse, "which accorded with a similar tradition among the Lolos."[2] The Li-so of Yung-ning, when questioned by me, gave themselves the name of Lu-su.

A very interesting contribution has quite recently been made to the literature that bears on the ethnology of China's Far West by the researches of Mr T. W. Kingsmill.[3] That scholar presents a formidable array of evidence from Greek as well as from Chinese sources to prove that the *Sinae* of the fourth century of our era were the inhabitants of *India extra Gangem*, namely the west side of what we call the Indo-Chinese peninsula, including Burma; that their capital, Thinae, was on the banks of the Irrawaddy, between Bhamo and

[1] Mr G. C. B. Stirling, quoted in *Gazetteer of Upper Burma*, pt. i. vol. i. p. 588.

[2] *Gazetteer of Upper Burma*, pt. i. vol. i. p. 616.

[3] *The Manlse and the Golden Chersonese*, and *Ancient Tibet and its Frontagers*, by T. W. Kingsmill, in vols. xxxv. and xxxvii. of the *Journal* of the Royal Asiatic Society (China Branch).

Mandalay;[1] that they, "if not identieal with the widely-extended people of the Shans," had at least a close ethnological connection with that race; that they and kindred races sprang from the great Maurya family of north-western India; and that to them is due the wide prevalence of Indian political influence and Indian art in the greater part of south-western China as well as throughout the Indo-Chinese peninsula and neighbouring islands. According to this view, which certainly receives some support from history, tradition, philology, and much miscellaneous evidence, the Man-tzŭ were originally of Mauryan stock, but allied themselves with the Böd tribes or Tibetans, with whom their migrations had brought them into close contact.[2]

An apparent difficulty in tracing Shans and Man-tzŭ and other tribes to a common origin in north-eastern India consists in the generally recognised affinity between the Chinese and T'ai peoples.[3] According to the commonly-accepted view the Shans sprang from somewhere in north-western China and were gradually pushed southwards as the Chinese race extended itself. De Lacouperie considered that the cradle of the Shan race was "in the Kiulung mountains, north of Ssuch'uan and south of Shensi, in China proper."[4]

[1] The name still survives in the province of Theinni and in the classical name Tien (滇) for the Chinese province of Yunnan. The connection between Tien and Theinni was pointed out by Terrien de Lacouperie in his introduction to Colquhoun's *Amongst the Shans*, p. xlviii.

[2] The fable is that a Mauryan woman was married to a Tibetan dog and that their progeny were the Man-tzŭ.

[3] See above, p. 275 (footnote 2).

[4] Introduction to Colquhoun's *Amongst the Shans*.

Mr Kingsmill's theory would perhaps gain more ready acceptance if we premised that the so-called Indian people from whom he supposes the Mantzŭ and others to have sprung were themselves not of Indian origin but had entered India at some remote period—probably before either Aryans or Dravidians set foot in the peninsula—either as peaceful immigrants or as an invading host, from the countries that lay to the north-east.[1]

Our knowledge of the early history of the Maurya family is unfortunately exceedingly scanty, and it is impossible to trace it to its pre-Indian home. To confine ourselves to their Indian history, the Mauryans seem to have sprung from the Licchavis, the strongest members of the powerful Vaggian confederation that dwelt near the Lower Ganges, north-east of the kingdom of Magadha. Just before the time of the Buddha—about the seventh and sixth centuries B.C.—a fierce contest for the mastery of northern India was waged between the kingdoms of Magadha and Kosala. This contest, as Dr Rhys Davids points out, "was decided in the time of the Buddha's boyhood by the final victory of Magadha."[2] About 320 B.C. the Mauryan dynasty under Chandragupta (Sandrakottos) overthrew that of Dhana Nanda and seated itself on the throne of Magadha, which, under a strong ruler, became more powerful than ever. From this time onwards till the extinction of Chandragupta's dynasty about 190 B.C., the Licchavi or Mauryan element was the main source of the strength of Magadha, which became the supreme

[1] See Note 41 (p. 438). [2] *Buddhist India*, p. 260.

power in the Indian peninsula. The royal adventurer Chandragupta Maurya was the contemporary and rival of Seleukos Nikator. Chandragupta handed on to his son Bindusāra and his grandson Asoka (the famous Buddhist "Emperor of India") the crown of one of the most powerful monarchies the world had known.[1] The capital of the Licchavis (as distinct from the Magadhans) was the city of Vesâli, which was probably situated about 25 miles north of the Ganges, north-east of Pataliputra (the modern Patna), which was the Magadhan capital. Buddhist records give us some remarkable particulars about Vesâli. "A triple wall encompassed the city, each wall a league distant from the next, and there were three gates with watch-towers. In that city there were always 7707 kings to govern the kingdom, and a like number of viceroys, generals and treasurers."[2] In another place we are told that these numerous royal persons were "all of them given to argument and disputation."[3] Allowing for Oriental exaggeration, these assertions certainly seem to imply that Vesâli, and the people whose capital it was, occupied a unique position in the political system of India.[4] There cannot have been many cities, even in that paradise of philosophers, which, in pre-Buddhistic days, or indeed at any other period, harboured thousands of disputatious kings. The so-called "kings," however, were probably only the heads of the free

[1] See Note 42 (p. 439).
[2] Introduction to *Jâtaka*, No. 149. (Cowell's ed., vol. i. p. 316.)
[3] *Ibid.*, No. 301 (vol. iii. p. 1).
[4] See Note 43 (p. 439).

families. Vesâli was really the metropolis of a number of federated republics, the influence of which extended far beyond the boundaries of Hindustan.

The Licchavis may well have pushed eastwards into China and Indo-China long before the Mauryans gave India its first imperial dynasty; though if we find traces of their influence in western China it seems not improbable that this is due to the fact that after their migration to India they succeeded in maintaining a friendly intercourse with their Eastern kinsfolk. In either case, the Licchavis (and through them the kingdom of Magadha[1]) must have possessed, in the days of the struggle against Kosala, an enormous advantage over their rivals in being able to draw an inexhaustible supply of strength from Indo-Chinese countries to which the Kosalans had no access.

I have no space here to discuss the various arguments that Mr Kingsmill adduces to prove that the Man-tzŭ, Lolos and allied tribes, and perhaps the Shans, are the descendants of the Mauryas—some being more or less mixed with the Böd and Kiang[2] elements of Tibet. Suffice it to say that he traces the Mauryan element in tribal names and place-names, in decorative and

[1] "The struggle between Kosala and Magadha for the paramount power in all India was, in fact, probably decided when the powerful confederation of the Licchavis became arrayed on the side of Magadha." (Rhys Davids' *Buddhist India*, p. 25.)

[2] For the Kiang element, see Kingsmill, *Journal* of the Royal Asiatic Society (China Branch), vol. xxxvii. 29 and 34 *seq.* The Kiang appear to have been a branch of the Yüeh-ti or Lunar Race, to which reference is made on p. 49.

architectural art,[1] in Chinese records and tribal traditions, and by an analysis of the phonetic history of certain Chinese characters.

The fatal weakness of the Indo-Chinese tribes appears at all times to have been their lack of cohesive power. At one time it must have seemed as though their empire would rival that of their Indian kinsmen — if kinsmen they were — in Magadha, and for centuries it might have seemed a doubtful question whether they or the Chinese were to be the masters of the vast country we now know as China. The great kingdom of Tien —which included the greater portions of Burma and Yunnan — was for centuries a formidable obstacle in the way of Chinese expansion towards the south, and it is only within comparatively recent years that Chinese suzerainty has been accepted by western and southern Ssuch'uan. The Shan kings of Tien or Nan-Chao sometimes arrogated to themselves the title of Huang-ti (Emperor), and frequently invaded Chinese territory. In 859 of our era one of these emperors besieged Ch'eng-tu, the capital of Ssuch'uan, and left "eighty per cent. of the inhabitants of certain towns with artificial noses

[1] It is to the "Mauryan" Man-tzŭ that Mr Kingsmill ascribes the excavation of the caves of Ssuch'uan (see pp. 46 *seq.*). He says that they were evidently the work of a people who had made considerable progress in the arts, and that the art in its predominant features approaches more nearly to ancient Indian types than to Chinese (*Journal* of the Royal Asiatic Society, China Branch, vol. xxxv. p. 93). As I have already stated, there is not much evidence of a strong artistic instinct in the decoration of the caves. I agree with Mr Kingsmill, nevertheless, in ascribing the art, such as it is, to Indian influences.

and ears made of wood."[1] To this day there are thousands of square miles of nominally Chinese territory in which Chinese law is unknown, and with the administration of which no Chinese official dares to meddle. Had these various tribes—many of whom have the right, according to Mr Kingsmill's theory, to claim a common Mauryan ancestry—produced a few great rulers endowed with a genius for organisation, their history might have been at least as splendid as that of the Manchus and the so-called Mongolians, both of which peoples have given emperors to China. It is indeed possible that a dynasty of Mauryan blood did actually succeed for a few brilliant years in seating itself on the Chinese throne, though the evidence to this effect is far from conclusive. Mr Kingsmill, not content with identifying the Sinae with a people belonging to the same race as the Mauryans, has also found reason for identifying the Seres with the Man-tzŭ: that is to say, with a race descended from Mauryans and Tibetans. He conjectures that the people of the State of Ts'in (Ch'in) were connected with "the Mans in the south" rather than with "the Chinese in the north." He points out that we can trace the word Ts'in[2] and its homologues to an ancient pronunciation *Ser*,[3] and that when Virgil and

[1] *Gazetteer of Upper Burma*, pt. i. vol. i. p. 267.

[2] 秦, pronounced Ch'in in modern Pekingese.

[3] In this connection Mr Kingsmill explains that the character *hsiang* (象), which means "elephant," was also originally pronounced Ser. I have already mentioned a mountain-pass called the Ta Hsiang Ling which is supposed to be named after either P'u Hsien's elephant or Chu-ko Liang. (See p. 117 and Note 14.) To the south of that pass there is another named the Hsiao Hsiang Ling, or Small Elephant

other Roman writers mentioned the *Seres* they were making use of a name which had become famous through the brilliant achievements of the Ts'in or Ser, who through the genius or good luck of Ts'in Shih Huang-ti had established a short-lived supremacy over the other peoples of the Chinese empire.[1] That ruler reigned from about 221 to 209 B.C., and therefore was almost a contemporary of the great emperor Asoka, who died only about eleven years before Ts'in Shih Huang-ti began to reign.[2] The famous episode of "the burning of the books" is said to have taken place about the year 213 B.C. It would be curious if it could be proved that, during the same century in which the great Mauryan emperor of Magadha was trying to inaugurate a new epoch of religion and peace by spreading the doctrines of the Buddha throughout southern Asia, another Mauryan ruler was sitting on the throne of China and inaugurating what he believed to be a new era of progress in north-eastern Asia by the destruction of the sacred books of China.

The Min-chia, whose characteristic features seem to dissociate them from the Mo-so in spite of their proximity of habitation, are probably connected more or less closely with the Shans. M. Vial refers to them in a passage which I

Pass, which must be crossed on the way to the Chien-ch'ang valley. Mr Kingsmill would perhaps translate the names of these passes as the Great and Small Passes of the Ts'in or Ser; in which case we may regard Ts'in Shih Huang-ti as being a third claimant to the honour of giving a name to this pass.

[1] See *Journal* of the Royal Asiatic Society (China Branch), vol. xxxvii. pp. 22-23.

[2] See Note 44 (p. 440).

translate as follows. "In 1394, Hung Wu, emperor of the Ming dynasty, caused a map of the empire to be prepared in which the Yangtse is made to form the southern limit of China. In 1400, Chien Wên or Hui Ti, who was Hung Wu's successor,[1] was dispossessed by one of his uncles and withdrew to Yunnan, where he lay hidden for thirty years. A great number of Chinese followed him and established themselves there. They now form the basis of this Chinese population that we call *pên-ti-jên* or Min-chia. They allied themselves to women of the indigenous race.[2] All these *pên-ti-jên* say that they came from a place called Kao Shih Ch'iao of the province of Nanking."[3] The war between Hui Ti and his rebellious but too successful relative, the Prince of Yen, is a matter of history; and it is also stated in the Chinese chronicles that when the emperor was overtaken by hopeless

[1] Hung Wu was the "reign-title" of the first emperor of the Ming dynasty, who reigned from 1368 to 1398. His successor, whose "reign-title" was Chien Wên, ruled from 1399 to 1402. With regard to the Yangtse being taken as the southern limit of China, this statement can only be accepted with an important modification, for all the southern provinces of China, including Yunnan, were at this time regarded as being within the empire, though the fact that they were chiefly inhabited by non-Chinese tribes made it somewhat anomalous to describe them as forming part of China proper. We have seen that Yunnan was annexed to the empire by Kúblái Khan in the thirteenth century. Towards the close of the following century the Yunnanese princes tried to reassert their independence, and the province was again reduced to complete submission by the generals of the emperor Hung Wu himself, who, in spite of his maps, never for a moment intended to relax the imperial hold on that distant province.

[2] By "indigenous race" M. Vial presumably means Lolos or Mo-so.

[3] That is, Kiang-su, the province in which Shanghai is situated. Nanking was at that time the capital of China.

defeat he escaped to Yunnan in the garb of a Buddhist monk. No doubt a number of faithful followers accompanied him into exile, but I am not aware of the evidence upon which M. Vial relies for his statement that they are the ancestors of the Min-chia. The Min-chia type is quite un-Chinese in appearance. That most members of the tribe speak Chinese is no strong argument in favour of their Chinese descent. It is a well-known fact that it was the deliberate policy of the Chinese emperors—especially in the early years of the present dynasty — to compel the conquered people of Yunnan to learn the language of northern China; and this policy was so wonderfully successful that at the present day nearly every one in Yunnan speaks a dialect which is easily intelligible to any one who has learned Pekingese. "The natives of Yunnan" as Baber said "were forced to learn the language of the north on pain of death." That a strain of pure Chinese blood must have mingled with that of the numerous races occupying Yunnan goes without saying; the mere presence of large Chinese armies on Yunnanese soil at times when campaigns lasted for a decade or more must of itself have tended to rub off the sharp edges of racial distinctions; but the special characteristics of the Min-chia are too well marked to justify the hasty adoption of the theory that they are the descendants of Chinese refugees from Nanking.

The number of different tribes who declare that they came originally from Nanking or elsewhere in the east is surprisingly large. I have already[1] referred to a tradition among the Chung-chia-tzŭ that they came from Kiangsi. The Miao-tzŭ of Kuei-chou apparently believe that they came "from the east." Prince Henry of Orleans records that the La'hu and Lolos both declared to him that they "came from Nanking ages ago,"[2] and mentions a similar tradition among the Li-so. That the Chung-chia-tzŭ, Miao-tzŭ, Lolo, La'hu, Li-so and Min-chia should have all come from the neighbourhood of Nanking seems scarcely credible, and the tradition with regard to most of them, if not all, may be dismissed as a fiction. But indeed I am aware of no theory about the Min-chia, or about Lolos, Mo-so, Li-so, Shans and the rest, that settles all difficulties and fits in with all the facts; and if one is tempted to put faith in any of the numerous hypotheses that have been advanced, it is only because a half-truth is not always "the worst of lies," and a permanent suspension of judgment is a source of discomfort to the mind that shuns the cheerless refuge of agnosticism.

[1] See above, p. 276.
[2] *Gazetteer of Upper Burma*, pt. i. vol. i. pp. 585-586.

CHAPTER XVI

TALI-FU TO BHAMO

At Tali-fu I found it impossible to hire mules or coolies for a journey to the Kunlon ferry, though during the cool weather the transport question would have presented no difficulty. To travel from Tali to Yün-chou, on the south of the Mekong, would have occupied, I was told, only seven days, and another twelve days' march would have brought me through the valley of the Nam T'ing to the Salwen ferry at Kunlon, the boundary of British territory. From there it is but four or five easy stages through the jungle to the British post of Lashio,[1] the headquarters of the Superintendent of the North Shan States, and from that point I could have taken train to Mandalay. In summer, however, and especially after the commencement of the rains, the Tali muleteers regard a journey through the Nam T'ing valley and the Shan jungles of the frontier as very deadly, and I found that even an offer of treble the usual pay would not induce a single man to come forward. The crossing of the Salwen valley on the way to Bhamo is also considered a very dangerous performance in the hot season; but that, after all,

[1] See below, p. 331.

is a matter of a few hours only, and there is no superstitious dread of any other part of the journey. I found it necessary, therefore, to abandon all idea of travelling to the Kunlon ferry, and rather reluctantly decided to take the well-known trade-route to Bhamo, through Yung-ch'ang and T'êng-yüeh.

So many Europeans in recent years have traversed this route that it is unnecessary for me to describe, in any detail, the characteristic features of a road which we all know so well from the graphic accounts of such experienced travellers as Baber, Colquhoun, Captain Gill and Dr Morrison. South-western China bears much the same appearance to-day as it did thirty years ago, and it may be doubted whether it was very different in the days of Marco Polo, though probably the roads were better. There is therefore very little need for me to describe this part of my journey with any minuteness.

I left Tali-fu on 25th May, and passed through the southern fortress-city of Hsia Kuan—where the trade is much brisker than at Tali-fu itself—after an easy ride of 6 or 7 miles. There my road left the lake and struck west into a ravine, and a few miles further on I reached the village of Ho Chiang-p'u. Next day we passed through Yang Pi, crossed a suspension bridge which was undergoing repair, and after a fairly stiff climb spent the night in a hamlet near the summit of a pass. On the 27th we crossed another pass of no great elevation, rode through T'ai-p'ing-p'u and one or two other small hamlets, and descended into a deep ravine in order to cross the Ch'ing Lien river by a suspension bridge, which, according to an inscription, was reconstructed in the eighteenth year of the present reign (1892), with funds raised by the public.[1] A few miles beyond, we halted for the night in the village of Huang-lien-p'u. Some arduous climbing the next day brought us to the small town of Yung P'ing, which, a year previously, had suffered terribly from the floods of a neighbouring river. As no inn was habitable, I was given accommodation in a schoolhouse.

On the 29th I left Yung P'ing by a new road, only recently opened to traffic, passed the villages of Hsiao T'ien Pa situated amid rice-fields, Hsiao Hua Ch'iao ("Little Flower Bridge"), and Ta Hua Ch'iao ("Big Flower Bridge"). Above the last-named village and overlooking it is a temple (the San Shêng Kung), in which I lunched. In the afternoon we climbed a steep pass from which an equally steep descent led to the village of Sha Yang, where we halted. Immediately on leaving this village next day we ascended and crossed a low ridge, and descended into a small valley cultivated with rice. We crossed a stream by a three-arched bridge built in 1888, called the "Stone Bridge of the Cry of the Phœnix" (Fêng Ming Shih Ch'iao). Beyond this is a row of stone tablets, some commemorating the virtues of incorruptible officials, and others recording the names of those who had subscribed funds for building the bridge.

[1] Baber describes the old bridge as "very dilapidated" when it was crossed by the Grosvenor Mission in 1876.

At the top of the next steep pass, which overlooks the deep trough through which flows the Mekong river (called by the Chinese the Lan Ts'ang Chiang[1]), there is a rather large temple much patronised and enriched by successful traders. The descent to the river's edge is very steep. "A series of short and dangerous zigzags," says Baber, "leads down to a bold suspension bridge of 60 yards span, striding the river at its issue from the darkest of gorges. The perpendicular walls are not 100 yards apart; from our confined position we did not venture to estimate their height."[2] Only the day before my arrival a man had been killed by a boulder which fell on his head as he was wending his way down to the river. One of my escort casually mentioned this to me just after we had passed the fatal spot. The man had been buried that morning close to the place where he was killed. The boulder was supposed to have been dislodged by a deer or a goat. On the east bank of the river, close to the bridge, is a stone tablet or shrine dedicated to the Spirit of the Mountain, and an inscription in which the bridge is described as the T'ai P'ing Ch'iao ("Great Peace Bridge"). The bridge is covered by a wooden arcade, from the roof of which are suspended several *pien* or boards bearing appropriate inscriptions in huge gilt letters. One of them has the four words, *Shan Kao Shui Ch'ang* ("The

[1] 瀾滄江.

[2] Captain Gill (*River of Golden Sand*) somewhat exaggerates the difficulties of what he calls "this desperate gorge."

mountain is lofty and the river is long")—which remark if wanting in imaginative insight at least expresses an obvious truth concisely and to the point. The cliffs on the west side of the river are likewise covered with short inscriptions, carved deeply into the rock. One of the largest of all consists of the four words, *Jên Li So T'ung*[1] ("Made a thoroughfare by the labour of man"). The construction of this great bridge is indeed an engineering feat of which any people might well be proud.

On leaving the river we had a stiff climb over a fairly well paved road to P'ing P'o, the inhabitants of which ought to be excellent mountaineers. They cannot go out of doors in any direction without having to ascend or descend a steep mountain-side. A further climb of nearly 3 miles, partly beside the bed of a stream which in the rainy season is said to be a foaming torrent but in dry weather is absolutely non-existent, brought us to our destination for the night in the village of Shui Chai. In the neighbourhood of this village I found some tombstones of a kind I had not hitherto seen, though I met with many similar ones thereafter. They are like stone drums or cylinders stuck end-wise into the ground, but slightly convex on the top. On some of the grave-tablets are inscribed the words, *Chia Ch'êng* ("The City Beautiful").

So far throughout my journey I had been remarkably fortunate as regards weather. The rainy season in western Yunnan usually begins

[1] 人力所通.

early in May, yet, except for some snow-storms, one day's rain at Li-chiang, and two or three heavy showers after leaving Tali-fu, I had met with nothing but the most brilliant sunshine. I knew, however, that once the rains began in earnest they would continue incessantly for many weeks to come, and for this reason I was anxious to reach Bhamo as quickly as possible. What became of the weather after I had reached the Irrawaddy valley was a matter of indifference: *après moi le déluge!* The next stage after Shui Chai was the city of Yung-ch'ang, and as I had to pay off my Tali muleteers there, and engage others to take me on to T'êng-yüeh, I sent on my servant post-haste to Yung-ch'ang to make the necessary arrangements in advance in order that I might not have to waste a day. Following him more leisurely, I left Shui Chai and rode along a winding road for about 6 miles to the summit of a pass from which we had a good view of a portion of the Yung-ch'ang plain. This range of hills separates the watershed of the Mekong from that of the much-dreaded Salwen. Soon after crossing the pass our road led us down the left side of a small mountain stream, and it was interesting to reflect that its waters were destined, like myself, for British territory. The first village on the west side of the pass was Niu Chio Kuan. It consisted of two huts in Baber's time, and though it has since then quintupled in size it is by no means an imposing centre of population. A mile further down the slope we reached Kuan P'o, a larger village, whence we descended to the edge of the Yung-ch'ang plain, and passed by the side of the village of Shih K'o Ts'un, which possesses a rather handsome and imposing temple, the Kuang Tsun Ssŭ.[1] I may note here that as one enters western Yunnan a tendency to over-decoration and ornateness in the architecture of temples is observable, but on the whole the effect is generally rather pleasing than otherwise, as carved and decorated doorways and fantastic gables often relieve the sordid meanness of the village dwelling-houses. No doubt the influence of non-Chinese races, akin to the Burmese or Shans, has been at work here.

The next village was Pan Ch'iao, a prosperous-looking place with a street of shops and many new buildings and ferocious dogs. One of the dogs, however, came to sorry grief in a conflict with my own bull-terrier, which—I will say it to his credit—seldom took the trouble to fight unless his antagonists were at least two in number. On leaving this village we were in full view of Yung-ch'ang city, with its curious pyramidal hill in the background. We entered by the north gate early in the afternoon. Within the city it almost seemed as though we were still traversing country roads, for we passed many wide open spaces, cultivated plots and a few isolated cottages, and the prickly pear was flourishing where one might have expected to find shops and paved streets. However, the whole city did not present this forlorn appearance, for a turning to the right

[1] 光尊寺.

brought us to a busy and populous quarter, and a further turn to the left led us into a lane in which inns abounded, showing that the city fostered a certain amount of trade.

I expected to find a fair assortment of foreign articles for sale here, but there were few. Tinned pineapples from a Chinese firm in Singapore, bearing a distinguished-looking label with the Royal Arms and the British lion, were to be bought for the equivalent of ninepence a tin; and "Finest Mineral Wax Candles, specially made for India," and sold by a well-known Rangoon firm, were also to be had for about one shilling per packet of five.

We have seen that the district of which Tali-fu is the centre, is the Carajan of Marco Polo. Its western limit appears to have been the Mekong river, and west of that was the old kingdom or state which Marco calls the Province of Zardandan. To its capital he gives the name of Vochan, and this city has been identified with Yung-ch'ang. This is the "Golden-Teeth" country, so named because the inhabitants were said to cover their teeth with thin movable plates of gold. Of this custom no vestige remains, and it is uncertain whether the people are represented by Shans or by some race connected with the Kachins. The inhabitants of the district were evidently regarded by the Chinese till quite modern times as an inferior race, for there is in the Chinese Penal Code a law to the effect that immigrant Chinese, visiting Yung-ch'ang for purposes of trade, must not ally themselves by marriage with the "outer barbarians" of that neighbourhood. The extraordinary practice known to us by the name (popularised by Tylor) of *Couvade* apparently existed in Yung-ch'ang in Marco Polo's time; and as he was doubtless unaware of its prevalence in many other parts of the world his testimony on the subject may be regarded as trustworthy. "And when one of their wives," says Marco, "has been delivered of a child, the infant is washed and swathed, and then the woman gets up and goes about her household affairs, whilst the husband takes to bed with the child by his side, and so keeps his bed for forty days; and all the kith and kin come to visit him, and keep up a great festivity. They do this because, say they, the woman has had a hard bout of it, and 'tis but fair the man should have his share of suffering."[1] Whether this explanation of the custom is the true one is perhaps open to doubt. It is hardly flattering to the kith and kin, who presumably did their best to relieve the man's monotony, and make matters as pleasant as the somewhat singular circumstances permitted.

The annals of Yung-ch'ang should prove of exceptional interest to the student of Chinese history, for they cannot but throw a flood of light on the relations between the various tribes and states that have striven for the mastery of western Yunnan and the great valleys of the Mekong and Salwen. Its first annexation to the Chinese empire may be assigned to the year

[1] Yule's *Marco Polo* (Cordier's edition), vol. ii. p. 85.

1277, when a great battle—vividly described by Marco Polo[1]—was fought in the Yung-ch'ang plain between the army of the Great Khan and the ambitious king of Mien, or Burma, the main strength of whose army consisted in a host of elephants. "Then might you see swashing blows dealt and taken from sword and mace; then might you see knights and horses and men-at-arms go down; then might you see arms and hands and legs and heads hewn off: and besides the dead that fell, many a wounded man, that never rose again, for the sore press there was. The din and uproar were so great from this side and from that, that God might have thundered and no man would have heard it! Great was the medley, and dire and parlous was the fight that was fought on both sides; but the Tartars had the best of it."

The population of Yung-ch'ang is still a very mixed one, but the Chinese language is spoken and understood by all classes, and the dialect differs little from that of the metropolitan province. The observant Marco Polo noticed among the people of Zardandan the prevalence of the custom of tatooing the body and legs: a custom which to this day is universal among the Shans and Burmese and allied races.

On arrival at my inn I found that all arrangements for the next stage of my journey had been duly made, and on the following morning I set out with two new riding mules—one for myself and one for my servant—and two baggage mules. The muleteers undertook to get us to T'êng-yüeh

[1] Yule's *Marco Polo* (Cordier's edition), vol. ii. pp. 98-104.

in five days, and kept their word. Our road led through the city past a temple dedicated to the God of Wealth and out of the south gate. I noticed the date "Kuang Hsü xxvi" (1900) on some of the bricks of the city wall, showing that a restoration had taken place recently. Unfortunately the authorities take no steps to prevent weeds and shrubs from growing in the interstices and on the parapet, and the roots must in course of time seriously affect the stability of the structure. Outside the gate we passed a Kuan Yin temple and went through a small suburb. The road then lay for about 4 miles southward over the plain and through the village of Wo Shih Wo (the "Sleeping Lion's Den"). The name is derived from a cave a few hundred yards above the village. The smell of the innumerable bats, not to mention the disquieting possibility of arousing the lion from his slumbers, would make the cave a disagreeable place to explore. The cave evidently penetrates some distance into the hill, though from the entrance it is difficult to say how far, as there is a turn to the left. It was very dark, and I did not venture far into the interior, as there was a steep slope made slippery by the constant dripping of water from the roof. The descent would have been easy enough—

> "Sed revocare gradum superasque evadere ad auras
> Hoc opus, hic labor est,"—

so I left the attempt to the next traveller.

From here the road wound steadily but not steeply up and over a range of hills, and brought us to the village of Hao Tzŭ P'u. We continued the ascent to the summit of a pass, and in the course of the corresponding descent reached the village of Lêng Shui Ching ("Cold Water Well"). Another 5 or 6 miles brought us down to a level plain and to our halting-place—the large village of P'u Piao. Here I found the accommodation bad, though it is a regular stage and there are several inns.

The next stage was a very short one, only about 7 miles, but it brought us to the edge of the "Valley of the Shadow of Death"—the chasm through which flows the Salwen—and my men would not dare to cross it unless they were quite fresh and had dosed themselves well with quinine. The road from P'u Piao offers no difficulties. The only villages we passed were several which bore the collective name of Fang Ma Ch'ang. Baber describes this place as being a ruined hamlet, but it has risen from its ashes since his day. Even as late as Baber's time this district was the scene of sanguinary strife between the imperial forces and a noted rebel chief. Baber actually saw the rebel camp on the hills opposite the road in the Fang Ma Ch'ang valley. No wonder he passed villages in ruins. Two miles further brought us to the end of our short stage—the miserable hamlet of Ta Pan Ching. A short distance behind it, on the slope of a wooded hill, is a small rock-temple. In it there are four sedent figures and two standing. A semicircular brick wall is built in front of them, so that their view, if they had eyes to see, would be distinctly circumscribed and lacking in variety. Just above the shrine, and nearly hidden by trees, is a picturesque little temple, and close by are a few graves.

Next morning, after dosing my men and myself with all the quinine that was likely to be good for us, I began the long winding descent into the valley of the Salwen, the Chinese name for which is the Lu Chiang or Lu Tzŭ Chiang.[1] I started on foot half an hour before my men, and did not see them until we all foregathered at the river. Soon after starting I came upon a stream of running water by the side of which was a tablet bearing a Chinese inscription to the effect that the water was dangerous to drink. Is it possible that the streams of this valley really contain some vegetable or mineral poison, and that it is from this fact that the valley derives its terrible reputation? The height of Ta Pan Ching above sea-level is 4,500 feet, while the bed of the Salwen lies at about 2,400; the actual descent was therefore 2,100 feet. It is not very steep, for the Salwen valley at this point is very much broader than that of the Mekong in the same latitude. After an easy and pleasant walk I reached the suspension bridge feeling quite as free from sickness as when I started.

I can offer no plausible theory to account for the traditional unhealthiness of the Salwen valley. To all appearance its verdant hills and broad slopes ought to be covered with cultivation and with the homes of thousands of industrious farmers. As it is, not a soul lives in the whole of that splendid

[1] 潞子江.

stretch of country except a few despised Shan or Pa I tribesmen, who are apparently the only people who can dwell there and thrive. Most travellers dash across as if they were flying for their lives,[1] and consider themselves fortunate if they are not struck down before they reach the heights overlooking the further side of the valley. Baber's account of its terrors, as they were described to him, is well worth quoting. "The morrow's journey would lead us across the Salwen — a river, to the native mind, teeming with portent and mystery. In western Yunnan this river is always spoken of with a certain awe. Governor Ts'ên himself had warned us to cross its valley with all haste. Often had we been told of the many varieties of malarious exhalations which shroud the hollow after sunrise: fogs, red, yellow and blue, of which the red is the most deadly and the blue next in the scale of mortality. General Thunder, who had never previously crossed, came to notify to us that he had determined to start before daylight, so as to get well beyond the river before the sun was up. Luckily for us, he said, the deadly flood was now spanned by a suspension bridge, but before its construction travellers had to pass in boats. In those days a gruesome monster, resembling in shape a huge blanket, would issue from the depths, and, wrapping passengers and

[1] This is especially the case with the Chinese who come from a long distance, and only know the Salwen by hearsay. My men (who belonged to Yung-ch'ang) treated the valley with a disrespect that was perhaps bred of familiarity, for they certainly did not unduly hurry themselves.

boat in his fœtid folds, would sink back into his native abyss."[1]

How far back these superstitions may be traced is difficult to say. Certainly in Marco Polo's time, in the thirteenth century, they were widely current; for, though he himself obviously did not cross the valley, he describes the whole region as "full of great woods and mountains which 'tis impossible to pass, the air in summer is so impure and bad; and any foreigners attempting it would die for certain." That travellers descending from the high Yunnan plateau into a steamy valley only 2,400 feet above sea-level may be seriously inconvenienced by the sudden change of temperature,[2] and perhaps become liable to attacks of fever, is not improbable; but as none of my own party succumbed to sickness, I am inclined to think that the Salwen has been unjustly maligned. My friend the Peking *Times* correspondent has told us "there can be little doubt that the deadliness of the valley is a tradition rather than a reality." In view of Dr Morrison's well-known accuracy, I am content to accept his opinion as the true one, more especially as it coincides with my own. Being a man of scientific and medical skill he would surely have sought out and annihilated Baber's blanket-fiend if it had existed.

[1] Royal Geographical Society's *Supplementary Papers*, vol. i. pp. 176-177.

[2] At Ta Pan Ching (4,500 feet) the shade temperature immediately after sunrise was 67° : in the temple at the Salwen bridge (2,400 feet) it was only 81° at midday. So even the change of temperature was not very serious.

After crossing the suspension bridge, which is similar in construction to those already noticed but is in two sections, I came to a small Pa I hamlet and a temple. Being in no hurry, and anxious to give the noxious vapours of the valley every opportunity of doing their worst on me, I paid a long visit to the temple and waited about an hour for the arrival of my caravan. I was told that the indigenous inhabitants of the valley were gradually increasing in numbers and bringing more of the land under cultivation, and that they were ruled by a *t'u ssŭ* or tribal chief who dwelt on the right bank of the river at a place about 10 miles to the south. A path leads thither along the river-bank.

The upward climb on the west side of the valley was not arduous, and the mules made the ascent without much difficulty in spite of the fact that a very heavy shower of rain turned the road into a running stream. It was curious to watch the rain-storm in the shape of a dense grey cloud rushing southwards through the valley. On looking back towards the river, then a couple of thousand feet below us, we had a fine view of the silver waters of the Salwen sparkling in brilliant sunshine; in a moment they were hidden by a rolling mass of dark vapour, out of which arose a strange parti-coloured rainbow in which orange and blue-green predominated. Its perfect arch crossed the whole breadth of the river-bed where the valley was narrowest, spanning the river like a fairy bridge. In five minutes the storm rolled on and the rainbow faded away, leaving me with the impression that I had never seen anything more beautiful or more strange. The fancy occurred to me that it was perhaps some such natural phenomenon as this that gave rise to the tradition recorded by Baber about the tinted fogs that varied in deadliness according to their colour.

We were all in a very wet and draggled condition when we arrived at the wretched wattle-and-mud hamlet of Hu Mu Shu, after a climb of about 3,100 feet above the level of the river. When we started next morning it was still raining, and in half an hour the clothes that we had dried with difficulty were again wet through. Our path lay to a great extent through thick forest, and the dripping of the leaves was almost as troublesome as the rain itself. We had a steady climb of about 8 miles to the hamlet called Hsiang Po ("Elephant's Neck"), and a further climb of 1,500 feet to the summit of a pass 8,730 feet high. There is a wooden gateway at the top. From here the road descends for about a mile, then ascends again and undulates, and finally goes rather steeply down to the hamlet of T'ai P'ing, where we halted for our midday rest. Pheasants abound in this district, but the jungle is so thick that it is hardly possible to leave the pathway in search of game. Our host at T'ai P'ing possessed some valuable European articles in the shape of a glass oil-lamp and two empty claret bottles probably left behind by some traveller more amply provided than myself with good things. The descent to the Shweli or Lung River was a steep and slippery ride in the course of which we descended about 8,500 feet. The river is crossed by a suspension bridge of the usual type. A mile or two further on we came to the village of Kan-lan-chan, where we spent the night in a very dirty inn.

Next day's stage presented no features of special interest. Early in the afternoon I descended to the T'êng-yüeh plain, which is studded with more or less prosperous villages, and soon caught sight of the semi-European buildings of the Chinese Imperial Customs and —more welcome still—the Union Jack floating over the gates of the British Consulate. There I was most hospitably received and entertained by Mr Ottewell, Acting British Consul, and enjoyed a two days' rest.

T'êng-yüeh is to be the terminus of the proposed British railway from Bhamo, regarding which negotiations have been in progress for some considerable time. That the trade between Burma and China by this route requires some stimulus is unquestionable. The officials in charge of the T'êng-yüeh Customs informed me that the volume of trade annually passing through their hands was not showing any elasticity, and that the Customs revenue barely served to defray the expenses of the establishment. Whether the railway will stimulate the trade to any very great extent is questionable; for caravans bound for Burma have already surmounted all serious obstacles, in the shape of mountain and flood, by the time they have reached

T'êng-yüeh, so that as far as they are concerned a railway would merely shorten by a few days a journey which already might have lasted months. Local traffic between the two termini will probably be found fairly remunerative, though very large returns can hardly be expected. If the railway could be carried on to Tali-fu, its ultimate success would be a certainty; but the engineering difficulties are very great, and the amount of capital required for construction would be enormous. From Tali-fu several branch lines might be constructed, one going south to the Kunlon ferry (a route which has already been surveyed) to meet the existing British line from Mandalay to Lashio, and another going north to Li-chiang. The main line should, of course, be carried eastwards to Yunnan-fu, which will very soon be in railway communication with French Indo-China and the port of Haiphong. The branch line from Tali-fu to Li-chiang—following the route traversed by myself[1] —would meet with no great difficulties, and would pass through a series of rich and populous valleys. Even if Li-chiang were a terminus it is probable that the local traffic would amply justify such a railway; though it would be better still if further branches could be carried on to Wei-hsi in the west, in order to intercept the Tibetan trade, and to Hui-li-chou or Ning-yüan-fu on the east, to tap the trade of the Chien-ch'ang valley, which might eventually include a great deal of the foreign trade of Ssuch'uan. It must be admitted that all these lines—with the exception of the branch from Tali

[1] Or the alternative route through the valley of Ho Ch'ing.

to Li-chiang—would be very costly to construct and to keep in repair. Meanwhile British enterprise seems content to restrict itself to the short line between Bhamo and T'êng-yüeh. This railway will doubtless fully justify its existence, but it is absurd to suppose that such a line will seriously compete with the French lines in the east of the province, or will have any appreciable effect in deflecting the trade of Yunnan from Tongking to Burma.[1]

At T'êng-yüeh I paid off the Tibetan servant who had accompanied me from Tachienlu, and the muleteers who had come from Yung-ch'ang, and engaged new mules and coolies to take me to Bhamo. I resumed my journey on 8th June. The path soon leaves the plain and mounts through extensive graveyards and over barren hills. Later in the day we descended, gradually but steadily, to a valley, narrow, but very extensively cultivated with rice and dotted with many villages. In many cases the recent rains had caused the inundated rice-fields to overflow into the road, which was often quite submerged. I lunched at the small village of Jê Shui T'ang, which, as its name implies, possesses a natural hot spring. We had now left the Yunnan plateau behind us, and had descended to the plains that slope gradually downwards towards the Irrawaddy. For the rest of the way to Burma I found that the vast majority of the population were Shans and

[1] Those interested in the railway question should consult Major Ryder's paper in the *Geographical Journal* for February 1903 (vol. xxi.) and Major Davies's remarks thereon.

Kachins, whose picturesque dresses are a pleasant contrast to the drab-coloured garments that generally content the less æsthetic Chinese. The women are remarkable for their headgear, which is similar to that worn by the isolated Shans whom I had seen in the Salwen valley. It consists of a tall dark turban that looks like a kind of antediluvian gentleman's top-hat that has been cruelly sat upon. Unfortunately the Shans, both men and women, are much given to disfiguring their mouths by chewing betel-nut—a disagreeable habit of an otherwise charming people. The drinking-water in this part of the country—as is generally the case in a land of padi-fields—must be used with great caution. I passed a clear flowing stream, by the side of which was the notification, *t'zŭ shui yu tu* ("This water is poisonous") —a warning which must be disconcerting to a thirsty wayfarer.

We spent the night of our first day from T'êng-yüeh in a roomy temple in the large village of Nan Tien. The next day was uneventful. We traversed execrable roads. Often it was difficult to know whether we were on the path or in a padi-field, for both were inundated, and we spent the greater part of the day in wading through a series of shallow and very muddy lakes. We spent the second night in the market village of Kau Ngai, and the third in Hsiao Hsin Kai ("Little Bhamo"). The purely Shan villages were generally enclosed within fences, and we did not see much of them; but I noticed that the native houses in the Chinese Shan States are less picturesque, and also apparently less clean and commodious than those of the Lao-Shans in the French Shan States and Siam. On 11th June the swollen rivers caused us even greater trouble than the flooded rice-fields, and at one point I feared we should have to wait till the waters subsided. Between the villages of Hsiao Hsin Kai and Lung Chang Kai we came to a river which, though doubtless an insignificant brook in dry weather, was then a swift and muddy river about 60 yards broad. There was nothing in the way of boat, bridge or ford, and our mules, with all the obstinacy of their kind, for a long time refused to leave the bank. Finally, my two baggage animals were relieved of their burdens, which were carried across in separate light loads on the heads of coolies. The latter were stripped to the skin, for the water was almost high enough to take them off their feet. One of them lost his footing, and let his load fall into the water; it was recovered, but most unfortunately it contained some rolls of exposed photographic films. The comparatively poor results of my journey from the photographic point of view — for dozens of films were utterly ruined—are largely due to that unhappy accident. The fact that I had so nearly reached my journey's end and had so far escaped any such mishap rendered it all the more vexatious. I crossed the river without any disaster to myself, but the drenching to which I was unavoidably subjected gave me an attack of fever, which was not shaken off for several days. It is not so easy to get rid of colds and fevers in the steamy tropical valleys of the Shan States as it is in the exhilarating climate of the Tibetan mountains. The latter part of the same day's journey (the fourth stage from T'êng-yüeh) was unexpectedly easy. I suddenly found myself on a good broad road, unmetalled, but well engineered. I followed this road the whole way to Bhamo, and it was not until my arrival there that I was given an explanation of so unusual a phenomenon as a carriage road in Chinese territory. It was the work of British engineers, and had been undertaken by the Government of Burma at the request and at the expense of the Government of Yunnan. The provincial funds have not yet permitted of the extension of the road to T'êng-yüeh, but it is to be hoped, for the sake of future travellers, and in the interests of trade, that something will be done to carry it over the rain-sodden plains. When we struck the British-made road we were about 70 or 80 miles from Bhamo, and between 20 and 30 from the British frontier. At 15 miles from the frontier we halted for the night in the village of Man-hsien, which is the administrative centre of a Chinese-Shan chief or sawbwa.[1] It is only a hamlet consisting of about thirty flimsy bamboo huts, several of which were shops for the sale of local produce.

On 12th June my day's journey began in Chinese and ended in British territory. Being too impatient to wait for my muleteers—who showed no emotion at the proximity of the British

[1] So called by the Burmese. The Shan word is *Sao-p'a*, which is the designation of a tribal chief or prince.

flag—I started on foot and walked the whole of the 15 miles to the frontier. There was a heavy shower in the early morning, but the sky soon cleared up, and for the rest of the day the fierce rays of a tropical sun beat upon me with all their strength, and taxed all the resisting power of the shilling umbrella I had bought at San Ying. The gradient of the road was excellent throughout, but being unmetalled it had been much damaged by the recent rains. In many places it was entirely blocked by landslips; at others it had been torn away by mountain floods. It was bordered by dense jungle on both sides. On the left, luxuriant vegetation covered the steep slope of a mountain; on the right was an abrupt descent into a ravine, in which one could hear but seldom see the roaring torrent below. In some places the landslips had brought down large trees, which lay across the road. My mules, I heard afterwards, had great difficulty in surmounting these various obstacles, and in some cases were forced to trample out a new road for themselves in the jungle. The road, good as it was, seemed to me a "fair-weather" road. There was a lack of bridges. Streams that might be non-existent in the dry season were then rushing over the road, wearing deep channels in its surface, or tearing it away altogether. There was also a lack of storm-water drains. These would at least do a little to prevent the torrential summer rains from making havoc of the roadway. Further, the wooded slopes adjacent to the road have not been sufficiently strengthened, and, under present conditions, serious landslips are bound to occur every year. Only an engineer has any right to speak with authority on such matters, but one may perhaps hazard the suggestion that the cemented roads of Hongkong, with their admirable and elaborate storm-drainage system, might with advantage be copied in Upper Burma in places where the roads are specially liable to landslips or floods. Probably, however, the great cost of such roadways would be prohibitive in a country which is, after all, thinly populated, and where there is little traffic.

In referring to the lack of bridges I must not forget the admirable iron bridge at Kamsa, 4 miles west of Man-hsien in Chinese territory. It spans a torrent which descends in a series of dazzling cascades. The highest of these, visible from the bridge, is a really fine waterfall, which would attract crowds of sightseers if it were in a more accessible country. The bridge is quite new, having been completed only in April 1905. Had it not existed, I should have found myself in a serious dilemma. The stream that flowed below it was a boiling torrent which neither man nor horse could ford or swim, and its course, above and below, was hidden by impenetrable jungle.

At the bottom of a narrow ravine 15 miles from Man-hsien there is a brook spanned by a log of wood. I saw no inscribed pillar, and no flags, nor was I challenged by any lynx-eyed Indian sentry; but this is the spot at which two great Empires meet. On the Chinese side were a few Shan huts, known collectively as Kulika. After climbing out of the ravine on the western side, I found the first evidence of British occupation: two small wooden bungalows surrounded by servants' sheds and outhouses. They were all empty and deserted, though some Shan pedlars were peacefully enjoying their midday slumber on one of the verandahs. The bungalows had probably been used by engineers and surveyors, but evidently they had not been occupied for some time. I took temporary possession of the one not selected by the Shans, and awaited there the arrival of my caravan.

After a meagre tiffin I again set off on foot amid enchanting tropical scenery. The views were not extensive, for the road lay through a gorge covered with thick jungle. Several hundred feet below the road I occasionally caught sight of the foaming waters of the T'ai P'ing rushing tempestuously through its confined bed. From a wide, majestic and apparently navigable river—for such it was while it flowed through the plains I had lately been traversing—it had become a series of boiling rapids noisily protesting against their confinement within so narrow a channel. Eight miles beyond the frontier I was not sorry to come within sight of the end of my long day's walk—the first of the trim little Public Works Bungalows[1] which a considerate Government has established at convenient distances along the main roads of Upper Burma for the use of officials and travellers. Here I was welcomed by a Kachin damsel, who, in the absence of the regular bungalow keeper, addressed to me soothing words which, I felt sure, must be meant to be words

[1] The name of the bungalow is Mong-kung-ka.

of welcome; and I made haste to interpret them as such. A walk of 23 miles at the hottest season of the year in a tropical country is not a task to be lightly undertaken every day; and when allowance is made for the manner in which I had lived for the past few months, in a country where European comforts are unknown, I may perhaps be pardoned for having given way to feelings of exultation at finding myself in a bungalow furnished—as it seemed to me—with the utmost luxury. A clean table-cloth, knives and forks and glass tumblers, long easy-chairs, a four-poster bed with mosquito curtains, and, above all, a bath, were things of beauty and wonder that seemed almost too good to be true.

My expedition from Weihaiwei to the frontier of Burma had occupied five months and six days. I had travelled from the most easterly prefecture in China (Têng-chou) to the most westerly (Yung-ch'ang); from the extreme north-east to the extreme south-west of China; over the loftiest passes in the empire, and through seven of its provinces. I had also traversed most of China's greatest rivers—the Yellow River, Yangtse, Min, Ya, Ta Tu, Yalung, Mekong, Salwen and Shweli. As to my condition at the end of this long and solitary journey, during the greater part of which I had partaken of the same coarse and frugal fare as my coolies and muleteers, I need only say that apart from a short attack of fever in the Shan plains beyond T'êng-yüeh I never had a day's sickness.

At the bungalow of Mong-kung-ka I was still some distance from Bhamo. At the earnest request of my guides, whose mules were exhausted, I spent three days in traversing the remaining 43 miles. On 13th June I halted at the bungalow of Kulong-ka, 30 miles from Bhamo. Next day, at the eighteenth milestone from Bhamo, I found myself on a metalled carriage road, as good as a first-rate country road in England, and followed it to the bungalow at Momauk, a small village inhabited by Shans and Kachins. On the 15th I left Momauk before 6 A.M., hoping to reach the travellers' Dâk bungalow at Bhamo, only 9 miles distant, without having to meet the critical eyes of the European residents. The very slender outfit with which I had started from Weihaiwei had long since disappeared. Peking furs and sheep-skin boots had served me well on the Tibetan mountains, but were hardly suitable for a tropical climate: and what remained of them I had given away to my followers at Tali-fu. Other garments had gradually fallen to pieces, and had been discarded one by one. I was now wearing Chinese straw sandals without socks, an old khaki suit patched with most inappropriate coarse blue cloth, and held together with string instead of buttons, and a huge, wide-flapping straw hat such as forms the headgear of Chinese Shans when working in the fields. The animal on which I had ridden from T'êng-yüeh was a shaggy Yunnanese pony. The saddle, which I had bought in Tachienlu, was of the kind generally used by the natives of eastern Tibet, with a high pommel tipped with metal, and a hard wooden seat covered with tightly-stretched yak leather. The stirrups were iron plates something like flat saucers, and the bridle was of rope and twisted bamboo. I had no desire to be thrust into the deputy-commissioner's dungeons on suspicion of being a head-hunting Wa, or an untamed Kachin, yet it was rash to expect any more hospitable reception in my present condition. My hopes of evading detection until I had emerged a new man from the shops of the shoemakers and tailors of Bhamo were doomed to disappointment. I covered the nine miles at my pony's quickest trot, and the houses of Bhamo were already in sight, when suddenly arose in front of me an ominous cloud of dust. A glint of sunshine shone on a brilliant array of polished arms, and quickly out of the dust advanced a body of Indian troops. The pleasure with which I should have welcomed the sight of a British mountain-battery and the sound of the tramp of the king-emperor's soldiers was damped by my painful knowledge of the ridiculous figure I must have presented. I hastily urged my pony into a friendly ditch while the detachment passed by, but I could not, unfortunately, escape the "stony British stare" of the commanding-officer. Half a mile further on, on entering the town, I met a solitary European on horseback, who in answer to my timid query kindly directed me to the Dâk bungalow. Half an hour afterwards I was arraying myself in ready-made garments of varying degrees of misfit in that admirable establishment well known to all residents in Upper Burma as "Kohn's."

CHAPTER XVII

BHAMO TO MANDALAY

A FEW years ago Bhamo was regarded by Europeans as far out of the reach of the ordinary traveller, and beyond the uttermost limits of what to the complacent Western mind constitutes civilisation. Since our soldiers took "the road to Mandalay" and ended an almost bloodless campaign in 1885[1] by annexing Upper Burma and deporting its misguided monarch, the little north-eastern frontier-town of Bhamo has entered upon a new phase of its somewhat dramatic history. It is now a considerable *entrepôt* of trade, and is bound to derive the full benefit of any future increase of overland commerce between China and Burma. It is therefore full of representatives of all the races of south-eastern Asia who meet there to exchange their varied goods. There is also a garrison, generally consisting of Indian troops, but sometimes of a British regiment as well; and their duty it is not only to watch the Chinese frontier—an easy task nowadays—but also to keep an eye on the wild Kachins and other lawless tribes of north-eastern Burma where there is still a

[1] The years of dacoit-hunting that followed were, unfortunately, far from bloodless; and it was during those years that the Burman learned to respect the British soldier.

vast tract of country "unadministered"—that is not yet brought under the direct control of the British Government. There is therefore a considerable English colony consisting of officers of the army and of the military police and a few civil officials. Of the latter, the chief is the deputy-commissioner. Like all members of the great service to which he belongs, he is a man who plays many parts and fulfils many functions. He it is who, in the eyes of the subject peoples, represents the imperial power of Great Britain. The "uncovenanted" service is represented by officers of the Public Works and Forestry, and other departments of government. That Bhamo is no longer a barbarous place outside the pale of civilisation is finally proved by the fact that it is now the residence of several English ladies who apparently find life not only supportable but even pleasant.

"There is a wonderful mixture of types in Bhamo. Nowhere in the world . . . is there a greater intermingling of races. Here live in cheerful promiscuity Britishers and Chinese, Shans and Kachins, Sikhs and Madrasis, Punjabis, Arabs, German Jews and French adventurers, American missionaries, and Japanese ladies." Such is the concise summing-up of Dr Morrison; and I may add that I found Bhamo much the same as it was when he visited it in 1894 except that the French adventurers and the Japanese ladies appeared to have fled to other pastures. But in another of his remarks I must confess I am unable to concur. "At its best," he says, "Bhamo is a forlorn, miserable and wretched station, where all men seem to regard it as their first duty to the stranger to apologise to him for being there." No such apologies were made to me; and if they had, I should have suspected that the apologist was taking an unnecessarily gloomy view of his surroundings. There are certainly many worse places in the East than Bhamo. It is within easy reach of Mandalay and Rangoon by steamer and train, and is therefore by no means so isolated as its position on the map might lead one to suppose. Its neighbourhood is picturesque; it has clubs and lawn-tennis courts; roads are good; there are many open spaces suitable for polo and the other games that the exiled Englishman loves, and its European houses are roomy bungalows surrounded by delightful gardens full of the glories of tropical vegetation. For part of the year the climate is no doubt trying. The town lies on the banks of the Irrawaddy, and is less than 400 feet above the sea-level. Before the rains break in early summer the temperature sometimes goes up to 100° Fahr. It was over 90° in the shade during the few days that I resided there. But that is cool compared with Mandalay, where the heat, at the end of the dry season, is sometimes excessive. I was told in Bhamo that the temperature at Mandalay about three weeks earlier was no less than 115° in the shade in the afternoon. But the dryness of the atmosphere both at Bhamo and Mandalay during the spring and early summer saves European constitutions from the disastrous results of a high temperature in a damp climate. The summer climate of Hongkong, where the thermometer rarely rises much above 90°, is on account of its excessive dampness far more trying than that of any part of Upper Burma.[1]

I remained at Bhamo from the 15th to the 18th June, during which time I was treated with the greatest hospitality by various local residents. On the morning of the 18th I started for Mandalay on one of the fine steamers belonging to the Irrawaddy Flotilla Company, and spent the next two days in a complete idleness, which, after months of arduous travelling, I found thoroughly enjoyable. The scenery of this part of the Irrawaddy is not as a rule very striking compared with the magnificence of some of the Chinese rivers, but its placid waters and the rich vegetation of its banks have a tranquil beauty of their own which is quite unique. Perhaps one of the most striking facts about Upper Burma is that it is one of the few countries where the works of human hands—native hands, at least—have not spoiled nature's own loveliness. A Chinese village is seldom a thing of beauty, except as viewed from a distance:[2] a Burmese village, on the contrary, hardly ever mars, and very often accentuates, the simple beauty of its surroundings. The houses—built of wood and bamboo—look as if they had grown out, and were still an integral part, of the virgin forest from which their materials have all been drawn. Like the statue which, according to the old Greek fancy, lay hidden in the shapeless block of marble until the artist's chisel released it

[1] The latitude of Hongkong is almost exactly the same as that of Mandalay and Calcutta.

[2] Some villages in Ssuch'uan may be said to be an honourable exception.

from its prison, so the Burmese village—as one might dream—was never created by the hand of man, but only lay buried in the primeval forest until the hour when the woodman's axe pruned the luxuriance of the jungle growths. Such, at least, was the impression that came to me as the throbbing steam-boat glided rapidly in the silver morning haze through the noiseless waters of the great river of Burma. A nearer acquaintance with the villages—for we often stopped to embark cargo or to land passengers—hardly convinced me that my dream was an idle one: for the finely-carved teakwood monasteries and the shining pagodas with their gilded summits, and, above all, the graceful figures and merry faces and tasteful dresses of the people themselves, all tended to intensify my first impressions. The sites of the stupas or pagodas are always singularly well chosen.[1] It is sad to reflect that some of the beauty of the Burmese riverside villages is gradually passing away in obedience to the dismal Western law of progress. The danger of fire and considerations of economy, coupled, I fear, with the partial decay of the exquisite taste which was once the Burman's birth-right, has brought about the introduction of new methods of building and foreign architectural designs. Most incongruous of all are the corrugated-iron roofs. Can the poor Burman be supplied with no roofing material less hideous? The Burmese are wise enough to retain their own national costume,

[1] "Est-ce la colline qui a été façonée pour la pagode, est-ce la pagode qui a choisi la colline, si bien faites l'une pour l'autre, ravissantes d'ensemble? Qu'elle est jolie, cette réflexion blanche, tombant de haut dans le cristal de l'eau!"—*Birmanie*, par Mme. Quenedey, p. 218.

a matter for which one should feel grateful; but the adoption of cheap black European umbrellas is almost as serious a lapse from good taste as the use of iron roofing, and is apparently recognised as such by the authorities. When the Prince of Wales was recently in Mandalay he was entertained by the Lieutenant-Governor at a water carnival. It took place on the waters of the moat close to the walls of Fort Dufferin—the old royal city — and such parts of the grounds as were open to the public were crowded with Burmese sightseers, dressed in their finest silks. The show of colour was unfortunately marred by enormous numbers of black umbrellas, used as sunshades. As a Burmese crowd (without umbrellas) is one of the most charming sights to be seen in Burma or anywhere else and was therefore well worthy of a prince's gaze, messengers were hurriedly despatched to inform the smiling crowd that in the presence of British royalty umbrellas must come down. The order was of course obeyed without a murmur, and the Prince of Wales had the pleasure of beholding in Mandalay a more brilliant and picturesque assemblage of his future subjects than he is ever likely to behold in the empire's capital.

The most striking scenery on the Irrawaddy below Bhamo is undoubtedly to be found in what is known as the Second Defile.[1] The river at this point flows through a comparatively narrow channel in a gorge which is overlooked by a great cliff

[1] The first is above Bhamo, where, owing to the dangers to navigation, steamers have temporarily ceased to run.

about 800 feet high. A few years ago I spent many happy days in a canoe, floating down the beautiful Nam-U,[1] from Muang Wa to Luang Prabang. A short distance above the mouth of the river, where it joins the Mekong, there is a stupendous limestone precipice—how lofty I should not dare to guess—which rises sheer out of the water on the right bank. In situation and appearance it is similar to the cliff in the Second Defile of the Irrawaddy, yet, if I can trust my own recollection, the Nam-U precipice is the loftier and more magnificent. As, however, the wild beauty of the Nam-U has never ceased to be a waking dream ever since I shot its rapids in my little canoe, and camped on its banks night by night at the edge of its silent and trackless jungles, it may be that its most striking features tend in my own mind to loom larger than the reality. In any case the Irrawaddy, too, can furnish food for lifelong dreams of beauty.

Having left Bhamo on 18th June I reached Mandalay on the morning of the 20th. Here—for the purposes of this book at least—I may regard my journey as at an end. In travelling overland from the capital of China to the old capital of Burma, I had carried out the pleasant task which I had set myself when I started from Weihaiwei almost half a year before. It were

[1] A large river of French Laos or the trans-Mekong Shan States. It is navigable only for canoes of the most primitive description, for it is full of dangerous rapids. It enters the Mekong a few miles above Luang Prabang. The scenery of this river, which I descended from its highest navigable point (Muang Wa) to its mouth, is exceptionally beautiful.

fitting, perhaps, that I should close this imperfect account of my journey with a description of the marvels of Mandalay; but I must decline a task for which no casual visitor can or should regard himself qualified. A week's residence in Mandalay is not sufficient to justify any one except the globe-trotter—for whom two days and a night may be sufficient—in attempting a description of one of the most curious and wonderful of the modern cities of Asia. In the palace grounds I was shown the magnificent monument which was erected to the memory of king Mindon,[1] father of the ex-king Thibaw. I was told that in a recent book about Burma, written by one who was too much pressed for time to sift his facts, there is a fine photograph of this monument which is described as "the tomb of king Mindon's favourite Terrier." There is a moral in this little story which we tourists would do well to take to heart.

Next to the numerous palace buildings with their gilded throne-rooms—no longer, thanks to Lord Curzon, used as a European club—the most interesting sights are outside the walls of the royal city. No student of Buddhism will omit to visit that wonderful collection of miniature temples known as the Kutho-daw, which contains the whole of the Buddhist Pali canon—a collection of sacred writings at least five times as long, be it remembered, as the whole of the Christian

[1] The founder of Mandalay, and second last king of Burma. He reigned from 1852 to 1878, and was succeeded by his son Thibaw, who reigned until his deposition by the British Government in 1885.

Bible—carved on nearly a thousand slabs of white marble. Each slab stands upright in a small pagoda and is fully exposed to view, though sheltered from the weather. The pagodas are about seven hundred in number, and are arranged in symmetrical order side by side, the whole forming a great square with a temple in the centre. This wonderful work was carried out by Mindon Min in 1857, simply as an act of religious devotion.[1] The other pagodas of Mandalay and its neighbourhood are very numerous, and each possesses interesting features of its own. The finest is perhaps the Maha Myatmuni, generally known as the Arakan Pagoda. It contains a fine brazen colossal image of the Buddha, nearly twelve feet high, in a sitting posture. Its peculiar sanctity is derived from the tradition that it was copied from life and is therefore a true image of the Buddha as he really was. In mediæval times wars were waged between several of the kings of Burma and Indo-China in order to settle the disputed right of its possession. I was surprised to find that religious scruples have not prevented the introduction of electric light into this temple; but the effect is far from displeasing. The lights in the recess containing the famous Buddha are so arranged that, while they strongly illuminate the image itself, the neighbouring parts of the pagoda, where I saw many girl-worshippers devoutly kneeling, are in deep gloom.

Starting from Mandalay as a centre I paid

[1] There is an interesting essay by Max Müller on the Kutho-daw in his *Last Essays* (Second Series).

several visits to other parts of Burma, where I remained altogether about six weeks. Among other places I visited Lashio, only a few days' journey by road from the Salwen at the Kunlon Ferry, and the furthest point yet attained by the railway. There I spent a few days as the guest of the Superintendent of the North Shan States.[1] At Maymyo, the charming European hill-station, I was kindly entertained by Sir Herbert White, K.C.I.E., Lieutenant-Governor of Burma, and later on was also his guest at Government House, Mandalay. Maymyo is only about four hours distant from Mandalay by train, but during that short distance the railway climbs a height of over 3,000 feet. Between Maymyo and Lashio I broke my journey for a couple of days, and, under the auspices of Mr D. G. Robertson, the British Adviser, I had the pleasure of meeting the reigning chief or sawbwa of the important Shan State of Hsi-paw. I had hoped to spend some weeks or months in the trans-Salwen portion of the province, for the purpose of studying something of the languages and customs of the numberless tribes that inhabit that fascinating and little-known country, and comparing them with what I knew of the allied tribes in French Laos, and those through whose territory I had recently passed in Chinese territory. As travelling in the Shan States is, however, practically impossible during the rains, I was obliged indefinitely to postpone the fulfilment of that part of my programme. As I hoped to return to the Shan States later on,

[1] Mr G. C. B. Stirling.

I commenced the study of the language and hired a Shan servant to accompany me during the remainder of my stay in Burma.

My next objective was the old capital of Pagan, on the left bank of the Irrawaddy, below Mandalay. I spent three days there, exploring the wonderful ruins of innumerable pagodas and monasteries which are all that remain of a city that was once not only the capital of a powerful kingdom but also one of the leading centres of learning and religion in south-eastern Asia. The secular buildings have nearly all disappeared, but the remaining ruins possess many features of the greatest interest to archæologists. I could trace no sign of Chinese influence in the architecture and decoration of this dead and vanishing city, though it is alleged—on doubtful authority—that the conquering Chinese arms did once at least penetrate as far as Pagan. Here, as elsewhere in Burma, the Chinese invasions do not appear to have left any lasting results or to have affected in any way the art of the country.[1]

Leaving Pagan I continued my journey down the Irrawaddy, and reached Rangoon on 15th July.

The conviction that a tour through Burma must leave in the minds of most Europeans is that the country is to be congratulated on its people and that the people are to be equally congratulated on their country. That Burma itself is one of the fairest of lands, every traveller can see for himself; and so far as I could judge from my

[1] See Note 45 (p. 440).

VIEW AT PAGAN, IRRAWADDY RIVER, BURMA.

[To face p. 332.

own short experience and from what was told me by sympathetic British residents, the Burmese are perhaps the most cheerful, generous and hospitable, and on the whole the most attractive people in Asia. But one very commonly hears them also characterised as frivolous, incorrigibly lazy, thriftless, superstitious, untruthful, and lacking in courage and tenacity of purpose. Many European travellers and others have come to the conclusion that these sad deficiencies in the Burman's character are gradually bringing about the ruin and extinction of his race. They point to the fact that the population of Rangoon is far less than half Burman; that Chetty money-lenders, cooks and labourers from Madras, and Chinese merchants and shopkeepers, are gradually monopolising the industry of the country, while the Burman looks on with apathy at his own displacement from the fields, kitchens, shops and counting-houses in which his Indian and Chinese rivals wax rich and fat. In many European houses—perhaps in Lower Burma the great majority—there is not a single Burman servant, all the duties of cook, coolie, table-servant and valet being discharged by suave, noiseless and obedient natives of India. The only people who seem to be able to attract Burmese servants, and keep them for any length of time, are members of the Civil Service, who, with their knowledge of the language and familiarity with the national customs and ideals, are better able than any other aliens to sympathise with the Burman in his joys and sorrows, his likes and dislikes, and to understand something of his point of view. They make good masters, and earn their reward in retaining the services of loyal and attached Burmese servants. Of course there are many non-official Europeans who, with the instincts of gentlemen, treat their dependents quite as well and sympathetically as any one; while among the civil servants there are no doubt many who from the beginning to the end of their career in Burma never shake off the feeling of antipathy to the Oriental—coupled, probably, with a strong sense of racial superiority—which they had when they first came out to the East. But these exceptional cases only prove the rule; and it is strong testimony to the intrinsic worth of the Burman's character that the more thoroughly he is understood the more he is liked by those best qualified to judge. The versatile traveller who "does Burma" in the course of his round-the-world tour, and fills a notebook with comments on the character of the Burmese as a result of what he hears at the dinner-tables of Rangoon, would do well to exercise caution before he gives his notebook to the world. Do not some of us in China well know how prone the tourist is to echo the too-often ignorant and one-sided views about the Chinese that he may have heard expressed in the clubs and drawing-rooms of Hongkong and Shanghai? It seems that the situation in Burma is not dissimilar.

I should be courting a well-deserved retort if I were now to attempt, in a few irresponsible pages, a complete character-sketch of the Burman as he appeared to me during my too-brief sojourn in his beautiful country. Instead of doing so I will content myself with recommending the reader who is interested in Burma but cannot visit it to read and read again the books that have been written by such well-informed and sympathetic writers as Sir George Scott, Mr Fielding Hall and Mr Scott O'Connor. It is satisfactory to know from one of these writers that the Burmese are by no means likely to be crowded out of their own country by such vigorous workers as the Madrasis and Chinese. The immigration of these people enriches the Burman instead of impoverishing him. It enables him to withdraw from work which he cordially dislikes, and to devote himself to the tilling of his rice-fields, and to live the free life—and it is by no means an idle one—that he best loves. The Burmese are showing no signs of approaching extinction; on the contrary, they are multiplying with rapidity.[1] The Burmese, says Mr Fielding Hall, are "extremely prosperous now. There is less poverty, less sickness, less unhappiness than among any people I have seen East or West. If there ever was a people about whom pessimism sounded absurd, it is about the Burmese."[2] If there is, however, one characteristic of the Burman which appears to be beginning to show signs of decay—let us hope it is change rather than decay—it is his artistic sense. His art, like the art of India and Ceylon, is, it seems, becoming demoralised. But that is not due to the example or competition of any Oriental race; it is a result—be it said to our shame—of the English conquest.

[1] See Note 46 (p. 441). [2] *A People at School*, chap. xxiv.

As regards the common accusation that the Burman is untruthful, it appears to me that Mr Fielding Hall has effectually disposed of this in the book from which I have just quoted. He points out that because a Burman often lies to a European—whom he can hardly help regarding as an unsympathetic alien—that does not imply that he is a liar by nature. "Every man has many standards. He has one for his family, one for his friends, one for his own class, one for his own nation, and a last for all outsiders. No man considers a foreigner entitled to the same openness and truth from him as his own people. . . . The only way to estimate a people truly is to know how they treat each other, and how they estimate each other. . . . I should say, from what I have seen, that between Burman and Burman the standard of honesty and truth is very high. And between European and Burman it is very much what the European chooses to make it."[1] These remarks, I may add parenthetically, would apply with equal force to the relations between Europeans and Chinese.

The question of laziness and want of energy is a very interesting one, and is not so simple as it appears at first sight. Because the Burman is glad to leave the rough labour of coolies and the dreary duties of cooking foreign food and performing the routine work of house-servant to the Madrasi, and because he is seen smoking big cheroots and wearing silk clothes much too good to work in while his active wife carries

[1] *Op. cit.* chap. xxi.

on the business of the bazaar, the strenuous Englishman, who knows so well what incessant hard work has done in building up the greatness of his own nation, is at first inclined to regard him with scorn and impatience. Perhaps because I am conscious of a secret sympathy with a life of what I may call intelligent indolence, I am not disposed to execrate the Burman for a fault in which I am prone to share. But, as a matter of fact, the Burman is not so idle as he is believed to be. "Do not suppose," says the eloquent writer from whom I have quoted, "that the Burmese are idle. Such a nation of workers was never known. Every man works, every woman works, every child works. Life is not an easy thing, but a hard, and there is a great deal of work to be done. There is not an idle man or woman in all Burma."[1] In the face of a statement so emphatic as this, how is it that the vice of laziness is so often attributed to the Burman? The reason is not far to seek. The Burman lives in a rich country where the actual necessaries of life come easily. He may have to work hard at times, but he does not and need not labour from morning to night and day after day without intermission. He is content with little, for he is a frugal eater and, more often than not, a vegetarian. Money is of little value to him except to buy some of the novelties that are poured into Burma from English factories. No doubt the more he craves to possess these novelties, the harder he will have to work to get the money to pay for them: and

[1] Fielding Hall's *Soul of a People*, p. 125.

this is a fact that is already having a marked effect on the national habits. The Burman who has not become half-occidentalised does not aim at wealth for its own sake: he does not bow down and worship people who have money: Mammon has not yet secured a niche in his pantheon. He only wants enough to feed his relations and himself, to bring up his children in health and strength, and to clothe them with garments that are not only comfortable to wear but pleasant to the eye. If his fields produce more food than he needs, he sells the surplus, and spends the money in works of charity and religion and in graceful hospitalities. The consequence is that at certain seasons of the year—when harvests are over, for instance—he has many hours of what we might call idleness. He wants to live, as well as to be a mere machine for the manufacture of wealth.

The Burmese theory is one which many a robust and healthy-minded Englishman will absolutely reject, and perhaps it is as well that the Englishman should do so. There can be no progress, he will say, if men are only going to do sufficient work to bring them their daily food. To be strenuous and active, to be ready to face difficulties and strong enough to overcome them — these are the only ways to keep ourselves in the vanguard of progress and civilisation. But, after all, is there not a good deal to be said for the Burman's point of view, too? Are we quite sure that we always know what we mean when we speak of progress and civilisation? That there is a terribly sad and ugly side to the development of civilisation in Western countries—a sadness and ugliness chiefly noticeable in the great industrial centres—is a dreary fact which no Englishman is so likely to realise to the full as he who revisits his native country after a prolonged absence in the East. Even in the most squalid quarters of the most densely-populated cities in China I have never come across anything more painful and depressing than comes daily within the experience of those who, like East End missionaries, live in close proximity to the slums and poorer quarters of our great English cities. Unfortunately, the ugliness, if not the squalor, extends itself beyond the slums, though it assumes different forms among the middle and upper classes of our people. At the risk of having one's words stigmatised as cant and humbug, it is difficult to refrain from giving utterance to a feeling of wonder that so much of the energy and activity of the imperial British race should be devoted to social and political rivalries and the accumulation of material wealth, and that modern English life should be so strongly tainted with the vulgarity and brutality that come of sordid ideals. Make a Burman a millionaire: he will build pagodas, he will support monasteries, he will entertain his friends lavishly, he will exercise a graceful charity unheard of in the West,—and all these things he will go on doing until his money-bags are so empty that he can carry them on his back with a light heart. The process will not be a long one. Transport a hundred Burmans to work in an English workshop or factory: they will probably be all dead or mad in five years; or, what perhaps is worse, all the joy and buoyancy will have been crushed out of their souls for ever. This will not be on account of the hard work—they could work harder if necessary—but because of the mechanical nature of the labour, the long hours of sunless confinement, the deadly monotony, the wearisome routine. Englishmen consider themselves the apostles of liberty throughout the world. The Burman, if asked to give his candid opinion after a year's experience of English life, would probably say that the position of the vast majority of Englishmen was not much better than that of chained slaves.

The evils of our civilisation are perhaps less apparent to him who dwells in its midst than to him who observes it from afar, yet in England, too, there have been some sad-voiced prophets. The warnings of Ruskin, Carlyle and Froude, to mention few out of the many who have uttered oracles since the days when Sir Thomas More in his *Utopia* satirised the love of gold, seem to have fallen on ears that are deaf to every sound but the clink of coin upon coin. Even psychologists and metaphysicians[1] have condescended

[1] See, for instance, Mr R. B. Arnold's *Scientific Fact and Metaphysical Reality*, pp. 321-323. Professor William James, in his *Varieties of Religious Experience*, asks whether "the worship of material luxury and wealth, which constitutes so large a portion of the 'spirit' of our age" does not "make somewhat for effeminacy and unmanliness." He goes so far as to recommend, as a cure for some of our social diseases, the adoption of that form of asceticism which consisted in "the old monkish poverty-worship." Wealth-getting, he says, "enters as an ideal into the very bone and marrow of our generation." It is certain, he adds, that "the prevalent fear of poverty among the educated classes

to come into the arena of practical life to tell us plain truths about the falseness of our aims and the barbarities that we have masked with the forms of civilisation.

> "The world is too much with us; late and soon
> Getting and spending we lay waste our powers."

It is not commercialism and industrialism in themselves that are harmful: it is only too obvious that our national, or at least our imperial existence is dependent on our wealth, and that wealth can come only from flourishing industries and a world-wide commerce. The harm lies, as Wordsworth saw, in making wealth our deity instead of our servant, and "laying waste" the powers and faculties which are fit for nobler and higher

is the worst moral disease from which our civilisation suffers."—(Pp. 365-369.)

See also Professor W. R. Inge's *Personal Idealism and Mysticism*, especially pp. 175-176. I strongly recommend the reader who is interested in the pressing problems presented by the changing relations between the Occident and the Orient to read Dr Inge's book (especially Lectures IV. and VI.) in connection with Mr Percival Lowell's *Soul of the Far East*. Both are, as one would expect, able and well-written books, but they take diametrically opposite views of a very important question. Mr Lowell finds that the most notable characteristic of the East, and the secret of its fatal weakness, is what he calls its Impersonality, and that the peoples of the West, deriving an irresistible strength from the exact opposite—an intense Individualism—have nothing to fear from the impersonal civilisations of the East, which they will eventually overpower and crush. Dr Inge arrives independently at a similar belief as to the remarkable absence of individualism in the East, but so far from adopting Mr Lowell's interpretation of its results he finds in this Oriental Impersonality a very remarkable source of strength and permanence; while he prognosticates possible disaster to Western civilisation from the very fact that it is based on individualism. Already, he says, "it shows signs of breaking up from within." It seems possible that the events of the not-distant future will show that Dr Inge was right.

functions by forcing them to act as the apostles and missionaries of a false god. We are apt to speak contemptuously of pagan religions. Take down the most grotesque idol that grins upon his shelf in India, China or Central Africa, and put in its place the new god worshipped by Englishmen and Americans to-day, and who shall choose beween them as fit objects for adoration?

It is frequently taken for granted—naturally enough in commercial England—that the creation of new wants is one of the finest results of civilisation; that by artificially creating new desires among the people of a "backward" race, we not only enrich ourselves by finding new markets for our trade, but we elevate and ennoble such a people by compelling them to lay greater store on the accumulation of wealth in order that they may gratify those new desires. That it is unwise to accept any such theory as axiomatic may be at least tentatively suggested. "It is popularly supposed" said Ruskin "that it benefits a nation to invent a want. But the fact is that the true benefit is in extinguishing a want—in living with as few wants as possible."[1] To see the whole Burmese nation clad in Lancashire cottons, labouring with set teeth from morning till night, year after year, their pagodas deserted and ungilded, their gleaming blue sky polluted with the smoke of factory chimneys, their beautiful country turned into a vast hive of ceaseless and untiring industry,

[1] *Time and Tide*. See also an article by W. T. Seeger in the *Hibbert Journal* for October 1906, p. 75; and Sir Oliver Lodge's article in the same journal for April 1907, p. 527.

simply in order that wealth might grow and British trade prosper, would no doubt be a consummation most devoutly to be wished by the working classes of the ruling race, and also by the alien Government which would congratulate itself on "the unexampled prosperity of the country and the gratifying elasticity of the revenue." But, meanwhile, what of the happiness of the Burmese people? It is a poor answer to say that if they do not want European luxuries they are not compelled to buy them, and that if they despise money no one is going to force them to accumulate it.

If by civilisation we mean an enlightened progress towards the realisation of the happiness of mankind — without necessarily assuming the truth of the Utilitarian position that human action ought to be deliberately directed towards the attainment of the greatest possible sum of pleasures —there can be no doubt that the Burmese people are very high indeed in the scale of civilised races. Nothing is easier than to criticise such statements. Some will say that the happiness of a Burman is a matter of temperament rather than the result of the conditions of his social environment. The Christian who holds that his religion is the only true one, and that all others are false, will condemn the Burman, because, being a Buddhist and a nat-worshipper, he is a "heathen." The man of science will say that in spite of his tolerance and kind-heartedness and humanity, the Burman has made no discoveries worth speaking of in medicine, knows nothing of surgery, and has never invented any labour-saving machinery. In fairness it should be added—for we are still discussing civilisation—that the Burman is not fond of applying his intellect to the devising of mechanical contrivances for slaughtering his fellow-men. Whatever be the shortcomings of his civilisation, the Burman has made one momentous discovery, and it is to this point that I have been trying to lead up: he has discovered how to make life happy without selfishness, and to combine an adequate power of hard work with a corresponding ability to enjoy himself gracefully. "Put him on the river he loves," says Mr Scott O'Connor,[1] "with a swift and angry current against him, and he is capable of superb effort. Turn his beautiful craft, enriched with exquisite carvings, down stream, with wind and tide in his favour, and he will lie all day in the sun, and exult in the Nirvana of complete idleness. And this is not because he is 'a lazy hound,' as I have heard him called, but because he is a philosopher and an artist; because there is a blue sky above him which he can look at, a river before him rippling with colour and light; because the earning of pence is a small thing to him by comparison with the joy of life, and material things themselves but an illusion of the temporary flesh."

A few years ago I wandered alone, as I have said, through the wildest parts of the trans-Mekong Shan States and Siam. I had no credentials, no guide, no servants, and had no

[1] *The Silken East*, p. 37.

knowledge of the languages spoken around me. I was received everywhere with the utmost kindness and the most open-hearted hospitality. In village after village in the valleys of the Nam-U and Mekong I found myself an honoured guest. I could give numberless instances of the tact and fine feeling constantly displayed by my hosts in their dealings with the dumb and unknown foreigner who seemed to have sprung upon them from nowhere. Money did not come into the matter at all: it was of no use to my hosts, for there was hardly any trade, and all their food and clothes were prepared in their own villages. During several memorable weeks I travelled through a fairyland of beauty, sometimes on foot, sometimes in a canoe or on a raft. I saw much of the domestic and social life of the people, and so charming was all I saw that I fear my pleasure was not untainted with envy. It seemed to me that not a single essential of true civilisation was there wanting; I felt that all my preconceived notions of what civilisation really meant had been somehow distorted and must be pulled down and built up anew. During my few weeks in Burma I did not travel in the same way, and steamers and trains gave me little opportunity of seeing Burmese life from the inside; but from what came under my own notice, and from what was told me by others who knew, I have no doubt that where the Burman has not lost his national graces through contact with an alien civilisation he is just as courteous and tolerant and well-mannered and "civilised" as those neighbours of his of whom I have such golden memories.

No doubt one of the greatest achievements of a civilisation such as that of Laos or Burma consists in the spirit of peace and restfulness that it seems to embody. There is, of course, a fallacy in supposing that a contented feeling of "having arrived" is to be expected at all in this human life. Whether we believe in an existence beyond the grave or not, few of us dare to be so optimistic as to suppose that perfection in any form can be realised on earth, although we instinctively feel that we must not be satisfied with anything less. Yet when in some parts of south-eastern Asia we have once breathed that Nirvana-like spirit of restfulness and peace, may we not be pardoned if we find there a strange and magical beauty that all the wisdom of the West can never yield us? It may be, indeed, that our complex Western civilisation, in spite of its materialism and its grossness, contains germs of a higher perfection than ever Burma or Indo-China dreamed of. A full realisation of human capacities, to use the phrase of T. H. Green, can hardly be expected in a simple form of society which calls for no great effort and in which there is no great temptation to deviate from the normal in either an upward or a downward direction. Our strenuous Western life, ugly and brutal as much of it is, and besmirched with the stains of blood and toil, may yet give birth to ideals nobler than ever stirred the imagination of southern Asia. The mountain rent by torrents and chasms, or the ocean tearing with white fangs the face of a cliff, presents to human eyes and minds a spectacle that contains a deeper and grander meaning than can ever be conveyed by the fragile beauty of the royalest of flowers: and the rose, for all its loveliness, fades and dies. Still, let us not despise the beauty that is flower-like, even if we meet it in a land of alien faces: we know that "he is false to God who flouts the rose."

I have said that the Burman shows himself able, in play-hours, to enjoy himself gracefully. In the Burman—he is not alone among Orientals in this—there is no vulgarity. When he and his friends are having what we might call "a spree," he never behaves rudely or uproariously, nor does he get drunk.[1] His good taste and self-control are shown in his demeanour just as they are in his clothes. He is never a "bounder," either in manners or appearance. All these remarks apply with equal force to his women-folk. The Burmese woman, whatever her class may be and whatever her occupation, is always a lady. There may be much merriment, a great deal of noise, a considerable amount of good-humoured chaff, but no "mafficking." Can we say quite the same of "Merrie England"?

It is hardly fair to dwell on the brightest and most picturesque side of Burmese life — which no doubt has its dark side as well—and compare it with the gloomier and more horrible features of the social life of modern England. But what

[1] Of course there are exceptions, especially in the larger towns where Burmese and English civilisations have clashed.

I wish to emphasise is the one fact that the Burmese people of all classes are able to enjoy themselves — and do so most heartily — without the least admixture of "hooliganism," which a very large class of our own countrymen and countrywomen are too obviously unable to do.[1] If an intelligent Burman were to visit England and set himself to discover why it is that among the poorer classes of our great cities merry-making is apparently inseparable from hideous and raucous vulgarity, he would probably ascribe it to the effect of long hours of degrading and mechanical labour, the drudgery and incessant routine of daily life in the sunless workshop and the dismal office—work from which the victims, owing to strenuous competition, derive only the meanest subsistence, and through which all ideas of gracefulness and good taste are obliterated, and all sense of beauty utterly destroyed.

The most wonderful and beautiful feature of Burmese life I have barely referred to, and yet it would deserve a whole volume to itself. The greatest thing in Burma is the Buddhist religion. We have been told by several people who ought to know, that the real religion of Burma is not Buddhism but Animism;[2] that Buddhism is merely an outward label, and that what the Burman really

[1] "It is the way in which hours of freedom are spent that determines, as much as war or as labour, the moral worth of a nation. It raises or lowers, it replenishes or exhausts. At present we find, in these great cities of ours, that three days' idleness will fill the hospitals with victims whom weeks or months of toil had left unscathed."—Maurice Maeterlinck, *The Kingdom of Matter*.

[2] See the Burma Census Report for 1891 and Sir George Scott's *Upper Burma Gazetteer*, and his *Burma: a Handbook*, pp. 380-381.

MONASTERY AT PAGAN, IRRAWADDY RIVER, BURMA.

[To face p. 349.

worships is not the law of Buddha, but the nats and spirits that inhabit the rivers and mountains and forests. There is, of course, a considerable element of truth in this criticism, and it applies even more truly to the Shans than to the Burmese. I have had evidence of this in the neighbouring countries, when the Shan boys who guided my canoe down the rivers of Laos used to stop to offer up prayers to the river-nats whenever we came to a dangerous rapid. But to describe Buddhism in Burma as a mere label seems—though I say it with all deference to those who know better—to be an exaggeration. The Burmans not only "profess and call themselves" Buddhists, but they are brought up in the tenets of that religion from their earliest childhood, and before the British Government established secular schools they received all their education from Buddhist monks within the walls of Buddhist monasteries. The great majority do so still, though some are sent to the secular schools as well. Like the Siamese, all Burmese boys at some time or other wear the yellow robe and take the monastic vows. Most of them return as a matter of course to the secular life, but it would be contrary to all human experience to expect them to forget the religion they have been taught both at home and at school during their most impressionable years; and, as a matter of fact, throughout their lives they continue to have the greatest reverence for the yellow robe—the symbol, in their eyes, of all that is holy.

I would go so far as to say that the average

Burman of the present day is at least as much entitled to the name of Buddhist as the average Englishman or German is to the name of Christian.[1] The law of Buddha is certainly not broken by Burmans in the same lighthearted manner that European Governments and individuals consistently break the commands contained in the Sermon on the Mount: it is not contemptuously thrust aside as "an excellent ideal, but quite unworkable in practice." Buddhism, as it is taught and practised in Burma, is a beautiful religion. I never met a single European in Burma —I must admit that I did not come in contact with the Christian missionaries there—who had a single harsh word to say about the wearers of the yellow robe,[2] or the general effect of their teachings. Whatever their own religious views may be, all Europeans seem ready to acknowledge that Buddhism was and still is a great power for good, and that it will be a dismal day for the Burmese people when their religion decays or relaxes its hold upon them. Fortunately, there seems to be every reason to believe that it will not do so, that Buddhism is for the Burman, if for no other, a *κτῆμα ἐς ἀεί*. It seems strange to be told by one of the foremost living exponents of Burmese life and character that the professed religion of Burma is only "an electro-plating, a bloom, a varnish, enamel, lacquer, a veneer."[3] Surely this must not

[1] Perhaps that is not saying much after all. "In reality," said the German philosopher Nietzsche, "there has been only one Christian, and He died on the Cross."

[2] Here, again, there are, of course, exceptions. There are "black sheep" within the monastic fold as well as outside it.

[3] Sir George Scott, in *Burma: a Handbook*, p. 381.

be taken quite seriously. A "bloom," a "varnish," a "veneer" suggests something that may be more or less easily rubbed off, without materially affecting the substance on which it has been laid. Can it be held in good faith that Buddhism could be rubbed away like the bloom from a grape and leave the Burmese people substantially unaffected? Do the gentleness, the patience, the humanity, the kindness to animals, the winning manners and the limitless charity and generosity of the Burmese owe nothing to Buddhism? If Buddhism has had even a minor share in the shaping of the character of the modern Burman we dare not call it a mere bloom or varnish. That there is, however, a very broad stratum of animism in the various deposits that have helped through the shadowy centuries of an unrecorded past to build up the religious mind of Burma may be granted without dispute. Animism, as we know, is to be traced in the popular versions of all or nearly all the religious systems of the world. The eleventh book of the *Odyssey* is—as F. W. H. Myers has remarked—"steeped in animism,"[1] and we have only to turn to the eighth book of the *Æneid*[2] to find that even in the polished age of Augustus animistic ideas were far from dead. Brahmanism, Buddhism, Islam, the Greek and Roman mythologies, the popular semi-religious superstitions of China and Japan, and Christianity[3]

[1] See his *Greek Oracles*, pp. 8, 18, 20-21. (Eversley Series.)

[2] See ll. 349 *seq.*

[3] See Frazer's *Golden Bough*, vol. iii. p. 49, and vol. i. pp. 170-171 (2nd ed.). See also Tylor's *Primitive Culture*, vol. i. pp. 475-476, and ii. pp. 217-218 (4th ed.); and Rhys Davids' *Buddhist India*, chap. xii.

are all to some extent interpenetrated with animism, and it is only natural that in the case of Buddhism the animistic influences should be specially strong: for that faith enshrines, among the noble and simple moral teachings that all can understand, a profound philosophical system far beyond the comprehension of the average half-educated peasant; and it has always shown, perhaps, even too generous a tolerance of the alien opinions and practices with which it has come in contact.

We are told by the well-known writer on Burma from whom I have just quoted, that when in 1888 the *hti* (pinnacle) of the Shwe Dagon Pagoda at Rangoon was thrown down by an earthquake, a magnificent new one, costing 600,000 rupees, all collected by public subscription, was put up by gratuitous labour.[1] I am far from wishing to lay any emphasis on the significance of the mere voluntary expenditure of so large a sum of money, for we know that in Burma all wealth is dross, and that as judged by Burmese ideas few of the rich philanthropists of Europe would rank as other than mere misers; but the fact of the gift of *gratuitous labour* by a people who are constantly stigmatised as "lazy dogs" and haters of all kinds of hard work, is surely worthy of a moment's consideration. The average Briton is credited with being anything but lazy, yet what would Christian England say if the Primate were to call upon the British workman to give the work of his hands for nothing in the restoration of St Paul's Cathedral? The result

[1] Sir George Scott, *Burma: a Handbook*, p. 22.

of his appeal might possibly suggest in some minds the disquieting reflection that the Burmese were not the only people whose professed religion was a mere "varnish."

Any one who visits the pagodas and watches the people at their devotions—they make a far more beautiful picture, by the way, than the congregation of any European church, though that is not to the point—is not likely to see anything suggestive of the decay of Buddhism. There are, on the contrary, healthy signs of a renewed religious activity which, if guided aright, should lead to splendid results and silence all forebodings. Meanwhile, the jewelled pinnacle of "the greatest cathedral of the Buddhist faith"[1] — the Shwe Dagon Pagoda — still bears silent witness to the vitality and beauty of the religion which called it into being. So long as the Buddhist faith is a living force in Burma, there will never be wanting eager hands to dress the altars and lay gold-leaf on the dome of that splendid fane, and never will the grand and passionless face of the Lord Buddha be averted from the little Burmese children who with their fathers and mothers come to lay their gifts of flowers at the Master's feet. If Buddhism dies out of Burma the country will lose the most precious of all its possessions; and when the Shwe Dagon, deserted by its last pilgrim, crumbles away into a shapeless heap of bricks, the world's diadem will lose one of its most lustrous gems.

[1] Scott O'Connor, *The Silken East*, p. 128.

CHAPTER XVIII

CONCLUSION

FROM Burma I returned to north China by slow and easy stages, covering a period of two and a half months. As, however, I visited no part of the Far East which is not thoroughly well known to the ordinary tourist, I will spare my readers an account of peoples and localities which have been often and well described by others. Leaving Rangoon by steamer on 19th July, I reached Colombo on the 24th, and as the guest of Sir Henry Blake, G.C.M.G., then Governor of Ceylon, I spent six delightful weeks in touring through the island by train and motor-car. At Anuradhapura I obtained a seedling from the famous Bo-tree[1]—probably the oldest surviving historical tree in the world—and took it away to plant in the Public Gardens of Hongkong. I trust it is still there, and that it will do credit to its illustrious origin. From Ceylon I passed through Singapore, Hongkong and Shanghai, and

[1] A cutting from the sacred tree (a species subsequently known as the *ficus religiosa*) under which Gautama is believed to have sat when he attained Buddhahood, was brought from India to Ceylon about the year 245 B.C. and planted at Anuradhapura, then the Singhalese capital. It is still growing there, and is annually visited by countless pilgrims from all parts of the Buddhist world.

RUINS AT ANURADHAPURA, CEYLON.

[*To face p.* 354.

crossed thence to Japan. After nearly a fortnight in the island of Kyūshū I paid a short visit to Korea, and finally returned to Weihaiwei on 5th October, after an absence of exactly nine months. My faithful dog, which had accompanied me through all the vicissitudes of my journey and had never had a day's illness, died suddenly, shortly after my return to China.

After the various journeys that I have made in different parts of China, I am often asked how I have been treated by the Chinese people, and to what extent I have suffered inconvenience from their notorious hatred for foreigners. The reader who has been so indulgent as to follow me carefully through the preceding pages has probably a good idea of what my answer to such questions is likely to be. In the course of more than nine years' residence in China I have travelled in ten provinces, and have never had cause for a single serious complaint against any class or any individual. By the official classes I have almost invariably been treated with scrupulous courtesy, and at the hands of the people I have experienced only kindness and hospitality. It is hardly possible for me to cite a single exception to this rule; and if it were not for the fact that other Europeans—missionaries and travellers—have sometimes had a different tale to tell, I should have no hesitation in saying that no more kindly or hospitable people exist than the people of China. They have certainly not the charm and grace of manner that are so characteristic of some of the Shan tribes or the people of Burma, Siam and Japan, and it is sometimes a little disconcerting to see them hurrying their children out of sight in case the Western ogre should want to cut out their eyes to make into foreign medicine. There are Chinese and Chinese, and good manners are less characteristic of one locality than of another. My own experience of the peasantry of eastern Shantung, with whom I am best acquainted, goes to show that they are good-tempered, reasonable, orderly and law-abiding, inveterate gamblers, quick to appreciate a kindness, good husbands and devoted fathers, neither more nor less intelligent than others of their class elsewhere, rather too fond of flattering the foreign official because they think he is fool enough to like it, singularly lacking in the proverbial conceit of his race, full of humour, a liar in the law-courts but truthful and honest outside them, and courageous in facing hardship and disappointment. My slighter acquaintance with the agricultural classes of other provinces forbids me to attempt any general characterisation, and even in our little territory of Weihaiwei — about 300 square miles in extent, with 160,000 people—there are differences and exceptions which must modify any general statement. The people of Kuangtung —the province from which issue the majority of Chinese emigrants—are in my opinion less attractive than those of many other provinces. They have sturdy qualities, are sober and industrious, enterprising and independent, but are rather too truculent and too much given to brawling. But this applies only to the lower classes, and especially

A VILLAGE FAIR IN CHINA, WITH OPEN-AIR THEATRE.

[To face p. 356.

to the "rolling-stones" that find their way to the coast-ports, for the typical Cantonese gentleman would be an ornament to any society in the world.

That the Chinese people have in the past been misunderstood is due to a variety of quite unavoidable circumstances for which no one can be said to be responsible. The intolerable arrogance of the Chinese Court, up to very recent days, in all its dealings with other Powers, tended to spread the belief that this attitude was characteristic of the whole Chinese people. The admission of foreign merchants to certain "treaty ports" did not tend to bring about much change of feeling, for though the Chinese mercantile classes soon won, through their honesty and fair dealing, a liking or respect which they have never ceased to deserve, the European settlements early became the resort of the worst type of Chinese ruffian. The emigrants from Kuangtung and other provinces of south-eastern China have in the Straits Settlements, California and Australia proved themselves well-behaved and law-abiding members of society; but among them, too, there were many who left their country "for their country's good," and who, had they not prudently sought refuge on foreign shores, would have suffered a worse fate than mere exile. Great numbers of the coolies who were sent to work in the South African mines, and whose various malpractices there have raised so natural an outburst of disgust and indignation, belonged to the vicious and criminal classes of north China, and even the best of them were recruited from the lowest ranks of society. Chinese officialdom, needless to say, was only too delighted to see the last of them. Unfortunately, even a visit to Shanghai or Hongkong does not tend to modify very appreciably the unfavourable opinion of the Chinese which the average Englishman may have formed from his previous knowledge of that race. Whatever may be the cause—and several causes might be assigned—the lower-class Chinese of Hongkong probably have worse manners than any other inhabitants of the Chinese empire. The coolies who wilfully jostle Europeans in Queen's and Des Vœux Roads, and snatch watches and purses from ladies and children, the house-servants who are impertinent to their European mistresses in their masters' absence, and the shopkeepers who blink rudely at their foreign customers and remain seated, sleepily fanning their paunches, when according to their own canons of good manners they should be on their feet murmuring polite salutations — all these are persons to whom a glimpse of Western civilisation seems to have done nothing but harm. They have lost their own manners, and have altogether failed to acquire those of the Occident. For my own part, I may say that though I have travelled through a great part of China and visited many of her large cities, I have found nowhere such lack of manners as unfortunately characterises a large proportion of our fellow-subjects in Hongkong.

It must be admitted that the Chinese do not like foreigners. It is all the more creditable to them that their native courtesy — outside the

European settlements—so often prevents them from showing their dislike. Here and there, no doubt, a real friendship springs up between a foreigner and a Chinese, owing to qualities which each finds and appreciates in the other, but as a rule the feeling hardly goes beyond one of respect. Though many Chinese gentlemen in Hongkong are naturalised British subjects and are men of education and culture, they are practically excluded from the charmed circle of Hongkong "Society." It must be granted, of course, that a difficulty is introduced into the situation through the incompatible social customs of the two races, especially with regard to the position of women. But the difficulty is not, as it may be in the case of English and Hindus, an insuperable one. The total absence of caste-rules and the willingness of intelligent Chinese to relax the rigidity of their own social laws deprive Europeans of the excuse that friendly intercourse with the Chinese is from the nature of things an impossibility.

Dr Martineau tells us that the man who goes abroad and comes in contact with alien civilisations is at first chafed by every sound and sight of foreign things, and thinks he has left everything good behind him at home; but that as he grows accustomed to his surroundings he is "hit by many a happy phrase and won by many a graceful usage, and fairly conquered at last by a literature and art and national life which reveal to him an unimagined type of human culture."[1] Unfortunately all travellers and residents

[1] *A Study of Religion*, vol. i. p. 374 (2nd ed.).

in foreign lands are not so easily dragged out of their prejudices as this passage would seem to imply. Indeed, it is hardly an exaggeration to say that the stay-at-home Englishman is often more apparently sympathetic towards alien races than those who come in daily contact with them. This, however, is too frequently due to a most dangerous form of ignorance,[1] that has already—within the British Empire—caused a good deal of possibly irreparable mischief. In spite of warning after warning, many an Englishman is still apt to think that Orientals under British rule should be put in possession of all the political "rights" of the Briton at home, and is constitutionally unable to see that a political and social system which has been slowly created during centuries of national growth by and for men of his own race may prove not only detrimental but even ruinous to the true interests—political, social and moral—of his Oriental fellow-subjects. It is quite possible—I desire to lay special stress on this point—that a sympathetic and broad-minded Englishman may have the highest regard for the individuals of an Oriental race, the deepest admiration for many aspects of Oriental life and character, and the keenest appreciation of the many splendid achievements of the East in art, philosophy and religion, and that he may nevertheless consistently repudiate any concurrence with the illogical doctrine that what is good for one is good for all, and that the aspirations of the Englishman must

[1] See an excellent anonymous article in *Macmillan's Magazine*, vol. ii. No. 16, N.S. It is entitled "The White Man and the British Empire."

necessarily coincide with the aspirations of the Hindu or the Chinese. I would even go further, and say that the man who wishes to fit out the Oriental with a complete equipment of Western ideals proves thereby that he has either no understanding of or no true sympathy with Eastern peoples and Eastern modes of thought: and that if he tries to give practical effect to his theories he will prove himself that most dangerous of foes —the mischief-maker who comes in the guise of a smiling friend.

Every exiled Englishman who as a Government official is brought into direct contact with a large population of Asiatics is well aware that if his object is to win a certain kind of precarious popularity among those whom he assists in ruling, there is ready to his hand a cheap and nasty way of attaining his ambition. Fortunately for the honour of England and the stability of the Empire, he is generally content with the less dazzling rewards that come from the honest performance of duty. It has recently been reported by the newspapers that an English politician, a few hours after he had set foot on Indian soil for the first time, informed crowded Hindu audiences that he proposed to assist them in securing a constitution similiar to that possessed by Canada, on the ground that "what was good for the Canadians must be good for the Indians"; in consequence of which it was arranged by half-educated Hindu demagogues that he should be greeted with the plaudits of million-throated Bengal, garlanded with flowers and hailed as "an angel and not a man."

Meanwhile, scattered throughout India are hundreds of able and experienced Englishmen—members of the Civil Service — who are giving the best years of their lives to India and her people, who can speak the Indian vernaculars and know the Indian mind and character as well as they can be known by any foreigner, and who are carrying on day by day the great administrative work that saves India from chaos. Few of their names are known to the British public, and not one of them — so far as I am aware—has ever been hailed by a Hindu mob as "an angel." How is it that a roving politician has managed so quickly to out-run them all in the race for popularity? Perhaps, if the truth were known, most of them could, if they so desired, attain the dizzy elevation of this kind of angelhood without much difficulty; but the pity of it is that as time went on they would find the conditions of continued success growing ever more and more stringent, till at last they would have to be something greater even than angels to satisfy the expectations of their admirers. The young Englishmen of half a century hence might have cause to lament that their fathers had not limited their ambitions in this life to terrestrial instead of extending them to celestial promotion, and the young Hindus, as they sat amid the ruins of their violated temples or crouched under the lash of the Mohammedan, would perhaps bitterly wish that their sires had known how to give honour where honour was due, and had turned a deaf ear to the ignorant rhetoric of native and foreign demagogues.

But the Englishman at home, who in a spirit of misdirected generosity aims at conferring on the Asiatic all the political and other "blessings" (if indeed they are such, even in England) that he himself enjoys, oblivious of the fact that under Asiatic conditions the blessings may turn into curses, is guilty of a blunder no graver nor more dangerous than that committed by the Englishman abroad who acts on the other assumption that the Oriental was created to be the white man's slave. This attitude is unfortunately traceable among a certain class of Europeans in both India and China;[1] and in China it has certainly tended to widen the natural gulf that Nature has fixed between the hearts and intellects of East and West.

That the Chinese in general have no liking for the foreigner seems to me a matter for no surprise whatever. I think I am not far wrong when I say that the average young European comes to the East with a prejudice against the Chinese, and a distinct idea that they are his inferiors. Of course in a sense this form of national prejudice exists all the world over. The English schoolboy used to believe that every

[1] Herbert Spencer, in the *Principles of Ethics*, speaks of "the many who, in the East, tacitly assume that Indians exist for the benefit of Anglo-Indians." He is right in saying it is tacitly assumed; for few go so far as to say openly that the Indians are destined by Nature to be exploited by the White races. But the tacit assumption often leavens their thoughts and discourses on "the native question." One recent writer, indeed, distinctly states that "it is an inexorable law of progress that inferior races are made for the purpose of serving the superior; and if they refuse to serve, they are fatally condemned to disappear" (W. H. Brown, *On the South African Frontier*). But who is to decide which are "the inferior races"?

Englishman was as good as three Frenchmen.[1] The French of the Middle Ages used to retort that Englishmen had tails, which is just what many educated Chinese of the present day believe of the Miao-tzŭ tribes. The ancient Greeks called every one else "barbarian." In our own day we have it on the word of an emperor that the real "salt of the earth" are the people of Germany: more recently, indeed, the salt has been metamorphosed "into the block of granite upon which the Lord God can complete His work of civilising the world."[2] Yet was it not only a few years ago that a statesman assured us that the torch of civilisation had now definitely passed to Russia? It was a Russian statesman, of course, who said so: and the Englishman or the American may smile at the self-assurance of this or any other nation that arrogates to itself the rôle which, as he has always been convinced, exclusively belongs to the Anglo-Saxon. Yet this kind of national partiality—provided it is accompanied by a belief in the principle of *noblesse oblige*—is by no means to be sneered at or despised. "The sense of greatness keeps a nation great," and an honest belief in our own lofty destiny will stand us in good stead in the day of trial. If two nations of equal powers and resources come to blows, and one of them happens to be actuated by a belief, lacking to the other, in its "divine mission," we need be in no doubt as to the side on which victory will declare itself. But the feelings with which

[1] See Shakespeare, *King Henry V.*, Act iii. Sc. 6.

[2] The *Times*, 4th Sept. 1907.

Europeans and Chinese too often regard each other are different in kind from the national prejudices that we know so well and make allowances for in the West.

In our relations with China we have been constantly offended by the air of superiority that is assumed towards us by the Chinese Government and by Chinese officials. They used to call us "barbarians" even in official documents, just as the street urchins of Canton still hail us as "foreign devils"; and we can never forget that Chinese officialdom used to do its best to humiliate us in our relations with the Court at Peking in a manner which was altogether intolerable. Of course, the Chinese were wrong in assuming a non-existing superiority, and they have had to pay bitterly for their arrogance. But is it not the case that we, as individuals and as Governments, have shown in different but not less provocative ways just as much unreasonable arrogance in our treatment of the Chinese? "The Chinese complain," writes a fair-minded American diplomatist,[1] "that an air of proprietorship is constantly manifested in unreasonable demands and impertinent criticisms, in denunciation of any of their officials who manifest a disposition to protect native interests, and that it practically amounts to a refusal to recognise China as the property of the Chinese. They object, perhaps unreasonably, against the application to their empire of those two well-known declarations, said to have been made by the unanimous voice of a religious body: 'Resolved,

[1] Mr Chester Holcombe, in *The Real Chinese Question*, p. 242.

that the righteous shall inherit the earth. Resolved, that we are the righteous.'"

Many Europeans not only hold the view that Chinese civilisation is inferior to that of Europe—which is doubtless to a great extent true, though there is another aspect of that question—but they are strongly convinced that the Chinese represent a lower type of humanity—that they are, in fact, less far advanced in the scale of evolution than Europeans. An educated Englishman once told me that the Chinese were evidently a mean and inferior people, because when you whacked a Chinese coolie in the streets of Canton[1] he did not hit you back. This argument is curiously typical of the aggressive attitude which is so often assumed by Europeans not only in their dealings with Chinese, but also in their relations with all other Oriental races, whose lack of "grit" is supposed to be proved by the fact that they are not so ready with their fists as we are. One of the most enlightened Hindus of our own day—the late Swami Vivekananda—quotes as a curious instance of this attitude a remark that was made to him in London. "What have you Hindus done?" said an English girl, full of the pride of race. "You have never even conquered a single nation."

Now, setting aside all considerations of national prejudice and patriotism, is it a fact that the Chinese are as a race inferior to the peoples of the West? The question, when we examine it closely, has really very little to do with political

[1] *Mutato coelo mores mutantur!*

strength or military efficiency, or (*pace* Mr Benjamin Kidd) relative standards of living, or even the usual material accompaniments of what we call an advanced civilisation; it is a question for the trained anthropologist and the craniologist rather than for the casual observer of men and manners. The Japanese people are now much more highly civilised, according to Western notions, than they were half a century ago, but it would be ludicrously erroneous to say that they are now a higher race, from the evolutionary point of view, than they were then. Evolution does not work quite so rapidly as that even in these days of "hustle." The Japanese have advanced, not because their brains have suddenly become larger, or their moral and intellectual capabilities have all at once made a leap forward, but because their intercourse with Western nations, after centuries of isolated seclusion, showed them that certain characteristic features of European civilisation would be of great use in strengthening and enriching their own country, developing its resources, and giving it the power to resist aggression. If the Japanese were as members of the genus *homo sapiens* inferior to us fifty years ago, they are inferior to us now. If they are our equals to-day—and the burden of proof certainly now rests on him who wishes to show that they are not—our knowledge of the origin and history of Eastern peoples, scanty though it is, should certainly tend to assure us that the Chinese are our equals too. There is no valid reason for supposing that the Chinese people are ethnically inferior to the Japanese. They have preserved their isolated seclusion longer than the Japanese, because until very recently it was less urgently necessary for them to come out of it. They have taken a longer time to appreciate the value of Western science and certain features of Western civilisation, because new ideas take longer to permeate a very large country than a small one, and because China was rich in the possession within her own borders of all the necessaries of life.

Many Europeans, dazzled and blinded by the marvellous inventions and discoveries of modern times, and the huge strides made by physical science, are apt to conclude too hastily that our ethnical superiority is sufficiently proved by the fact that all or nearly all such achievements are due to the white races only.[1] Even the Japanese, we are often reminded, are after all only our imitators, and being so must necessarily be our inferiors. If an artist were to make so excellent a copy of the Madonna di San Sisto as to deceive connoisseurs into the belief that it was the original, he would not thereby elevate himself to an equality with Raphael. But surely it is much too soon to make generalisations about the relative development of Eastern and Western nations from the few facts at our command. It is only during the last

[1] I earnestly commend to the reader's notice an admirable leader in the *Times* of 15th January 1907, which closes with these words: "Altogether it seems to be time for the white races to take a fresh survey of the whole situation, and to recognise that, in the changed conditions, the old haughty and dictatorial attitude stands in need of modification."

one or two hundred years that science has achieved her greatest triumphs in Europe, and it is with the aid of those triumphs of science and partly as a direct result of them that European civilisation has progressed during that time. Yet even with us popular opinion has not always been on the side of advancing science. I once heard a charming old lady declare that balloons or air-machines of any kind would never be successful, because the Almighty in His wisdom had decreed that mankind was to restrict its movements to the solid earth, and that even the attempt to make such machines was—like the building of a certain mythical tower that we have all heard of—an act of impiety which would certainly bring down divine vengeance. Yet the man who now denies that we are within measurable distance of the conquest of the air—especially if he denies it on religious grounds—is not likely to be listened to with much respect at the present day. Many persons—pious and other—were strongly opposed to the construction of railways in England in the early part of the nineteenth century. We grew impatient with the Chinese, because, until very recently, they showed similar reluctance to the introduction of railways and machinery into their own country, thus proving that they were oblivious of the enormous economic benefits that such innovations had conferred upon every country that had adopted them; yet we do not regard the University of Oxford as having been the last stronghold of barbarism in England, because that venerable corporation for a long time opposed the approach of a railway to its classic halls, nor do we consider that Lancashire was less civilised than the rest of England in the eighteenth century, because its cotton-spinners rose in their thousands to resist by force the introduction of Sir Richard Arkwright's spinning-frame. If we are willing to admit that Oxford and Lancashire did not act from a mere blind hostility to modern inventions as such, we should at least be willing to enquire whether the opposition of the Chinese has not also been due to other causes than mere barbarism or lack of intelligence.

I do not think it can be seriously contended that the civilisation of China to-day is on the whole lower than that of Europe in the comparatively recent days of the thumb-screw and the Holy Office, and it is possible that in the K'ang Hsi period (1662-1722) China was as civilised as most of the countries of Europe were at the same period. In that case it is not much more than two hundred years since European civilisation began to move ahead of that of China—a very short period in a nation's history, and almost infinitesimal from the point of view of the evolution of mankind.[1] Our racial superiority to

[1] Lest it may appear that I am under-rating the speed with which evolutionary forces have operated among the European races during the last few centuries, I venture to quote the words of one whose opinion is likely to be listened to with respect, and who was the last man to minimise the significance of the conquests made by science. "There can be no doubt that vast changes have taken place in English civilisation since the reign of the Tudors. But I am not aware of a particle of evidence in favour of the conclusion that this evolutionary process has been accompanied by any modification of the physical or the mental characters of the men who have been the subjects of it. I have not met with any grounds for suspecting that the average

A TEMPLE-THEATRE IN NORTH CHINA.

[*To face p.* 371.

the Chinese may be an anthropological truth, but it cannot be deduced merely from the fact that during the most recent portion of our national existence we have invented steam engines or wireless telegraphy or quick-firing guns or turbine battleships or even party government.

That Chinese civilisation has for many years been allowed to get into a very bad state of repair is, of course, an undoubted fact. Not to mention the various terrible outbursts of hatred against foreigners, for which the aggression of foreign Governments has generally been to a great extent responsible, no excuse can be found for the atrocities committed in the Chinese criminal law-courts, or the unsatisfactory position of women, or the binding of girls' feet, or the defective educational system, or the low state of the arts of medicine and surgery, or the corruption of the official classes and the numberless administrative abuses. All these and many other evils must be rectified before China can expect to take her proper place in the front rank of the nations of the world. That she is now making an honest endeavour to rectify them in the face of immense difficulties must, I think, be apparent to all observers, but we cannot expect that great social and political changes can be introduced into so enormous a country as China merely by the issue of a series of imperial decrees, and it is but

Englishmen of to-day are sensibly different from those that Shakespeare knew and drew. . . . In my belief the innate qualities, physical, intellectual and moral, of our nation have remained substantially the same for the last four or five centuries" (T. H. Huxley, *Prolegomena to Evolution and Ethics*).

too probable that before she can enter upon the heritage that is rightly hers, China has yet to pass through a terrible ordeal of fire. It is also far from unlikely that in the early stages of her new career she will be forced by circumstances into various reactionary phases which may give foreigners the mistaken impression that she is about to fall back again into her old lethargy and somnolence.

Some of the existing features of Chinese civilisation are so admirably suited to the genius of the people that they might with great advantage be allowed to remain almost unchanged. If everything goes into the melting pot, China will lose almost as much as she can ever hope to gain. It is a great mistake, for example, to suppose that the Chinese system of government is thoroughly bad. The Government has failed so often and so signally to uphold the dignity of China in her quarrels with other Powers that we are apt to regard the whole system as rotten, inside and out. We are told so much about official corruption and the inhumanities of Chinese gaols and the cruel acts of oppression practised by the ruling classes and their underlings, that some may be surprised to learn not only that there are hundreds of admirable officials, zealous and single-minded in the discharge of their duties, but that the majority of the people of China are quite unconscious of being oppressed, and would be bewildered if one were to suggest that such was the case. The "squeezes" of the officials and their subordinates are thoroughly well recognised by every one concerned, and acts of real extortion are by no means so common as Europeans believe, though there have no doubt been several serious cases of malversation of funds subscribed by Chinese and foreigners for such laudable objects as famine relief. It is true, moreover, that the official classes have often shown a cynical disregard for the sanctity of private property, and this has compelled many rich Chinese to invest their money in Shanghai and Hongkong. As regards the ordinary "squeezes," the imperial Government knows quite well that the salaries paid to the officials do not amount to a living wage, and that to eke out their slender incomes they must pocket fees and percentages which have no legal sanction.

The criminal convicted in a Chinese court is well aware that he must fee his gaolers — that is practically part of his punishment for being a criminal. The party to a civil lawsuit knows equally well that he cannot hope to get a hearing till he has paid something to every one connected with the court, from door-keeper to magistrate's secretaries, and that if he wins his case he will have to pay more: but he, too, knew all this before he decided to go to law, and he regards all these payments much as we should regard a solicitor's bill of costs. Real acts of extortion and oppression are often practised in individual cases, but it is a strong light that beats upon the judgment seat of a Chinese official, and if he becomes notorious for such acts he must have exceedingly influential support if he expects to escape denunciation and disgrace. It is the sale of offices, the selfishness of the highest ruling classes, the ignorance and prejudices of the court, the malversation of funds that ought to be devoted to paying for fleets and armies and public works, that China suffers from so bitterly to-day, not the comparatively small extortions practised by local officials.

Even taking extortion and "squeezes" into consideration, China is a lightly-taxed country; and we should remember that in times of famine or other distress it is quite common for the Government to remit all direct taxes throughout the whole area affected. A Chinese magistrate is held responsible for the peace and well-being of his district just as a father is held responsible for the conduct of his son. The people whom he rules know this very well, and are fully conscious of their own power to ruin his official career if he consistently tries to extort more than the recognised "squeezes," or is guilty of any gross acts of maladministration.[1] In connection with civil lawsuits, intentional miscarriages of justice are far less frequent than is usually supposed. The parties may be required to pay what we should call bribes, and sometimes the hearing of a case is intentionally postponed from day to day

[1] A few years ago a certain Chinese magistrate in a district very near Weihaiwei was much disgusted, on arriving at his post, to find that the opportunities for "squeeze" were so severely limited that he was likely to remain a poor man. On his own responsibility he decided to tap a new source of revenue, and issued a proclamation to the necessary effect. In a few days the populace was up in arms, the magistrate's official residence was pulled to pieces (it is still almost a ruin), and he was himself a disgraced fugitive.

until the bribes offered are sufficiently large; but the important point to notice is, that all this bribery does not necessarily imply a miscarriage of justice. Considering the wide areas over which Chinese district magistrates preside, and the slight amount of supervision exercised over their proceedings, it is not an exaggeration to say that great numbers of them are able and well-meaning officials who have an honest desire to benefit the people committed to their charge and to serve their country loyally. We find, too, that the men who show such qualifications in a conspicuous degree are almost sure of rapid advancement; nor do they fail to earn the respect and affection of the people whom they rule, for there is no one quicker than a Chinese to realise when he is well governed, and perhaps no one more appreciative.

The social organisation of China, especially for an agricultural people, is in many respects thoroughly sound. In ordinary times — that is, when no extraordinary events such as famines or political troubles occur to complicate matters—China is one of the most profoundly peaceful countries in the world. The fact that hated foreigners can safely go through the country from end to end without any means of self-protection is in itself a striking proof of this. The people are singularly law-abiding. There are no policemen in the European sense except in a few large cities like Peking, Ch'êng-tu and K'ai-fêng-fu, where Western institutions are beginning to be copied, and yet there is probably a smaller percentage of crime in China than in any country in Europe. This is partly due, no doubt, to the naturally peaceful and industrious character of the people, but it is an almost necessary corollary of their semi-patriarchal village system and the responsibility of each family for the good behaviour of all its members. In the three hundred and ten villages of the leased territory of Weihaiwei the policy of the British Government has been to rule the people as far as possible in the way to which from time immemorial they have been accustomed. The village organisation is maintained, and in the courts of the two British magistrates the law that is administered is the law of China (tempered by local custom), so far as such law and custom are not repugnant to British conceptions of justice and morality. In my own district, which is nearly 200 square miles in extent, and contains about two hundred villages with nearly a hundred thousand inhabitants, there are eight police constables permanently stationed at headquarters, ready to be sent out to discharge any duties that may be necessary, but apart from them there is not a policeman in the district. During a recent period of six months—including the winter months, which are always the season for serious crime in north China—the cases of robbery reported to the police were three in number. Out of about eighty cases in which during the same period imprisonment or fines were imposed, nearly half were gambling cases and the rest of a more or less trifling nature. When riding through the villages of the territory I do not remember to have seen more than one intoxicated man, and he had been to market and

THE GRAVE OF "JIM," WEIHAIWEI.

[*To face p.* 376.

sold all his pigs. During more than two years in Weihaiwei I have tried Englishmen and Japanese for being "drunk and disorderly," but never a single Chinese. I must hasten to explain that the absence of crime and disorder in Weihaiwei is not in the least degree due to any reforms introduced by the British Government: the neighbouring districts under Chinese rule are just as well behaved, if not, indeed, rather more so. Perhaps I should add that civil lawsuits in Weihaiwei are exceptionally numerous. Such cases are decided by the two British magistrates in accordance with Chinese law and are conducted in the Chinese language. The only expense which a litigant incurs is a shilling or two for hiring a petition-writer to state his case, and even this outlay he can avoid if he happens to be an educated man and can write out an intelligible statement for himself, or get a friend to do it for him. There are no court fees, no "squeezes," and solicitors and barristers are unknown. I am not quite satisfied that the facilities offered to litigants in our courts in Weihaiwei are altogether beneficial in their results. Litigation has become so cheap and easy that it is often resorted to before the least serious attempt has been made by the parties to come to an amicable settlement out of court. The British magistrates are called upon to decide such trumpery questions that if a litigant were to submit them to a Chinese tribunal the magistrate would probably order him to be flogged for needlessly stirring up litigious strife. By taking cognisance of the simplest village disputes it may be that we are gradually weakening the solidarity of the village organisation, which, if once destroyed, can never be restored; and we are possibly storing up a good deal of trouble for the Chinese officials who will resume their functions in Weihaiwei on the expiry of our lease.

If the high development of literary and artistic tastes is to be taken as a criterion of civilisation it is not likely that even in this respect Europe has much cause to throw contemptuous glances at China. But many of those European collectors who admire and are willing to pay enormous prices for specimens of Chinese porcelain[1]—much of it stolen from private houses in Peking and elsewhere—are perhaps not aware of the high standard which Chinese artists have reached in other directions. Fine examples of their pictorial art are still not very numerous in Europe, or at least are not easily accessible to the public, though the British Museum contains, among other Chinese drawings and paintings, characteristic sketches by such famous artists as Lin Liang of the Ming dynasty. But the rapidity with which the art of Japan has gained the admiration of Europe is proof enough that Chinese art—to which that of Japan owes its most characteristic qualities and nearly all its inspiration—will some day arouse no less enthusiasm among the art critics of Europe. An English critic, who is also a poet—Mr Laurence Binyon—says of the landscape painting of the Sung dynasty (the tenth

[1] The *Times* of 15th December 1906 reports the sale at Christie's of a pair of vases of the K'ang Hsi period for 3,700 guineas, and a pair of beakers of the Yung Chêng period for 3,100 guineas.

to the thirteenth centuries of our era) that "not till the nineteenth century in Europe do we find anything like the landscape art of China in the Sung period,—a disinterested love of beauty in nature for its own sake, regardless of associations imposed by the struggles of existence. . . . To the Sung artists and poets, mountains were a passion, as to Wordsworth. The landscape art thus founded, and continued by the Japanese in the fifteenth century, must rank as the greatest school of landscape which the world has seen."[1] In art, as in literature and politics, the great days of China lie in the past, but there are probably more artists at work at the present day in China than anywhere else, and the zeal and enthusiasm with which they execute their best work—generally without any expectation of material reward — is a sure indication that the artistic sense of the Chinese is still full of vigorous vitality, and may lead to great results in the future.

In music it must be admitted that China lags as yet far behind Europe. It has been reported of one of the foremost pianists and composers of the present day that when he visited California and heard Chinese music for the first time, he volunteered the opinion that "it really was music," a truth which some of us perhaps might be inclined to doubt. If an intelligent Chinese who had never before been outside his own country were taken without previous instruction to the performance of an Italian opera, or had the privilege of hearing the *Agnus Dei* of Mozart's 1st Mass or Meyerbeer's *Qui in manu Dei requiescit* as sung,

[1] Quoted in Professor Giles' *Chinese Pictorial Art*.

for example, in Magdalen College Chapel, he would be merely puzzled. The music would be devoid of meaning to him, and he would probably regard it as unintelligible noise. Yet, after all, a musical ear—apart from the almost universal liking for simple melody—is by no means too common even in Europe, and an average Englishman would repudiate the idea that he was less civilised or less highly evolved than a German because he had less appreciation of the wonders of harmony. Time was—not so very long ago—when Wagner's music was regarded in England as a kind of joke; and few people are really able to understand and appreciate the grandest music of the nineteenth century—though they often think they do—without some previous training. Some are even frank enough to confess that it bores them, much as it would bore a man who did not understand Greek to listen to a reading from Sophocles. But are the Chinese capable of being musically trained? Judging from a few cases within my own knowledge, I am inclined to think they are. But in any case we should remember that music as we understand it is the youngest of the arts, and time only can show whether all the great music of the future is to be exclusively a Western product.

As regards literature, the difficulty of the Chinese written language has no doubt stood in the way of spreading a knowledge of the Chinese masterpieces in Europe, and most of the translations that exist are—even when verbally exact—far from reproducing the spirit of the original.

The probability is that in future the best translations will come from the pens of native scholars. Mr Ku Hung-Ming,[1] graduate of a Scottish university, has rendered good service to Europe in giving us what are perhaps the best existing English translations of a portion of the Confucian classics. Yet the ignorance still shown even by European residents in China of the extent and richness of Chinese literature is very remarkable. Some time ago, in conversation with an Englishman who had lived many years in China, I happened to allude to the works of one of the most famous of Chinese poets. My friend had never heard his name, and was surprised to learn that China had any poets at all. Professor Giles, with his happy gift of apt translation and paraphrase, has turned into good English verse[2] a few short specimens of the beautiful poetry of the T'ang and Sung dynasties, and the contents of his little volume must have surprised some Western readers who had little idea that while the Mercians and West Saxons were still struggling for supremacy in England under their Ecgberhts and Beorhtrics, such exquisite flowers of poesy were springing up on the soil of distant China. Yet the translations that have already appeared in foreign languages are but a trifle compared with the wealth of poetry that still remains unknown to Europe; and Chinese poetry, like that of all other languages, loses half its beauty when clothed in the words of an alien

[1] Author of *Papers from a Viceroy's Yamen*, and other works.
[2] *Chinese Poetry in English Verse* (Shanghai and London: 1898).

tongue. A Chinese gentleman's education is not regarded as complete if he cannot clothe his ideas in graceful verse; nor does he, like the English schoolboy who seldom meddles with Latin hexameters and Greek iambics when his education is "finished," neglect this pleasant accomplishment when he has left the halls of learning. Such poetry, naturally, is rarely of a high order; but though the published poetry of the present day is poor compared with that of the past—even in England we have not always with us singers of the Elizabethan standard—the great poets of China are still quoted and read with the same appreciation as of old. That real poetic feeling is far from extinct may be seen by any English reader who peruses Mr C. Clementi's translation of the Cantonese Love-songs,[1] which are quite modern. The genius of Chinese poetry tends to be elegiac and idyllic. It is seldom or never intensely lyrical, even when it is intended for a musical accompaniment, like the love-songs just referred to. But if Chinese literature can boast of no Shelleys or Swinburnes, there are many writers whose poems may well be compared with the best work of our English elegiac and descriptive poets, such as Gray. It must, I think, be admitted that the Chinese language is not the most perfect existing vehicle for poetical expression. We need only take a single test-line from Homer — say line 198 of *Odyssey* xi., — or a couplet from Shelley—say lines 5 and 6 of the third stanza of *The Question*,—to realise a rhythmical music and

[1] Published by the Clarendon Press, 1904.

movement of which the Chinese language is, I fear, incapable; yet the words used by Lafcadio Hearn to describe the best Japanese poetry may with equal justice be applied to the idyllic poetry of China: "compositions which, with a few chosen syllables only, can either create a perfect coloured picture in the mind, or bestir the finest sensations of memory with marvellous penetrative delicacy."[1]

All that I have said of the amenities of Chinese civilisation will no doubt bewilder some readers who have never visited the country and who never think of China unless it happens to figure conspicuously in the newspapers in connection with wars and massacres. They have had detailed accounts of how ruffianly hordes of cut-throats tried to exterminate the Europeans in the legations at Peking, and every now and then they hear of the brutal murder of a missionary and his family. But does it never occur to them to ask what has led to such outbreaks? Surely these murders and outrages are not committed from sheer love of blood and slaughter? If such frenzied attacks are made from time to time upon foreigners, surely they cannot result from a mere loathing of fellow human beings who happen to belong to a Western land? It is well to seek information on such points, for the questioner may rest assured that the fault has not always been on the side of China, that these ebullitions of frenzy do not spring from mere wild barbarism, and that a real or fancied wrong is invariably at their root. For

[1] Lafcadio Hearn's *Kokoro*, p. 335.

the Chinese are as keen as the proudest race in Europe to resent insult or injustice. It is no doubt true that on occasions when the Chinese find their own antiquated fighting implements totally inadequate to enable them to meet on equal terms the powerfully-armed and well-drilled soldiers of Europe, they will then, in frenzy and desperation, and stung with a sense of wrong, be guilty of grave crimes against humanity, choosing moments when their victims are few and defenceless to strike them in the dark; but they are not actuated by mere savagery and lust of blood. Nor are they cowards. That they will flee panic-stricken from a foe armed with the most deadly modern weapons of precision, is true enough: so would have fled the fathers of the splendid heroes who recently beat the best soldiers and sailors of one of the foremost Powers of Europe, yet no one dares to assume that the fathers of the Japanese soldiers of to-day were cowards. Let us hesitate before we condemn the Chinese as a cowardly race because they shrink from facing odds which we Englishmen are never called upon to face ourselves. Let us at least wait till they have met us on equal terms, armed with weapons as good as our own, and led by officers trained in the art of war.[1]

Many will excuse Western aggression in China and in the Orient generally on many grounds: even Kiaochou will have its apologists. But can any fair-minded gentleman of England, Germany, France or Russia say with perfect sincerity that

[1] See Note 47 (p. 442).

the military Powers of Europe have behaved chivalrously towards the East? Have they not too often acted as bullies, too often taken advantage of their brute strength? Even so, the apologists may say, the methods of nations cannot and must not be the same as those of individual men. Conduct that the public-school boy would denounce as caddish becomes statecraft and *la haute politique* when nation deals with nation. Yet is it not conceivable that if we treated the East with the same chivalry and courtesy which the well-bred English gentleman in private life shows to those who are weaker or humbler than himself, we might before many years are past find in China a loyal and powerful friend instead of a possible sullen and suspicious foe? It should never be forgotten that the true Oriental — even more than the Englishman bred at Winchester and New College — is a firm believer in the truth embodied in William of Wykeham's old motto, *Manners makyth man*; and nothing is more certain than that if we want China to welcome us as teachers, as engineers, as builders of railways, as merchants, as missionaries or as capitalists we must approach her with frankness and courtesy, not with professions of altruism covering only greedy selfishness, not with the sinister motives of Chaucer's "smyler with the knyf under the cloke."

As far as British relations with China are concerned, by far the brightest sign of the times is the willingness of our Government to assist China in stamping out the curse of opium—almost as great a curse as alcohol in our own country—and in doing what in us lies to prevent the further dismemberment of the empire. That this is a policy which commends itself to all Englishmen who have fairly considered the questions at issue, I have very little doubt; but it is to be feared that there will always be some who, from selfish dread of losing some material advantage which they hoped to gain from exploiting China, will always be ready to urge a narrower policy. They are indignant at the idea of the subjects of a foreign Power obtaining any valuable concessions or rights in England itself—as when the newspapers report the acquisition of Welsh coal-fields by a syndicate of Germans—yet they are intolerant of the cry of "China for the Chinese." Fortunately, the English Press of Hongkong and Shanghai is generally very fair-minded in its attitude towards international questions, and the intelligent and sympathetic view which it has taken of some of the recent regrettable episodes in Anglo-Chinese relations at Shanghai and elsewhere must go far towards broadening the ideas of many of its readers. Yet too often, I am afraid, the European in China almost prides himself on the fact that he has no liking for or sympathy with the Chinese; and those who are convicted of showing such sympathy are as often as not stigmatised as "pro-Chinese"—apparently the worst offence of which any Englishman in China can be guilty. In the treaty ports one often hears the very foolish remark made, that the acquisition of a scholarly knowledge of the

Chinese language and literature leads to a kind of softening of the brain: "that way madness lies." This attitude is analogous to that of the modern man of business, who, having had only a commercial or technical training himself, and regarding all education merely as a means for acquiring money and "getting on," scoffs at what he knows nothing about, and ridicules those who maintain the advantages of a study of Greek. Without a knowledge of that language it cannot, of course, be expected that they should take to heart a valuable old warning:

πᾶς τις ἀπαίδευτος φρονιμώτατός ἐστι σιωπῶν.

China has only recently begun to awake from her old lethargy, and in her recent attempts to assert her independence and to repudiate foreign interference it must be admitted by her best friends that she has already made some grievous and foolish mistakes that may cost her dear. More than one Western Power watches these mistakes with sullen interest, sword in hand. It is to be hoped for China's sake that the statesmen who are to guide her fortunes during the next few years—which will too probably be years of strife and bloodshed—will not attempt to compress the work of a century into a year; and it is to be hoped that the great Western Powers for their own sakes will show reasonable patience in dealing with the blunders which in the course of so vast a work as the readjustment of the social and political forces of China must from time to time be committed by her responsible leaders. Chinese patriotism, for the first time since the history of

European relations with China began, is becoming a force to be reckoned with. Crude manifestations of this patriotism have recently given rise to unfortunate incidents and to acts which Europe and America cannot be expected to sympathise with or to admire; indeed, in some cases the West is undoubtedly right in insisting that China should show a proper respect for her treaty obligations. But surely this is not the time to show selfish hostility to the new hopes and ideals of a great people who are struggling in the throes of regeneration. The next fifteen years will probably be decisive in determining the whole course of China's future history. If wise statesmanship brings her successfully through her present struggle she need have no fear for the remoter future. She will then be on the way to become one of the greatest nations — perhaps the greatest — in the world, and I know of little in her past history to discourage the hope that she will use her great powers for the good of mankind and the preservation of the world's peace.[1]

After all, it is only in recent years that we have begun to realise how large the world is—a curious fact when we consider how the advance of science has tended to the annihilation of space. The Roman empire and the *pax Romana* were of such enormous importance for all the races that now people Europe that we have hardly yet rid ourselves of the old idea that the Romans at the period of their widest dominion ruled the world; yet we ought to know now that the Mediter-

[1] See Note 48 (p. 443).

ranean "world" was only a fraction of our globe, and by no means the only civilised fraction. The Chinese called their country "The Middle Kingdom," meaning that it was the centre from which all civilisation and all light and learning radiated. The countries outside China, when their existence was known of at all, were regarded as more or less civilised according as they were nearer to or further removed from that brilliant centre. Those that were altogether beyond the reach of China's influence were outside civilisation; they were countries on the fringe of the world, inhabited by barbarians. Our own attitude has hitherto been very much the same. We who have inherited, more or less directly, the civilisation and culture of Rome and Greece have for centuries past regarded ourselves as "the world." When we began to have relations with Eastern countries we found that somehow or other we could not make Oriental culture and civilisation quite fit in with our preconceived notions of those things. We regarded the East—especially China—with a kind of mingled contempt and amusement. Even to this day superficial writers cannot deny themselves the pleasure of dwelling on what to their minds are the oddities and absurdities of Chinese life: and so we have humorous descriptions from their pens of how everything in China is distorted and "upside down"—the writers forgetting that some of the salient features of our own civilisation must be quite as ridiculous when looked at from the Chinese standpoint. But the truth is, of course, that neither Europe nor China has any right to regard the other as a subject for caricature. The time has come when we should realise that Europe and North America are not "the world"; that even the glorious heritage handed down to us by Greece, of which we are so justly proud, did not include everything that was worth having or worth knowing; that we people of the West have a monopoly neither in virtue nor in culture; and that the Far East, as well as the Far West, has inherited something of the wisdom of the ages. When we have realised these things it may then be possible for East and West to meet in friendship and frankness instead of with mutual suspicion or contempt, each ready to give the other something of the best that it has inherited from its own past. It may then be that we shall begin to trade with China in something more than cottons and silks, machinery and rifles; that a commerce will be inaugurated of which political economy knows nothing, in which customs tariffs will be unnecessary, and in which sympathy and tolerance, not money, will be the medium of exchange.

APPENDIX A: VOCABULARIES

English.	Yung-ning Li-so.	Yung-ning Moso.	Muli (Njong).
One	t'i	chih	ti
Two	nyi	nyi	nö
Three	sa	so	son
Four	li	ru	zhi, or zha
Five	nga	nga or ua	ngo
Six	ch'u	k'uo or k'o	t'ru
Seven	shih	shih	hnö, hnyi
Eight	hi or hei	ho	shüeh
Nine	gu	gu	yö, or yi
Ten	t'zŭ	ts'e or t'zŭ	ka-te
Eleven	t'zŭ t'i	t'zŭ chih	ka-ti
Twelve	t'zŭ nyi	t'zŭ nyi	ka-nö
Thirteen	t'zŭ sa	t'zŭ so	ka-son
Fourteen	t'zŭ li	t'zŭ ru	ka-zhi
Fifteen	t'zŭ nga	t'zŭ nga	ka-ngo
Sixteen	t'zŭ ch'u	t'zŭ k'o	ka-t'ru
Seventeen	t'zŭ shih	t'zŭ shih	ka-hnö
Eighteen	t'zŭ hi	t'zŭ ho	ka-shüeh
Nineteen	t'zŭ gu	t'zŭ gu	ka-yö
Twenty	nyi-t'zŭ	nyi-t'zŭ	na-ha
Twenty-one	nyi-t'zŭ-ti	nyi-t'zŭ-chih	na-ha-ti
Thirty	sa-tz'ŭ	so-tz'ŭ	so ha
Forty	li-tz'ŭ	ru tz'ŭ	ra ha
Fifty	nga-tz'ŭ	nga tz'ŭ	ngo ha
Sixty	ch'u-tz'ŭ	k'o tz'ŭ	t'ru ha
Seventy	shih-tz'ŭ	shih tz'ŭ	hnö ha
Eighty	hi tz'ŭ	ho tz'ŭ	sho ha
Ninety	gu tz'ŭ	gu tz'ŭ	yö ha
One hundred	t'i hya	...	shi
Yesterday	a nyi	a nyi	pu-she
To-day	ni-nyi	nyi	pu-ne
To-morrow	na ha	su nyi	shim-pu
Day after to-morrow	...	...	ko-se-nö
Three days hence	...	...	ko-de-nö
Spring	sa nga ha	nyi so-le	cha pei
Summer	sha ha	dje so-le	mi-ni-bü
Autumn	ho li mi	ch'u so-le	drou-pa
Winter	mu ts'u	ch'ih so-le	gu-pa
I, me	ngo, nga	nya	a
Old	...	...	mi gi
Young	...	...	djen
Large	...	chih	she-mö
Small	...	dji	k'o dze mö
Come	lö ha	yi ze	yu
Go	dja ha	hü, or hsü ze	shon

Pa-U-Rong Hsi-Fan.	Pa-U-Rong Lolo.	Tibetan.	Remarks.
ta	ta	chig.	Compare *Wa*: te; *Karen*: ta; *British Li-so (Lee-saw)*: hti.
nyi	ni	nyi.	Compare *Cantonese*: yi; *Karen*: nö; *British Li-so*: nyi.
zi	son	sum.	Compare *Chinese (Mand.)*: san; (*Cantonese*): sam; *Siamese and Lao*, sam.
ri	zhi	zhi.	
nga	nga	nga.	Compare *Cantonese*: ng; *Shan, Siamese and Lao*: Ha.
tru	dru	d'rug.	
dun	dun	dün.	
dji	zhei	gye.	
gu	gu	gu.	Compare *Cantonese*: kao.
ka-den	tchi	chu.	
...	...	chug chig.	
...	...	chu nyi.	
...	...	chug sum.	
...	...	chug zhi.	
...	...	chug nga.	
...	...	chug d'rug.	
...	...	chug dün.	
...	...	chug gye.	
...	...	chug gu.	
nya ka	...	nyi shu.	
...	...	nyi shu chig.	
zi ka	...	sum chu.	
ra ka	...	zhib chu.	
nga ka	...	ngab chu.	
tru ha	...	dr'ug chu.	
nya ha	...	dün chu.	
sho ha	...	gye chu.	
gu ha	...	gub chu.	
ta ra	...	gya.	
...	...	k'a sa.	
...	...	d'e ring.	
zha di	zhom bi	sang.	
...	...	nang (-nyi).	
...	...	zhe (-nyin ga).	
...	djang-u	chi-ka.	Moso *so-le* means a period of three months.
...	mêng-i	yar-ka.	
...	mo dzon	tön-ka.	
...	...	gün-ka.	
...	...	nga.	*Cantonese*: ngo.
...	...	nying-ba.	
...	...	lo zhön-ba.	
dja	...	ch'en-po.	
ka-ta	...	ch'ung.	
...	ba-lu	yong-wa; leb-pa.	
...	...	p'eb, dro.	

English.	Yung-ning Li-so.	Yung-ning Moso.	Muli (Njong).
Eat	dza dza	...	dzu
Sleep	yi dja	lei zhi	k'o zhi
Beat	di	la	dzu
Kill	si	k'o	ne se
Man	...	hyi (strong aspirate)	me
Year	...	du k'u	gu
Month	ha po ti ma	le, or hle me	zhi
Moon	ha po	le, or hle me	hli
Day	t'i nyi	t'i nyi	nyi
Sun	mi mi	nyi me	nyi
Star	...	...	dru
Cloud	...	...	hlieh wei
Rain	...	...	kwi
Snow	...	...	p'u
Wind	...	...	mo-ho
Sky	mu	mu	me nyi
Fire	a-tu ko	hle dji	ma tre
Water	yi ta	dji	djö
Hill	...	dji na me	don
Stone	mu ti	...	yom-pa
Earth (soil)	ne hö	djĭ	dja
Wood	ssŭ	ssŭ	hsieh
Gold	shih	ha	ngei
Silver	p'ü	ngu	nyou
Iron	hu	shi	she
Copper	...	...	ni
Bone	hao-to	shang-ö	ra-ka
Grass	...	...	zhon
Rice	...	...	tch'e
Tobacco	...	...	ye
Barley	...	...	mi-dji
Silk	...	...	go-ch'en
Tea	...	...	dje
Yak, cow	...	ye	roa
Water-buffalo	...	dji ye	...
Dog	a-na	k'u	ka-dra
Goat	a-ch'ih	t'zŭ	la
Pig	...	...	dzö
Fowl	...	a	ro
Hare	...	...	...
Sheep	...	...	...
Father	pa-pa	a-da	a-so-an
Mother	ma-ma	a-me	ma-ma
Elder brother	a-bu	a-mu	a-pei
Younger brother	ke-zei	ke-ssŭ	ko-an
Head	wu-dü	wu-k'ua	k'o
Hair	wu-ts'ü	...	ko ma
Ears	...	...	ne dju
Nose	na-k'o	nyi ga	hne zhon
Teeth	...	...	hsru
Tongue	...	...	hle
Fish	...	...	...
Mouth	...	...	k'a no
Hand	...	lo k'ua	zheru

Pa-U-Rong Hsi-Fan	Pa-U-Rong Lolo.	Tibetan.	Remarks.
...	...	za-wa.	
abi	...	nyal-wa.	
...	...	dung-wa ; zhu-wa.	
...	...	sö pa ; se pa.	
nyi	mi	mi.	
go	...	lo.	
yi	...	da wa.	
hli nyi	cha pa	da wa.	
nyi	...	nyin ; nyi ma.	
ru ra	ru ra	nyi-ma.	
...	me drü	kar-ma.	
...	...	trin-pa.	
...	...	ch‘ar-pa.	
za tri-bu	...	k‘a wa ; g‘ang.	
ri-ru	...	lung-po ; lhag-pa.	
ngi ru-ru	ni ru-ru	nam.	
na tsa-tsa	ma	me.	
dji	dji	ch‘u.	
o	...	ri.	
...	...	do.	
...	dra	sa.	
hsieh	...	shing.	
ngei	...	ser.	
dja-ha	she ha	ngül.	
ra-ha	...	chag.	
sa-ha	...	zang.	
ro	...	rü-pa.	
rong	rong	tsa.	
bre	...	dre.	
...	...	t‘a ma.	
...	...	ne ; tsam-pa.	
...	...	g‘o-ch‘en.	
...	hla	j‘a ; sö j‘a.	*Chinese* : ch‘a.
dzo zhu	...	b‘a mo ; dri ; dzo.	
...	...	...	
ma hla mi	...	k‘yi.	
kü-na	...	ra.	
dja	...	p‘ag-pa.	
...	ra-ma	j‘a.	
na hra	...	ri b‘ong ; yö.	
rong	...	lug.	
...	ko-tron	p‘a ; yab.	
...	k‘un yon	a ma ; yum.	
...	...	a j‘o ; j‘o la.	
...	...	nu-o.	
...	k‘o	go.	
ko ma	...	tra.	
...	ch‘u hsin	na (spelt rna).	
ra t‘on	ra t‘on	na (spelt sna).	
...	ra hu	so.	
...	...	...	
jü	...	nya.	
du ka	ng ken	k‘a.	
...	ya ba	lag-pa.	

English.	Yung-ning Li-so.	Yung-ning Moso.	Muli (Njong).
Black	a-lu ma	...	nya ka-ka mö
White	p‘u-cha ma	...	tr‘on mö
Red	p‘u shih chih ma	...	nye mö
Blue	ni ch‘u ma	...	nyi na na mö
Green	...	...	...
Yellow	...	...	nyö mö
This	...	...	o tei
That	...	...	dei pei
Arm	...	...	...
House	hyi	yi k‘ua	djih
Eyes	me to	nya lü	mi-a
Fingers	...	lu	hla-dzu
First finger	...	lu nyi	ku zhi hla-dzu
Second finger	...	lu so	son pa hla-dzu
Third finger	...	lu ru	zhi pa hla-dzu
Fourth finger	...	lu nga	nga-pa hla-dzu
Thumb	...	lu mi	ta ma
Finger-nail	...	...	...
Last year	...	...	zhei p‘u
Next year	...	...	zhei k‘u
Heart	...	...	hua
Fast	...	...	tr‘om p‘u
Slow	...	...	tei tei p‘u
Horse	a-mo	rouen	kwei
Stand	...	...	di ch‘in
Walk	...	...	shi ki
Blood	...	...	se
North	hung go lo	hung gu lo	...
South	i ch‘i me	i ch‘i me	...
East	mi mi tü ga[1]	nyi me tu[1]	...
West	mi mi gu ga[2]	nyi me gu[2]	...
Son, boy	nga za	zo	...
Daughter, girl	za mu za	mi zo	...
Go fast	mi mi ze	...	...
Go slow	za zu	...	...
Bed	...	...	...
Civil official	...	ssŭ p‘in	...
Road	...	zha me	...
Flower	...	ba ba	...
Tree	...	ssŭ tzŭ	...
Go up	...	kö be be	...
Go down	...	me ch‘a be	...
Feet	...	k‘ö ts‘e	...
Die, dead	...	le shih	...
Face	...	pa k‘ua	...
No, not	...	me be	...
Yes, be, is	...	k‘ë	...
Late	...	hua k‘o	...
Early	...	nya	...
Have	...	t‘e djo	...
Good	...	djei	...
Bad	...	mo djei	...
Body	...	...	...
Book	...	...	...

[1] Literally, "The side where the sun rises."

[2] Literally, "The side where the sun sets."

Pa-U-Rong Hsi-Fan	Pa-U-Rong Lolo.	Tibetan.	Remarks.
nyi na-no	na-na	nag-po.	
p'u li-li	ko lu-lu	kar-po.	
hu li-li	...	mar-po.	
...	...	njön-po.	
ngu li-li	...	jang-k'u.	
...	...	ser-po.	
...	i-bei	di.	
...	o-bei	d'e.	
ya	ya	lag-pa.	
...	ra-ba	k'ang-pa.	
byu	...	mig.	
...	o-dzu	dzüg-g'u.	
...	dan-yi-da	...	
...	som bü	...	
...	...	...	
...	...	...	
...	dza	t'e-po.	
...	ndra	sen-mo.	
ya bi	zha bi	na-ning.	
ya k'u	ya k'u	dri-lo.	
gya du	...	nying.	
tr'a p'u	...	gyog-po.	
ku-ku	...	g'a-li.	
dü	dü	ta.	
...	du-mu	lang-ne ; de-pa.	
...	re-bro	dro-wa.	
...	...	tr'ag.	
ch'a	...	ch'ang.	
lo	...	lho.	
lu	...	shar-ch'og.	
djong	...	nub-ch'og.	
...	da ngi ; bu ts'a	pu ; pu-g'u.	
...	ko ma sha ; me ji	b'u mo.	
...	...	gyog-pô dro.	
...	...	g'a-li dro.	
...	dra	nya t'ri.	
...	ko ta	pön po.	
...	...	lam.	
...	...	me-tog.	
...	sem-bu	sing-dong ; shing.	
...	...	yar.	
...	...	mar.	
...	...	kang-pa.	
...	...	ch'i wa ; k'oshi song.	
...	...	dong ; ngo.	
...	...	ma ; ma re.	
...	...	la so ; yö pa.	
...	...	ch'i po.	
...	...	nga po.	
...	...	yö pa.	
wu lat	...	yag po ; zang-po.	
za ru	...	ngen-pa.	
lu bu	...	zug po ; lü.	
gi gu	...	pe-ch'a.	

APPENDIX B: ITINERARY

Date.	Name of Place.	Remarks.
Jan. 6-9, 1906	Weihaiwei to Peking (威海衛：北京)	By steamer and train.
„ 13-16	Peking to Hankow (漢口)	By train.
„ 19-30	Hankow to Ichang (宜昌)	By steamer.
Feb. 2-12	Ichang to Wan-hsien (萬縣)	About 200 miles in "Red-boat."
„ 13	Fu-tzŭ-p'u (福自鋪)	Village.
	Fên Shui (分水)	Large village ; good inn.
„ 14	Shang Ku Ling (响鼓嶺)	Village.
	Liang-shan (梁山縣)	District city.
„ 15	Sha Ho P'u (沙河鋪)	Village.
	Lao Yin Ch'ang (老音塲)	Village.
	Yüan Pa I (元壩驛)	Village.
„ 16	Huang Ni Pien (黃泥邊)	Village.
	Ta Chu (大竹)	District city ; good inn.
„ 17	Chüan Tung Mên (眷東門)	Large village.
	Li Tu (李渡)	Small town on Ch'ü River.
„ 18	Crossed Ch'ü River (渠河)	Ferry.
	Wu Chia Ch'ang (吳家塲)	Busy unwalled town.
	Ch'ing Shih Chêng (青石正)	Large village.
„ 19	Lo Chia Ch'ang (羅家塲)	Village.

Date.	Name of Place.	Remarks.
Feb. 19	T'iao Têng Ch'ang (跳登塲)	Village ; bad inn.
„ 20	Lao Chün Ch'iao (老君橋)	Village.
	Shun-ch'ing-fu (順慶府)	Prefectural city on Chia-ling River. Good inn named the Shang Shêng Tien (上陞店).
„ 21	Wu Lung Ch'ang (五龍塲)	Village.
	P'êng-hsi-hsien (蓬溪縣)	District city.
„ 22	Kuan Shêng Tien (關聖殿)	Village.
	T'ai Ho Chên (太河鎮)	Small town on right bank of Fou Chiang. Many pottery factories and shrimp-shops. River navigable for narrow boats.
„ 23	Kao Fên Tsui (高墳嘴)	Village ; good inn.
	Kuan Yin Ch'iao (觀音橋)	Bridge and village.
„ 24	Lu Pan Ch'iao (魯板橋)	Village.
	Ta Sang Tun (大桑墩)	Village.
„ 25	Hsing Lung Ch'ang (興隆塲)	Large village.
	Chao Chia Tu (趙家渡)	Small town.
„ 26	Yao Chia Tu (姚家渡)	Village.
	Ch'êng-tu-fu (成都府)	Capital of Ssuch'uan. Elevation, 1,500 feet above sea-level.
Mar. 1-4	Ch'êng-tu to Chia-ting-fu (嘉定府)	By boat. Chia-ting is a small prefectural city at junction of Min, Ya and Ta Tu Rivers. Elevation, 1,100 feet.

Date.	Name of Place.	Remarks.
Mar. 6 . . .	Chia-ting to Omei-hsien (峨眉縣)	Omei-hsien is a small district city at the foot of Mount Omei, 1,500 feet.
„ 7-10 . . .	Mount Omei (峨眉山)	11,000 feet.
„ 11 . . .	Omei-hsien to Chia-chiang (夾江)	Small town on Ya River.
„ 12 . . .	Hung-Ya-hsien (洪雅縣)	District city
	Chih-kuo-chên (止戈鎮)	Small village ; bad inn.
„ 13 . . .	Kuan Yin Ch'ang (觀音場)	Small village.
	Ts'ao Pa (草壩)	Small town.
„ 14 . . .	Ya-chou-fu (雅州府)	Prefectural city, 2,500 feet.
„ 16 . . .	Fei Lung Pass (飛龍嶺)	3,600 feet.
	Shih-chia Ch'iao (石家橋)	Small village ; good inn.
„ 17 . . .	Jung-Ching-hsien (滎經縣)	Small town, 2,300 feet.
	Huang-ni-p'u (黃泥舖)	Small village, 3,870 feet.
„ 18 . . .	Ta Hsiang Ling (大相嶺)	Pass, 9,200 feet.
	Ch'ing-ch'i-hsien (清溪縣)	Small district city, 5,750 feet.
„ 19 . . .	Fu Chuang (富庄)	Small village, 3,900 feet.
	Ni (I) T'ou I (宜頭驛)	Small village ; good inns ; 4,900 feet.
„ 20 . . .	Fei Yüeh Ling (飛越嶺)	9,000 feet ; steep pass.
	Hua-lin-p'ing (花林坪)	Small village, 7,100 feet.
„ 21 . . .	Lêng Chi (冷磧)	Large village, 4,700 feet.
	Lu Ting Ch'iao (瀘定橋)	Small town on the left bank of Ta Tu River, 4,850 feet. Suspension bridge.

Date.	Name of Place.	Remarks.
Mar. 22	Ta P'êng Pa (大烹壩)	Hamlet.
	Wa Ssŭ Kou (瓦寺溝)	Small village near junction of Tachienlu River and Ta Tu River, 5,300 feet.
„ 23	Tachienlu (打箭鑪)	Small city, 8,400 feet.
Apr. 15	Chê To (折多)	Scattered hamlet, 10,650 feet.
„ 16	Solitary house.	
	Chê Ri La	Two passes : the higher about 17,400 feet.
	A Te	Scattered hamlet, 13,000 feet.
„ 17	Du Sz Drung	Village, 10,800 feet.
	Dza Ri K'u	Village.
	Ring I Drung	Village.
	Bridge and village.	
	Ba Lu	Village.
	P'un Bu Shi	Solitary house.
„ 18	Octagonal towers.	
	Ch'un Bo	Solitary house.
	Large house	Residence of T'u Pai Hu, 11,400 feet.
„ 19	Bridges.	
	Sho Ti Ba Dze	Village.
	Tan Ga La	Pass, 15,000 feet.
	Tu (*Chinese*, Lu Li)	Village.
„ 20	Bridge.	

Date.	Name of Place.	Remarks.
Apr. 20	Dro Dse Drung (*Ch.* San Chia-tzŭ : 三 家 子)	Village.
	Na K'i (*Ch.* Hsia Ch'êng-tzŭ : 下 城 子)	Village.
	Long Obo.	
	Dra Shê	Village.
	Octagonal tower.	
	Ri Wa (*Ch.* Wu Chia-tzŭ : 五 家 子).	
	Ko Ri Drung (*Ch.* Chung Ku : 中 古)	Hamlet, 13,000 feet.
„ 21	Dji Dju La	Pass, 17,500 feet.
	Dur (*Ch.* Hei Lao : 黑 老)	Village, 12,500 feet.
„ 22	Wu Shu La (*Ch.* Wu Shu Shan : 五 樹 山)	Pass, 15,500 feet.
	Wu Shu (*Ch.* Wu Shu : 五 樹)	Village, 11,000 feet.
„ 23	Sin Go La	Pass, 15,000 feet.
	Nai Yu La	Pass, 16,000 feet.
	Hlan Go La	Pass, 17,200 feet.
	Gur Dja (*Ch.* Yin Cho : 銀 棹)	Village, 12,000 feet.
„ 24	Ri Go La	Pass, 16,500 feet.
	Pu Ti La	Pass, 10,800 feet.
	Pei T'ai (*Ch.* Pai T'ai : 白 臺)	Village, 10,000 feet.
„ 25	Lan Yi Pa	Valley with one house.
	Hsin Yi La	Hill from which signal-gun is fired.
	Pa-U-Rong	Flourishing cluster of villages overlooking valley of Yalung, 7,700 feet.

Date.	Name of Place.	Remarks.
Apr. 27	Yalung River (Nya Ch'u, or Chin Ho) (鴉礱江)	Crossed by single-rope bridge. River, 7,500 feet.
	Dju Mu	Hamlet, 9,000 feet.
„ 28	Tê Ben	One house, 10,000 feet.
„ 29	Pa Sung	Hamlet.
	Ten Ba K'a	Hamlet, 10,800 feet.
„ 30	Pass	12,500 feet.
	Hu Dra	Solitary house, 10,100 feet.
May 1	Two ruined huts.	
	Wa-chin Gompa, or Lha-k'ang	Lamasery, 9,600 feet.
	Ta K'oa	Hamlet.
„ 2	Dje Ru	Hamlet.
	Tong Yi Bridge	Over Li Ch'u or Litang River.
	Wu	Hamlet.
	Obos and Chorten	Camp in the open, 9,000 feet.
„ 3	Bridges.	
	Ku-Dze	Hamlet.
	Muli (木裏)	Lamasery and headquarters of lama-prince of "Huang-Lama," 9,500 feet.
„ 6	Solitary house	9,500 feet.
„ 7	Shi Li La	Pass, 15,500 feet.
	Li She Tzŭ	Mo-so hamlet, 11,000 feet.
„ 8	Li Rang Tzŭ	Hamlet, the last in "Huang-Lama" and in Ssuch'uan.

Date.	Name of Place.	Remarks.
May 8	Boundary of Ssuch'uan and Yunnan Provinces.	
	Djo Dji	Village.
	Wo La	Village.
	Yi Ma Wa	Village.
	A-ko Am-ni Wa	Village.
	A-gu Wa	Village.
	Yung-ning-t'u-fu (永寧土府)	A Mo-so town with a lamasery. Chief centre of district ruled by Mo-so chief, on whom Chinese Government has conferred hereditary rank of Prefect; 9,500 feet.
„ 10	Ge Wa Ya K'ou	Pass, 13,000 feet.
	Solitary hut.	
„ 11	Lan Ga Lo	House.
	La Ka Shi	Village.
	Ferry	Yangtse River, 5,200 feet.
	Fêng K'o	Village, 7,200 feet.
„ 12	Shrine and spring.	
	Cottages.	
	Camp in forest.	
„ 13	Go Ka A	Pass, 15,000 feet.
	T'o Ko Sho	Hamlet.
	Camp in forest.	

Date.	Name of Place.	Remarks.
May 14	Ming Yin Chi (鳴音汲)	Village, 9,200 feet.
	Camp	8,900 feet.
„ 15	Pass	10,600 feet.
	Bridge over Hei Shui (黑水)	8,900 feet.
	Three passes	Highest about 11,000 feet.
	Stony plateau	Overlooked by snowy peaks, 18,500 feet.
	Li-chiang plain and villages.	
	Li-chiang (麗江府)	Prefectural town: seat of native chief, and also of Chinese Prefect and Magistrate, 8,200 feet.
„ 18	Shang La Shih (上喇是), or Lashi	Village, 8,100 feet.
	Pass	10,000 feet.
	Kuan Hsia (關下), or P'o Chiao (坡腳)	Village at north end of Chien Ch'uan plain.
„ 19	Tu Ho (渡河)	Village.
	Wa Ch'ang (瓦場)	Village.
	Chi Wu (雞勿)	Village.
	Chiu Ho Pa (九河壩)	Village.
	Mei Tzŭ (梅子)	Village.
	Shao Chin Ch'ang (哨金場)	Village.
	Chien-ch'uan-chou (劍川州)	Departmental city, 7,500 feet.
	Lake.	
	Han Têng Ts'un (漢登村)	Village.
	Hai Wei (海尾)	River and bridge.

Date.	Name of Place.	Remarks.
May 19	Tien Wei Kai (甸 尾 街)	Village.
„ 20	Hao Shou Bridge (蒿 壽 橋)	House, temple and bridge.
	Niu Kai (牛 街)	Village.
	Huo Yen Shan (火 燄 山)	Hill with hot springs.
	San Ying (三 營)	Small market town ; good inn.
„ 21	Ch'ang Ying (長 營)	Village.
	Ying-shan-p'u (映 山 舖)	Large village.
	Pai Sha Ho (白 沙 河)	Small river and canal.
	Chung So (中 所)	Village.
	Yu So (右 所)	Village.
	Lung Kai Tzŭ (龍 街 子)	Village.
	Têng-ch'uan-chou (登 川 州)	Small departmental city, 7,000 feet.
	Erh Hai (洱 海)	Lake of Tali-fu.
	Sha P'ing (沙 坪)	Village near north end of lake.
„ 22	Shang Kuan (上 關)	Walled village.
	Numerous villages.	
	Tali-fu (大 理 府)	Prefectural city, 6,700 feet.
„ 25	Hsia Kuan (下 關)	Busy town, 6,900 feet.
	Ho Chiang-p'u (河 港 舖)	Small village.
„ 26	Yang Pi	Small town, 5,160 feet.
	Suspension bridge.	
	Mountain hamlet	Not the usual stage.

Date.	Name of Place.	Remarks.
May 27	Pass	8,350 feet.
	T'ai-p'ing-p'u (太平鋪)	Hamlet, 7,370 feet.
	Suspension bridge	Over Ch'ing Lien Ho (清蓮河).
	Huang-lien-p'u	Village.
" 28	Chiao Kou Shan	Huts.
	Wan Sung An	Small temple.
	Yung P'ing (永平)	Small town.
" 29	Hsiao T'ien Pa (小田垻)	Village.
	Hsiao Hua Ch'iao (小花橋)	Village.
	Ta Hua Ch'iao (大花橋)	Village.
	Pass	8,150 feet.
	Sha Yang	Village.
" 30	Bridge of the Phœnix Cry (鳳鳴石橋).	
	Pass.	
	Mekong River (瀾滄江)	4,000 feet. Bridge of 60 yards span.
	P'ing P'o	Hamlet.
	Shui Chai	Village.
" 31	Pass	7,800 feet.
	Niu Chio Kuan	Village.
	Kuan P'o	Village.
	Shih K'o Ts'un	Village.
	Pan Ch'iao (板橋)	Village.

Date.	Name of Place.	Remarks.
May 31	Yung-ch'ang-fu (永昌府)	Prefectural city, 5,500 feet.
June 1	Wo Shih Wo (臥獅窩)	Village.
	Hao Tzŭ P'u	Village.
	Pass.	
	Lêng Shui Ching (冷水井)	Village.
	P'u Piao	Large village.
" 2	Fang Ma Ch'ang (放馬場)	Villages.
	Ta Pan Ching (大板井)	Hamlet, 4,500 feet.
" 3	Salwen River	Suspension bridge, 2,400 feet.
	Hu Mu Shu	Hamlet, 5,560 feet.
" 4	Hsiang Po (象脖)	Hamlet, 7,230 feet.
	Pass	8,730 feet.
	T'ai P'ing (太平)	Hamlet, 7,780 feet.
	Shwe-Li or Lung River	Suspension bridge, 4,300 feet.
	Kan-Lan-Chan (乾欖站)	Village, 4,810 feet.
" 5	Chin Chai P'u (金齋鋪)	Village.
	T'êng-Yüeh (騰越), or Momein	City. British Consulate and Chinese Imperial Customs. 5,365 feet.
" 8	Jê Shui T'ang (熱水塘)	Village.
	Nan Tien (南甸)	Village. Seat of a Shan Sawbwa.
" 9	Kau Ngai	Market village.
" 10	Hsiao Hsin Kai (小新街)	Village ; good inn.

Date.	Name of Place.	Remarks.
June 11	Lung Chang Kai	Village. Customs station.
	Man-hsien	Village. Seat of a Shan sawbwa.
„ 12	Kamsa Bridge	Iron bridge, completed 1905.
	Kulika	British frontier.
	Mong-kung-ka	First Government Bungalow.
„ 13	Kulong-ka	Government Bungalow.
„ 14	Kalachet	Bungalow.
	Momauk	Bungalow.
„ 15	Bhamo	Frontier garrison-town, on Irrawaddy, 361 feet.
„ 20	Mandalay	By steamer from Bhamo.

NOTES

NOTE 1 (p. 61)

MOUNT OMEI AND CHOU KUNG SHAN

There are vague traditions that Mount Omei was a centre of primitive nature-worship long before the days of Buddhism. There is a passage in the *Shu Ching* from which we learn that the semi-mythical emperor Yü (about the twenty-third century B.C.), after the completion of some of the famous drainage and irrigation works with which his name is associated, offered sacrifices on (or to) certain hills named Ts'ai and Mêng. It is a disputed point among the commentators where these hills are. Mêng is said to be one of the mountains that overlook Ya-chou, and we shall see in Chapter VIII. that one of those mountains is still the resort of pilgrims. As to Ts'ai, one commentator at least has inclined to the opinion that it must be looked for in the Omei range (see Legge's *Chinese Classics*, vol. iii. part i. p. 121). If this identification be correct, we must regard the brief notice in the *Shu Ching* as the oldest reference in extant literature to Mount Omei. The student of Chinese who wishes to pursue further the vexed question of Mêng and Ts'ai will find a discussion of it in the 16th *chüan* of the *Ssuch'uan T'ung Chih*. The probability seems to be that both Mêng and Ts'ai were close to Ya-chou, and that neither of them should be identified with Omei. Mêng seems to be one of the hills that lie to the south of the city; Ts'ai may or may not be the somewhat famous mountain generally known as Chou Kung Shan, or the Hill of Duke Chou, which is situated a couple of miles to the east. Chou Kung, who is said to have died in B.C. 1105, is perhaps chiefly known to Europeans as the legendary inventor of the famous "south-pointing chariot," but he is regarded by the Chinese as a pattern of many virtues. His zeal for the public good was so great that he seems—if we may believe Mencius — to have anticipated the all-night sittings of the House of Commons. His merits indeed were of so extraordinary a nature that, as we know from the *Lun Yü*, Confucius regarded it as a sign of his approaching dotage that for a long time he had ceased to dream of Chou Kung.

Other people besides Confucius were in the habit of dreaming of this great and good man. The hill near Ya-chou, according to a story preserved in the official annals of Ssuch'uan, owes its name to a dream-vision that came to the famous Chinese general, Chu-ko Liang. This distinguished warrior flourished in the second and third centuries of our era. He made his name by his successful campaigns against the Wild Men of the West—the Man-tzŭ and others — and on one occasion when he was proceeding at the head of his army to inflict chastisement upon them he spent a night on the slopes of the Ya-chou Hill and dreamed that Chou Kung paid him a visit. He regarded this as of such happy omen for the success of his expedition that he immediately caused a temple to Chou Kung to be erected on the auspicious spot. Since that time, the hill—which may or may not have been already sacred, under the name of Ts'ai, to the memory of the Emperor Yü—has always been known as Chou Kung Shan. The fame of the general Chu-ko Liang has almost rivalled that of Chou Kung himself. This "darling hero of the Chinese people," as Professor Giles calls him, has had temples erected in his honour in many towns of Ssuch'uan, and he is a well-known and popular figure on the Chinese theatrical stage.

NOTE 2 (p. 65)

BODHIDARMA

Bodhidarma (達 摩 大 師) is the original of the *Ta Mo* so often found in Ssuch'uanese temples. Catholic missionaries, struck by the sound of the name and the fact that Ta-Mo is sometimes found wearing an ornament shaped like a Christian cross, have clung to the idea that Ta-Mo was no other than the Apostle St Thomas. (See *Croix et Swastika*, by Father Gaillard, pp. 80 *seq.*) Bodhidarma is regarded as the founder of the Zen sect in Japan. Japanese children know him well, for he is a conspicuous object in the toy-shops in the form of the legless Daruma. (See Lafcadio Hearn's charming essay in *A Japanese Miscellany.*)

NOTE 3 (p. 70)

"GODS" IN BUDDHISM

On this subject may be consulted the passage on the "Eel-wrigglers" in the Brahma-gâla Suttanta, translated by Rhys Davids in the *Sacred Books of the Buddhists*, vol. ii. Buddhism refrains from denying, rather than distinctly affirms, the existence of the Brahmanical gods; but these gods, if existent, are regarded as neither omnipotent nor immortal. They are subject to the law of karma just as man himself is subject. The Arahat is greater than any "god" because released from all change and illusion, to which the "gods" are still subject. (See Rhys Davids, *Hibbert Lectures*, pp. 210 *seq.*, 4th edn.) The abolition or retention of the Brahmanical deities would really make little or no difference to the philosophical position of canonical Buddhism.

NOTE 4 (p. 71)

NIRVANA

The view of Nirvana set forth in the text is that taught by Professor Rhys Davids, the veteran scholar to whom all European students of Buddhism owe so deep a debt of gratitude. (See his *Buddhism*, *Hibbert Lectures*, *American Lectures*, and his valuable contributions to the *Sacred Books of the East*. With regard to Nirvana, see especially his *Questions of King Milinda*, vol. i. pp. 106-108 and vol. ii. pp. 181 *seq.*) As regards the *tanha* or "thirst" for existence, which according to the Buddhist theory keeps us in the net of illusion and prevents the attainment of Nirvana, Huxley (*Evolution and Ethics*) mentions as a curious fact that a parallel may be found in the *aviditas vitae* of Stoicism.

The Japanese views of Nirvana are set forth clearly and authoritatively in Fujishima's *Le Bouddhisme Japonais*. "Selon les écoles du Mahâyâna, ce qui est vide au dedans et au dehors c'est l'existence composée et visible (*samkrita*) : l'anéantissement de ce vide n'est donc pas lui-même le vide, mais plutôt la plénitude." The author goes on to quote from a sutra which declares that "illusion passes away; reality remains; that is Nirvana." To an English reader this naturally recalls some of Shelley's lines in *Adonais*, too well known to quote. Japanese Buddhism has, of course, developed somewhat on lines of its own. The popular Buddhism of Japan is portrayed with rare insight by Lafcadio Hearn, as in his *Gleanings from Buddha-Fields*, pp. 211 *seq.*

Among recent attempts to escape from the pessimistic conclusion that, according to strict Buddhism, Arahatship must lead after all to complete extinction, Schrader's interesting essay in the *Journal* of the Pali Text Society, 1904-1905, is worth consulting. The question is one of deep philosophic interest, but a discussion of it cannot be attempted in the narrow space at our disposal here.

NOTE 5 (p. 76)

THE MAHAYANA

For explanations of the rise of the Mahayana, see (among many other authorities) Max Müller's *India*, p. 87 (1905 edn.) and his *Last Essays* (First Series) pp. 260 *seq.* (Longmans: 1901); see also p. 376 in R. Sewell's essay on *Early Buddhist Symbolism* (J.R.A.S., July, 1886). For the growth of the Mahayana and kindred schools in China, the works of Beal, Edkins, Eitel and Watters are among the first that should be consulted. There is still a great deal that is mysterious in the early history of Mahayana and allied systems, and it is reasonable to hope that the discoveries recently made, and still being made almost daily by Stein and others in Chinese Turkestan and neighbouring regions, will throw a flood of light on the whole subject, and perhaps destroy many existing theories regarding the history of Buddhism during the ten or twelve first centuries of the Christian era.

NOTE 6 (p. 86)

ANTIQUITIES OF MOUNT OMEI

As Baber's discovery of the *chüan tien* or spiral-shaped brick hall and the bronze elephant which it contains aroused very natural enthusiasm among persons interested in Far Eastern antiquities, and is still repeatedly referred to in connection with Chinese archæology, it is with hesitation that I suggest a doubt as to whether either the building or the elephant is as old as Baber—and others after him—have supposed. (See *Supplementary Papers*, R.G.S., vol. i. pp. 34–36, and Archibald Little's *Mount Omi and Beyond*, pp. 64-5.)

In the 41st *chüan* of the *Ssuch'uan T'ung Chih* there are two passages relating to the Wan-nien Ssŭ, and one of them Baber apparently overlooked. It was written about 1665 in commemoration of a restoration of the Wan-nien and Kuang Hsiang monasteries under the auspices of a Provincial Governor. In it occur some remarks of which the following is a rough translation. "From the T'ang to the Sung dynasties the name of the monastery was *Pai Shui P'u Hsien Ssŭ*. In the time of Wan Li of the Ming, its name was changed to *Shêng-shou Wan-nien Ssŭ*. As originally built (*yüan chien*) it contained a *tsang ching ko* (*i.e.* a library) consisting of a revolving (circular?) spiral structure of brick, strongly built, of exceptionally delicate workmanship, very lofty and imposing, and of a beauty unsurpassed in the world." Now the existing *tien* is a most curious building of a foreign (probably Indian) type, but to describe it as lofty and imposing and of delicate and elaborate workmanship would be to spin a traveller's yarn of the baser sort. How, without impugning the good faith of the chronicler, can we reconcile such a glowing description with existing facts?

When we learn from the local records that the Wan-nien Ssŭ has been several times destroyed by fire, the obvious supposition is that the original splendid structure described in my quotation perished with the rest of the monastic pile. Baber himself points out that the tusks of the elephant inside the *tien* are of late date, the old ones having been "melted off," he was told, "by the intense heat." It seems natural to suppose that when the rebuilding of the monastery took place (and it was rebuilt, as we know, late in the sixteenth or early in the seventeenth century, and again about 1665) the monks had neither funds nor skill sufficient to enable them to restore the *chüan tien* to its pristine magnificence, and contented themselves with putting up a much smaller and meaner building, preserving as far as possible the original peculiarities of design.

This, however, is mere supposition. I now return to our Chinese authorities, and in the 9th *chüan* of the *Omei-hsien Chih* I find an allusion to the Wan-nien Ssŭ by one Li Hua Nan (李化楠), an official who apparently flourished in the seventeenth century. He states most emphatically that the monastery was restored or rebuilt in both the Sung and the Ming periods, but had undergone such complete destruction by fire that nothing was left *except a chüan tien belonging to the period of Wan Li*. Wan Li was the reign-title of a Ming emperor who reigned from 1573 to 1619. That the *chüan tien* was *carefully and thoroughly restored* under Wan Li is admitted by the authority quoted by Baber himself: the only question seems to be whether the restoration left enough of the original building to justify our regarding it as a veritable monument "fifteen centuries old"—as Baber conjectured—or whether, as the evidence seems to indicate, the restoration was such that we have only a small and inferior copy of "a lofty and imposing building, of a beauty unsurpassed in the world."

No one, so far as I know, has yet drawn attention to the fact that the spiral building of the Wan-nien Ssŭ is not—or was not—the only building of its kind on Mount Omei. Among the few monasteries on the lower slopes of the mountain which I did not enter is the Hua Yen Ssŭ (not to be confused with the temple of the Hua Yen Ting mentioned on page 91). It was not till after I had left the province that I came across a description of this monastery, which made me much regret that I had not visited it. I translate the following passage from the *Omei-Shan Chih* (quoted in the 41st *chüan* of the *T'ung Chih*): "There is a very ancient and wonderful revolving (circular?) spiral building (有 磚 螺 殿 極 其 古), and a tablet of the Shao Hsing period of the Sung dynasty, on the left side of which are carved the words '15 *li* to Omei-hsien' and on the right the words '70 *li* to the summit of the mountain.'" The words used to describe the shape of the "revolving spiral" building are identical—so far as they go—with those applied to the brick edifice in the Wan-nien Ssŭ: and the whole passage certainly implies that, whatever the date of the spiral building in the Hua Yen Ssŭ might be, it was at any rate prior to the Sung dynasty. The next visitor to Mount Omei should not fail to examine the curiosities of the Hua Yen Ssŭ; a close inspection of its spiral building—if it still exists—and a comparison of it with that of the Wan-nien Ssŭ might assist us in assigning a date to the latter, and might perhaps prove that however old the latter may be it is not without a rival in mere antiquity.

So much for the brick building. What is to be said about the bronze elephant that Baber so properly admired, and which he believed to be "the most ancient bronze casting of any great size in existence"?

Li Hua Nan, the writer who ascribes the *chüan tien* to the Wan Li period, goes on to add a piece of information which is much to our purpose. "There is a P'u Hsien 1 *chang* 6 *ch'ih* in height, with a gilded body, riding a bronze elephant, set up in the *Jên Tsung period of the Sung dynasty.*" The sentence is somewhat ambiguous, for the date might refer to the image of P'u Hsien only and not to the elephant. Baber believed, on artistic grounds, that the P'u Hsien was of much later date than the elephant. On the whole, however, it seems probable that Li Hua Nan referred to both images. The Jên Tsung reign lasted from 1023 to 1063, so that if we select the middle of the period we may assign the elephant approximately to the year 1043. This cuts many centuries off the age of the elephant as reckoned by Baber.

There is no reason for doubting whether so fine a bronze casting of an animal unknown to China could have been made as late as the eleventh century. There were still Buddhists in India at that time, and Chinese pilgrims had not yet given up the habit of visiting India in search of relics and *pei to yeh* (palm-leaf manuscripts). Indian Buddhists, too, frequently came to Mount Omei. There is, indeed, no necessity for mere guess-work, for the monastic and provincial records contain ample evidence that the casting of large bronzes for Buddhist shrines was, during the Sung period at least, a regular industry in the city of Ch'êng-tu.

The numerous miniature "Buddhas" that line the walls of the present *chüan tien* have attracted the attention of several European visitors, and perhaps deserve a few words of comment.

Some are the property of pilgrims who leave them in the holy building in order that they may acquire sanctity, but the greater number are evidently antique and seem to be of uniform pattern. Baber was informed that they were of silver—darkened with age and the smoke of incense. Mr Archibald Little says they are of bronze. I made my own enquiries on the matter and was assured by the monks that they were of iron. Where did they come from? I conjecture that they are the images that once adorned a vanished hall of the Wan-nien Ssŭ, known as the *San Ch'ien T'ieh Fo Tien*—Pavilion of the Three Thousand Iron Buddhas. I cannot find any history of this building, but from a poem by Ku Kuang Hsü, a Ssuch'uan chief justice of the Ming dynasty, I gather that it was remembered but had disappeared by his time. It existed in the Sung dynasty, for it is mentioned by one Fan Ch'êng Ta (范成大) who visited it during that period. The number of the images is easily explained as an allusion to the three thousand disciples who are said to have sat at the feet of P'u Hsien in the days when, according to the legend, that great Bodhisattva expounded the Good Law amid the forests of Mount Omei.

NOTE 7 (p. 86)

"BUDDHA'S TEETH"

The most famous of the supposed teeth of Buddha is, of course, the celebrated relic preserved in Kandy. The Buddhists of Ceylon will have none of the story that the original tooth was ground into powder by a pious Portuguese archbishop of the sixteenth century, and they firmly believe that the genuine relic still reposes in Kandy at the Malagawa Vihara. China possesses, or is supposed to possess, several of the alleged Buddha's teeth, but they seem to have acquired no more than a local reputation. One—similar in appearance to that of Mount Omei—is described by Fortune as being in possession of a monastery at Fu-chou. A writer in the *Fan Ju Tzŭ Chi* (范汝梓記), commenting upon the specimen in the Wan-nien Ssŭ, remarks that it weighs 15 catties, equivalent to about 20 lbs. He says that in the Ching Yin (淨因寺) in Ch'êng-tu there is one that weighs $3\frac{1}{3}$ lbs., and another in the Chao Chiao Ssŭ (昭覺寺) in the same city that weighs $9\frac{1}{2}$ lbs. He goes on to describe a far more remarkable specimen that had the singular property of producing out of its own substance myriads of other *shê li* or Buddhistic relics, some of which flew off into space while others fell on the floor and knocked against the furniture with a jingling sound. This surprising tooth appeared by special command

2 D

before the emperor, but we are not informed whether the *séance* was a successful one. Our historian shows something of a tendency to indulge in frivolous speculations regarding the capacity and measurements of the mouth that could accommodate teeth of such monstrous sizes and singular properties, and he points out that according to tradition a true Buddha's tooth is always marked with certain sacred symbols, such as the *dharma chakra* or Wheel of the Law.

Marco Polo mentions a great embassy sent by the emperor of China to Ceylon in 1284 for the purpose of obtaining certain relics of "our first father Adam," such as his hair and teeth and a dish from which he ate; and he remarks that the ambassadors, besides acquiring the dish, which was of "very beautiful green porphyry," and some of the hair, "also succeeded in getting two of the grinder teeth, which were passing great and thick." It need hardly be said that the monarchs of the Yüan dynasty took a very considerable interest in Buddha, but none at all in "our first father Adam." That they sent embassies to Ceylon for Buddhist relics is probably true, for the fact is mentioned in Chinese Chronicles; but it is impossible to say whether any of the numerous "teeth of Buddha" that have appeared in different localities in China formed part of the relics then brought from Ceylon. (The notes appended to Cordier's edition of Yule's *Marco Polo*, vol. ii. chap. xv., should be consulted by all interested in the subject of the migrations of Buddhist relics.)

NOTE 8 (p. 89)

THE K'AI SHAN CH'U TIEN

The name of this monastery shows that it claims to be one of the original religious foundations of Mount Omei. According to tradition it was here that P'u Kung, as related in Chapter VI., was gathering herbs when he came across "in a misty hollow" the tracks of the lily-footed deer that led him to the mountain-top. The monastery is supposed to have been founded in commemoration of the occurrence.

NOTE 9 (p. 95)

TA SHÊNG SSŬ OR GREAT VEHICLE MONASTERY

The old name of this monastery was Hua Ch'êng (化城), and the name was chosen by its founder, "a holy monk from the foreign countries of the West," who said that the scenery reminded him of his native country. Tradition says that he built the original hermitage of the bark of trees; hence the additional name *Mu-p'i* by which the foundation was known for centuries afterwards. One of the stories about this part of the mountain is that two hungry pilgrims were fed with fruit here by a wonderful white monkey.

NOTE 10 (p. 102)

"THE GLORY OF BUDDHA"

Several Chinese descriptions of the Fo Kuang will be found in the chronicles of Mount Omei and of Omei-hsien, notably those of Ho Shih Hêng (何式恒) and Yüan Tzŭ Jang (袁子讓). According to the latter, there are more than five colours. He describes the appearance somewhat as follows. The central circle is of jade-green; the outermost circle consists of a layer of pale red, and the successive inner circles are of green, white, purple, yellow and crimson. Each beholder, he says, sees his own shadow in the mist of the central circle.

A crude drawing of the "Glory" may be noticed near the upper left-hand corner of the Chinese plan of Mount Omei, which is reproduced in this book.

NOTE 11 (p. 108)

"THE HOLY LAMPS"

Among good Chinese descriptions of this phenomenon may be mentioned those of Yüan Tzŭ Jang (袁子讓) of the Ming and Ho Shih Hêng (何式恒) of the present dynasty. Both writers have been mentioned in the preceding note. The former wrote a delightful account of his visit to Mount Omei. It is in a flowing unpedantic style, and it proves that its writer had a keenly observant eye and a great liking for old-world legends combined with a power of working them up into a graceful narrative.

NOTE 12 (p. 109)

THE HSIEN TSU TIEN, CHUNG FÊNG SSŬ AND TA O SSŬ

The *Hsien Tsu Tien* represents the earliest of the Mount Omei monasteries, and is said to have been built by P'u Kung in the reign of Ming Ti of the Han dynasty after the famous episode of the lily-footed deer. Probably if the searchlight of strict historical enquiry were to be turned on the legends and records of Mount Omei, it would be found that the mountain knew nothing of Buddhism until the third or fourth centuries of our era. It is a significant fact that some of the legends about P'u Kung—the herb-gathering official who followed the deer and first saw the "Glory"—state or imply that he belonged to the Chin period, which did not begin till the year 265. There is more than a likelihood that the historians of such ancient monasteries as the Hsien Tsu Tien and the Wan-nien Ssŭ deliberately ante-dated their foundation in order to throw back the beginnings of Omei's Buddhistic history to the earliest possible period. It is almost inconceivable that Omei can have become the resort of Buddhist monks during the very reign of the emperor who is credited with the first introduction of Buddhism into China.

According to the monastic chronicles, the earliest name of the monastery we are considering was P'u Kaung Tien, "The Pavilion of Universal Glory." The name was subsequently altered to Kuang Hsiang Ssŭ (光相寺), and so it was known during the T'ang and Sung periods. In the time of Hung Wu, first emperor of the Ming, it was rebuilt and roofed with iron. Associated with it were four small bronze pagodas, some of the remains of which are still lying on the ground within the precincts of the present Chin Tien (which was apparently first built in the reign of Wan Li of the Ming). A thorough restoration—carried out during a period of three years—took place in the second half of the fifteenth century. At the end of the Ming period it was utterly destroyed—presumably by fire. It was again rebuilt during the reign of K'ang Hsi of the present dynasty under the auspices of a Provincial Governor named Chang (see note 6, paragraph 2), and minor restorations on a smaller scale have taken place more recently.

The *Chung Fêng Ssŭ* or Half-way Monastery bears the alternative name of "The Gathering Clouds," an allusion to the fact that here the upward-bound pilgrim enters into the region of mist. It dates from the Chin dynasty (about the third century of our era) and was restored in the Sung and Ming periods.

The *Ta O Ssŭ* is an ancient foundation rebuilt in the first year of K'ang Hsi (1662). It is one of the principal religious houses on the mountain, and has a finer site than most of its rivals. An alternative name is Fu Shou An. This name is due to the fact that the words Fu Shou — "Happiness and Longevity"—were carved on a neighbouring rock by a celebrated recluse of the Sung dynasty named Hsi I, known as the Wizard of Omei.

NOTE 13 (p. 114)

YA-CHOU-FU

The military importance of this city was very great so long as the tribal chiefs and Tibetans had not been reduced to comparative quiescence. The commander-in-chief of the military forces of the province was permanently stationed at this frontier city. (*Shéng Wu Chi*, 11*th chüan*.)

NOTE 14 (p. 117)

THE TA HSIANG LING

There is a small unsettled controversy regarding the name of the Ta Hsiang Ling. It is possible that the mountain owes its name not to the legend of P'u Hsien's elephant, but to the famous general Chu-ko Liang (see note 1). Devout Buddhists are bound to hold that the name means "The Great Elephant," and this is the view taken in all Buddhistic accounts of western Ssuch'uan and in the maps issued by the monks of Mount Omei. But other authorities—including the official *Topography* and the *Shéng Wu Chi* (5th *chüan*)—give the central character not as 象 (*hsiang*, elephant) but as 相 (*hsiang*, minister of state), thereby changing the mountain's name into "The Great Mountain of the Minister." This minister is none other than Chu-ko Liang, who is said to have crossed the mountain during his western campaigns. The "Small Elephant Pass" in the Chien-ch'ang Valley is similarly metamorphosed into "The Small Mountain of the Minister," and for a like reason. This latter mountain, however, is also known officially as the Nan Shan or South Mountain. (寧遠府南山土名小相嶺嘗以武侯經過得名: *Shéng Wu Chi*, *loc. cit.*)

This note will throw a light on a passage that occurs in Mr

Archibald Little's *Mount Omi and Beyond* (pp. 204-205) and exonerate Captain Gill from the charge of inaccuracy.

It may be worth mentioning that a neighbouring mountain bears the officially-recognised name of Shih-tzŭ Shan, or Lion Hill, but the *T'ung Chih* explicitly states that this is owing to its peculiar shape. There is nothing in the contour of the Ta Hsiang Ling to suggest an elephant.

NOTE 15 (p. 120)

CH'ING-CH'I-HSIEN

This little town has had a variety of names during its long and chequered history, and it frequently changed hands. Its position was for centuries somewhat analogous to that of Berwick-on-Tweed during the Anglo-Scottish border wars. The *T'ung Chih* states that it passed into the hands of the Chinese after one of the numerous "pacifications of the West," in the 30th year of Han Wu Ti (111 B.C.), but it was lost to China many times after that. Its present name and status as a magistracy date from the eighth year of Yung Chêng (1730). This was an epoch in which a series of able Chinese emperors were making determined and, on the whole, successful efforts to reduce the Wild West to obedience.

NOTE 16 (p. 121)

THE LIU SHA RIVER

The Liu Sha is also known as the Han Shui or Chinese water. It is said to rise in the "Fairy's Cave" (*hsien jên tung*) in the Fei Yüeh range. Thence it flows to the Shih Chien Shan or Trial-of-the-Sword Hill and joins the Chien Shui (澗 水) and thereafter enters the Ta Tu. According to the *Huan Yü Chi* (寰 宇 記) an evil miasma arises from this river every winter and spring, causing fever.

NOTE 17 (p. 122)

THE FEI YÜEH LING AND HUA-LIN-P'ING

This great pass has for centuries been regarded by the Chinese as a very important strategic point in connection with their western wars. During the eighteenth century, when strenuous warfare was being carried on against the Chin Ch'uan chiefs and others, the summit of the pass was permanently held by a Chinese guard, and the village that lies at the mountain's western base—Hua-lin-p'ing—was garrisoned by a considerable body of troops.

NOTE 18 (p. 124)

THE TA TU RIVER

The Ta Tu (Great Ferry) is said to derive its name from the fact that it was crossed by the ubiquitous Chu-ko Liang. In the neighbourhood of Chia-ting it is commonly known as the T'ung, and above Wa Ssŭ Kou its two branches are always known as the Great and Small Chin Ch'uan. (*Shêng Wu Chi, 5th chüan.*)

NOTE 19 (p. 126)

LU TING BRIDGE

The *Ssuch'uan T'ung Chih* makes the following remark in connection with the suspension bridge at Lu Ting. "Formerly there was no bridge. The waters of the river are swift and turbulent, and boats and oars cannot be used. Travellers used to cross by hanging on to a rope stretched across the river—a dangerous proceeding." (We shall see, when we come to the Yalung, that rope bridges are still in use.) In the fortieth year of K'ang Hsi (1701) it was decided with imperial sanction to construct an iron suspension bridge, not merely for the convenience of travellers to and from Tibet, but also to facilitate the military operations which during the reigns of K'ang Hsi, Yung Chêng and Ch'ien Lung were carried on with great vigour against the Tibetan tribes. The bridge is accurately described in the *Chih* and in the *Hsi Tsang Tu K'ao* as being 31 *chang* 1 *ch'ih* in length and 9 *ch'ih* broad, and as possessing 9 chain-cables supporting wooden planks, and side-railings of cast-iron. A *chang* is 11$\frac{3}{4}$ English feet, and a *ch'ih* about 14$\frac{1}{10}$ English inches. The bridge is similar in construction to those that span the Mekong, Salwen and other rivers in Yunnan. They are remarkable examples of Chinese engineering skill, and never fail to astonish European travellers who behold them for the first time.

The completion of the Lu Ting bridge seems to have had a considerable moral effect on the border tribes, for the *Chih* contains the names of dozens of *t'u ssŭ* (tribal chiefs) who immediately afterwards submitted to Chinese overlordship and consented to pay tribute. The more remote chiefs came in later, but most of those in the neighbourhood of the road to Tachienlu and the Ta Tu River hastened to become vassals of China during the five first years of the eighteenth century. The vassalage consisted—and for the most part still consists—merely in the payment of a small annual tribute. But the chiefs of the Greater and the Smaller Chin Ch'uan — the country that includes the valley of the Ta Tu and its branches above Wa Ssŭ Kou—resisted Chinese encroachments for many years in a most vigorous and courageous manner, and it was not till the reign of Ch'ien Lung, towards the end of the century, that the resistance of the last Chin Ch'uan *roitelet* was finally quelled — with the usual accompaniments of slaughter and devastation. Even as it was, the Chinese owed their ultimate success more to the assistance rendered them by other tribal chiefs—of whom the Ming Chêng Ssŭ or King of Chala was the most important—than to their own military skill. The war is well described—though from an exclusively Chinese standpoint—in the *Shêng Wu Chi* (聖武記).

NOTE 20 (p. 129)

TACHIENLU

The Chinese characters (see Itinerary) used for the name Tachienlu are three separate words signifying *strike, arrow, forge.* These characters were originally chosen merely to represent the sound of the Tibetan name Tar-rTse-Mto or Dartsendo (derived from the names of the streams that meet there), but Chinese archæologists contrived to forget this and insisted upon finding an interpretation of the word that would suit the meaning of the three Chinese characters. Accordingly they constructed an ingenious legend to the effect that the famous Chu-ko Liang—always as useful in literary as he used to be in military emergencies—came to Tachienlu in the third century of our era, and ordered his lieutenant, Kuo Ta, to forge arrow-heads there for the imperial army. The actual forge is said to have been in a cave on a hill at a short distance to the north-east of the city. The proof of the absolute truth of this story consists in the incontrovertible fact that the hill in question is called the Kuo Ta hill to this day, and there is a cave in it. The story is further embellished by the statement that when the forge was in use a blue-black ram ran round the hill and frightened away the barbarians (*i jên*) so that the good work could proceed without interruption.

An ancient name of the Tachienlu district is said to have been Mao Niu Kuo—the Land of Yaks.

NOTE 21 (p. 129)

SINO-TIBETAN TRADE

Chinese accounts of Tachienlu as a trading centre may be found in the *Hsi Tsang T'u K'ao*, the *Tachienlu T'ing Chih* and the more easily accessible *Shêng Wu Chi*. In the fifth volume of the last-named work the town is aptly described as being (from the commercial point of view) the hub of a wheel —the centre at which all the spokes meet.

NOTE 22 (p. 136)

THE KING OF CHALA

Tachienlu is not a correct name for the state as a whole: it is strictly applicable only to the city. The state may be described as Chala or as Ming Chêng. Ming Chêng (明 正) corresponds with the Chinese title of the king—Ming Chêng Ssŭ (明 正 司)—which was conferred upon an ancestor no less than five hundred years ago. The meaning of the Chinese words—"bright" and "correct"—are of no consequence. The word "Chala" we have already discussed on page 136.

The king's Chinese rank is that of a *hsüan wei shih ssŭ* (宣 慰 使 司)—one of the numerous titles invented by the Chinese for their vassal chiefs. This title carries with it the Chinese rank 3b. As a *hsüan wei shih ssŭ* the king of Chala takes precedence of the chiefs of Litang and Batang, his neighbours on the west, both of whom are *hsüan fu shih ssŭ* (宣 撫 使 司) with Chinese rank 4b. All three take precedence of the ruler of Muli, who is an *an fu shih ssŭ* (安 撫 使 司), with rank 5b. (For an explanation of these titles and ranks, see Mayers' *Chinese Government*, 3rd edn., pp. 46-47. The Chinese official hierarchy consists of nine ranks, subdivided into a higher and a lower grade, or *a* and *b*.) Special decorations may be and often are conferred upon an individual chief, and these may carry with them the "button" of a superior rank: the button and its privileges, however, are not hereditary. The rank of the chiefs *quâ* Chinese officials does not affect their position *quâ* rulers of native states. The "kings" of Litang, Batang and Muli are within their own borders quite as powerful as the "king" of Chala. The latter, however, holds his kingship by strict hereditary right, whereas the "regalities" of Litang and Batang are not necessarily hereditary, though in practice they may be generally so. The kingship of Muli is hereditary in one family (see page 215), but as the king is also a lama, and therefore a celibate, the descent can only be collateral.

It must be remembered that there are many other semi-independent kings and chiefs along the borderland of Burma, Tibet, Turkestan and Mongolia. Some are the vassals of China, others the vassals of Tibet, while there are probably some even to-day who pay no tribute and acknowledge no suzerain. Few of these chiefs, however, have the importance and dignity of those mentioned in this note.

The greatest length of the state of Chala, from Rumi-changu on the north, to Lo Jang and Muli on the south, is 1,050 *li* (say 350 miles); the greatest breadth, from Lu Ting on the east, to the Yalung on the west, 400 *li* (say 133 miles). Under the king's control are 49 sub-chiefs, including 1 *t'u ch'ien hu* (土 千 戶) and 48 *t'u pai hu* (土 百 戶). A *t'u ch'ien hu* nominally presides over 1,000 households, a *t'u pai hu* over 100. These terms, however, are quite elastic in meaning. The former takes precedence of the latter, but he does not necessarily control a wider territory, or a larger population. The population of the whole state—not including Tachienlu—consists of 6,591 households. (This is the figure given in the *Ssuch'uan T'ung Chih*, the latest edition of which belongs to the nineteenth century.) The number seems a small one, but a Tibetan household—the members of which are all farm-hands or herdsmen—is generally large, though the average family is so small that the population of Chinese Tibet is probably—apart from Chinese immigration—at the present time stationary. The annual tribute payable to China by the king himself amounts to 161 taels 7 candareens—a sum which, according to our reckoning, amounts to about £25. His 49 sub-chiefs or headmen pay between them a further tribute of about 180 taels 9 mace 2 candareens—equivalent to about £27. The total revenue raised by China out of this large tract of country is, therefore, only slightly over £50 a year. But this amount was assessed at a time when the tael was worth far more than it is worth now, and its purchasing power in the Tibetan states is in any case considerably greater than in the east of China; moreover, the money is not, strictly speaking, a tax, but a mere acknowledgment of China's suzerainty. *Ula* (see pp. 136-137) is the real tax paid to China by the tributary states of the west, and China exacts it in case of need to the grim uttermost. Over and above the exaction of *ula* and the payment of tribute the people are, of course, obliged to pay taxes to the king himself. The king's powers in the matter of taxation appear to be unlimited, for the principle of "no taxation without representation" has not yet been accepted as a political axiom in the state of Chala. But the only direct tax consists of a kind of *likin*, or toll on merchandise in transit; this is ample to defray the cost of administration, and the king's private exchequer is apparently chiefly dependent for its supplies on the revenues of his hereditary property, which are very considerable. The king of Chala succeeds in doing what the kings of England used at one time to get into serious trouble for not doing—he "lives of his own."

The position of the *t'u ch'ien hu* and *t'u pai hu* is a peculiar one. Though they are under the jurisdiction of the king, they may be regarded as possessing a certain amount of independence. The *Ssuch'uan T'ung Chih* states that the king became a vassal of China in the year 1666, but his *t'u ch'ien hu* did not follow suit till 1700, while the 48 *t'u pai hu* all "came in" together in 1701 (the fortieth year of K'ang Hsi). The Suzerain Power, however, is careful to differentiate between the great vassals and the little ones: the king of Chala—like others of his rank—receives, in return for his homage, sealed "letters of authority" and a stamped warrant; each *t'u pai hu* receives only the warrant. All these formalities are of small practical consequence: the Chinese insist upon controlling the high-road to Lhasa, and upon receiving their just dues in the shape of *ula* service and tribute, but otherwise the kings and *t'u pai hu* of the western border are just as free as they were before they "tied their heads"—as the Tibetan saying goes—to the emperor of China. It may be worth while adding that the king of Chala is expected to prostrate himself before the imperial throne at Peking once in twelve years. In practice it appears that he does not do so with great regularity. The expenses entailed by such a journey—chiefly in connection with the valuable presents always expected by the Court on such occasions—must be a very severe tax on his majesty's privy purse.

The first appearance of a ruler of Chala in Chinese history may be assigned to the first years of the Ming dynasty, in the second half of the fourteenth century, when the king showed his good-will to his mighty neighbour by assisting the imperial troops in the frontier warfare of those days. In the fifth year of Yung Lo (1407) he received the title of Ming Chêng Ssŭ, and in the fifth year of K'ang Hsi (1666) his successor definitely abjured his allegiance to Tibet and became a vassal of China. In 1771 the king—whose name was Chia Mu Ts'an—received official recognition from the emperor for his valuable assistance against the Chin Ch'uan rebels, and received a Peacock's Feather and the "button" of the Second Rank. Twenty years later his successor had a similar honour conferred upon him for like services, and in the fourteenth year of Chia Ch'ing (1809) the king went with a retinue to Peking to do homage to the emperor. Since then the history of the little state has gone through few vicissitudes; but, now that the relations between China and Tibet are going through a process of re-adjustment, it is probable that the new administrative arrangements will tend to the gradual effacement of the powers and privileges of all the Sino-Tibetan kings and chiefs, including the ruler of Chala, and the conversion of their territories into magistracies and prefectures under the direct control of China. Perhaps this is a fitting time, while "the old order changeth, yielding place to new," to put on record some account of systems of government and constitutions that no doubt have in the past fulfilled some useful purposes, but seem destined before long to pass utterly away.

NOTE 23 (p. 155)

HEIGHTS OF PASSES

With regard to the elevations given in this book it is very necessary to say that those referring to localities between Tachienlu and Li-chiang must be regarded as tentative and provisional only. Future travellers, better equipped with instruments than I was, will doubtless find much to correct. My readings were for the most part dependent on aneroids, which are very untrustworthy at great altitudes. Wherever possible, I have accepted the results of previous travellers, especially those of such accomplished surveyors as Major Davies.

NOTE 24 (p. 157)

POPULATION OF YALUNG WATERSHED

M. Bonin appears to have had the same experience. He states that in travelling from Chung-tien *viâ* Muli to Tachienlu—a journey of about a month's duration—he did not meet a single Chinese. "All the inhabitants," he says, "belong to the Tibetan race." (*Bulletin de la Soc. de Géog.*, 1898, p. 393.)

NOTE 25 (p. 161)

RACE-TYPES OF YALUNG WATERSHED

These people owe their tall and well-built frames to their non-Tibetan blood. It is probably the "Man-tzŭ" blood that tells. "The stature of the Tibetans of Lhasa," says Colonel Waddell, "is even less than that of the Chinese, and considerably below the European average; whilst the men from the eastern province of Kham are quite up to that standard." (*Lhasa and its Mysteries*, p. 347.) Kham or Khams includes or included the greater part of Chinese Tibet.

NOTE 26 (p. 186)

ATTITUDE OF MULI PEOPLE TOWARDS STRANGERS

M. Bonin states that he had to spend ten days in negotiation before he was allowed, in 1895, to cross into the Muli country. He approached it from the Yunnan side. (*Bulletin de la Soc. de Géog.*, 1898, p. 396.) Major Davies informs me that he also had difficulty in persuading the people of Muli to allow him to cross the Yalung in the course of his journey from Mien-ning-hsien. It was doubtless owing to the friendliness and tact shown by these travellers and by Mr Amundsen that I met with no opposition on entering the country.

NOTE 27 (p. 187)

EXPLORATION OF THE TA LIANG SHAN

It is reported that the country of the Independent Lolos (the Ta Liang Shan) has at last been traversed by a European. The successful traveller was a French officer named D'Ollone. (See *Geographical Journal*, October, 1907, p. 437.) The account of his journey should be awaited with interest.

NOTE 28 (p. 190)

THE PA-U-RONG T'U PAI HU

The *t'u pai hu* of Pa-U-Rong (Pa-U-Lung according to the Pekingese sound of the Chinese characters) is to be accounted one of the most important of all the 49 sub-chiefs of the king of Chala, if the amount of tribute paid is the test of importance. His annual tribute is 7 taels, whereas the single *t'u ch'ien hu* only pays a little more than 9 taels. The highest of all the tributes is that of the *t'u pai hu* of Rumi Cho-rong, in the northern part of the state. His payment is 12 taels 5 mace. The Pa-U-Rong *t'u pai hu* nets a modest revenue by causing travellers and merchants who cross the Yalung at this point to pay him a small toll.

NOTE 29 (p. 191)

NAME OF THE YALUNG

M. Bonin calls the Yalung the *Rivière Noire*, apparently supposing its Tibetan name to be Nag Ch'u (ནག་ཆུ་) "Black Water." But I know of no authority for this. The true Tibetan name appears to be Nya(g)-ch'u (ཉག་ཆུ་). The *nya(g)* re-appears in the tribal or district name Mi-nya(g) or Miniak (Menia), མི་ཉག་; and the Chinese "Yalung" is an attempt to pronounce the Tibetan *Nya-Rong* (ཉག་རོང་) or "Valley of the Nya."

NOTE 30 (p. 197)

THE CHIN SHA CHIANG

It may not be generally known that according to the Chinese authorities there are *two* rivers bearing the name of Chin Sha Chiang. One is the *Ta* (Great), the other the *Hsiao* (Small) Chin Sha Chiang, and *the "small" one is the Yangtse*. In a first attempt to identify the Ta Chin Sha Chiang—which must obviously be a very great river—we are apt to be much puzzled; for we read of it as flowing from western Tibet and also as flowing through Burma into the "Southern Ocean." But the mystery is explained when we remember that the great river of southern Tibet—the Tsangpo or Yaru Tsangpo (literally "Upper River") —used to be believed not only by Chinese but also by European geographers to be the main feeder of the Irrawaddy. We now know that the Tsangpo is no other than the main upper branch of the Brahmaputra: or rather we assume it from much circumstantial evidence. No European has yet followed the course of the Brahmaputra up to the point where it receives the icy waters of the Tibetan Tsangpo—which hurls itself over the edge of the Tibetan plateau and creates there a series of waterfalls that must be among the grandest sights in the world—but we now know, from the reports of our native surveyors, the approximate position of the falls.[1] The country between Assam and Tibet is unfortunately inhabited by tribes that are apparently violently hostile to all strangers. Their own domestic habits are of a somewhat repellent nature: it is said,[2] for instance, that on occasions of the

[1] See Waddell's *Lhasa and its Mysteries*, pp. 434 *seq.*
[2] *Op. cit.*, p. 439.

celebration of marriages it is the genial custom of one of the tribes to serve up the bridegroom's mother-in-law at the nuptial banquet.

The Chinese geographers know the Tsangpo by its Tibetan name (calling it the Ya-lu-tsang-pu-chiang, where *chiang* is tautological) but they also call it the Great (*Ta*) Chin Sha Chiang; and readers of their topographical works must beware of confusing this river with the Small (*Hsiao*) Chin Sha Chiang of China: though when the adjective is omitted the river referred to is always the Chinese river, and therefore identical with the Yangtse.

NOTE 31 (p. 213)

MULI

I have adopted the spelling "Muli" instead of "Mili" on the authority of the *Ssuch'uan T'ung Chih.* The Chinese characters there given are 木 裏 (Mu-li), and though I have seen others used I think there can be no doubt that the *T'ung Chih* is the best authority to follow.

NOTE 32 (p. 216)

KHON

The name of the third lamasery was given to me as Khon, but I observe that Mr Amundsen calls it Kang-u, and locates it half-way between Muli and the Yalung, almost due east. Major Davies's map, again, places a lamasery named K'u-lu at almost the same spot. K'u-lu, Khon and Kang-u are probably one and the same place, and as Major Davies's route seems to have led him past it the name given by him is probably the correct one. It seems strange that the residences of the *k'an-po* should all be within a comparatively short distance of each other. If the real object of the periodical movements of the "Court" were to enable the *k'an-po* to keep in close touch with all parts of his territory, it would naturally extend its peregrinations somewhat further afield.

NOTE 33 (p. 217)

OFFICIAL TITLES IN MULI

Most of these official titles are well known in connection with the administrative arrangements of all the great lamaseries of Tibet; but the authority of the Muli officials is not confined to the management of lamaseries.

NOTE 34 (p. 219)

THE KING AND PEOPLE OF MULI

The ruler of Muli holds the rank, *vis-à-vis* the Chinese suzerain, of an *An Fu Ssŭ* (see note 22). In his own territory he is a *gyal-po* or king, but he is also a lama, and the succession must therefore go to a collateral branch of the "royal" family. In practice, the heir is generally a nephew who has been inducted into Lamaism at an early age, and has risen high in the hierarchy. The king of Muli first became tributary to China in the seventh year of Yung Chêng (1729). He received from the Chinese Government sealed "letters of authority" and a stamped warrant similar to those bestowed on the king of Chala. The greatest length of the territory, from the frontier of the Litang principality on the north to the territory of the Ku-Po Chu *t'u ssŭ* on the south, is 900 *li* (say 300 miles); its greatest breadth is from the frontier of Chala on the east to that of Chung-tien on the west, 1,300 *li* (say 430 miles). These distances, as in the case of Chala, are measured by length of actual paths, and not by bee-lines. Though the Yalung forms the eastern boundary at Pa-U-Rong, the Muli territory extends for a distance of some scores of miles across the Yalung further south. According to the *Ssuch'uan T'ung Chih* (published in the first half of the nineteenth century) the total number of *i jên* ("barbarians") under the king's rule comprises 3,283 households. This figure hardly enables us to assess the present population, which—if we include the large body of lamas—can hardly be judged to be less than 25,000. It should be remembered that there are no towns in Muli, very little trade, and great areas of mountainous country practically uninhabitable. The king's annual tribute consists of 120 piculs of buckwheat (16,000 lbs.) estimated in cash value at 74 taels 4 mace and 3 horses, each valued at 8 taels, or a total of 24 taels for the three. The total tribute thus amounts (in money-value) to 98 taels 4 mace. These assessments of value were, of course, made many years ago. Probably re-assessments are made from time to time, as otherwise the monetary values would bear no proper ratio to the value of the articles forming the basis of the tribute. Payment is made at Yen-yüan-hsien, and is supposed to be applied to the expenses of the local military establishment. It is the custom of the country that one out of every three, or two out of every five, male members of a family enter the priesthood. All the lay population can be called upon for military service; but it is hardly necessary to say that the king keeps no standing army, and his people are only called to arms when serious disputes arise with the neighbouring Tibetan chiefs. The *T'ung Chih* goes on to say that the people of the land of Muli consist of six different kinds of Barbarians: (1) *lamas*; (2) *Chia-mi* or *Chieh-mi* (呷 迷); (3) *Yüeh-ku* or *Yo-ku* (約 古); (4) *Hsü-mi* (虛 迷); (5) *Mo-so*; (6) *Hsi Fan*. The lamas, of course, are not a distinct race; the Mo-so and Hsi Fan are discussed in Chapter XV. of this book; as for the three others, the remarks made upon them in the *T'ung Chih* leave us very much in the dark. The characteristics of the *i jên* are dismissed in four lines. We are told that the Chia-mi and Yüeh-ku are very like one another, and that the women allow their hair to hang over their shoulders. The Hsü-mi males cultivate a queue, and the women do up their hair into a pointed coiffure. They are docile, and of an amiable disposition. The Mo-so and Hsi Fan are like each other, and honest and tractable by nature. Their clothes are made of woven cloth, and their coats button under the left arm (*tso jên; cf.* the Confucian *Lun Yü*, p. 282, Legge's edn.) The men wear queues and the women do up their hair. They live by agriculture. They are fond of hunting wild animals. This is all the *T'ung Chih* has to tell us about the people of Muli. The section ends with the laconic remark that lawsuits are decided by the *k'an-po*.

Chinese customs certainly seem to be losing rather than gaining ground in Muli: the queues worn by some of the men do not hang down the back but are coiled round the head; and it is not a mark of respect, as in China, to uncoil the queue. Moreover the front of the head is not shaved, as in China. The remarks about the women are true enough: a large proportion wear their hair loose, so that they look like rather overgrown and unwieldy school-girls; the rest have more or less elaborate coiffures, but the female fashions of China in this respect are totally ignored. I will leave the task of identifying the Chia-mi, Yüeh-ku and Hsü-mi to some future investigator with more time and leisure than fell to my lot. Tibetans, Li-so, Man-tzŭ or Lolos, Kachins and Mo-so are all doubtless to be found among the people of Muli, and it seems not improbable that the predominant type is Mo-so.

NOTE 35 (p. 222)

THE LANGUAGE-TEST OF RACE

The collection of hastily-compiled and doubtless very inaccurate vocabularies to be found in Appendix A need not be taken as indicating any belief in the value of such lists of words from either the philological or the ethnological point of view. They are given merely for what they are worth, as an infinitesimal addition to the small stock of general knowledge that we already possess with regard to the tribes of western China. The old faith in language as a sure test of race has long been given up. A page or two of skull measurements would help us more towards settling the racial problems of western China than the completest equipment of grammars and dictionaries. Unfortunately the methods employed by many of the tribes for the disposal of their dead will seriously hamper the investigations of the craniologist who, in the hopes of a rich harvest of inexorable bones, may take his measuring-tape to the graveyards of western China.

NOTE 36 (p. 226)

HIGHEST HABITATION ON THE GLOBE

The land of Muli is as wild and mountainous as that of Chala. It was between Muli and the Yalung that M. Bonin discovered what he believes to be the highest inhabited station on the globe, at a height of 16,568 feet, "a hamlet occupied in the dead of winter by a few yak-herdsmen." The mines of Tok-ya-long in western Tibet, he says, which have hitherto been considered the highest habitation in the world are 525 feet lower, and moreover are not inhabited all the year round. There are other spots both in Muli and Chala, probably of a greater height than 16,000 feet, that are inhabited, though the huts are probably not occupied in winter.

NOTE 37 (p. 233)

FEMALE CHIEFS

In the Shan States female rulers are apparently not uncommon. (See *Gazetteer of Upper Burma*, pt. i. vol. i. p. 262.) For an interesting note on several Tibetan "queens" (derived from native and Chinese sources) see Rockhill's *Land of the Lamas*, pp. 339-341. Sa-mong is better known as So-mo. A recent European visitor to this country says that the "queen" or *nü-wang* of So-mo is only a myth, "the real monarch being actually a man, who for some obscure reason calls himself a Queen." (W. C. Haines Watson, *A Journey to Sung-p'an*, in *J.R.A.S.* (*China*), vol. xxxvi., 1905.) The *Ssuch'uan T'ung Chih* contains references to several female *t'u ssŭ*. A female *t'u pai hu*, with a territorial name of six syllables, is mentioned as becoming tributary to China in K'ang Hsi 60. She paid 20 taels annually as "horse-money." The *Ch'ang Kuan Ssŭ* of Sung Kang is—or may be—a woman. One is mentioned as receiving honours from China in K'ang Hsi 23. Another female *ch'ang kuan ssŭ* in the Chien-ch'ang Valley (Hu-li-ho-tung) is described as being a tribute-payer to the extent of ten horses a year.

NOTE 38 (p. 246)

LI-CHIANG-FU

An old name of Li-chiang was Sui (巂), and its inhabitants, in the days of the Early Han dynasty, appear to have been known as the K'un Ming (昆 明). Their fierceness and lawlessness were instrumental in preventing the Emperor Wu Ti, in the second century B.C., from establishing a trade route from China to India through their territory. (See T. W. Kingsmill's *Intercourse of China with Eastern Turkestan*, *J.R.A.S.*, January 1882.)

NOTE 39 (p. 259)

THE REBELLION IN YUNNAN

The best account of the Mohammedan rebellion is to be found in M. Émile Rocher's *La Province Chinoise du Yunnan*, vol. ii. pp. 30-192. The origin of the rebellion is to be traced to a comparatively trifling dispute among miners, which took place in 1855 in a mining centre situated between Yunnan-fu and Tali-fu. The Mohammedan section of miners, who all worked together, aroused envy and hatred because they had struck richer veins of metal than the "orthodox" Chinese miners in a neighbouring locality, and the result was a violent dispute which ended in blows. The official who was responsible for good order in the district was seized with panic and fled to Yunnan-fu, where he submitted reports that were unjustifiably hostile to the Mohammedans. The latter meanwhile had rendered themselves masters of the situation, and drove their opponents off the field. The people of the neighbouring town of Linan avenged this insult by attacking the Mohammedans in overwhelming force and expelling them to the forests. This was the beginning of a series of bloodthirsty combats, which in a short time set the whole province in a blaze, and caused the loss of millions of human lives.

So far as race went, the Mohammedans of Yunnan were no other than ordinary Yunnanese. They were marked off from their fellow-provincials solely by their religion. This, however, was sufficient to cause them to be treated almost as foreigners, for they had little intercourse with orthodox Chinese, and seem to have intermarried among themselves. Whether the Mohammedans of Yunnan and other parts of China were—and are—strict observers of the rules of their religion is a doubtful point. Rocher says of the Yunnanese Mohammedans that "they have preserved intact the beliefs of their ancestors, and they rigorously observe the rules imposed upon them by the Koran." Other observers, however,—including Mohammedan natives of India—have scoffed at their co-religionists of Yunnan, declaring that they know nothing of the tenets of Islam, and obey none of the rules of their faith except that of abstinence from pork. I have myself seen Chinese Mohammedan children undergoing the pains of having page after page of Arabic drilled into their little heads, though both they and their teachers admitted that they did not understand the meaning of a single word. The fact remains, however, that some Chinese Mohammedans do still occasionally make the pilgrimage to Mecca; and well-attended Mohammedan mosques may yet be found in at least half the provinces of China.

Chinese Mohammedans have often proved a thorn in the flesh of the official classes, not only in Yunnan, but also in Kansu and elsewhere. Yet it cannot be said that they have shown much of that fiery religious fanaticism which has sometimes characterised Islam elsewhere. The great rebellion in Yunnan did not originate in any religious dispute, and it would never have developed into a war that lasted nearly twenty years and laid waste a province, if only a few able and impartial officials had given their attention to the matter in its early stages.

Two circumstances helped to prolong the struggle. The first was the great T'ai P'ing rebellion in eastern China, which rendered the central Government powerless to deal effectually with the situation in Yunnan; the second was the military skill of the Mohammedan leaders, which led to the concentration of the whole Mohammedan strength in the hands of a few able men.

The history of the war cannot be sketched here. It may be sufficient to say that at one time nearly the whole province was in the hands of the Mohammedan rebels; even Yunnan-fu itself capitulated to their victorious arms. Before this took place, the great Mohammedan leader, Tu Wên-hsiu, had already greatly distinguished himself in the west of the province. Against the will of the viceroy, who committed suicide, the officials had in 1856 planned and carried out a massacre of all Mohammedans found within a radius of 800 *li* from the capital. The news of the massacre naturally roused in Tu Wên-hsiu intense feelings of indignation and hatred against the provincial Government which had sanctioned an act of such hideous barbarity, and his natural abilities and high reputation for courage and integrity soon singled him out for leadership. His first great victory secured him the city of Tali, which became the Mohammedan headquarters. In 1867 he was proclaimed Imam or Sultan, and Tali became the capital of a short-lived Mohammedan state. It was held till 1873, when Tu Wên-hsiu, faced by hopeless odds, surrendered it and poisoned himself. Before this time the genius of General Gordon had put an end to the T'ai P'ing rebellion, and the imperial Government was in a position to oppose the Sultan with an overwhelming force. Only one result was possible. With the capitulation of Tali and the death of Tu Wên-hsiu the Mohammedans were able to make no further headway against the imperial troops.

One of the most terrible results of this hideous civil war was the recrudescence of the deadly disease now too well known to us all as the plague. After the war the pestilence gradually spread far beyond the limits of the province, and is still the annual scourge of south China and India. It is probable, however, that plague has for many centuries been endemic in the valleys of western Yunnan. The accounts given of it by such writers as Rocher and Baber, who witnessed its ravages in Yunnan long before the fatal year when it was first observed in Hong Kong (1894), are of great interest. The curious fact that rats always seemed to be attacked before human beings was noted by Rocher many years before the disease began to be studied by medical experts. (See Rocher, *op. cit.*, vol. i. p. 75; vol. ii. pp. 279-281.)

NOTE 40 (p. 273)

CHINESE OFFICIAL ACCOUNTS OF WESTERN TRIBES

Several volumes of the official Provincial Annals of Yunnan are devoted to a most elaborate quasi-ethnological enquiry into the various tribal communities of that province. Unfortunately, the conscientious industry of the compilers coupled with their bland credulity and lack of critical training led them to fill their pages with a great deal of matter that is useless and misleading. The numbers and names of the tribes are quite unnecessarily multiplied, and there is hardly any attempt at classification or at the tracing of origins. Subdivisions of the same race are treated as entirely separate, and any similarities between them are either ignored or merely mentioned as unexplained facts. Yet it must be admitted that as descriptions of tribal customs and as store-houses of tradition and folk-lore the ethnological sections of the Annals are by no means to be despised. The *T'ung Chih* of Ssuch'uan is less satisfactory in this respect than that of Yunnan.

NOTE 41 (p. 284)

THEORY OF INDIAN ORIGIN OF TRIBES

It seems quite clear that the Licchavis—or the great Vaggian or Vrijian clan-system to which they belonged and from which the Mauryans sprang—were neither Aryans nor Dravidians. In all probability they were of Kolarian or Munda race. The Kolarians seem to have entered India from the north-east—just as the Aryans afterwards entered it from the north-west—and extended themselves over vast areas from which they were subsequently driven by Dravidians and Aryans. They must have originally come from the countries that lay to the east, which we now know as Burma, China and Indo-China. They probably left many of their Kolarian kinsfolk behind them, and it may have been through keeping up communications with the latter that they were able to introduce into their old homes something of the new culture and civilisation that they acquired in their new homes in India. The Kolarian dialects are known to be akin to those of certain tribes in Burma, and so far as personal characteristics are concerned a description of the Kolarian tribes as they are known to-day in parts of Bengal would be applicable, word for word, to some of the peoples of Indo-China and Yunnan. "The Kolarian people," says Mr J. F. Hewitt, who lived among them, "may generally be described as gregarious, excitable, turbulent when roused, but generally peaceable and good-humoured. They are brave and adventurous, witty, and very fond of amusement, not given to work more than is necessary, and as a rule very careless of the future." (*J.R.A.S.*, vol. xx. p. 330.) It must be remembered, however, that the Burmese people, to whom these words are also applicable, are now believed by the best authorities to have come from "the Mongolian countries north of Magadha." (Sir George Scott's *Burma*, p. 66.)

Many of the tribes of western China—some of the Lolos and Min-chia, for instance—are often described as possessing a type of features that is almost European; and Mr Kingsmill seems to derive from this fact some support of his theory of their Indian (Aryan) origin. "The distinctive colouring," he says, "closely approximates to the Aryan type of the Indian peninsula," etc. (*J.R.A.S.* (China Branch), vol. xxxv. p. 95.) But the Mauryans themselves, as we have seen, were not of Aryan origin. The Licchavis are referred to in Manu as one of the "base-born" castes for that very reason—in spite of the fact that they possessed great power and prestige and very wide influence. It seems very doubtful whether an Aryan emigration from India to China took place at any time. India always offered full scope for all Aryan energies; indeed we know that the Aryans by no means became so universally predominant, even in India, as one might gather from the early and wide extension of their language and religion. If there really is an Aryan element among the tribes of western China it would be curious to speculate on the possibility of its having come by a non-Indian route.

NOTE 42 (p. 285)

CHANDRAGUPTA AND ASOKA

Chandragupta's reign probably began in 320 B.C., and his grandson Asoka ruled from ? 264 to ? 228. The chronology is not yet absolutely fixed, but I rely with some confidence on the dates recently selected by J. F. Fleet (*J.R.A.S.*, October 1906, pp. 984 *seq.*) who, it may be remarked incidentally, assigns the death of the Buddha to B.C. 482.

NOTE 43 (p. 285)

VESÂLI AND THE LICCHAVIS

For further information regarding Vesâli and the Licchavis see W. W. Rockhill's *Life of the Buddha*, pp. 62 *seq.*, and 203 (*footnote*), Dr Rhys Davids' *Buddhist India*, pp. 40-41, and two articles by Mr Vincent Smith in the Royal Asiatic Society's *Journal* for April 1902 and January 1905. One of Mr Rockhill's Tibetan authorities connects the Licchavis with the Sakyas or Çakyas to whom the Buddha himself belonged. "The Çakyas," says this authority, were "divided into three parts, whose most celebrated representatives were Çakya the Great (the Buddha), Çakya the Licchavi, and Çakya the Mountaineer. Grya Khri btsan po, the first Tibetan king, belonged to the family of Çakya the Licchavi. Many other Buddhist sovereigns of India and elsewhere claimed the same descent." This note is of interest as showing the wide extent and long duration of Licchavi influence, and the desire of powerful races and kings to trace a connection with the family of the Buddha. "Çakya, the Licchavi" may, of course, have become a member of the clan by adoption. Caste-rules (even supposing they precluded adoption) did not hold good among the Licchavis, who were not

Aryans. With respect to the possible connection of the Buddha's family with the Licchavis, all that can be said for certain is that the Licchavis were among the earliest and most devoted supporters of the Buddhist faith, and that Vesâli soon became a city of great religious importance. Buddhism, indeed, was less of an Aryan religion than people have been in the habit of supposing. The Sakyas themselves were almost certainly an Aryan people; we know that their exclusiveness and intense pride of birth brought about the destruction of their capital at the hands of Vidūdabha. But it seems quite clear that Buddhism progressed most rapidly and won its greatest victories among people of non-Aryan race, and this not only in foreign lands but in India itself. Buddhism did not achieve its wonderful successes in India in the third century B.C. and afterwards by means of the conversion of Brahmans. It is far truer to say that Buddhism spread on account of its adoption by northern non-Aryan tribes which, in spite of Aryan conquests, remained very powerful both in numbers and in political influence. (See on this point B. H. Baden-Powell's *Notes on the Origin of the "Lunar" and "Solar" Aryan Tribes*, *J.R.A.S.*, April 1899, pp. 298-299.

NOTE 44 (p. 289)

THE SERES

The Seres are mentioned by Virgil, Strabo, Lucan, Pliny and Pomponius Mela. Lucan seems to have supposed that they were an African race—neighbours of the Ethiopians. Such ignorance in Nero's age may be excused when we remember the wild theories prevalent in mediæval Europe as to the local habitation of Prester John!

NOTE 45 (p. 332)

ARCHÆOLOGICAL WORK

Some valuable work—of special interest to the student of Buddhism—has quite recently been carried out at Pagan by Mr I. H. Marshall and Dr Sten Konow. (See *J.R.A.S.*, October 1907, pp. 1003 *seq.*) It is earnestly to be hoped that that Government will some day see fit to provide for the proper support of the Archæological Department, which cannot be expected to carry out good work at Pagan or elsewhere without funds. Every year's delay will render the work of excavation more difficult and more costly. It is not pleasing to observe that the Archæological Departments of India, Burma and Ceylon are all starved. Only a few weeks after the conclusion of the recent Franco-Siamese treaty it was announced in the French press that steps were being taken forthwith to carry out some expensive archæological and preservative work at the magnificent ruins of Angkor Wat, which are within the Cambodian territory acquired by France under the treaty. Is England always to lag behind France in matters of this kind?

NOTE 46 (p. 335)

THE BURMESE LABOUR QUESTION

One aspect of the labour question in Burma does not seem to have attracted the attention it deserves. In spite of Mr Fielding Hall's optimism, the belief that the apathetic Burman is being shouldered out of his own country by more hard-working immigrants, especially natives of India, is a very prevalent one, not only among European observers, but even among some classes of the Burmese themselves. At present no Burman dares to raise a protest against the influx of labourers, who, if they do not utterly crush him in the course of the struggle for existence, may at least degrade him from the high level of comfort and social well-being in which he now lives. The day may come when the Burman will demand that this alien immigration be interdicted. If he does so, what will be the attitude of the Government? Probably anything but sympathetic. The White races of Australia, British Columbia and California object to the influx of Chinese and Japanese labourers for reasons practically identical with those that would actuate the Burman, and if their attitude is a justifiable one can it be argued that the Burmese attitude would not be equally so? The Burman would doubtless be told by the European, whose material interests in Burma depend on the unrestricted immigration of hard-working aliens, that his country cannot be allowed to go to waste; that if he, through his laziness, will not develop it to the utmost, some one else must be found who will develop it in his stead. But the Chinese and Japanese might if they were strong enough—and perhaps some day they will be strong enough — knock at the gates of Australia, Canada and the United States, and demand admission on precisely similar grounds. No one will deny that the scarcity and high price of labour in those countries have seriously retarded, and are still retarding, nearly every form of industrial and agricultural development; yet the Yellow races are excluded on the grounds that they would lower the White man's standard of living, and that they are in the habit of sending their earnings out of the country. I do not say the White man's attitude is unreasonable: but I do not see how, on our own principles, we could refuse to restrict the immigration of black aliens into Burma if the Burmese people — on grounds identical with those that actuate our own conduct in Canada and elsewhere—demanded that we should do so. Such action would no doubt be an artificial restriction of natural economic tendencies, and so might bring its own punishment in the long-run; but the same remark applies to the policy adopted in our own colonies.

We have recently become so much accustomed to hear of the antagonism and rivalry of interests between East and West—as if all Eastern countries represented one set of immutable ideals and all Western countries another — that we are apt to lose ourselves in a mist of generalities. The East has problems of its own to solve, some of which reproduce in a more restricted area the racial problems that are beginning at a late hour to agitate the minds of statesmen in Europe and America. The European speaks with half-hearted contempt (behind which lurks a secret dread) of a Yellow Peril: the Burman is disquieted by a no less threatening Black Peril that is already within his gates, and his gates still stand open with a dangerous hospitality.

NOTE 47 (p. 384)

MILITARY QUALITIES OF ORIENTALS

The British officers who trained and led the recently-disbanded Chinese Regiment are known to have formed a high opinion of the personal courage of the Chinese as represented by the men of that regiment. When it is remembered that the very existence of the regiment as a unit in the British Army was an anomaly, and that at Tientsin and Peking the men fought as mercenaries against their own countrymen, the fact that they behaved well under fire is all the more noteworthy. It may be taken for granted that even the Japanese soldier, if ordered to charge an unruly mob of his own countrymen, would hardly show the brilliant daring that he displayed before Port Arthur.

When Europe was startled by the news of some of the great Japanese victories in Manchuria, an English newspaper made the somewhat hasty suggestion that the Japanese were "scientific fanatics," and the phrase was caught up and repeated with approbation by many. Why fanatics? Simply because the Japanese troops had behaved with such unheard-of heroism that Europe was unable to reconcile such conduct with its own ideas of what constituted bravery. What many Englishmen said, in effect, was this: "The conduct ordinarily shown by British troops in action is bravery; to go beyond this is fanaticism.

The criterion of true courage is the average conduct of the average British soldier on the field of battle." The Japanese who with reckless gallantry gave their lives for emperor and country on the battle-fields of Liao-tung, and who considered it a disgrace to return home without a wound, were fanatics. Well, if so, it is a kind of fanaticism that every European Government would like to see spread among its own fighting-men when the day of battle comes.

NOTE 48 (p. 388)

"THE YELLOW PERIL"

With some people the antipathy to the Oriental amounts to a positive horror, inexplicable even by themselves in ordinary language, and very often based on no personal experience. "I know not," said De Quincey, "what others share in my feelings on this point; but I have often thought that if I were compelled to forego England, and to live in China, among Chinese manners and modes of life and scenery, I should go mad. The causes of my horror lie deep, and some of them must be common to others. . . . In China, over and above what it has in common with the rest of southern Asia, I am terrified by the modes of life, by the manners, by the barrier of utter abhorrence placed between myself and them, by counter-sympathies deeper than I can analyse. I could sooner live with lunatics, with vermin, with crocodiles or snakes." When we have made all allowances for the excited utterances of an opium-dreamer, these words indicate the existence of intensely strong feelings of racial antipathy, and there is no reason to regard De Quincey as the only European who has entertained such feelings. Does our subliminal consciousness retain dim ancestral memories of mighty struggles waged æons ago for the survival and supremacy of our own racial type? And does it harbour a vague prophetic dread of a more terrific warfare yet to come?

What is perhaps at the root of this horror of Asiatics felt by some Europeans is an instinctive feeling that the world is not large enough to contain or afford free play for the energies of both races; coupled perhaps with an ugly doubt whether, in spite of all the great material achievements of the West in recent years, the European type is after all the fittest to survive in the struggle for existence. Huxley long ago reminded us that the "survival of the fittest" does not necessarily imply the survival of the "best" or most highly developed. He points out, for instance, that if certain conceivable changes were to come about in atmospheric conditions, the law of the survival of the fittest might bring about the extinction of all living things except "lichens, diatoms, and such microscopic organisms as those which give red snow its colour."[1] They would be the sole survivors of the struggle for existence because they alone were adapted to the new environment. It may be that at some future period in the course of the struggle—though long before we have reached the lichen and diatom stage—certain conditions may prove hostile to the continued existence of the White races and favourable to that of the Yellow. Lafcadio Hearn, who in spite of his "de-occidentalisation" admitted the superiority of the Western races — without explaining what he meant by "superiority"—expressed the belief that in the "simple power of living" they are immensely inferior to those of the East. "The Occidental," he says, "cannot live except at a cost sufficient for the maintenance of twenty Oriental lives. In our very superiority lies the secret of our fatal weakness. Our physical machinery requires a fuel too costly to pay for the running of it in a perfectly conceivable future period of race-competition and pressure of population." He conjectures that some day the Western peoples may be crushed out of existence, their successors scarcely regretting their disappearance "any more than we ourselves regret the extinction of the dinotherium or the ichthyosaurus." Why indeed should they? When we consider how seldom the memory even of our own dead ancestors touches our sympathies or prompts an affectionate thought it will not seem strange that in the days to come the victorious Yellow man may regard the extinct White man with no more emotion than the visitor to a museum now regards the wire-linked bones of a prehistoric monster. No creature that is doomed to failure in the struggle for existence need look to the conquerors for the least sign of pity or sympathy. The poor dodo has vanished from the scene of its joys and sorrows for ever, but that is not the reason why the nightingale's song is sometimes a sad one. No less cheerfully warbles the thrush because the great auk will flap his ineffectual wings no more. Even the crocodile refrains from shedding tears over the fossil remains of the Triassic *stagonolepis*.

It behoves us to remember that victory in the struggle for existence is not a victory once and for all. The doom of the conqueror in this fight is that he must never sheathe his sword. The prize goes always to him who deserves it, but no rest is allowed him when the battle is over. New challengers are ever pressing into the lists, and the challenged must go ever armed and with lance in rest.

The grim tragedy once enacted periodically at Aricia might be interpreted, not too fancifully, as a miniature representation of the more terrible struggle that is for ever in progress through-

[1] See *Evolution and Ethics*, pp. 80-81 (Eversley edn.).

out the whole world of animate nature. The guardian of the Golden Bough—

> "The priest who slew the slayer,
> And shall himself be slain"—

retained his position and his life only so long as they were not challenged by one more vigorous or more dexterous than himself.

The great nations of the West have won their material pre-eminence by overcoming weaker competitors, who in their turn had once been conquerors. They will keep their prizes so long as they deserve to keep them, and no longer. Exclusion laws and trades-unions and cunning appliances wrought by scientific and intellectual skill may stave off the day of disaster, but if the White races have no better support than such things as these, for them the day of doom will assuredly dawn.

Yet a struggle for predominance among great sections of the human race need not imply actual physical warfare. If the Yellow races are to be supreme, it will be partly because the White races have suicidally contributed to their own ruin. If White men become too intensely careful of the individual life, and too careless of the welfare of the race; if they allow luxury to sap their energies and weaken their moral fibre; if they insist too strongly on "rights" and show too slack a devotion to "duty"; if they regard the accumulation of wealth as the be-all and end-all of existence; if selfishness impels their young men to avoid matrimony, and their young women to shun the duties of maternity; if they give way to these and other social vices to which our age bears witness, they cannot reasonably expect to compete advantageously with people who have no craving for luxury, and scarcely know what it means; who look not to wealth as a means for individual aggrandisement; who are at all times willing to sink personal interests in the larger interests of family and clan; who are tireless and uncomplaining workers; among whom parenthood is a religious necessity, and artificial restrictions of the birth-rate are practically unknown; and whose women are free from political aspirations and willing to do their duty at the domestic fireside and in the nursery.

The Yellow Peril, then, is no mere myth: let so much be granted. Yet the recognition of its existence need not drive us to utter pessimism, so long as our faults are not irremediable, and our virtues not reduced to inactivity. The shaping of our fate lies, to some extent at least, in our own hands, and, after all, the outlook for the West is not entirely gloomy. The mere proximity of a peril does not make the brave man falter and tremble; on the contrary, it braces his nerves, and increases his alertness. If the East has qualities and virtues that make for great strength, it is no less clearly lacking in other qualities and virtues that still find a home in the West. The Yellow

Peril, so far from driving us to a cowardly despair, may and should have the effect of raising our courage, ennobling our ideals, up-rooting our selfishness and purifying Western society. It may enable us to see that in some respects our aims have been false ones, and that our views of the essentials of progress and of civilisation must be partially modified. The recognition of the existence of our own diseases may lead to the discovery of the means of cure. The East has begun in recent years to learn some valuable lessons from the West; is it not time that we returned the compliment? If we could but bring ourselves to do so, perhaps at no very distant period the Yellow Peril might turn out to be the White Salvation.

GENERAL INDEX

The references in Roman numerals are to the Notes

INDEX OF NAMES

The references in Roman numerals are to the Notes

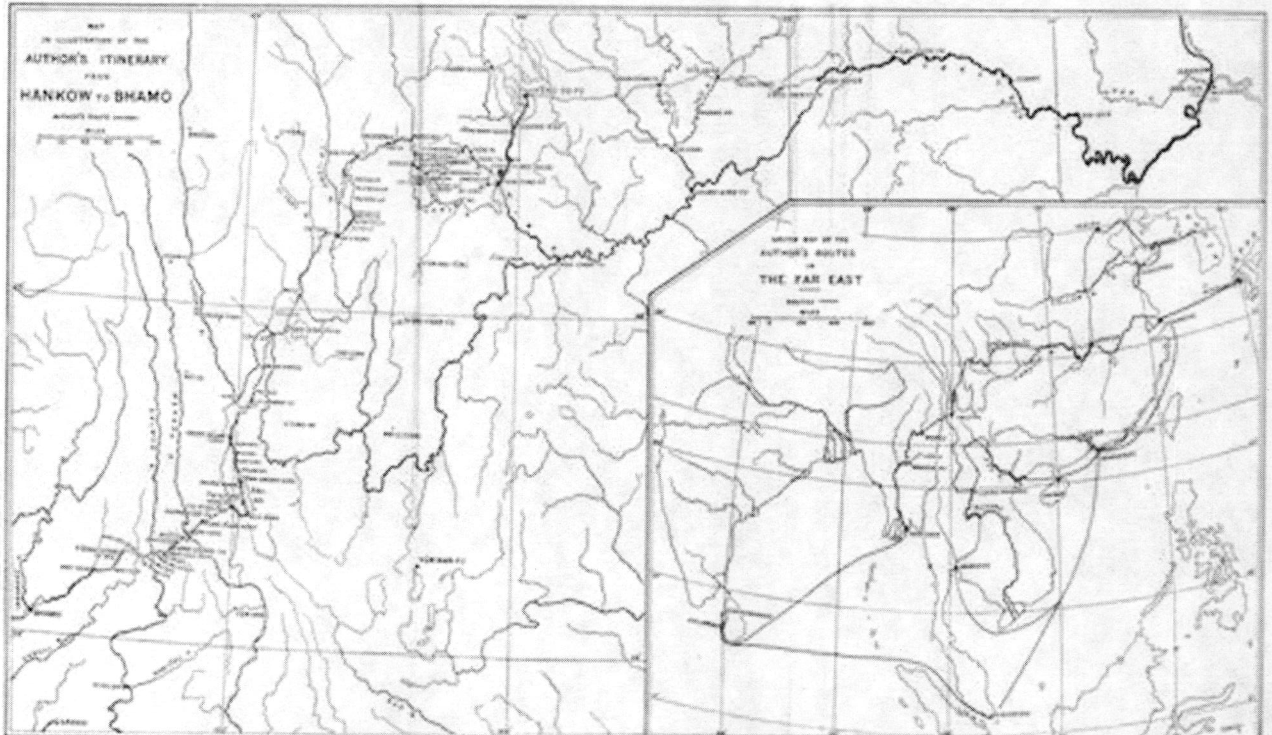
MAP
AUTHOR'S ITINERARY
FROM
HANKOW TO BHAMO
THE FAR EAST